INUYASHA ™

VOL. 22
Action Edition

Story and Art by
RUMIKO TAKAHASHI

English Adaptation by Gerard Jones

Translation/Mari Morimoto
Touch-Up Art & Lettering/Bill Schuch
Graphic Design/Yuki Ameda
Editor/Avery Gotoh
Supervising Editor/Michelle Pangilinan

Managing Editor/Annette Roman
Director of Production/Noboru Watanabe
Vice President of Publishing/Alvin Lu
Sr. Director of Acquisitions/Rika Inouye
Vice President of Sales & Marketing/Liza Coppola
Publisher/Hyoe Narita

Printed in Canada.

Published by VIZ, LLC
P.O. Box 77010
San Francisco, CA 94107

Action Edition
10 9 8 7 6 5 4 3 2 1
First printing, June 2005

 store.viz.com

www.viz.com

INUYASHA

VOL. 22   Action Edition

STORY AND ART BY
RUMIKO TAKAHASHI

CONTENTS

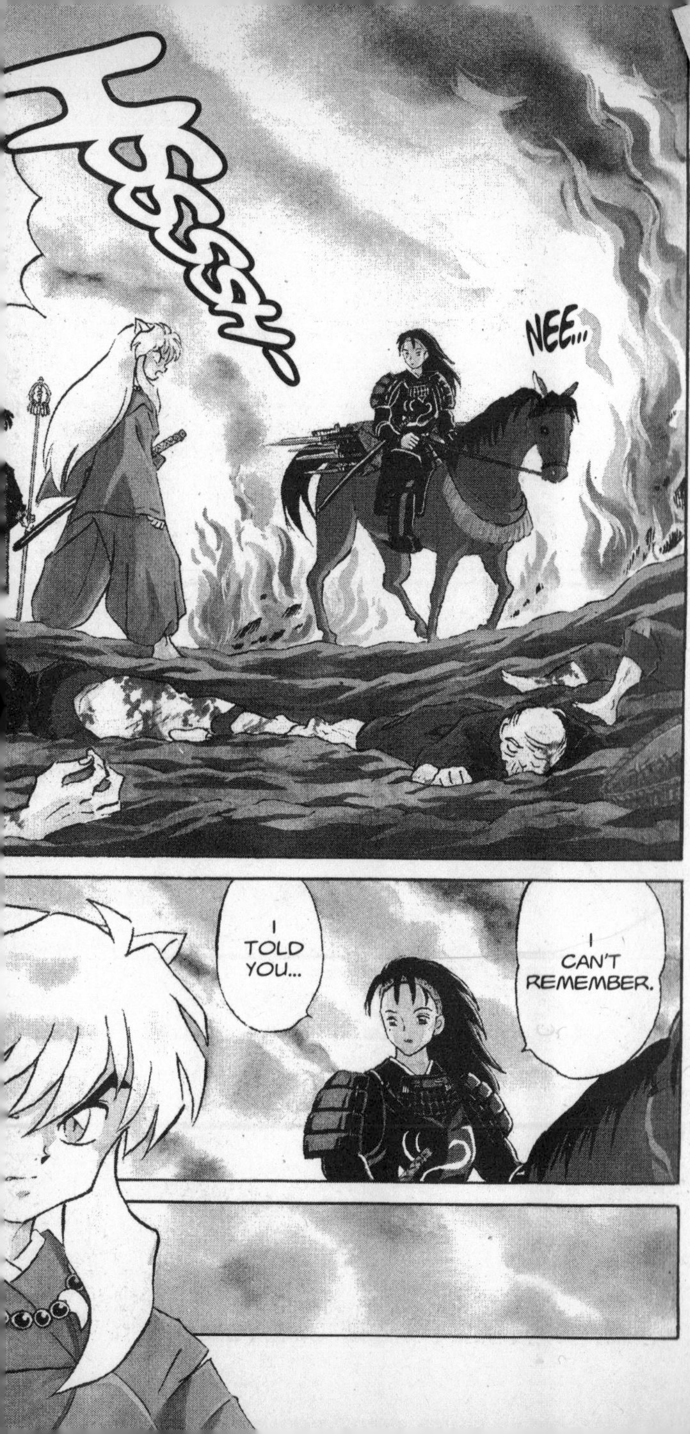
NEE...
I TOLD YOU...
I CAN'T REMEMBER.

THE STORY THUS FAR

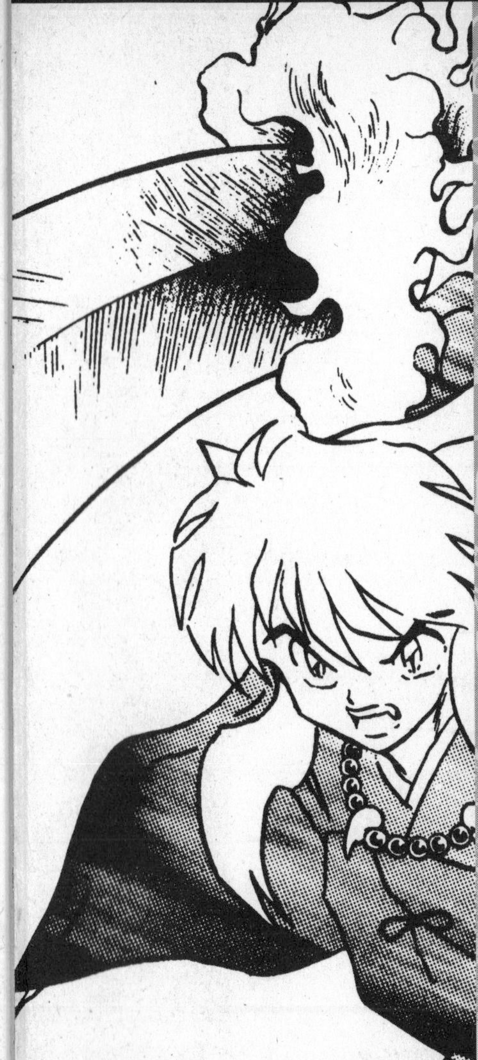

Long ago, in the "Warring States" era of Japan's Muromachi period (*Sengoku-jidai*, approximately 1467-1568 CE), a legendary dog-like half-demon called "Inu-Yasha" attempted to steal the Shikon Jewel—or "Jewel of Four Souls"—from a village, but was stopped by the enchanted arrow of the village priestess, Kikyo. Inu-Yasha fell into a deep sleep, pinned to a tree by Kikyo's arrow, while the mortally wounded Kikyo took the Shikon Jewel with her into the fires of her funeral pyre. Years passed.

Fast-forward to the present day. Kagome, a Japanese high school girl, is pulled into a well one day by a mysterious centipede monster and finds herself transported into the past—only to come face to face with the trapped Inu-Yasha. She frees him, and Inu-Yasha easily defeats the centipede monster.

The residents of the village, now 50 years older, readily accept Kagome as the reincarnation of their deceased priestess Kikyo, a claim supported by the fact that the Shikon Jewel emerges from a cut on Kagome's body. Unfortunately, the jewel's rediscovery means that the village is soon under attack by a variety of demons in search of this treasure. Then, the jewel is accidentally shattered into many shards, each of which may have the fearsome power of the entire jewel.

Although Inu-Yasha says he hates Kagome because of her resemblance to Kikyo, the woman who "killed" him, he is forced to team up with her when Kaede, the village leader, binds him to Kagome with a powerful spell. Now the two grudging companions must fight to reclaim and reassemble the shattered shards of the Shikon Jewel before they fall into the wrong hands....

THIS VOLUME Locked in battle with Ryôkotsusei—the same demon responsible for his father's death—Inu-Yasha may have a chance at victory...but not if he can't master the "Backlash Wave" (Bakuryû-ha). Meanwhile, when Kagome is bitten by Tsubaki's familiar, the Shikon Jewel shards themselves are affected. What can it mean for the shards to turn black...?

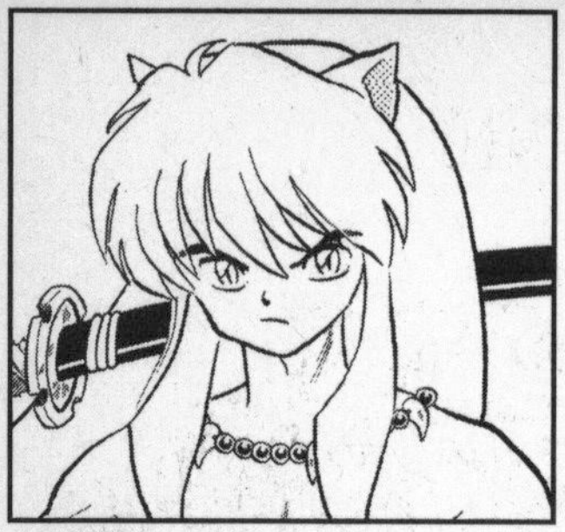

INU-YASHA
Half-demon hybrid, son of a human mother and demon father. His necklace is enchanted, allowing Kagome to control him with a word.

KAGOME
Modern-day Japanese schoolgirl who can travel back and forth between the past and present through an enchanted well.

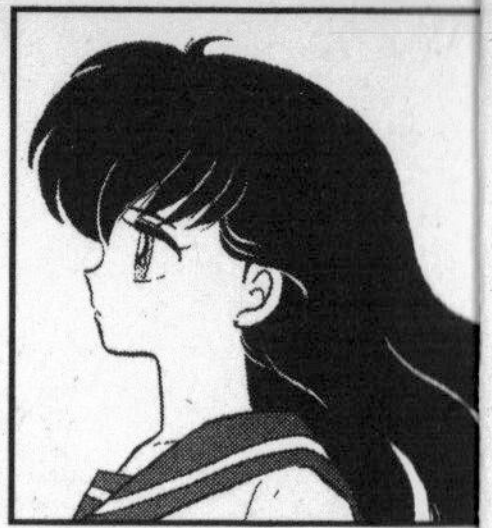

MIROKU
Lecherous Buddhist priest cursed with a mystical "hellhole" in his hand that's slowly killing him.

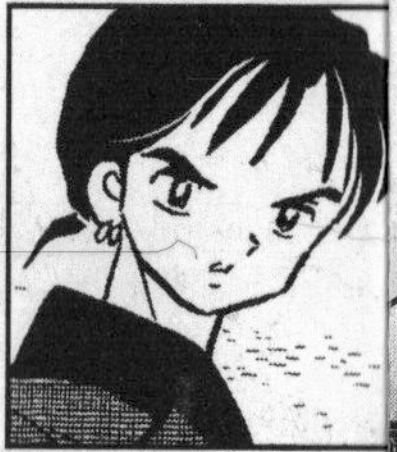

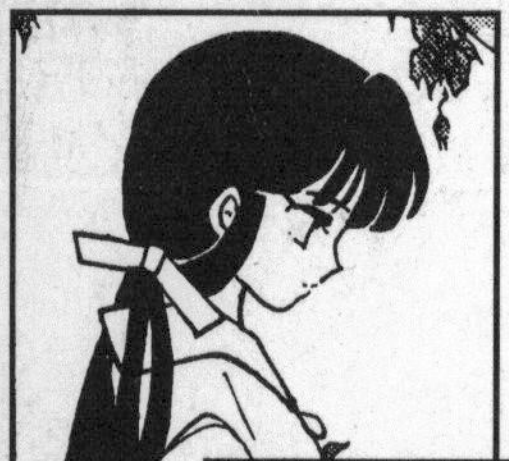

KIKYO and KAEDE
Once older and younger sisters, Kikyo's initial death and Kaede's long human life have put them half a century apart.

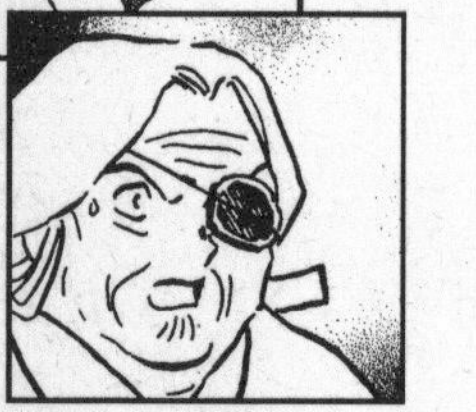

SANGO
"Demon Exterminator" or slayer from the village where the Shikon Jewel was first born.

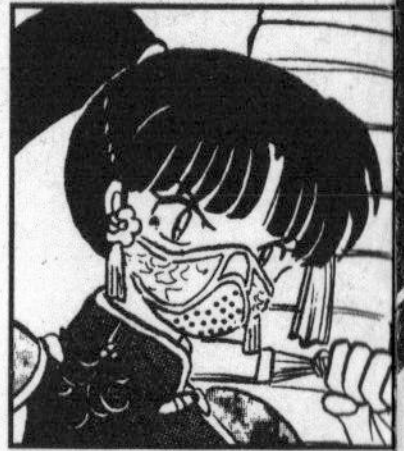

KAGURA
A demon created by Naraku from parts of his body, Kagura—the Wind Demon—is Naraku's second incarnation. Unlike others, however, Kagura resents Naraku's control over her and aids him only for her own survival.

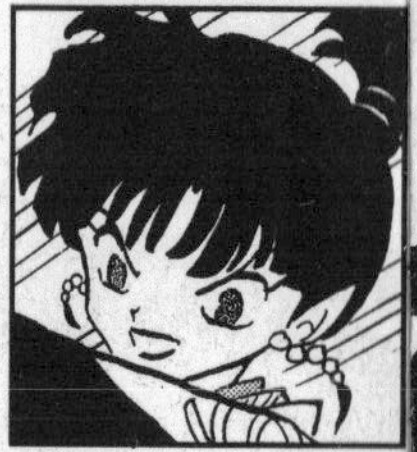

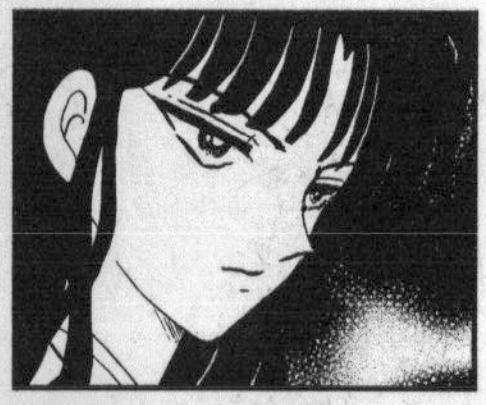

NARAKU
Enigmatic demon-mastermind behind the miseries of nearly everyone in the story.

ONIGUMO
A one-time thief whose face and body were so badly burned even Kikyo was unable to do much for him; the love he feels for Kikyo is the one thing that seems to remain in an otherwise faceless sea of lost memories.

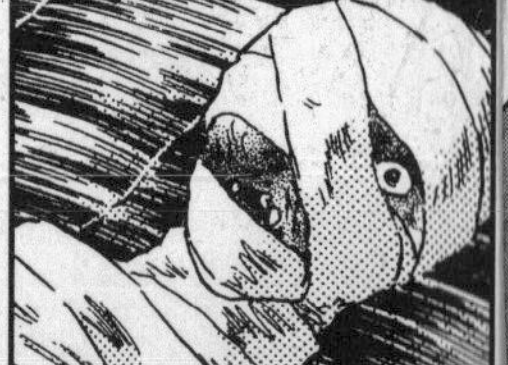

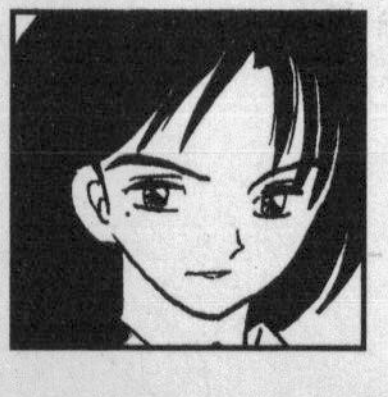

MUSO
Strange, faceless man who steals face after face from others, in search of just the right one for himself.

SCROLL O

PEERL

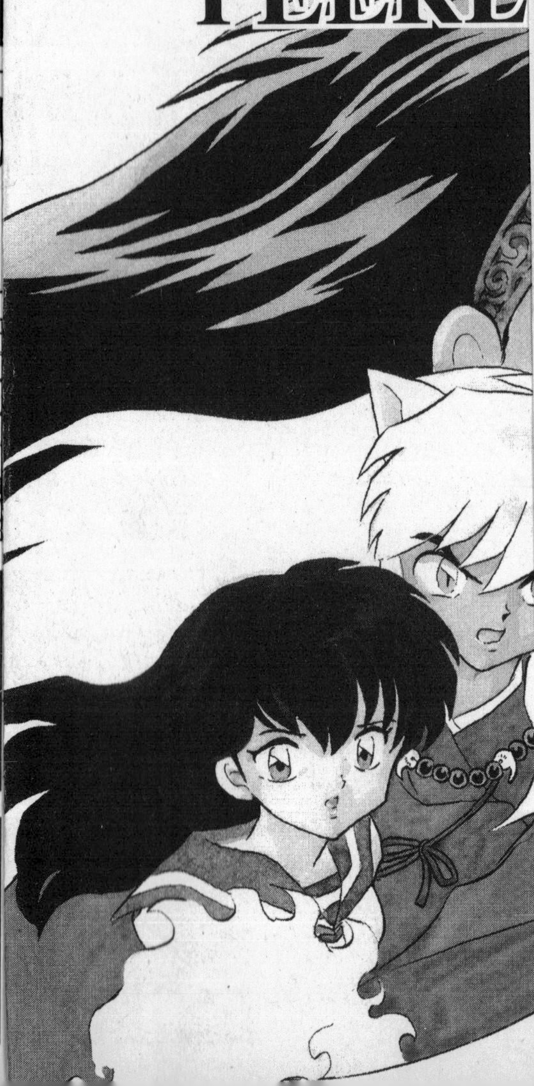

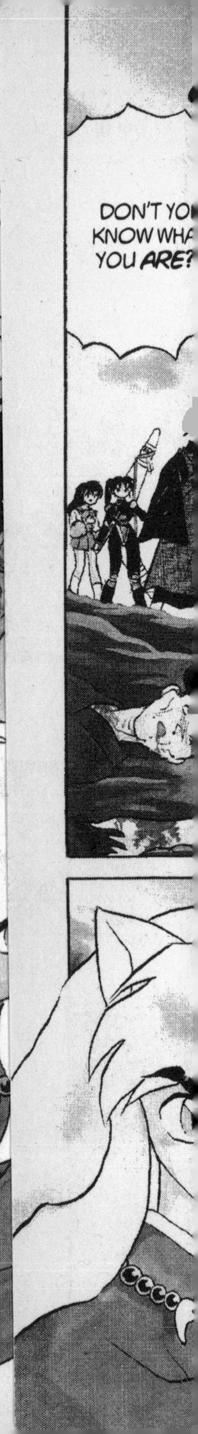
DON'T YO
KNOW WHA
YOU ARE?

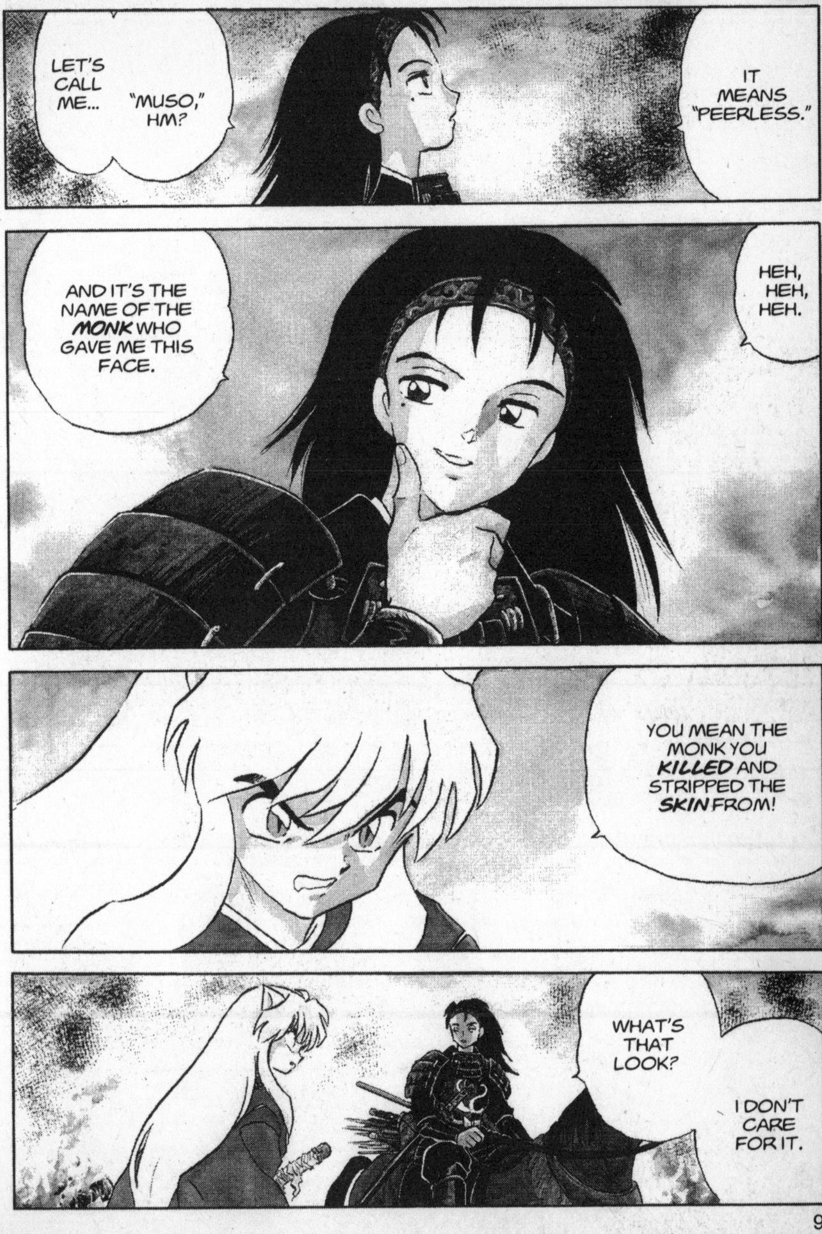
LET'S CALL ME... "MUSO," HM?
IT MEANS "PEERLESS."
AND IT'S THE NAME OF THE MONK WHO GAVE ME THIS FACE.
HEH, HEH, HEH.
YOU MEAN THE MONK YOU KILLED AND STRIPPED THE SKIN FROM!
WHAT'S THAT LOOK?
I DON'T CARE FOR IT.

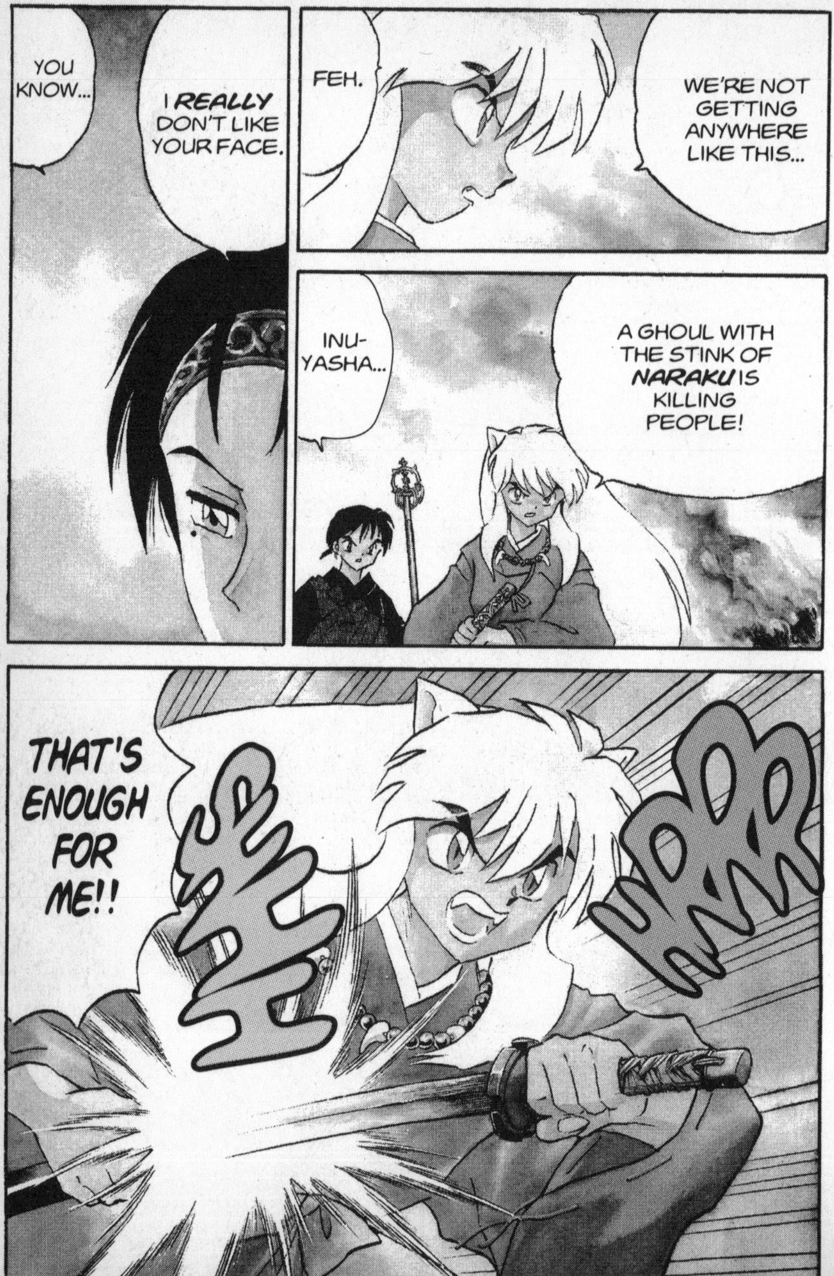
YOU KNOW...
I **REALLY** DON'T LIKE YOUR FACE.
FEH.
WE'RE NOT GETTING ANYWHERE LIKE THIS...
INU-YASHA...
A GHOUL WITH THE STINK OF **NARAKU** IS KILLING PEOPLE!
THAT'S ENOUGH FOR ME!!

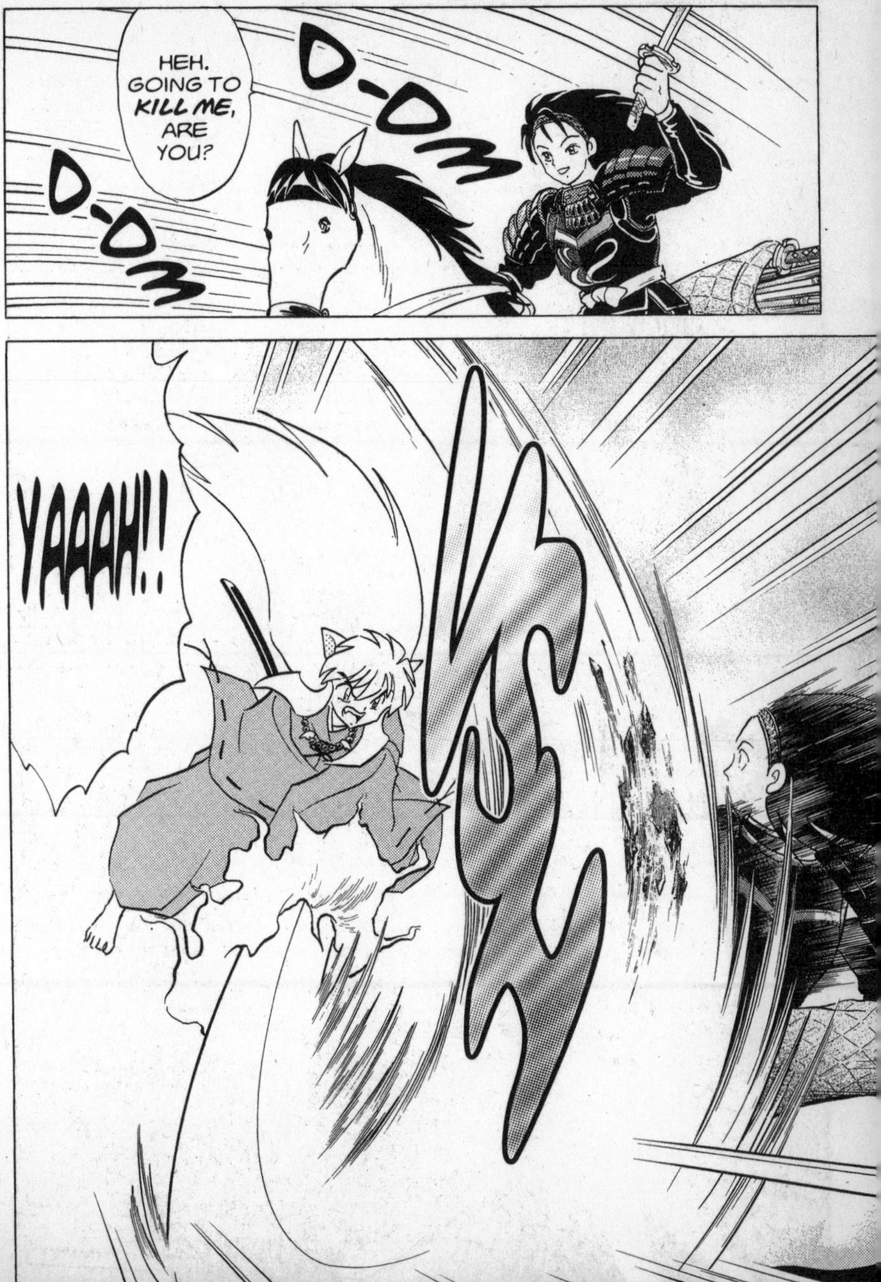
HEH. GOING TO KILL ME, ARE YOU?
D-DM
D-DM
YAAAH!!

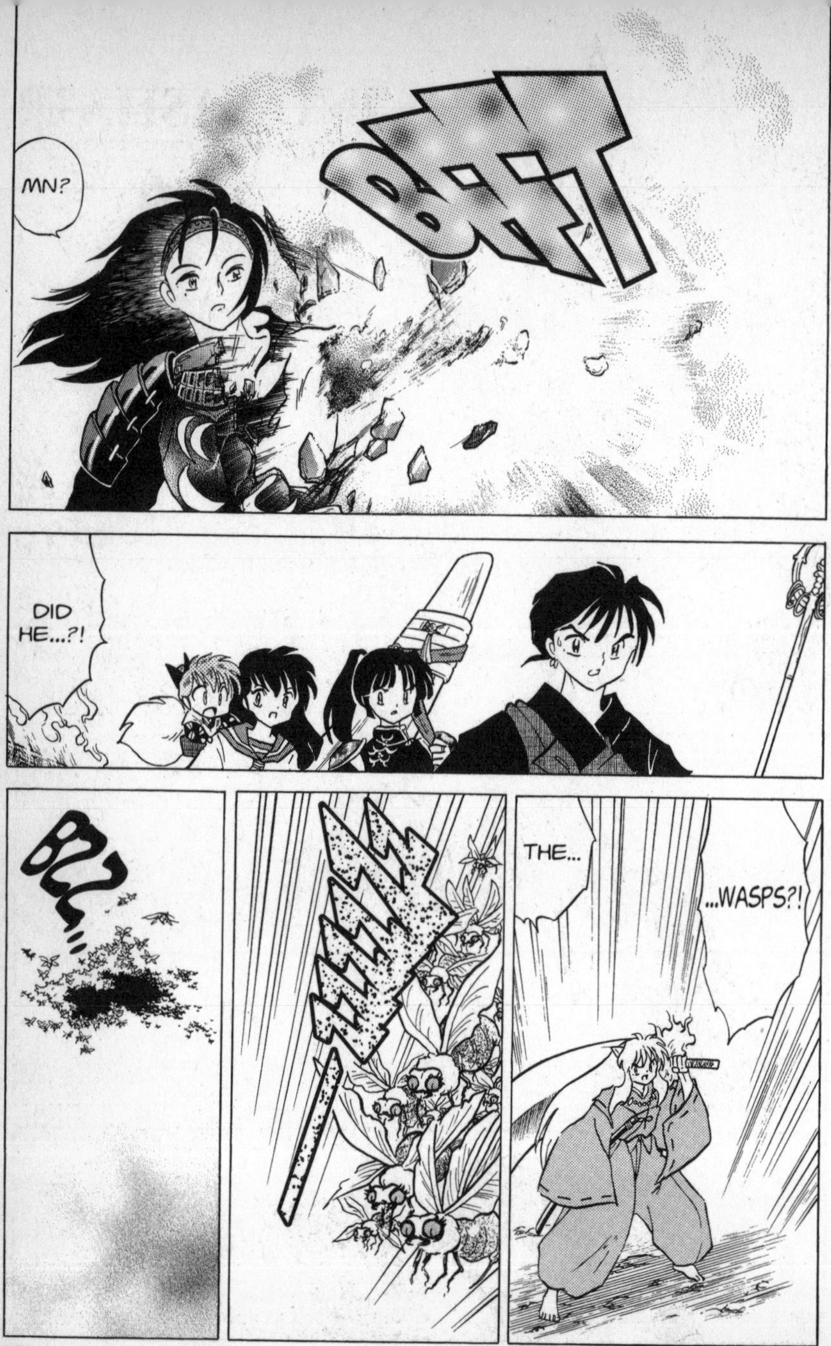
MN?
DID HE...?!
BZZ...
THE...
...WASPS?!

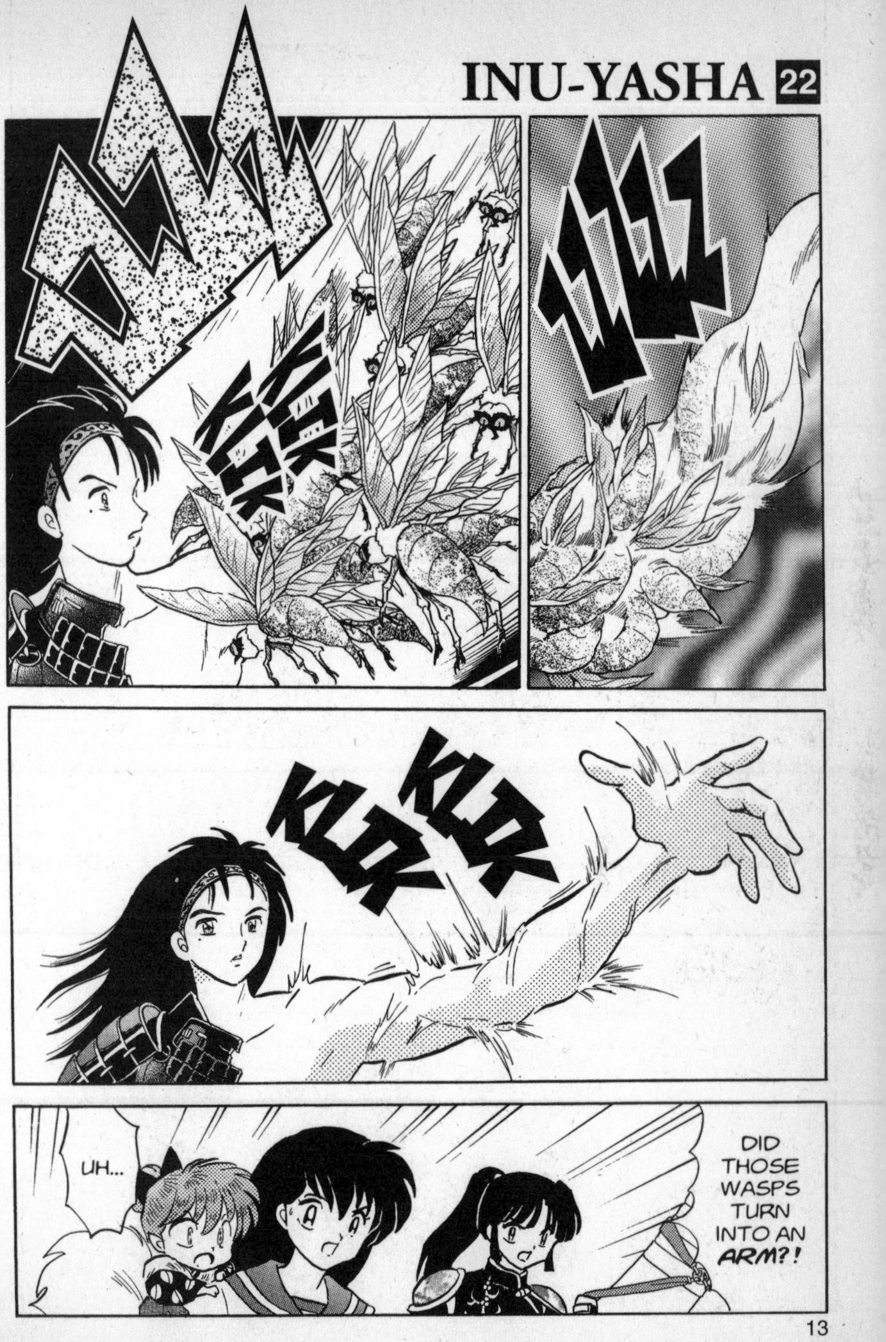
KLTK KLTK
KLTK KLTK
UH...
DID THOSE WASPS TURN INTO AN *ARM*?!

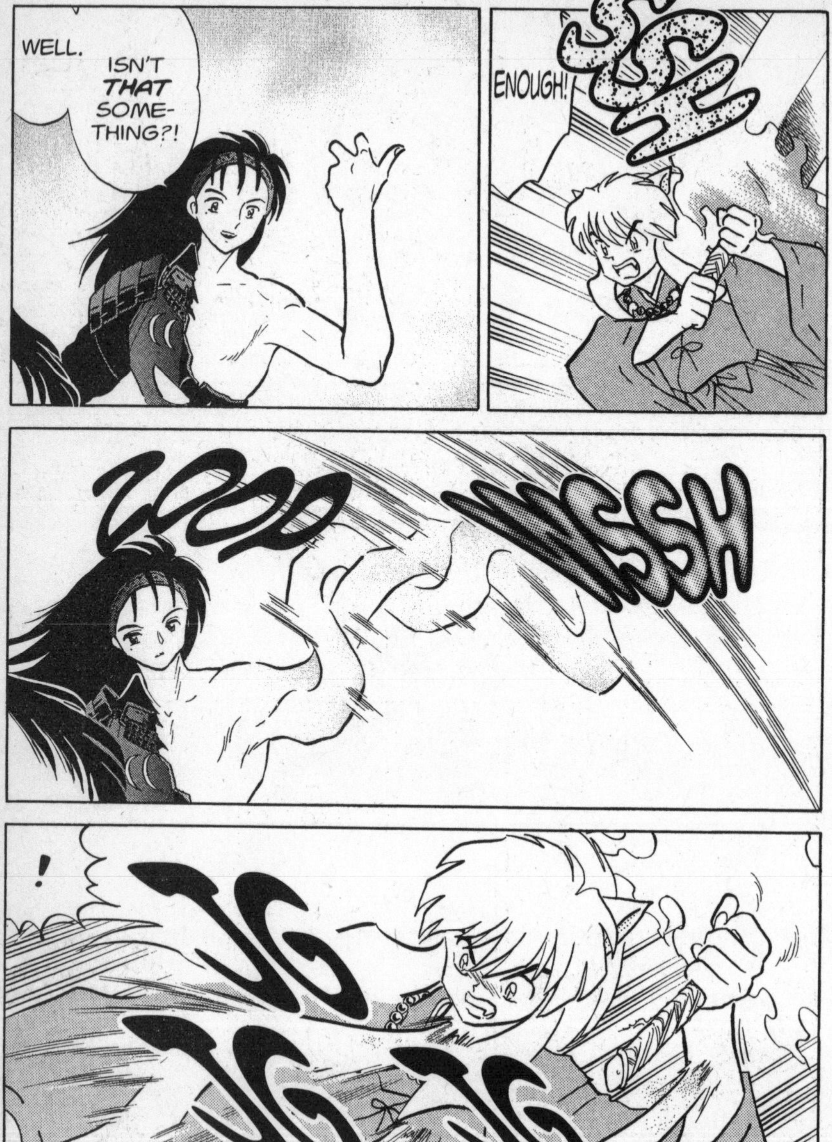
WELL.
ISN'T **THAT** SOME-THING?!
ENOUGH!
!

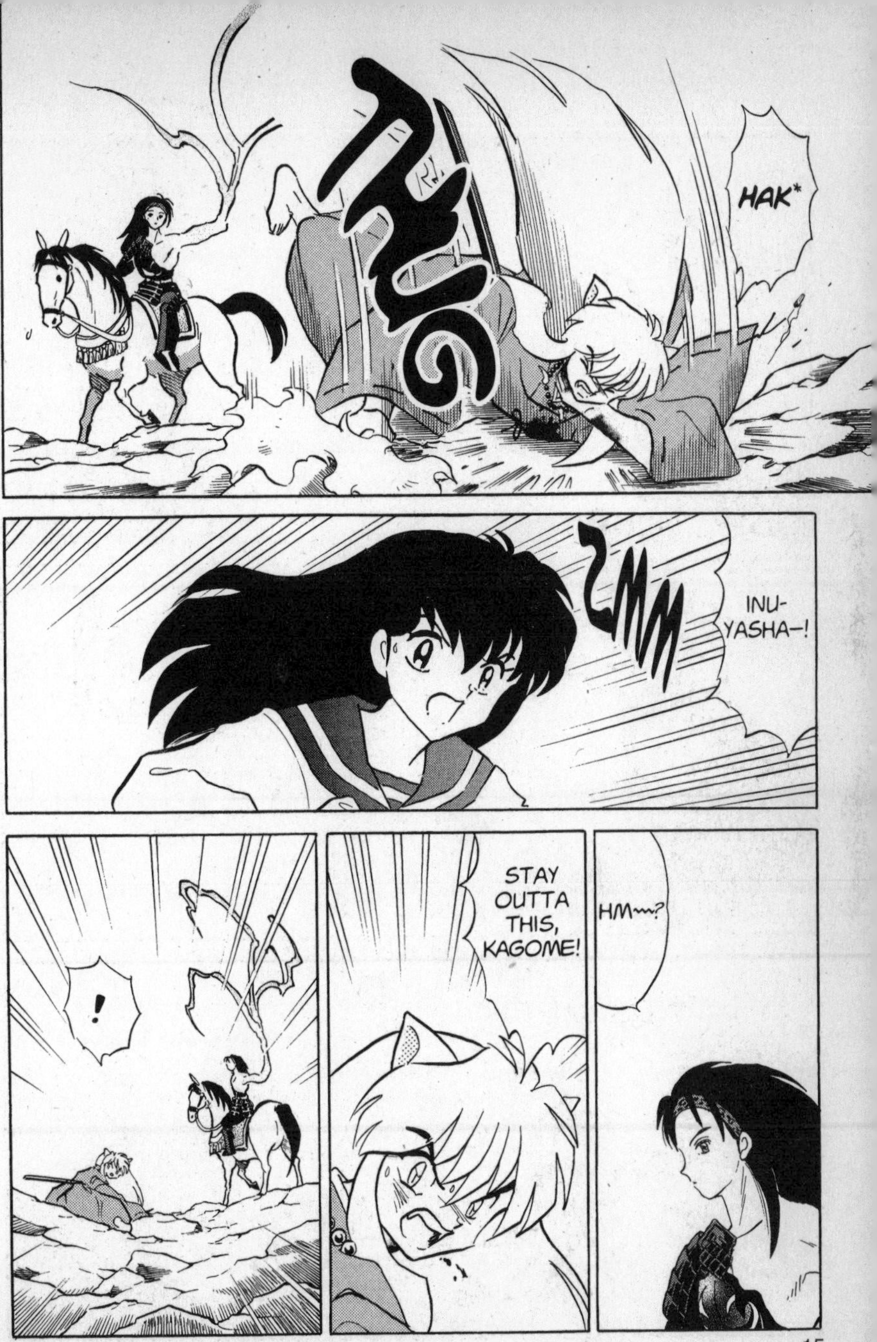
THUD
HAK*
INU-
YASHA—!
!
STAY
OUTTA
THIS,
KAGOME!
HM~?

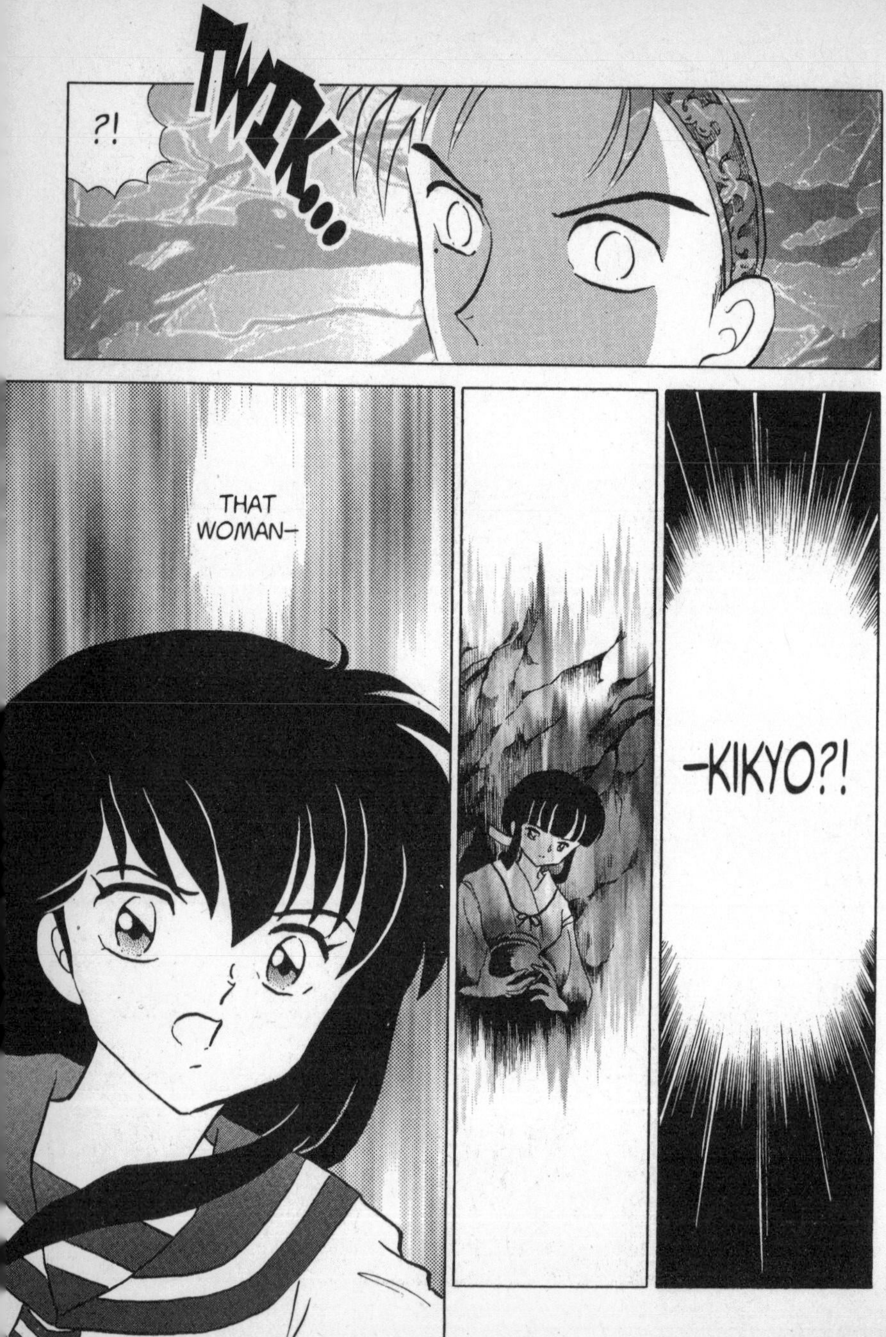
?!
TWEK...
THAT WOMAN–
–KIKYO?!

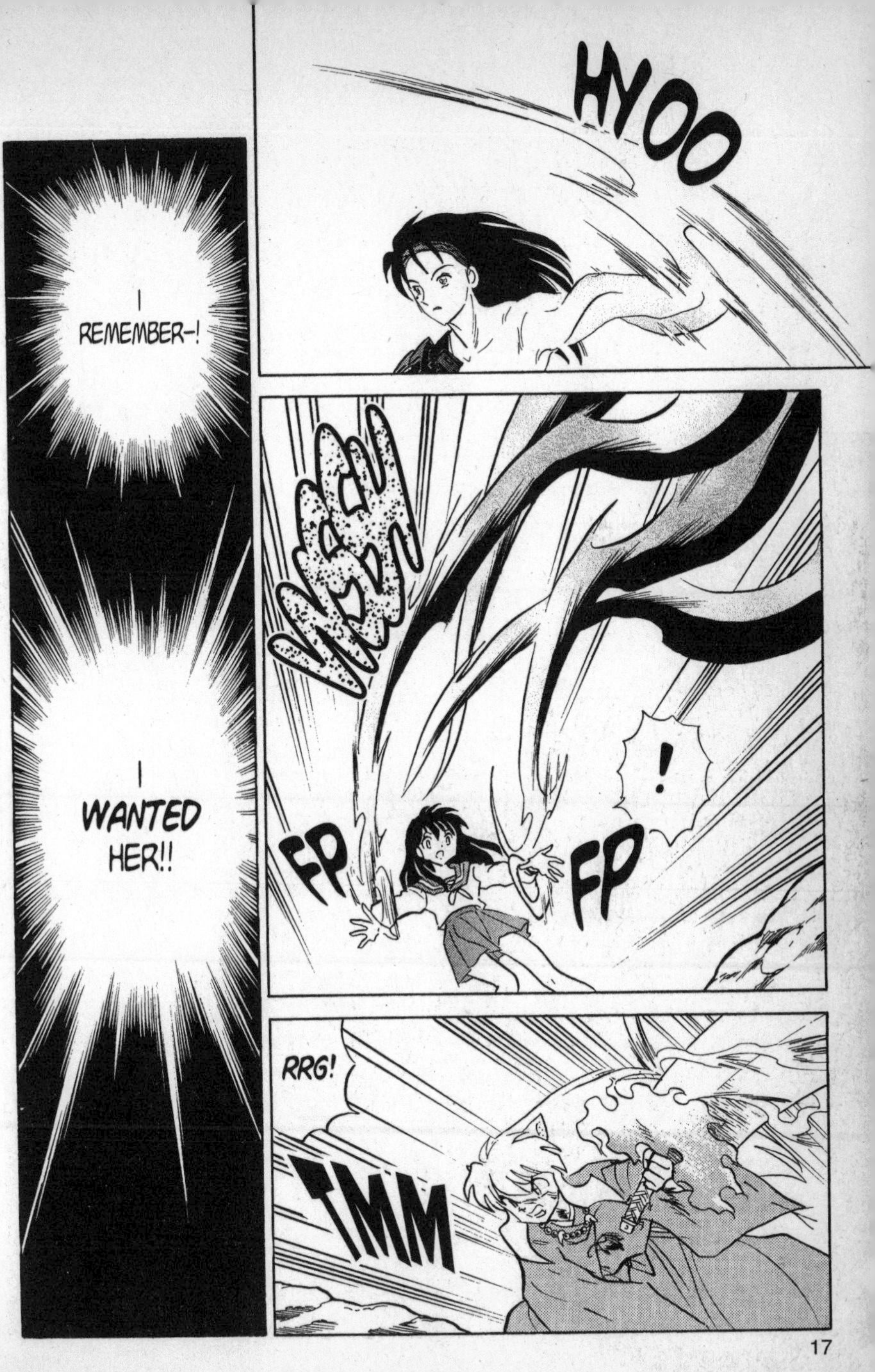
I REMEMBER–!
I WANTED HER!!
HYOO
FP
FP
!
RRG!
TMM

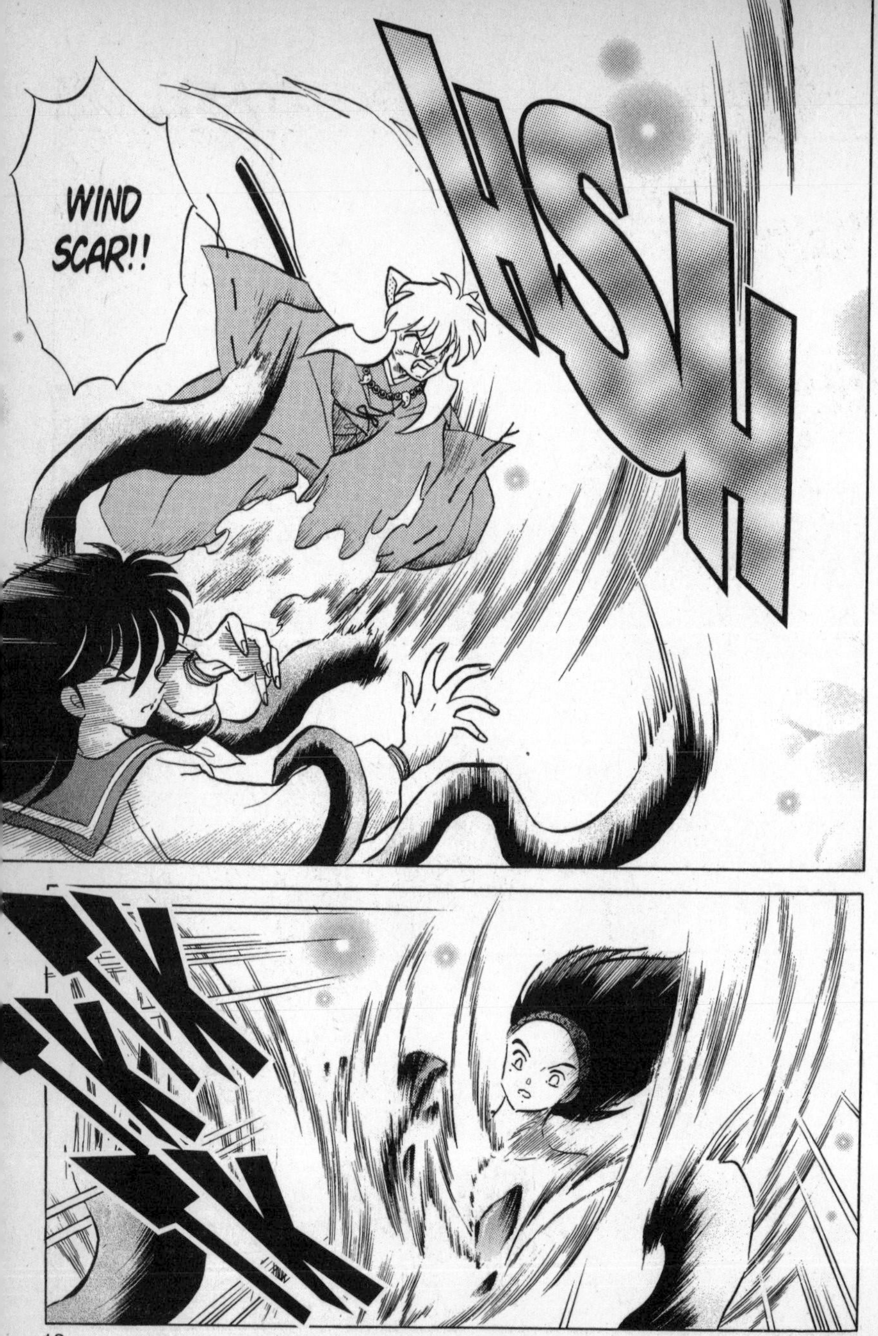
WIND SCAR!!

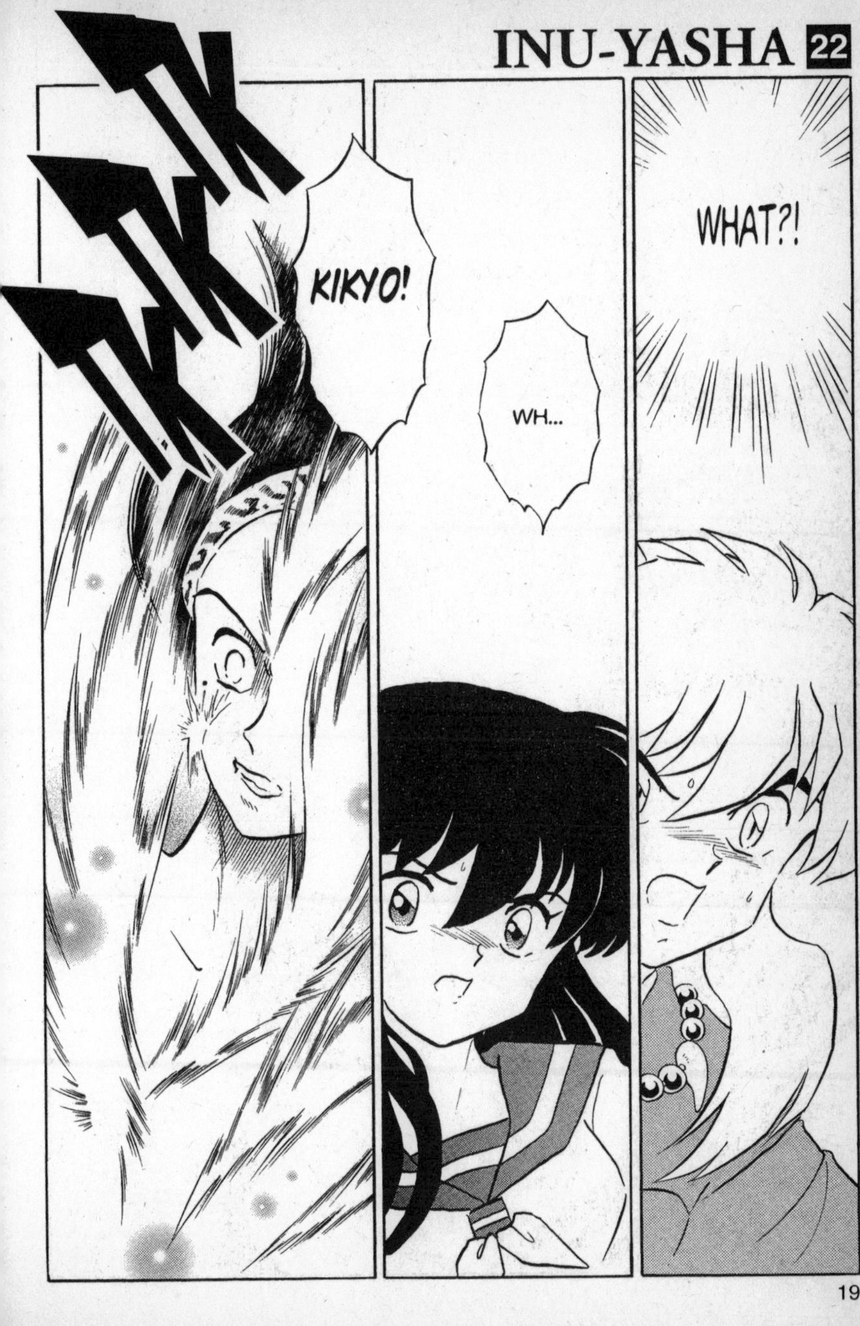
KIKYO!
WH...
WHAT?!

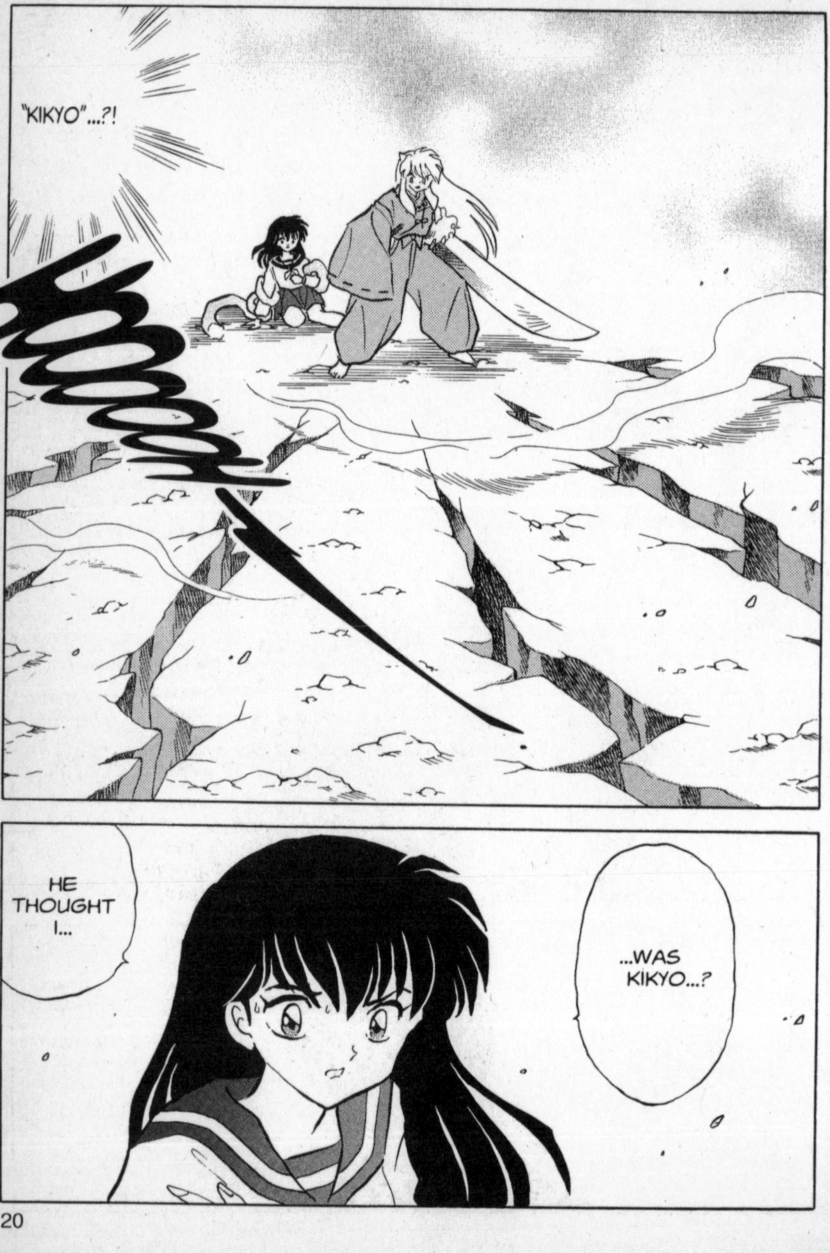
"KIKYO"...?!
HE THOUGHT I...
...WAS KIKYO...?

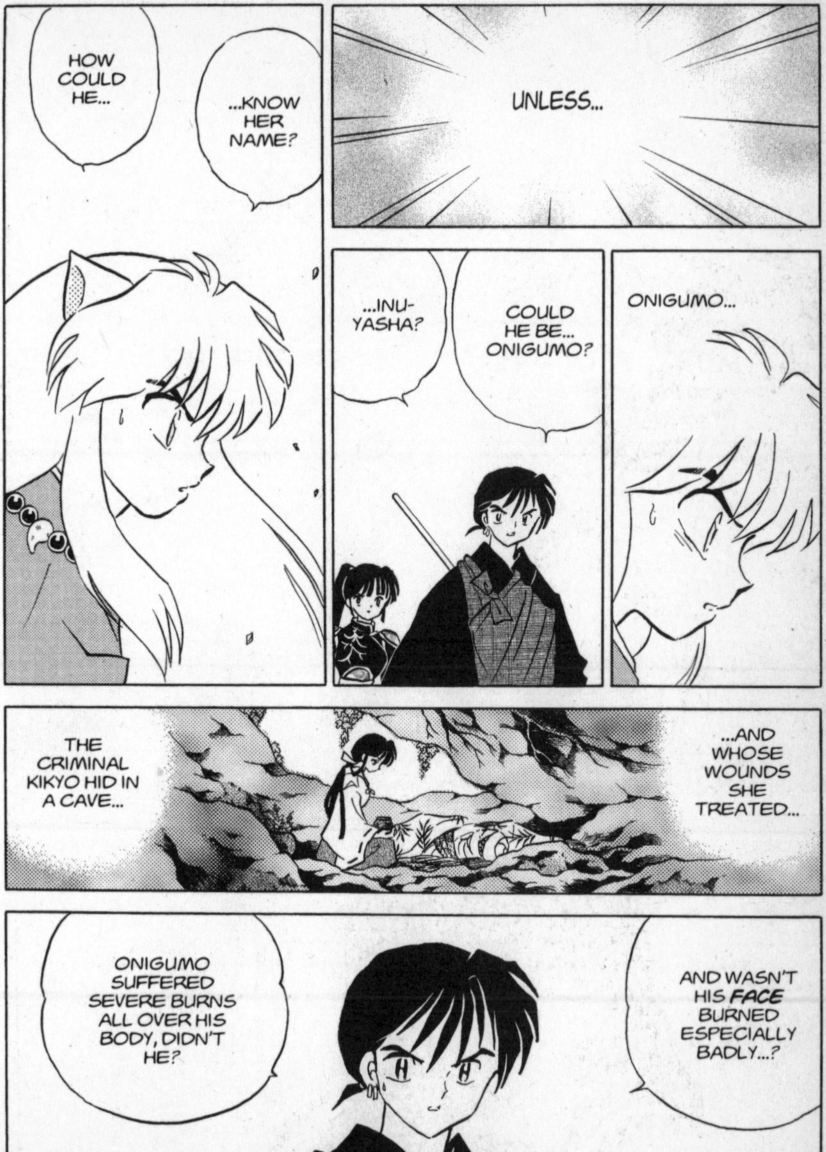
HOW COULD HE...
...KNOW HER NAME?
UNLESS...
...INU-YASHA?
COULD HE BE... ONIGUMO?
ONIGUMO...
THE CRIMINAL KIKYO HID IN A CAVE...
...AND WHOSE WOUNDS SHE TREATED...
ONIGUMO SUFFERED SEVERE BURNS ALL OVER HIS BODY, DIDN'T HE?
AND WASN'T HIS *FACE* BURNED ESPECIALLY BADLY...?

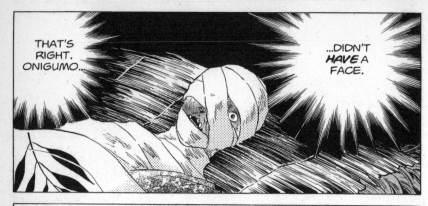

THAT'S RIGHT. ONIGUMO...

...DIDN'T **HAVE** A FACE.

AND HE HELD THOSE FEELINGS FOR KIKYO IN HIS HEART...

...HIS **TWISTED** HEART...

...THAT BECAME THE DARK CORE OF **NARAKU** WHEN ONIGUMO OFFERED UP HIS BODY TO THE DEMONS.

DEEP INSIDE NARAKU, THAT HEART STILL BURNED—

AND NOW— SOMEHOW—

...IT *EMERGED* FROM NARAKU'S BODY—AND GAINED A *FORM!*

IS ONIGUMO'S HEART FINALLY DEAD?!

THE WIND SCAR STRUCK IT STRAIGHT-ON... THERE'S NO WAY IT COULD SURVIVE...

AND YET—

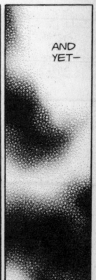

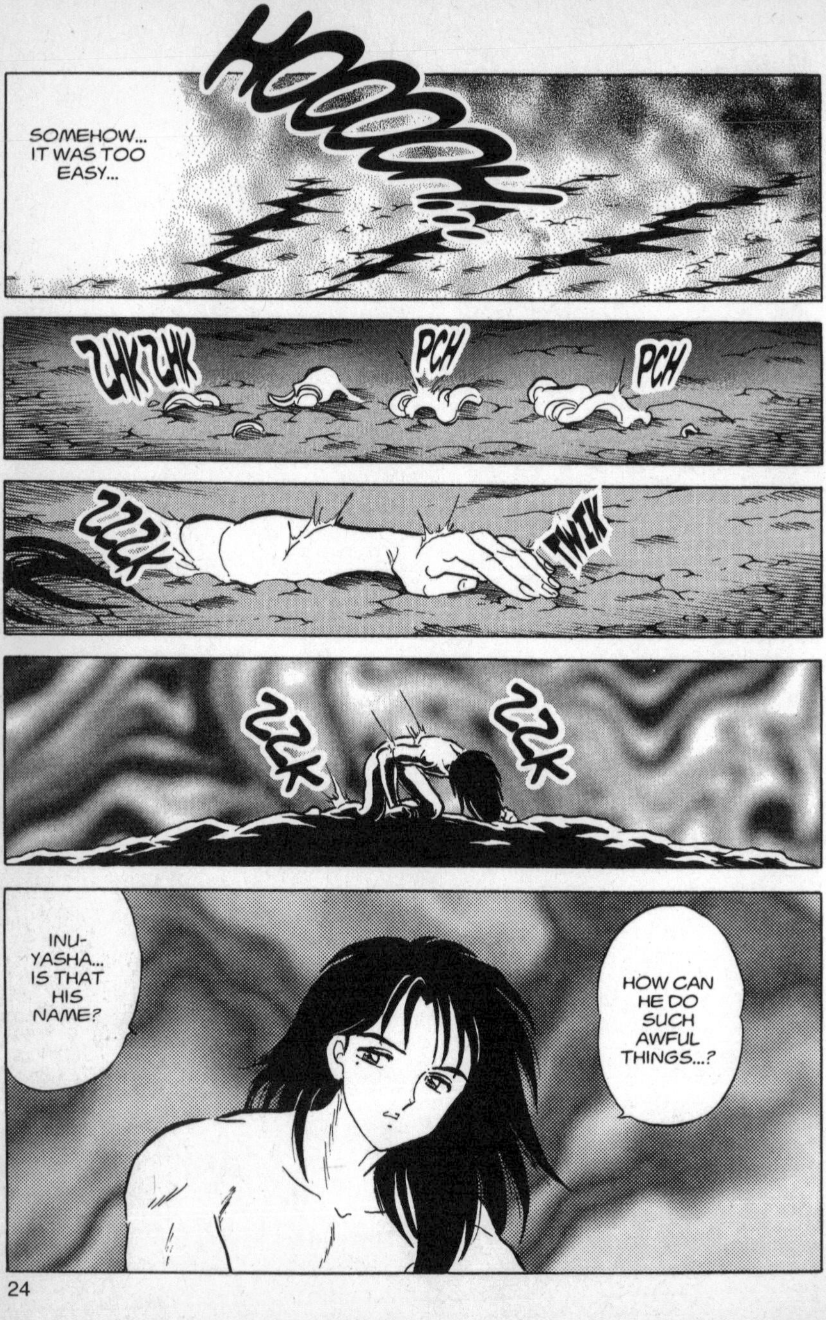
HOOOOH...
SOMEHOW... IT WAS TOO EASY...
ZHK ZHK
PCH
PCH
ZZZK
TWIK
ZZZK
ZZZK
INU-YASHA... IS THAT HIS NAME?
HOW CAN HE DO SUCH AWFUL THINGS...?

SCROLL TWO
ONIGUMO'S MEMORIES

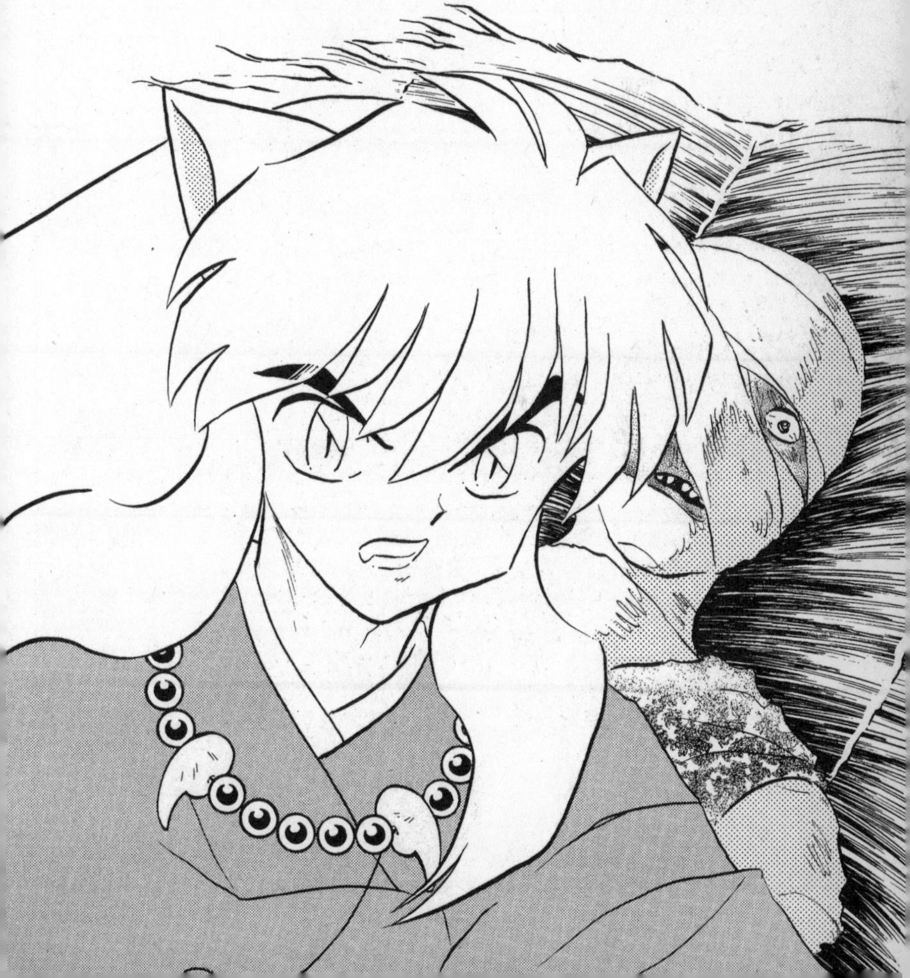

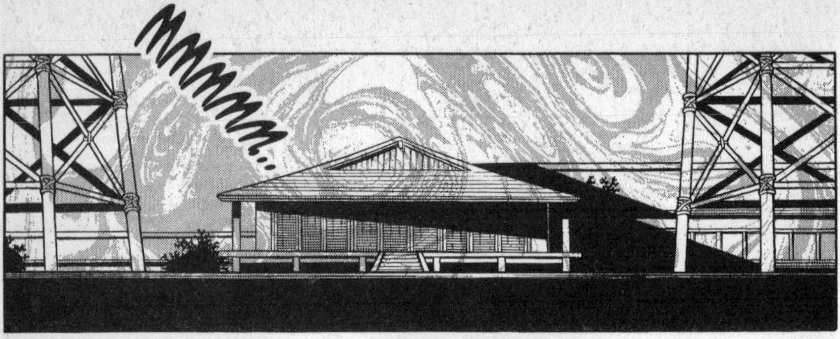
MMMMMM...

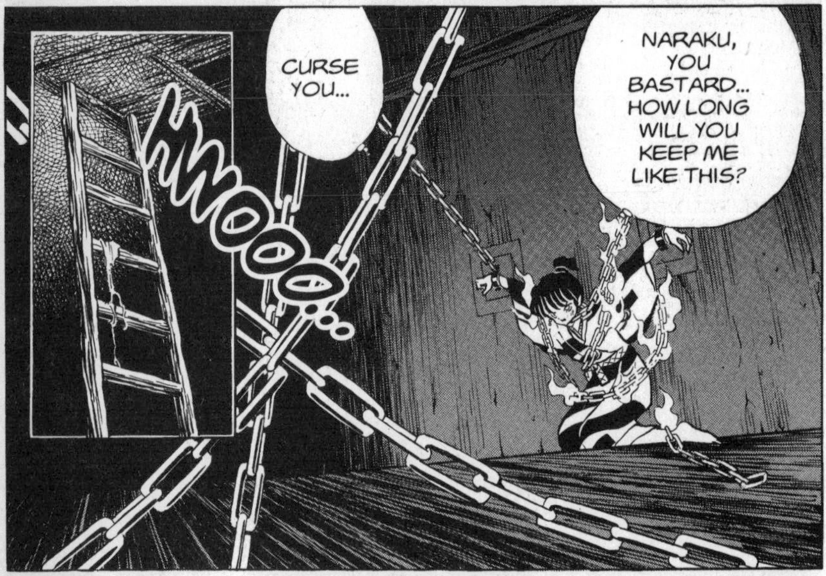
HWOOO...
CURSE YOU...
NARAKU, YOU BASTARD... HOW LONG WILL YOU KEEP ME LIKE THIS?

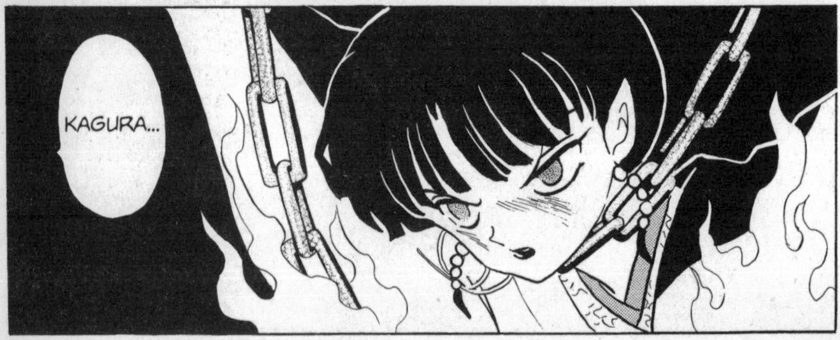
KAGURA...

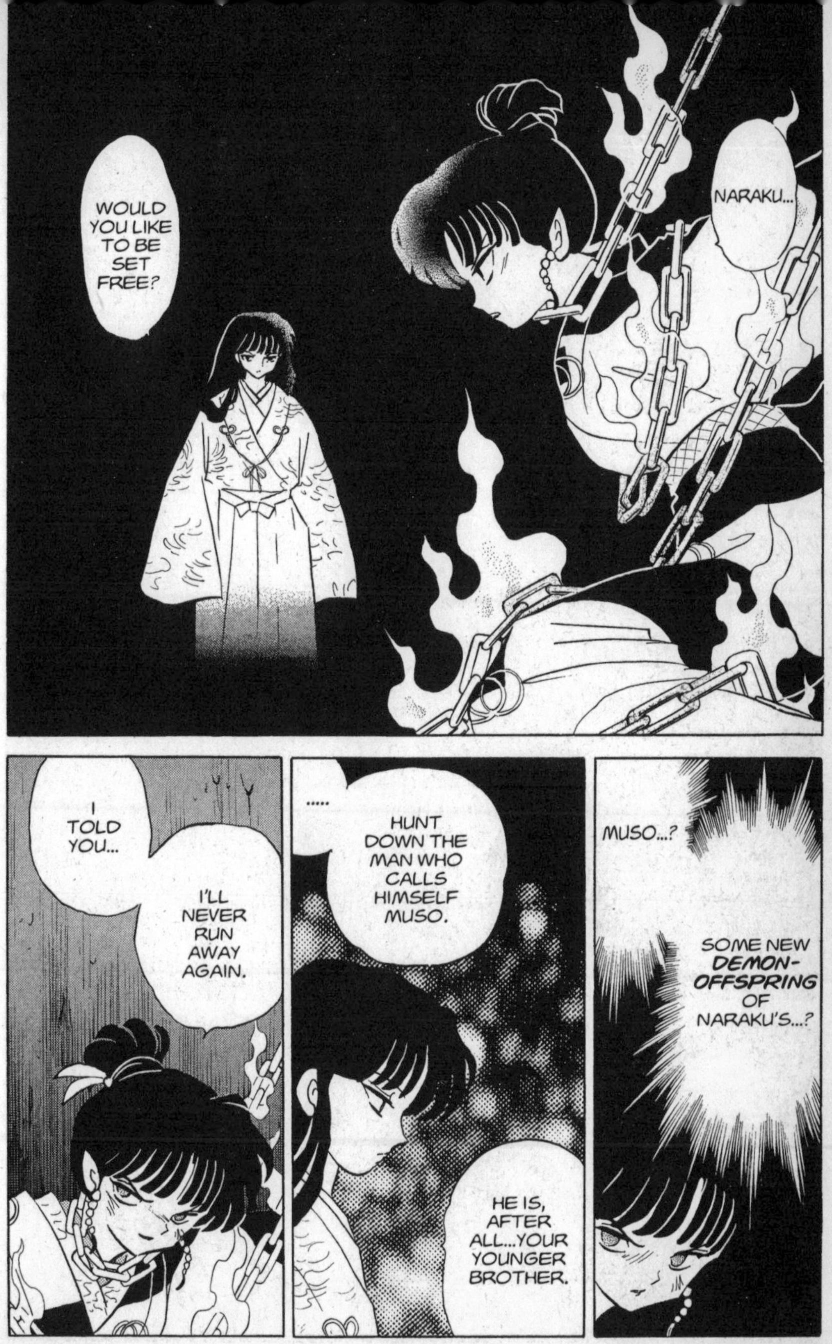
WOULD YOU LIKE TO BE SET FREE?
NARAKU...
I TOLD YOU...
I'LL NEVER RUN AWAY AGAIN.
.....
HUNT DOWN THE MAN WHO CALLS HIMSELF MUSO.
HE IS, AFTER ALL...YOUR YOUNGER BROTHER.
MUSO...?
SOME NEW DEMON-OFFSPRING OF NARAKU'S...?

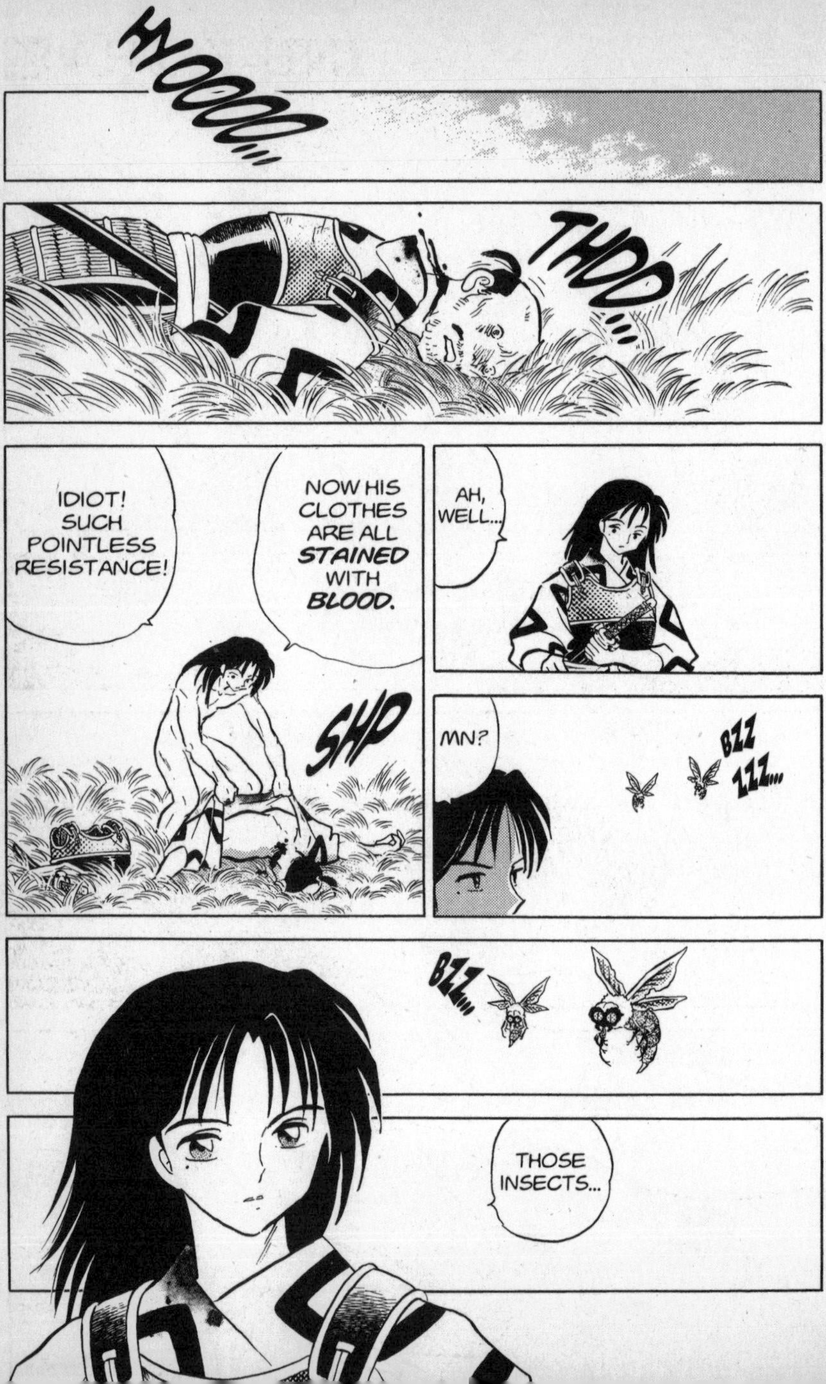
HYOOOO...
THDD...
IDIOT! SUCH POINTLESS RESISTANCE!
NOW HIS CLOTHES ARE ALL **STAINED** WITH **BLOOD.**
SHP
AH, WELL...
MN?
BZZ ZZZ...
BZZ...
THOSE INSECTS...

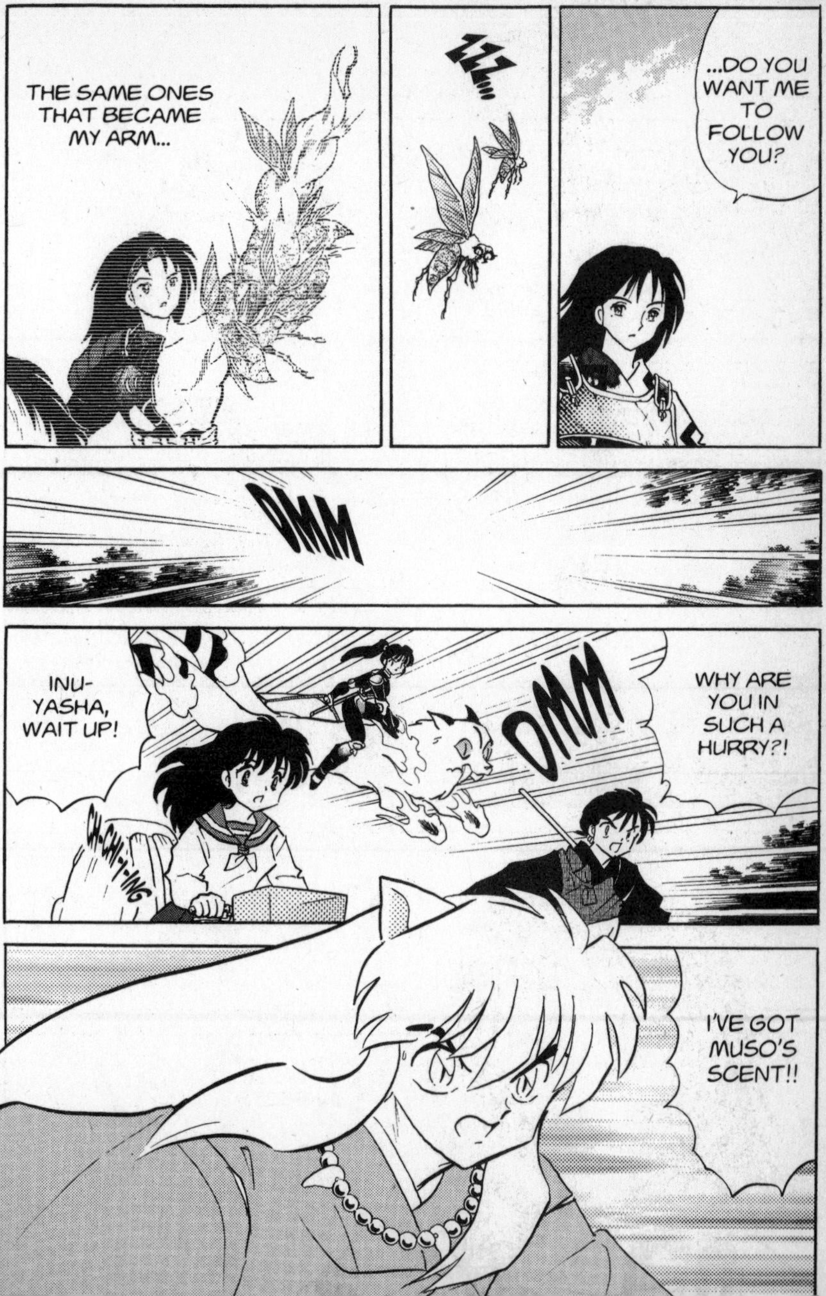
THE SAME ONES THAT BECAME MY ARM...
...DO YOU WANT ME TO FOLLOW YOU?
INU-YASHA, WAIT UP!
CH-CHI-I-ING
WHY ARE YOU IN SUCH A HURRY?!
I'VE GOT MUSO'S SCENT!!

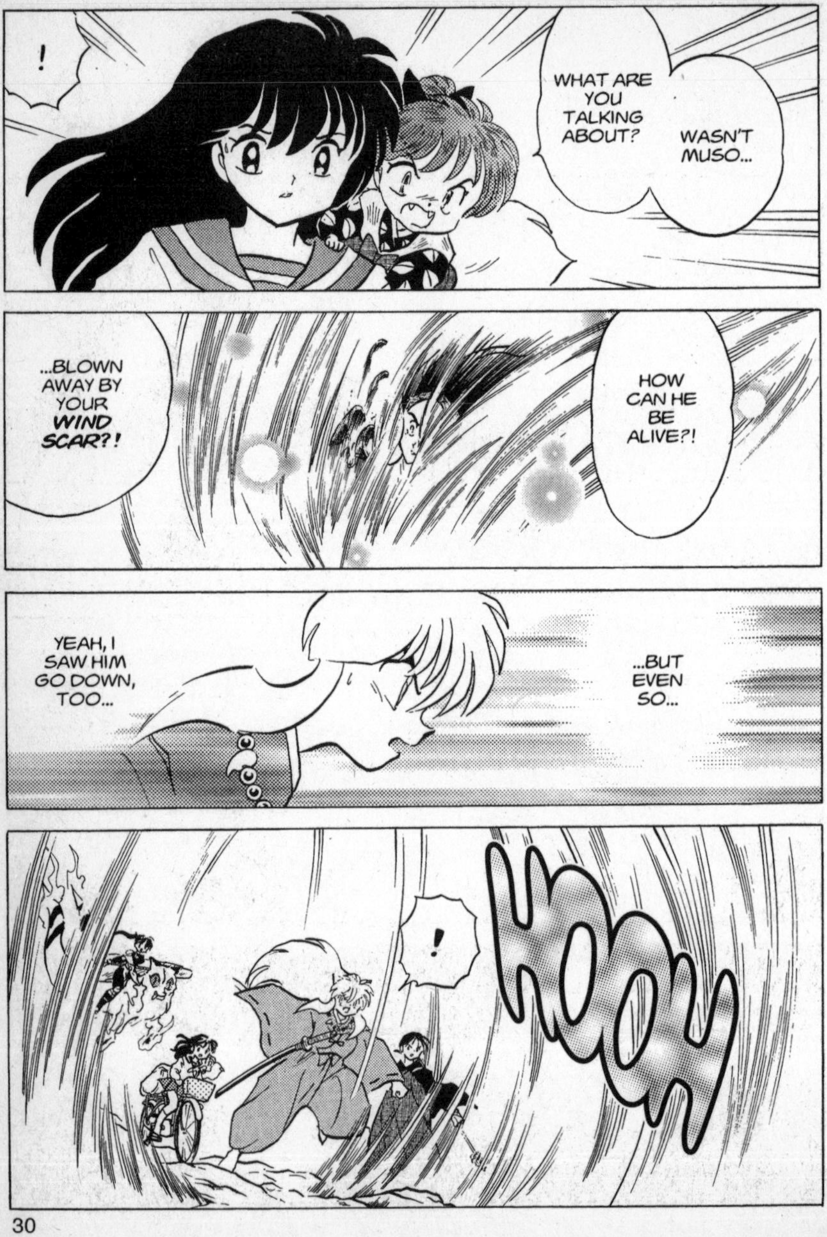
!
WHAT ARE YOU TALKING ABOUT?
WASN'T MUSO...
...BLOWN AWAY BY YOUR WIND SCAR?!
HOW CAN HE BE ALIVE?!
YEAH, I SAW HIM GO DOWN, TOO...
...BUT EVEN SO...
!
HOOOH

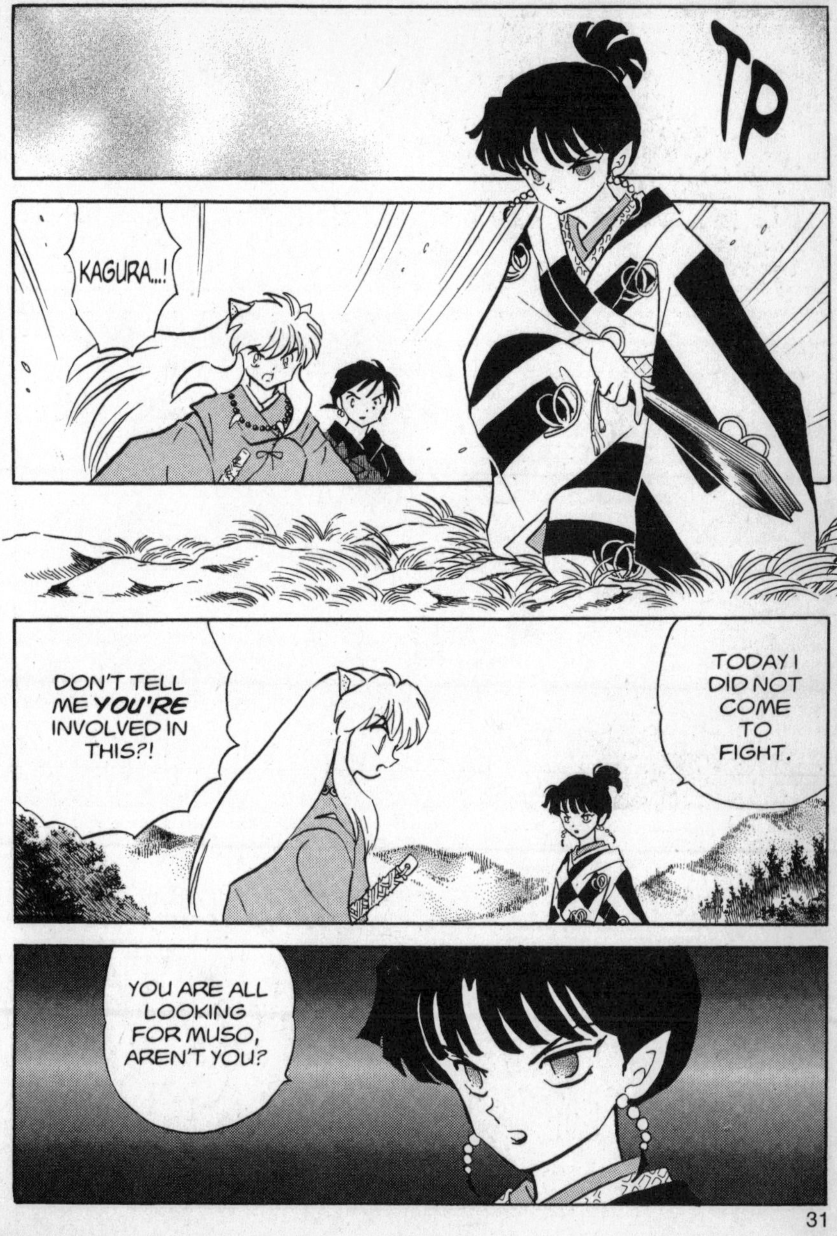
TP
KAGURA...!
DON'T TELL ME ***YOU'RE*** INVOLVED IN THIS?!
TODAY I DID NOT COME TO FIGHT.
YOU ARE ALL LOOKING FOR MUSO, AREN'T YOU?

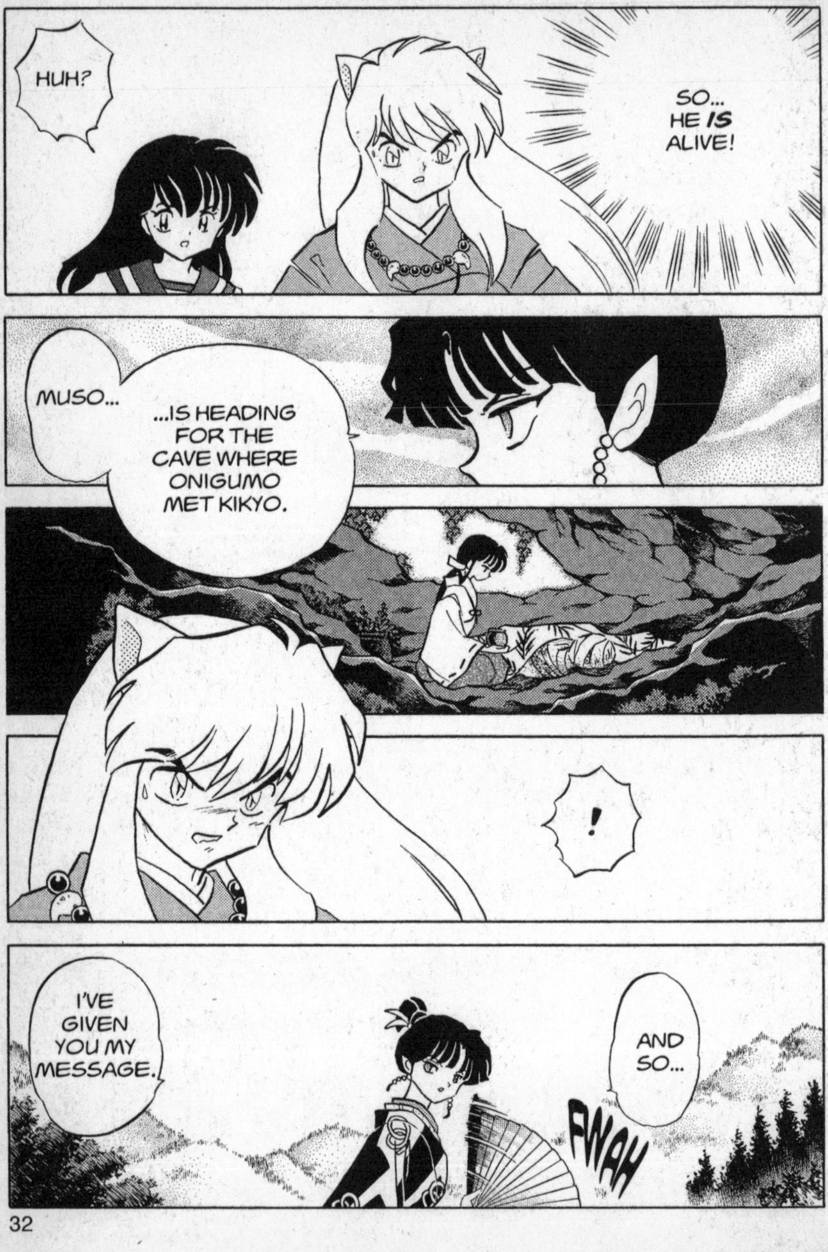
HUH?
SO... HE IS ALIVE!
MUSO...
...IS HEADING FOR THE CAVE WHERE ONIGUMO MET KIKYO.
!
I'VE GIVEN YOU MY MESSAGE.
AND SO...
FWAH

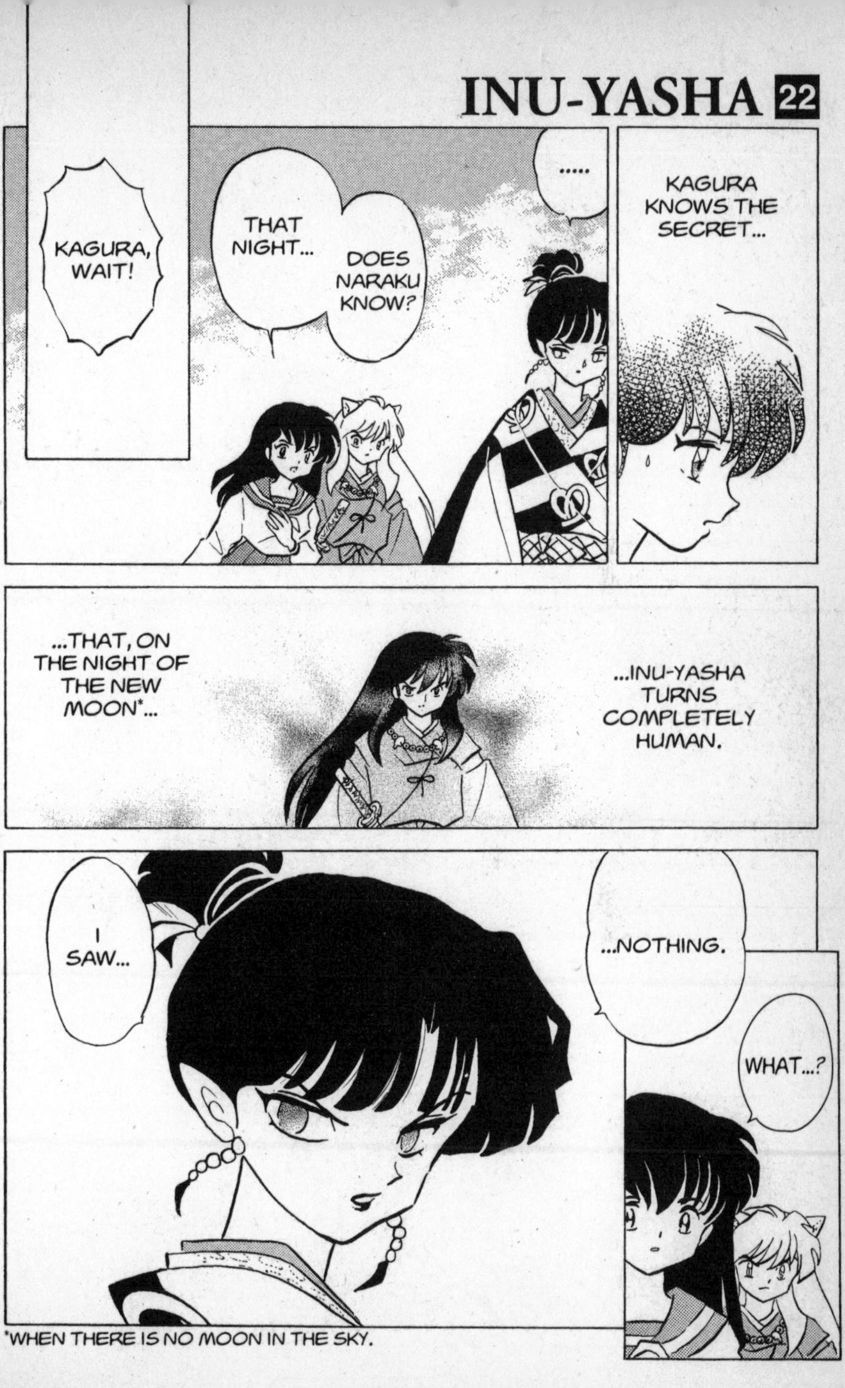
KAGURA, WAIT!
THAT NIGHT...
DOES NARAKU KNOW?
.....
KAGURA KNOWS THE SECRET...
...THAT, ON THE NIGHT OF THE NEW MOON*...
...INU-YASHA TURNS COMPLETELY HUMAN.
I SAW...
...NOTHING.
WHAT...?

*WHEN THERE IS NO MOON IN THE SKY.

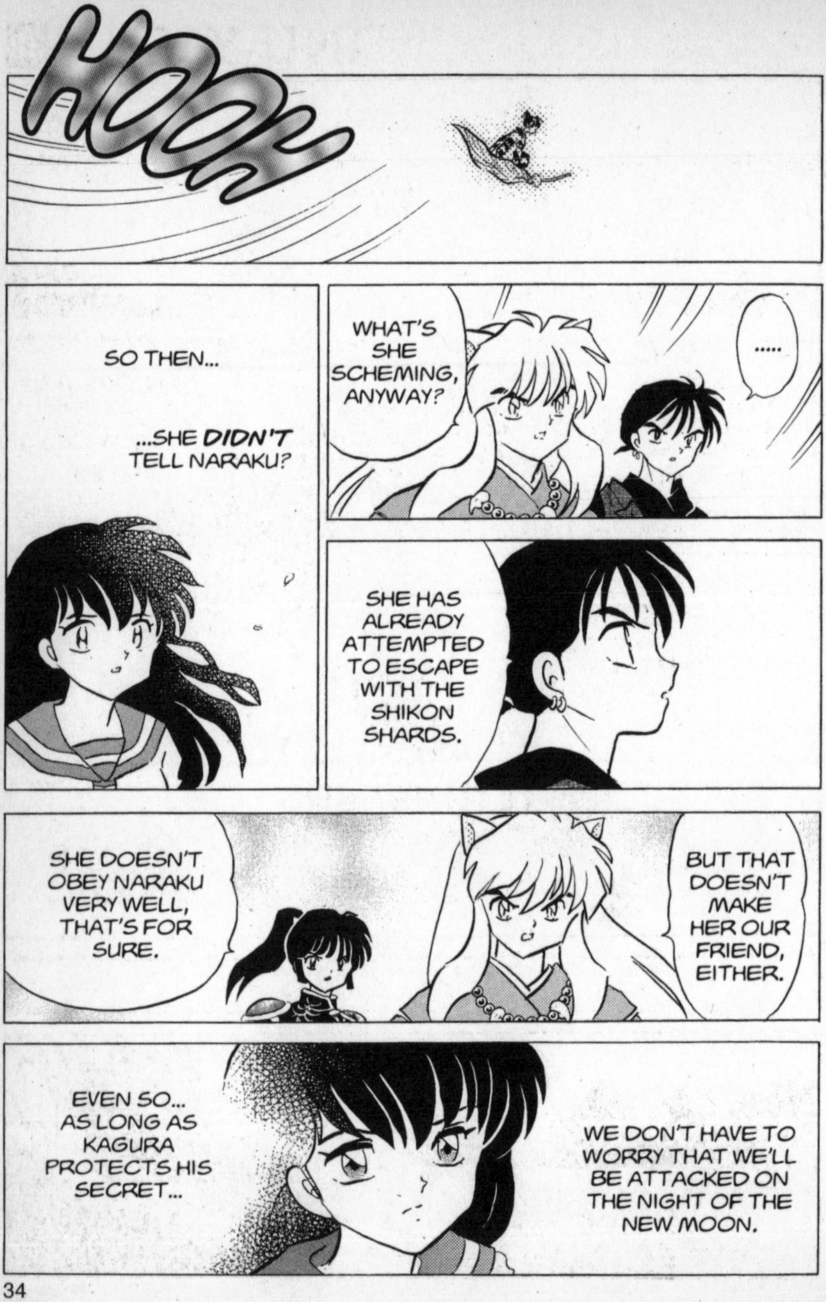
HOOOH
SO THEN...
...SHE **DIDN'T** TELL NARAKU?
WHAT'S SHE SCHEMING, ANYWAY?
.....
SHE HAS ALREADY ATTEMPTED TO ESCAPE WITH THE SHIKON SHARDS.
SHE DOESN'T OBEY NARAKU VERY WELL, THAT'S FOR SURE.
BUT THAT DOESN'T MAKE HER OUR FRIEND, EITHER.
EVEN SO... AS LONG AS KAGURA PROTECTS HIS SECRET...
WE DON'T HAVE TO WORRY THAT WE'LL BE ATTACKED ON THE NIGHT OF THE NEW MOON.

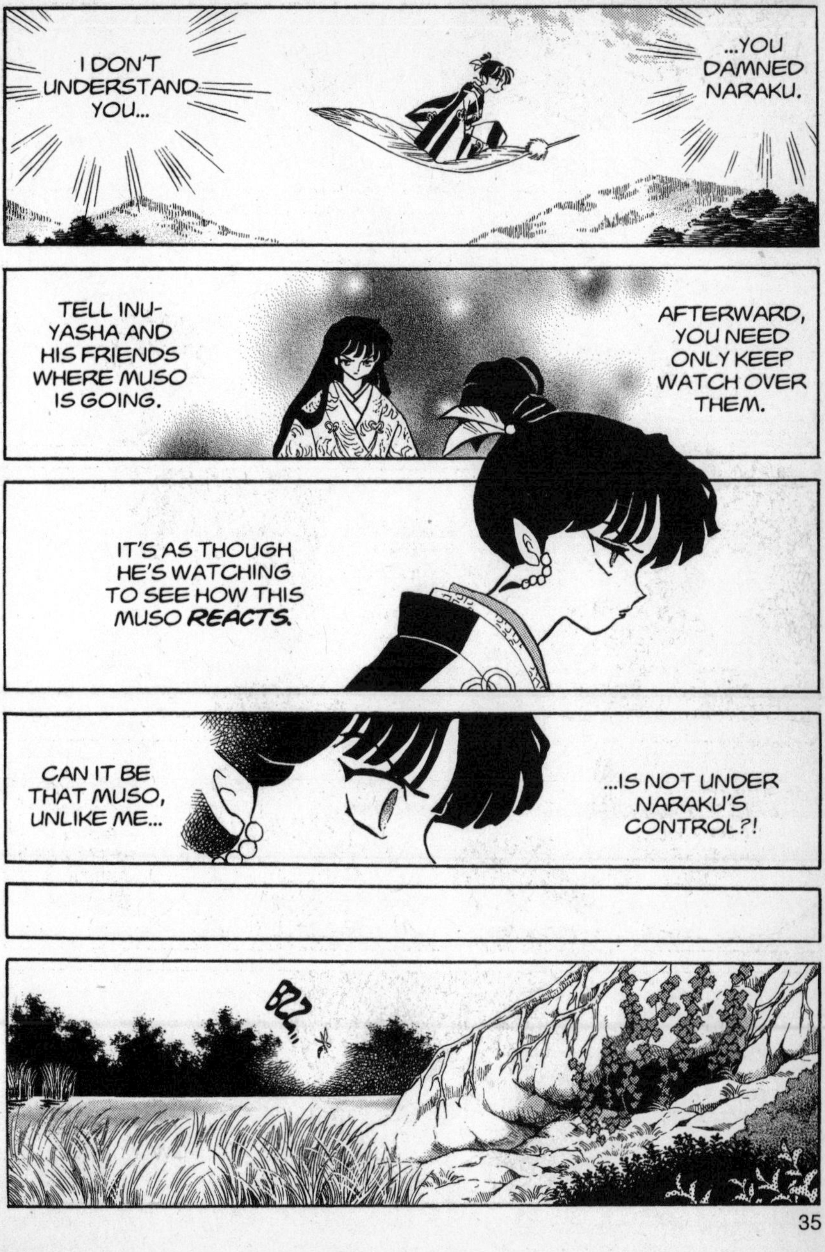
I DON'T UNDERSTAND YOU...
...YOU DAMNED NARAKU.
TELL INU-YASHA AND HIS FRIENDS WHERE MUSO IS GOING.
AFTERWARD, YOU NEED ONLY KEEP WATCH OVER THEM.
IT'S AS THOUGH HE'S WATCHING TO SEE HOW THIS MUSO **REACTS**.
CAN IT BE THAT MUSO, UNLIKE ME...
...IS NOT UNDER NARAKU'S CONTROL?!
BZZ...

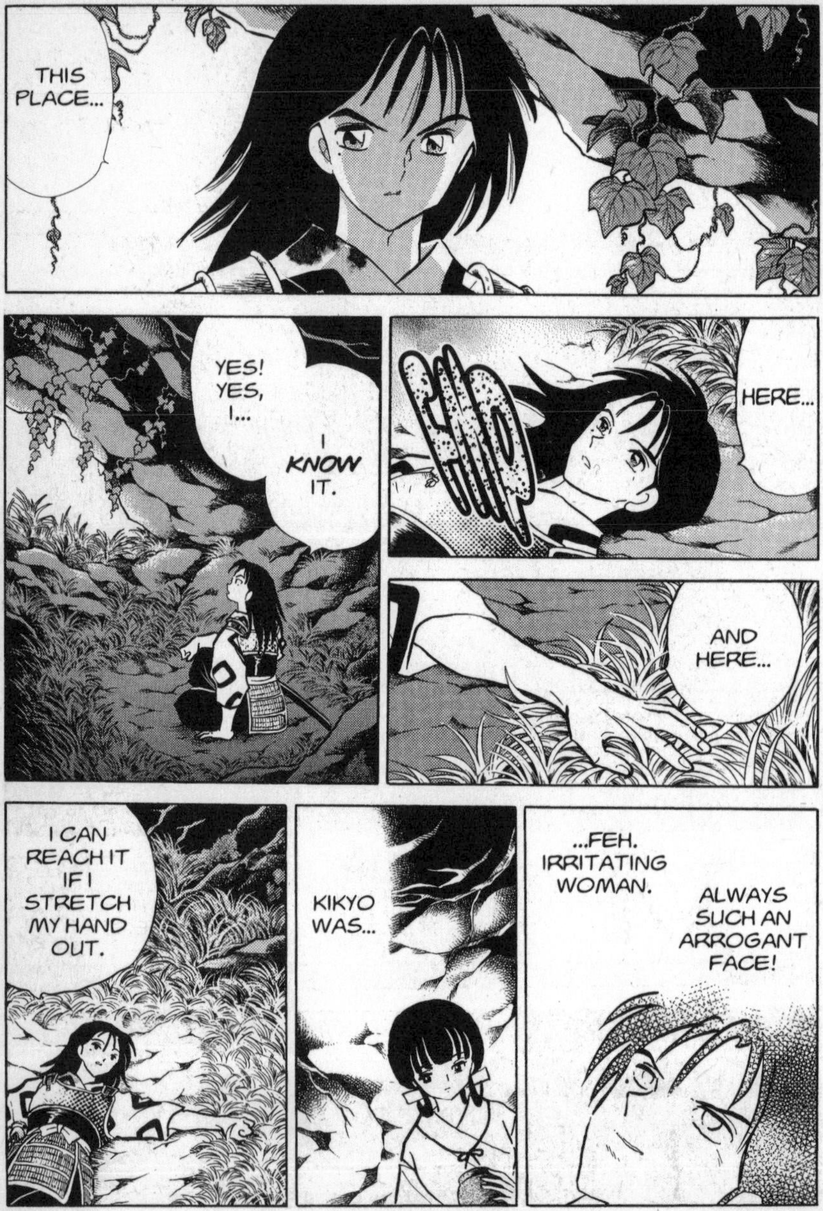
THIS PLACE...
YES! YES, I...
I *KNOW* IT.
HERE...
AND HERE...
I CAN REACH IT IF I STRETCH MY HAND OUT.
KIKYO WAS...
...FEH. IRRITATING WOMAN.
ALWAYS SUCH AN ARROGANT FACE!

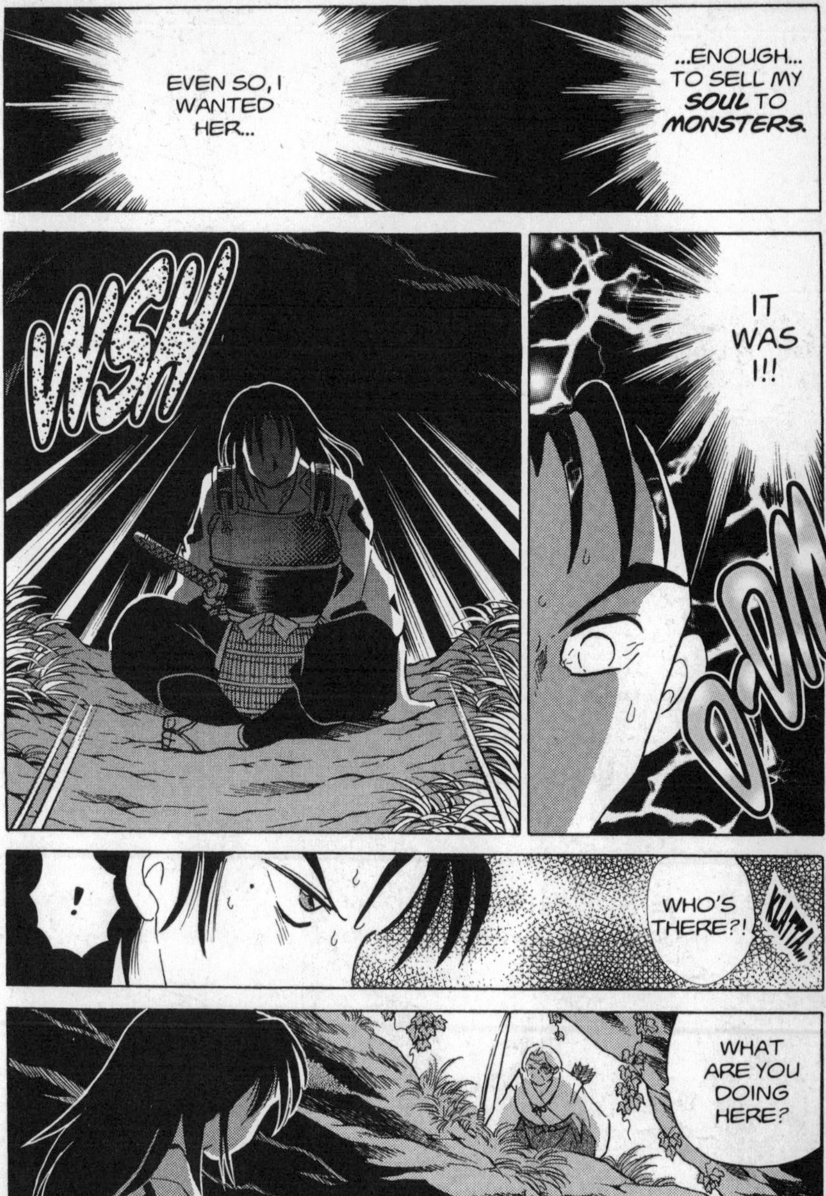
EVEN SO, I WANTED HER...
...ENOUGH... TO SELL MY **SOUL** TO **MONSTERS.**
WSH
IT WAS I!!!
D-DOM
!
WHO'S THERE?!
KLATTA...
WHAT ARE YOU DOING HERE?

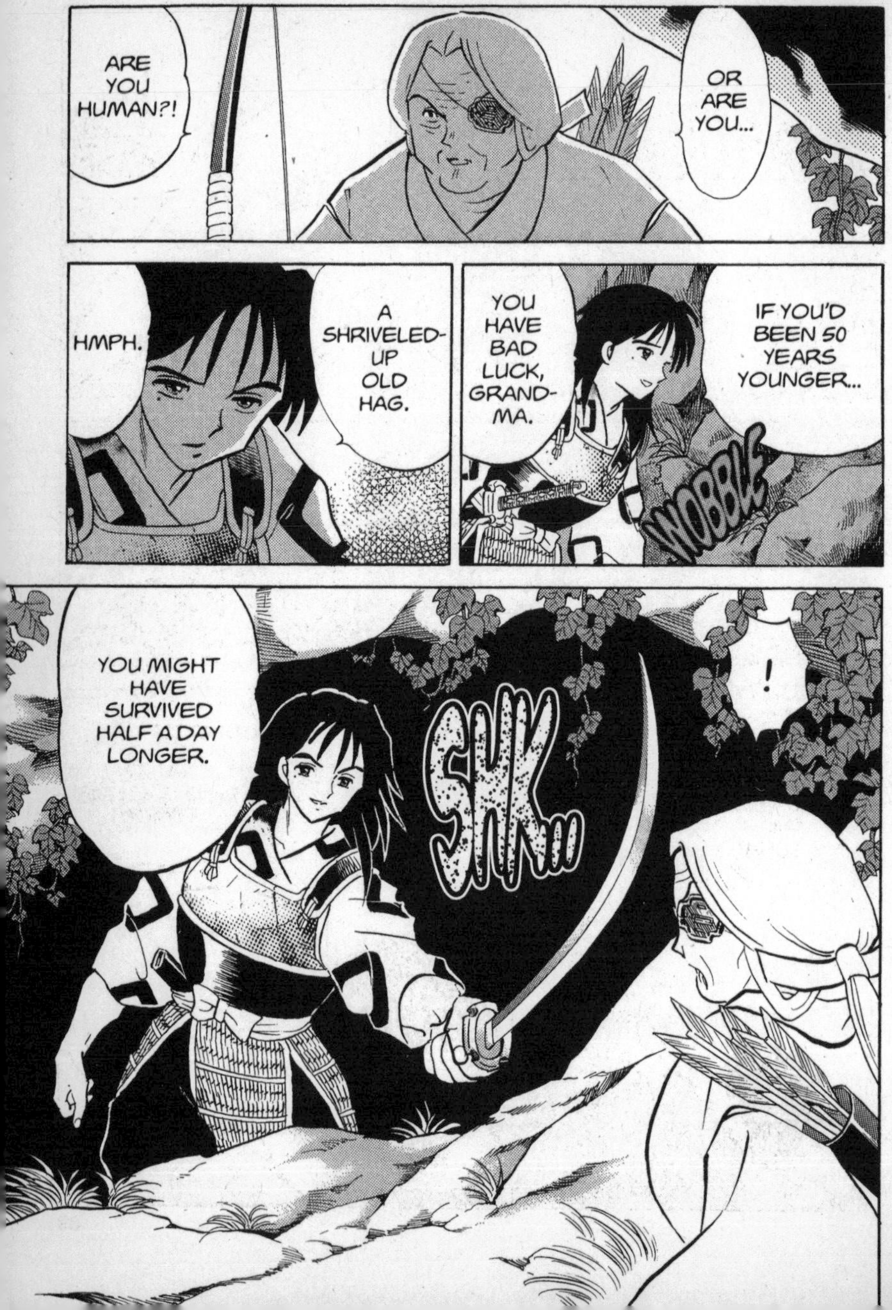
ARE YOU HUMAN?!
OR ARE YOU...
HMPH.
A SHRIVELED-UP OLD HAG.
YOU HAVE BAD LUCK, GRAND-MA.
IF YOU'D BEEN 50 YEARS YOUNGER...
WOBBLE
YOU MIGHT HAVE SURVIVED HALF A DAY LONGER.
SHK...
!

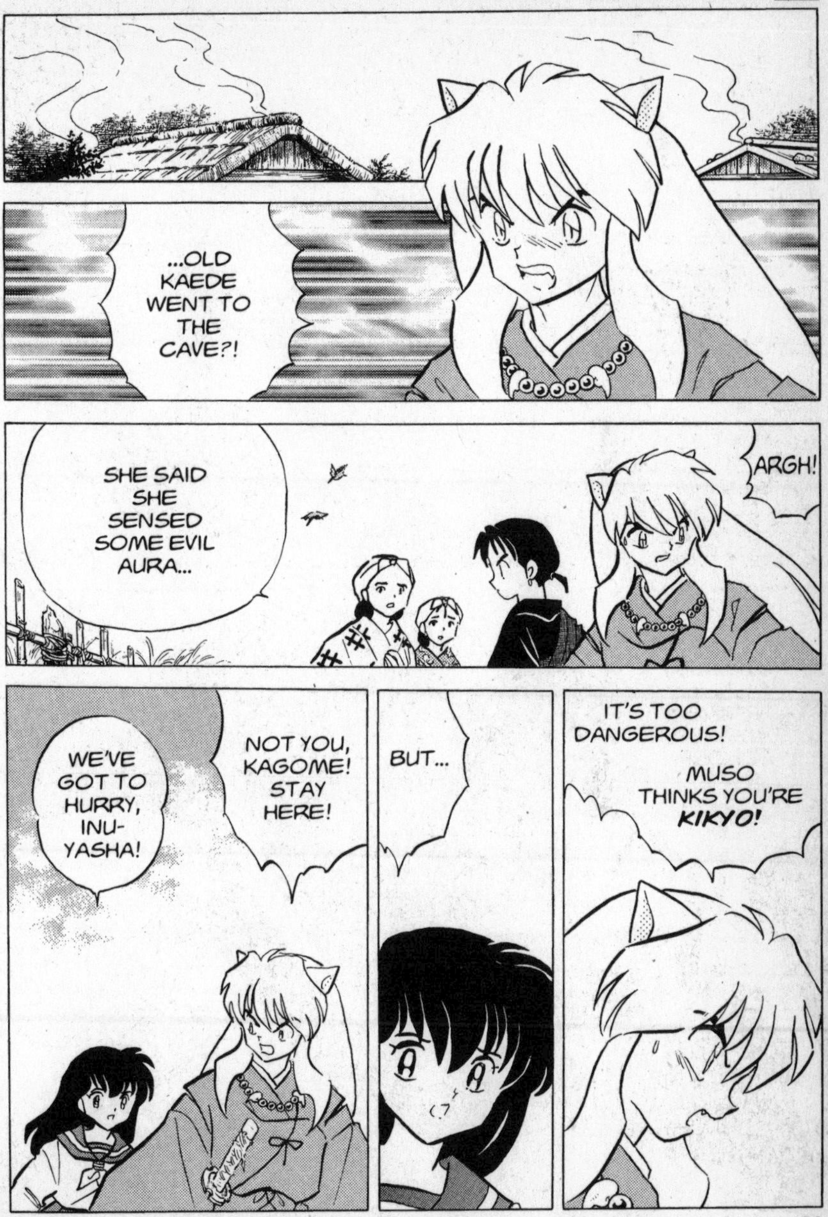
...OLD KAEDE WENT TO THE CAVE?!
SHE SAID SHE SENSED SOME EVIL AURA...
ARGH!
WE'VE GOT TO HURRY, INU-YASHA!
NOT YOU, KAGOME! STAY HERE!
BUT...
IT'S TOO DANGEROUS!
MUSO THINKS YOU'RE ***KIKYO!***

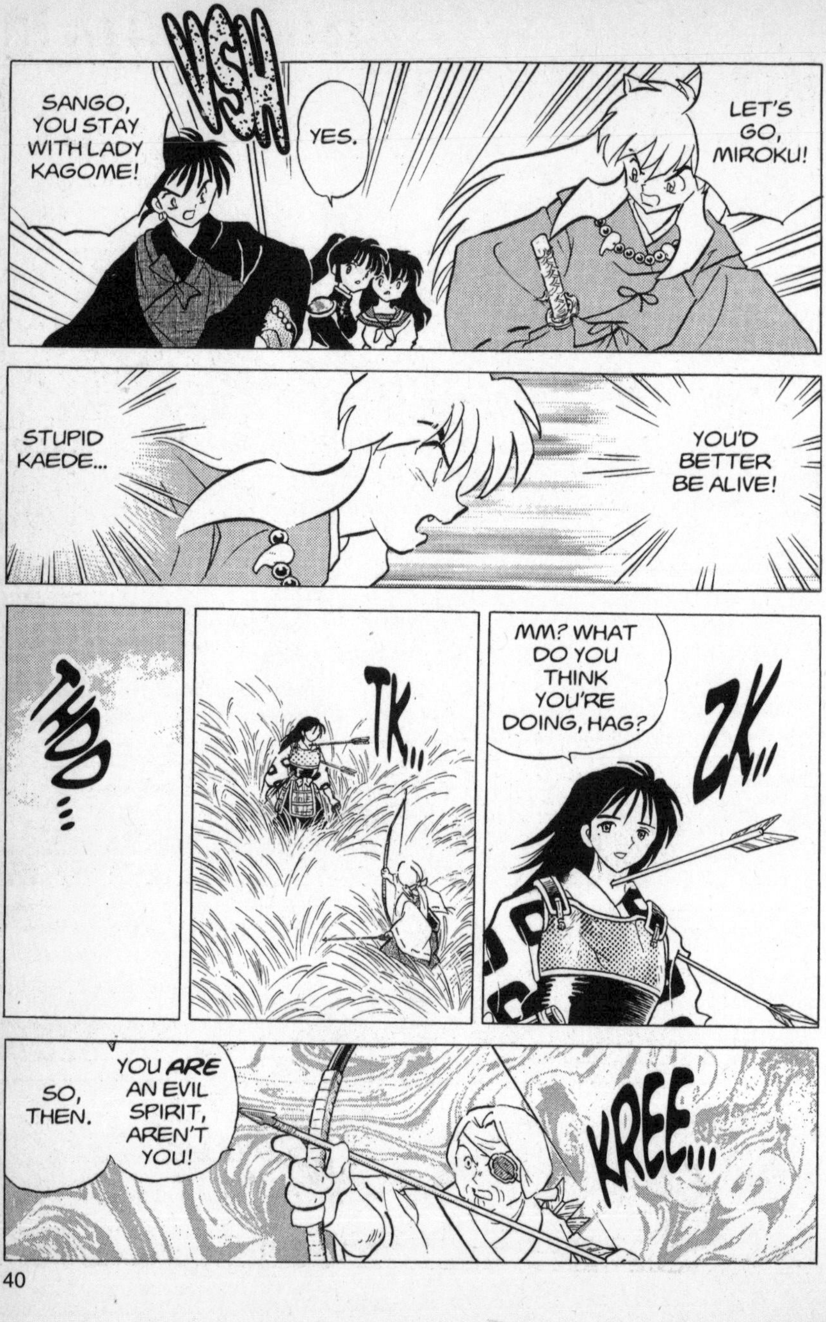
VSH
SANGO, YOU STAY WITH LADY KAGOME!
YES.
LET'S GO, MIROKU!
STUPID KAEDE...
YOU'D BETTER BE ALIVE!
THOD...
TK...
MM? WHAT DO YOU THINK YOU'RE DOING, HAG?
ZK...
SO, THEN.
YOU ***ARE*** AN EVIL SPIRIT, AREN'T YOU!
KREE...

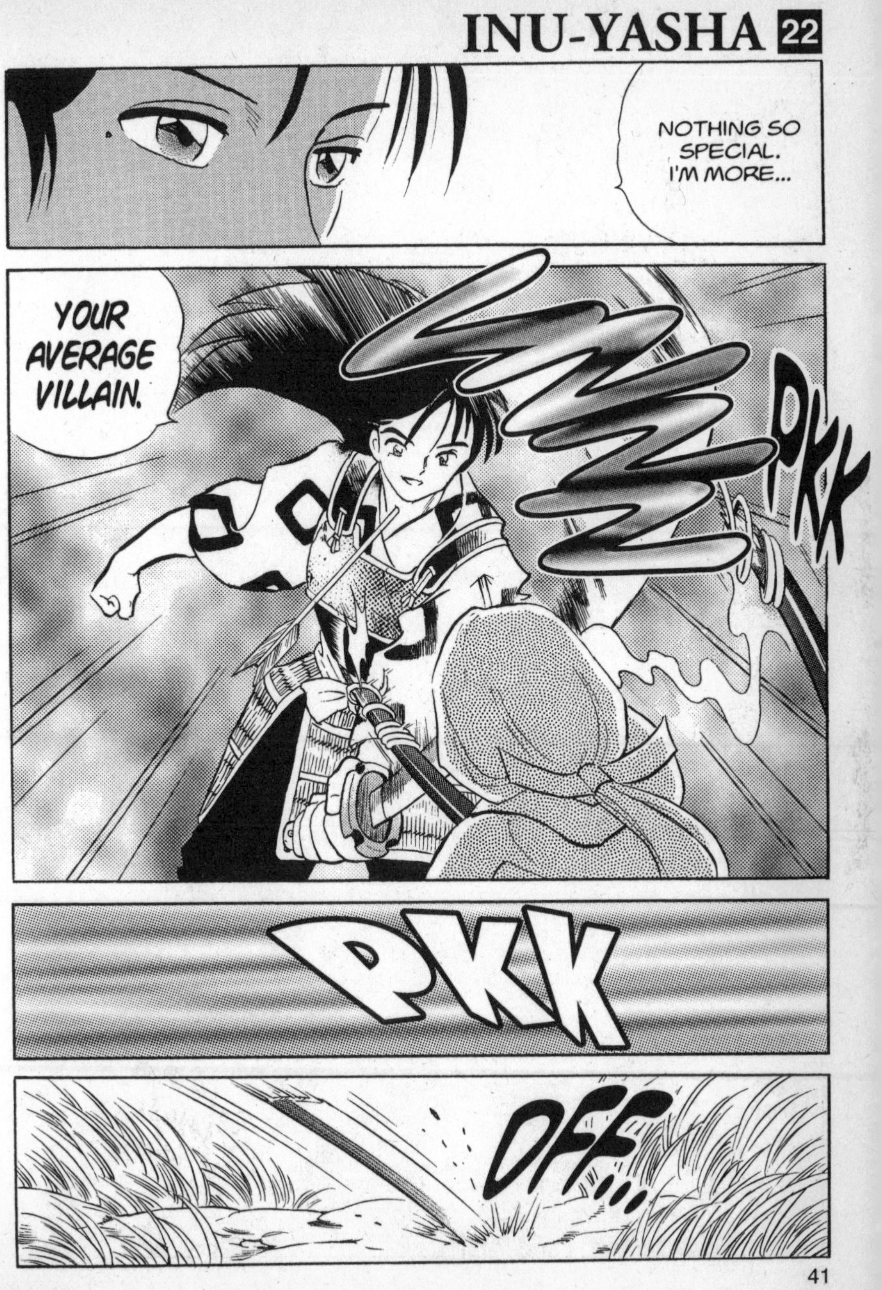
NOTHING SO SPECIAL. I'M MORE...
YOUR AVERAGE VILLAIN.
PKK
PKK
OFF...

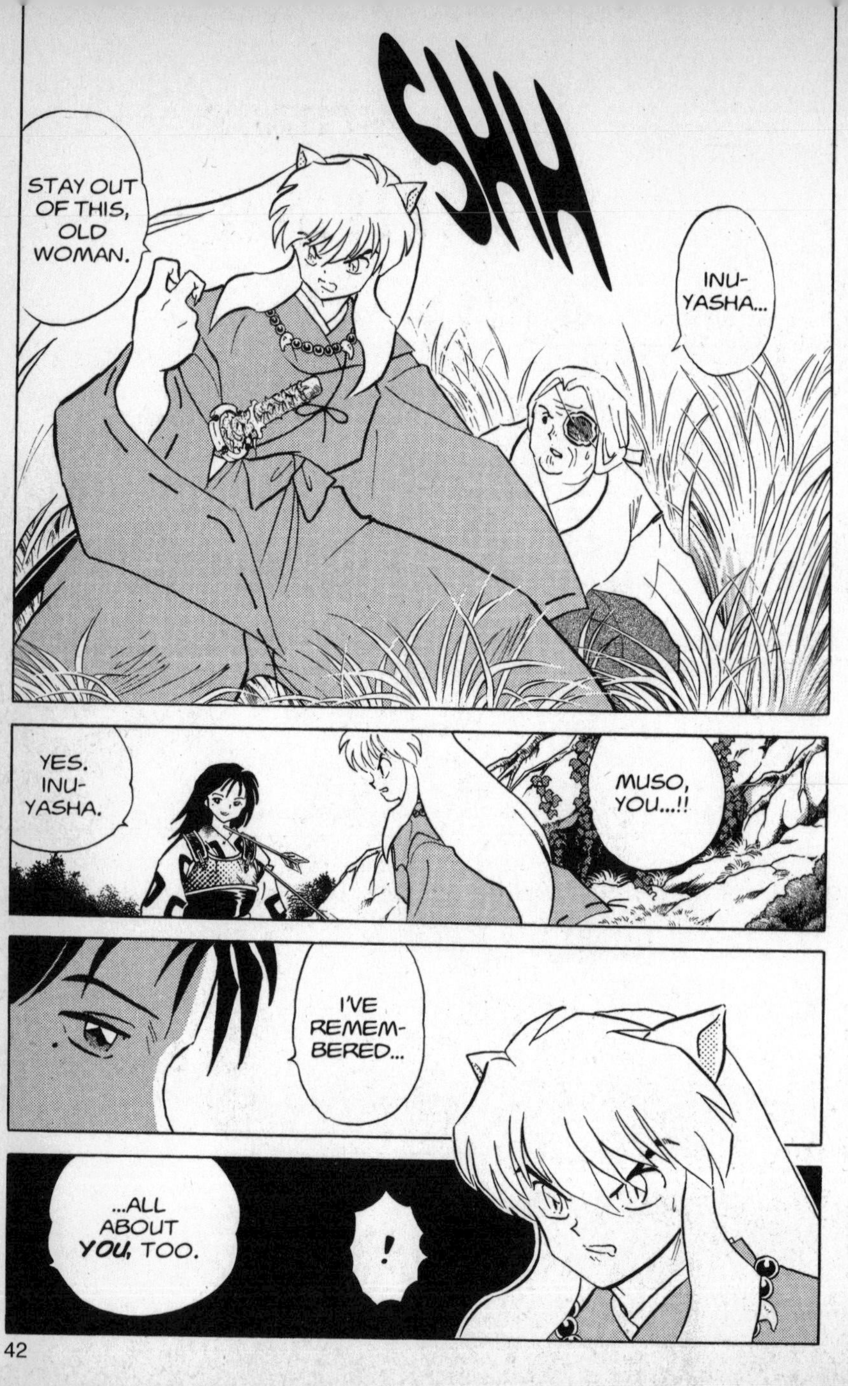
STAY OUT OF THIS, OLD WOMAN.
SHH
INU-YASHA...
YES. INU-YASHA.
MUSO, YOU...!!
I'VE REMEMBERED...
...ALL ABOUT YOU, TOO.
!

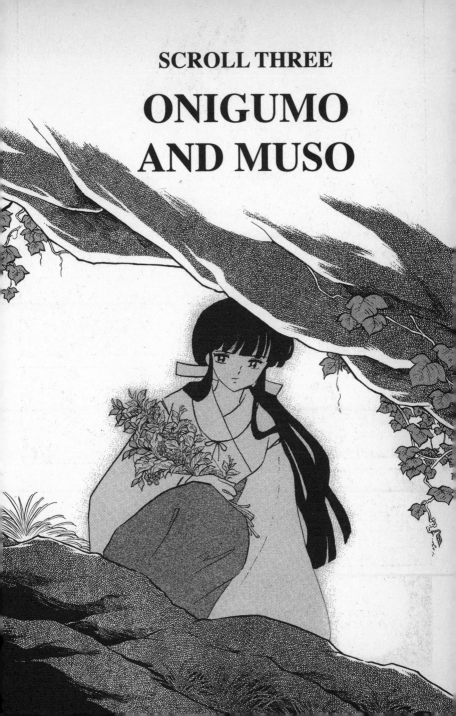

SCROLL THREE

ONIGUMO AND MUSO

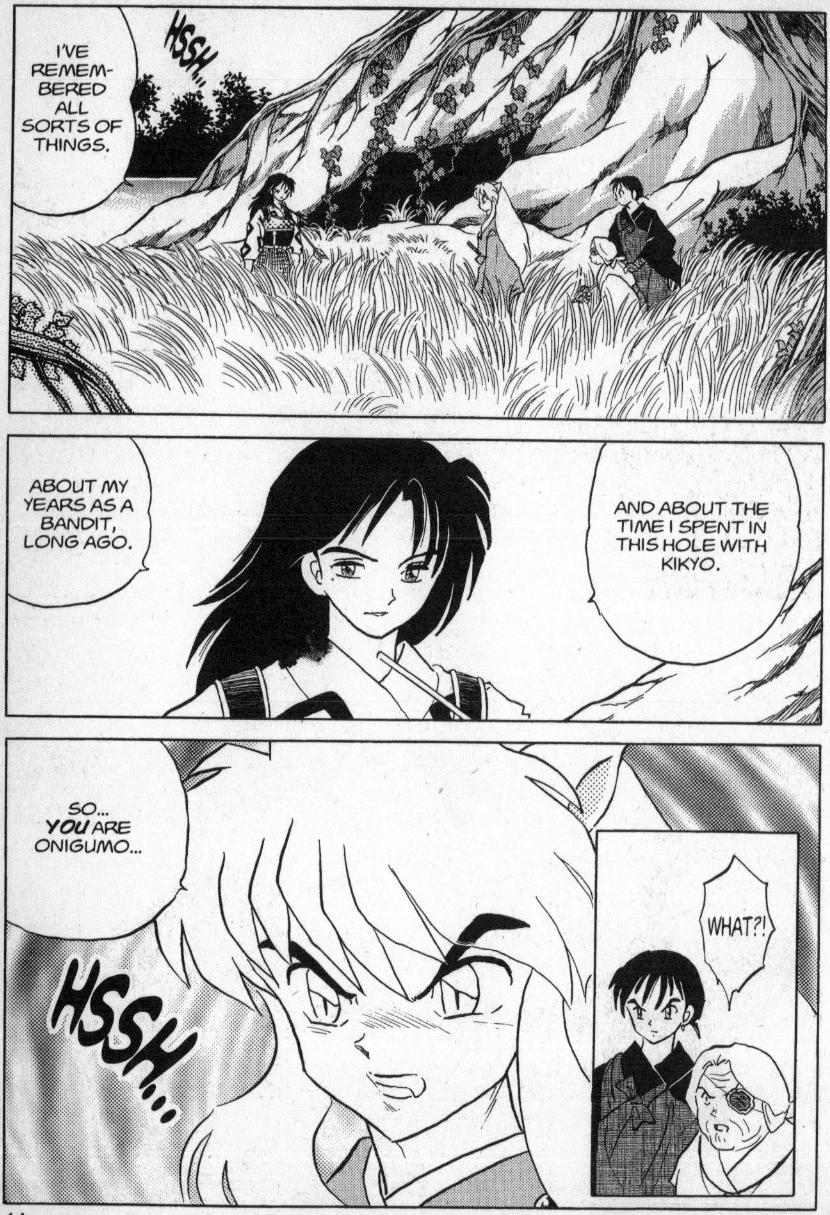
I'VE REMEMBERED ALL SORTS OF THINGS.
HSSH...
ABOUT MY YEARS AS A BANDIT, LONG AGO.
AND ABOUT THE TIME I SPENT IN THIS HOLE WITH KIKYO.
SO... YOU ARE ONIGUMO...
HSSH...
WHAT?!

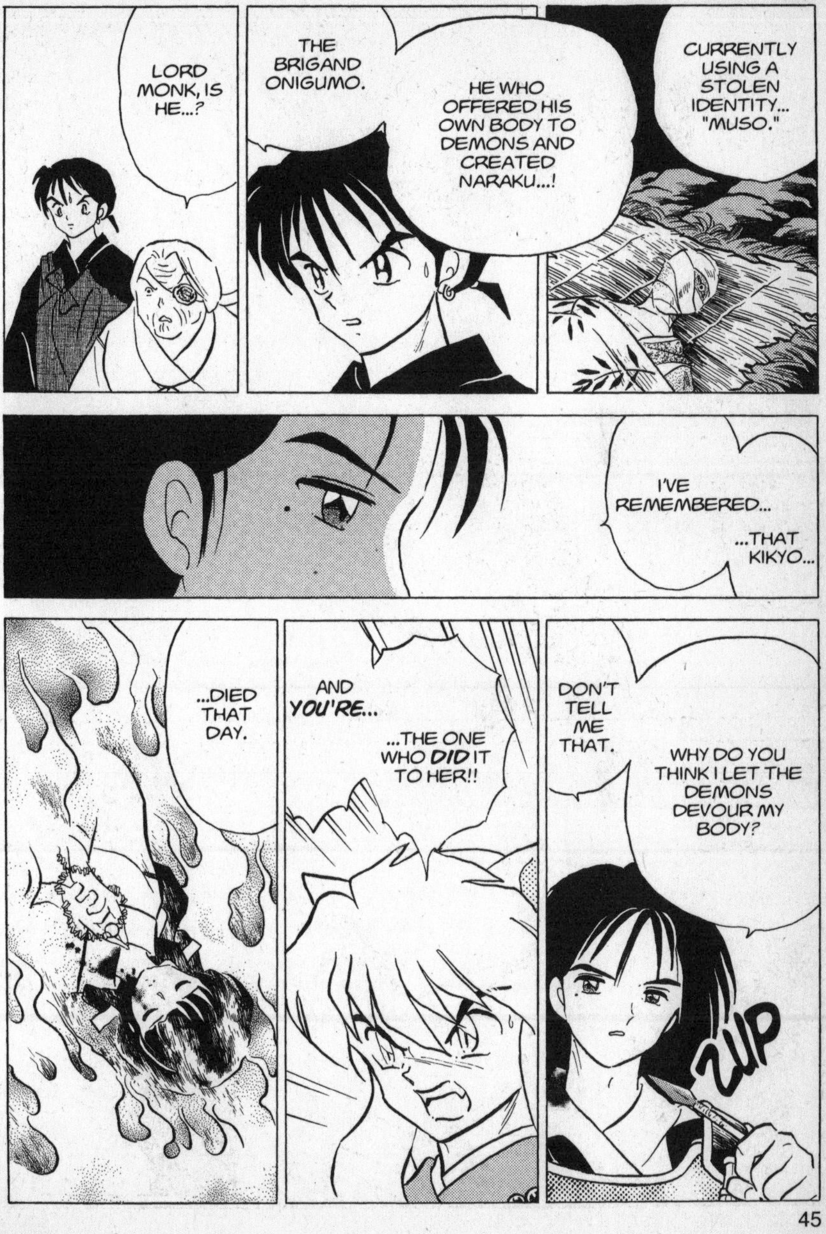
LORD MONK, IS HE...?
THE BRIGAND ONIGUMO.
HE WHO OFFERED HIS OWN BODY TO DEMONS AND CREATED NARAKU...!
CURRENTLY USING A STOLEN IDENTITY... "MUSO."
I'VE REMEMBERED...
...THAT KIKYO...
...DIED THAT DAY.
AND *YOU'RE*...
...THE ONE WHO *DID* IT TO HER!!
DON'T TELL ME THAT.
WHY DO YOU THINK I LET THE DEMONS DEVOUR MY BODY?
ZUP

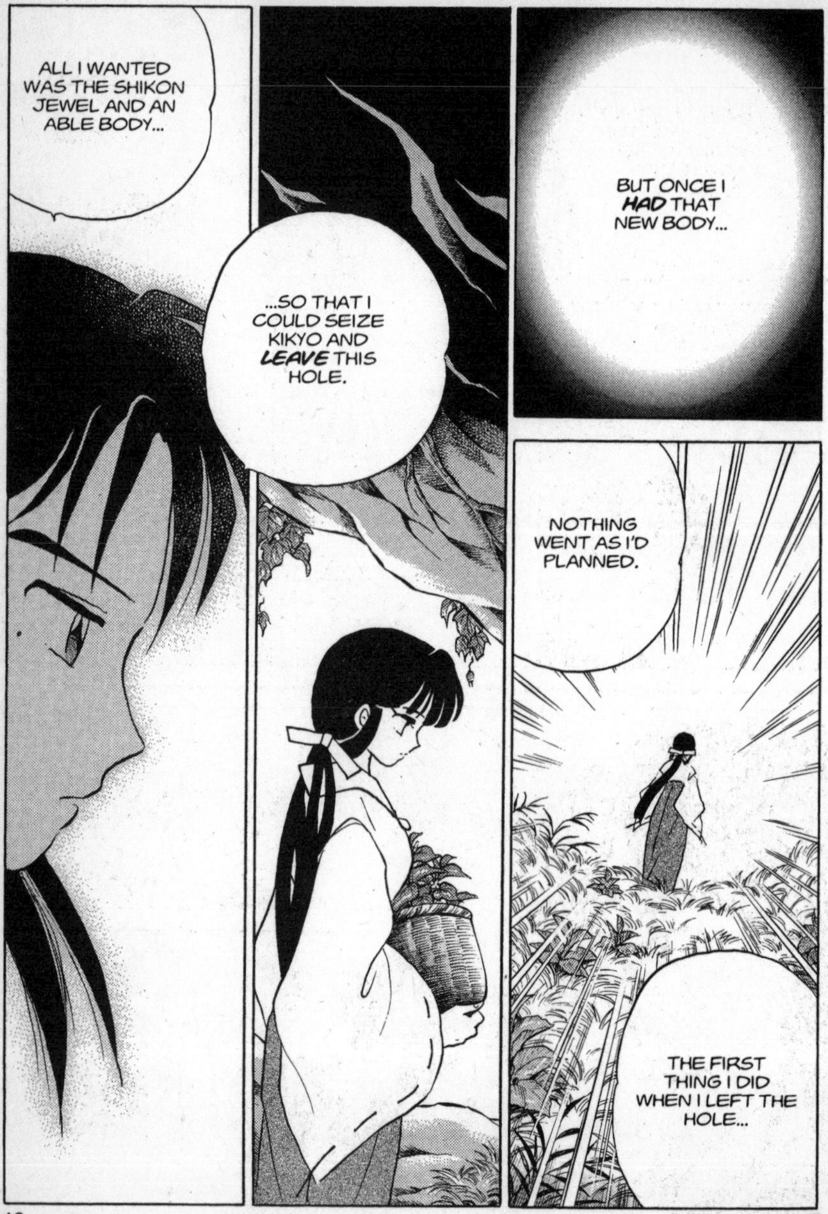
ALL I WANTED WAS THE SHIKON JEWEL AND AN ABLE BODY...
...SO THAT I COULD SEIZE KIKYO AND LEAVE THIS HOLE.
BUT ONCE I HAD THAT NEW BODY...
NOTHING WENT AS I'D PLANNED.
THE FIRST THING I DID WHEN I LEFT THE HOLE...

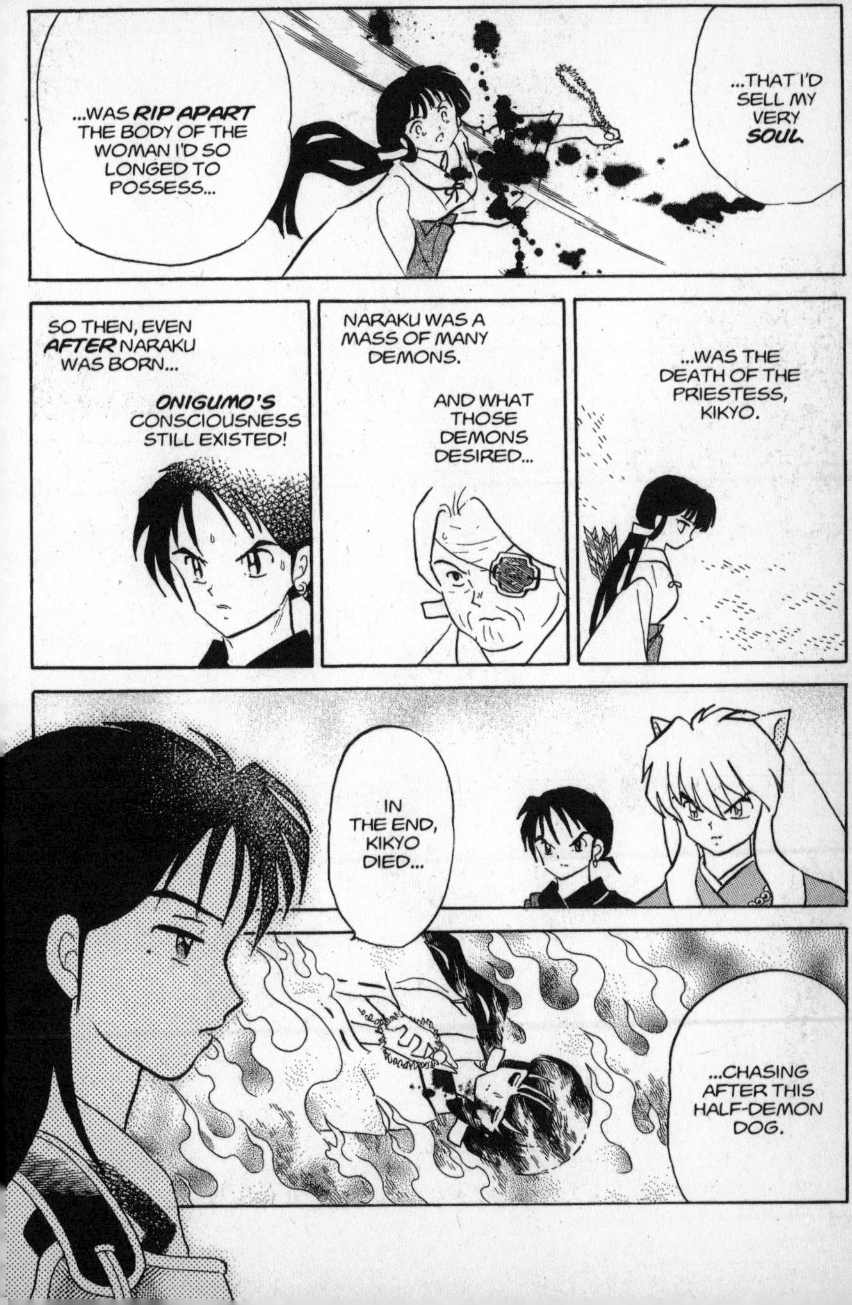
...WAS RIP APART THE BODY OF THE WOMAN I'D SO LONGED TO POSSESS...
...THAT I'D SELL MY VERY SOUL.
SO THEN, EVEN AFTER NARAKU WAS BORN...
ONIGUMO'S CONSCIOUSNESS STILL EXISTED!
NARAKU WAS A MASS OF MANY DEMONS.
AND WHAT THOSE DEMONS DESIRED...
...WAS THE DEATH OF THE PRIESTESS, KIKYO.
IN THE END, KIKYO DIED...
...CHASING AFTER THIS HALF-DEMON DOG.

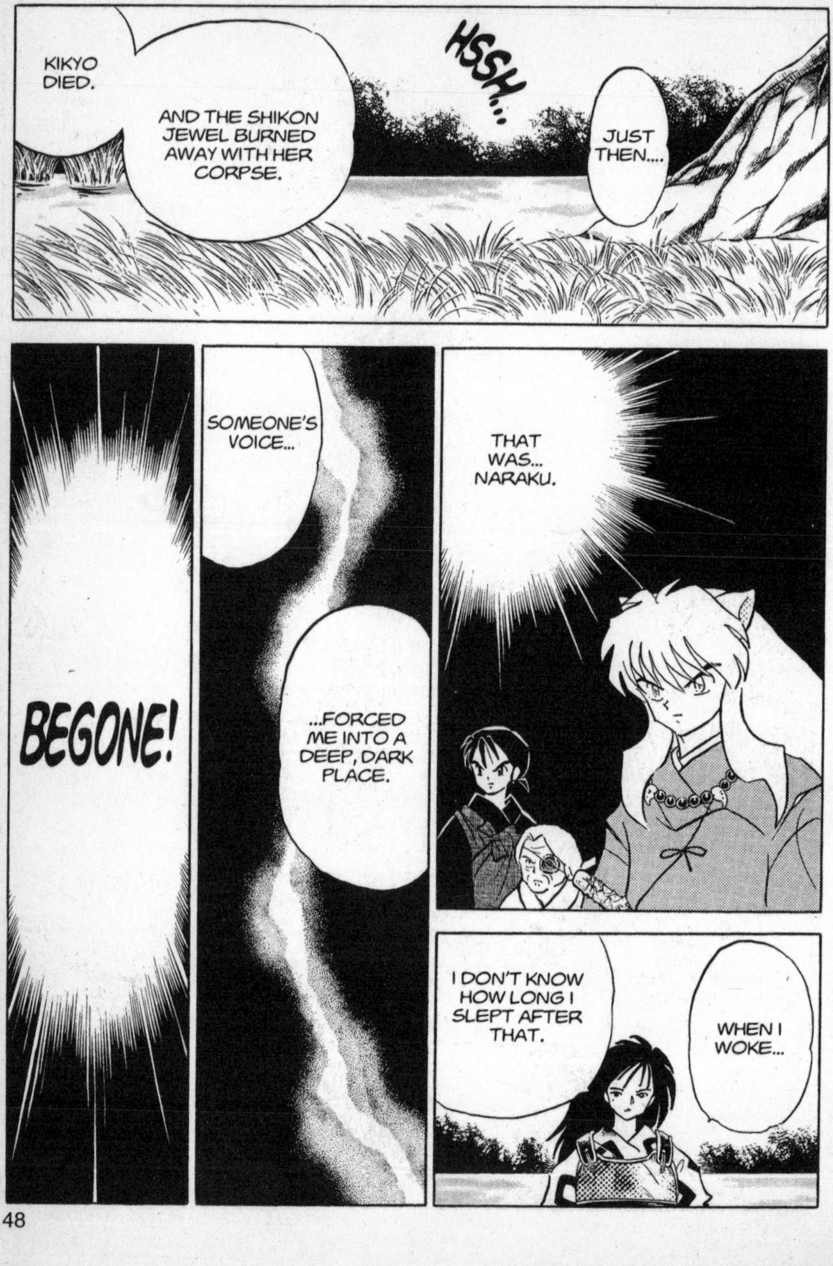
KIKYO DIED.
AND THE SHIKON JEWEL BURNED AWAY WITH HER CORPSE.
HSSH...
JUST THEN....
BEGONE!
SOMEONE'S VOICE...
...FORCED ME INTO A DEEP, DARK PLACE.
THAT WAS... NARAKU.
I DON'T KNOW HOW LONG I SLEPT AFTER THAT.
WHEN I WOKE...

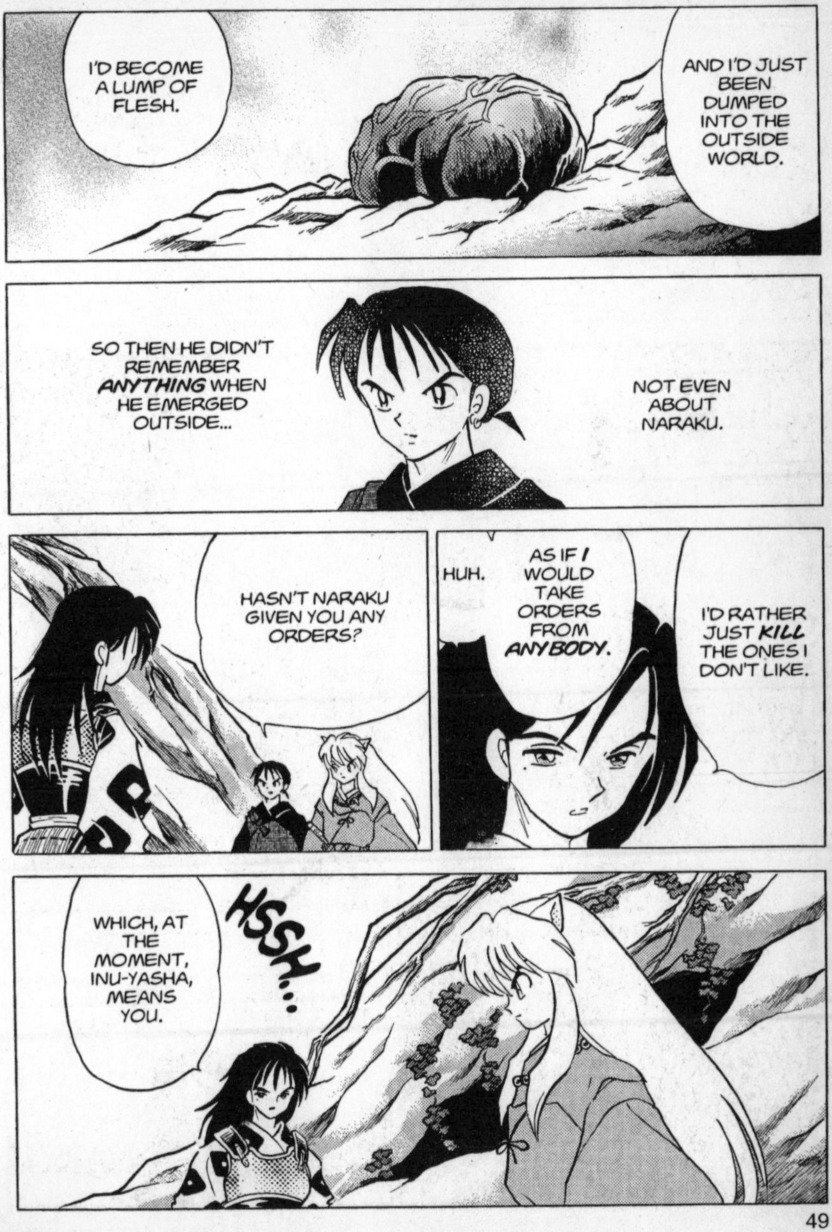
I'D BECOME A LUMP OF FLESH.
AND I'D JUST BEEN DUMPED INTO THE OUTSIDE WORLD.
SO THEN HE DIDN'T REMEMBER ANYTHING WHEN HE EMERGED OUTSIDE...
NOT EVEN ABOUT NARAKU.
HASN'T NARAKU GIVEN YOU ANY ORDERS?
HUH.
AS IF I WOULD TAKE ORDERS FROM ANYBODY.
I'D RATHER JUST KILL THE ONES I DON'T LIKE.
WHICH, AT THE MOMENT, INU-YASHA, MEANS YOU.
HSSH...

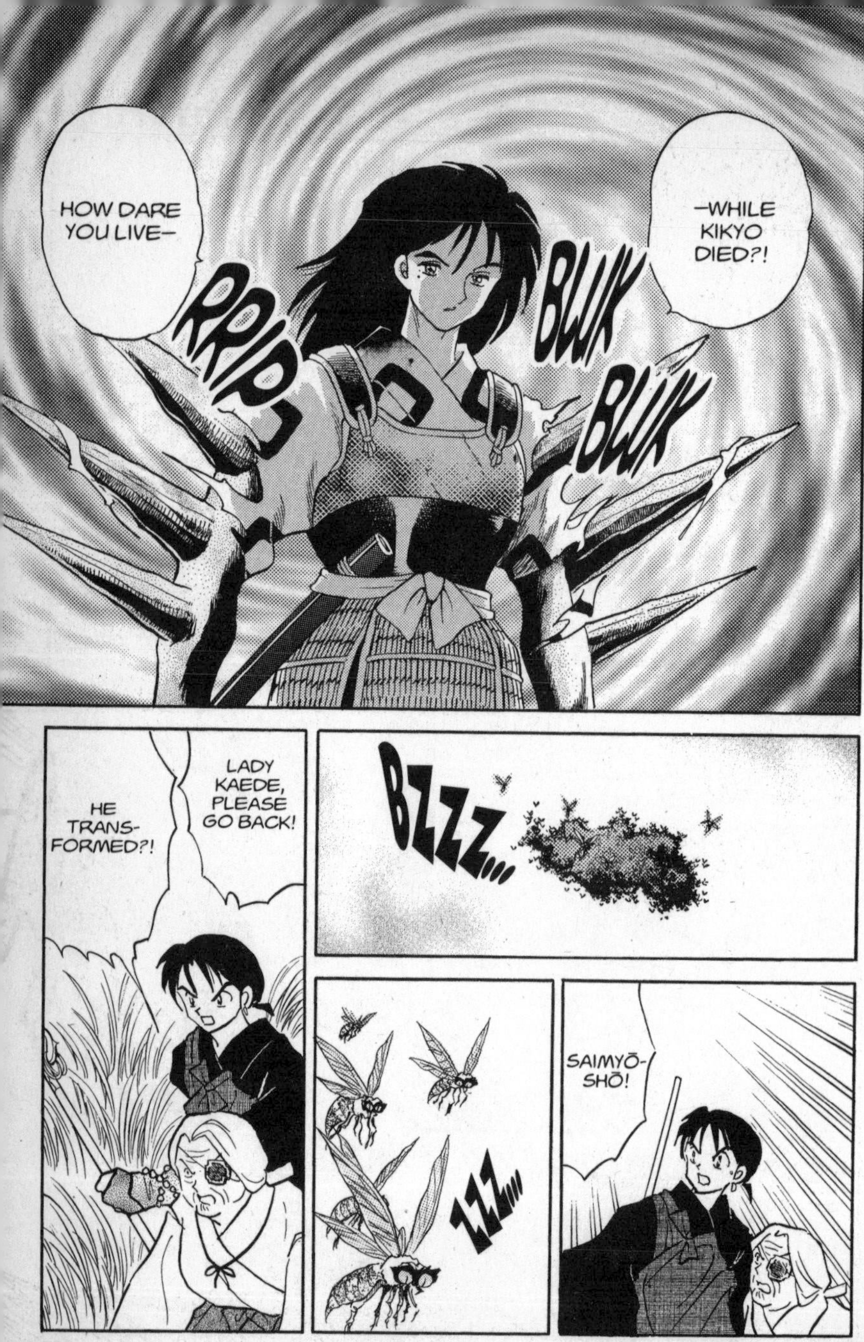
HOW DARE YOU LIVE—
RRIP
BLUK
BLUK
—WHILE KIKYO DIED?!
HE TRANS-FORMED?!
LADY KAEDE, PLEASE GO BACK!
BZZZ...
ZZZ...
SAIMYŌ-SHŌ!

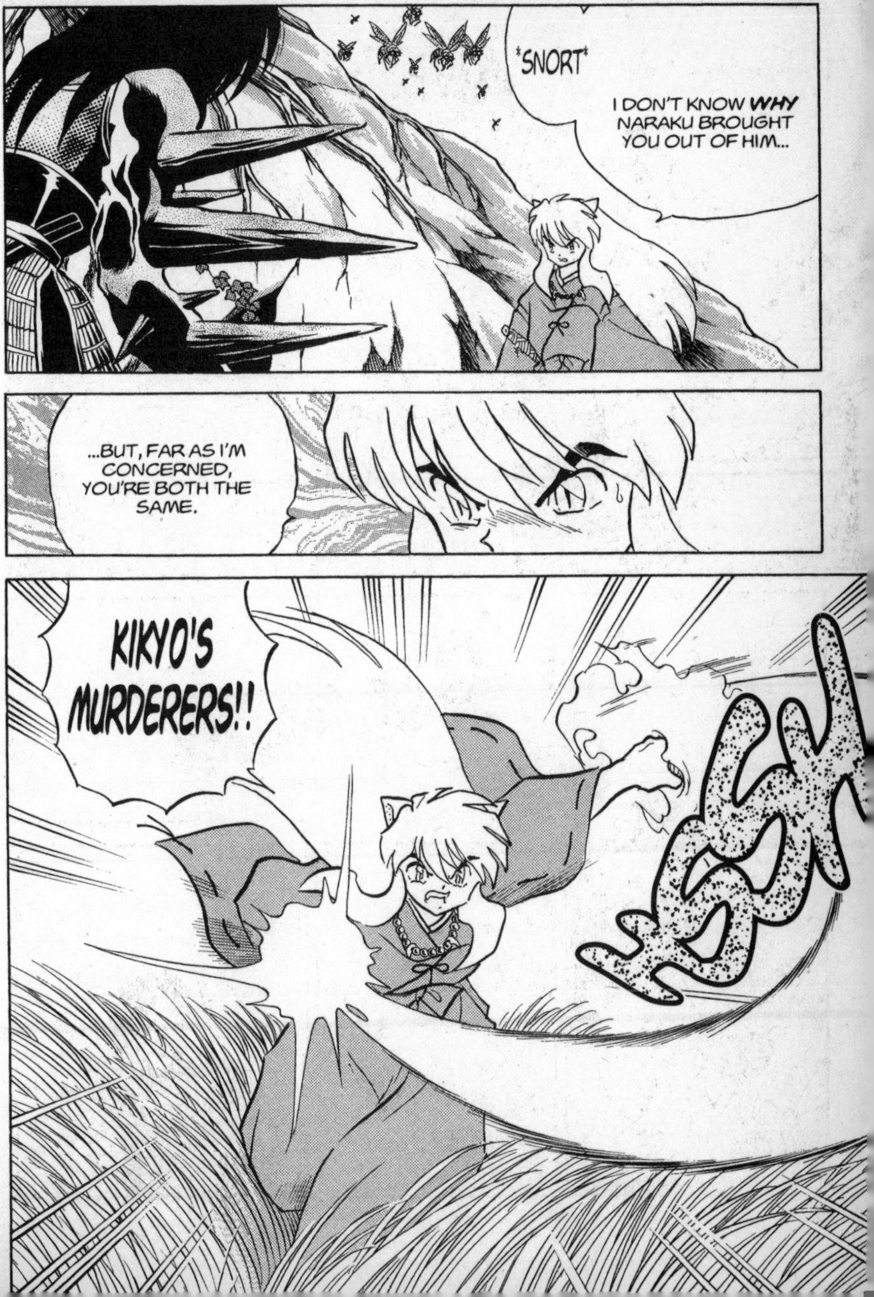
SNORT
I DON'T KNOW **WHY** NARAKU BROUGHT YOU OUT OF HIM...
...BUT, FAR AS I'M CONCERNED, YOU'RE BOTH THE SAME.
KIKYO'S MURDERERS!!

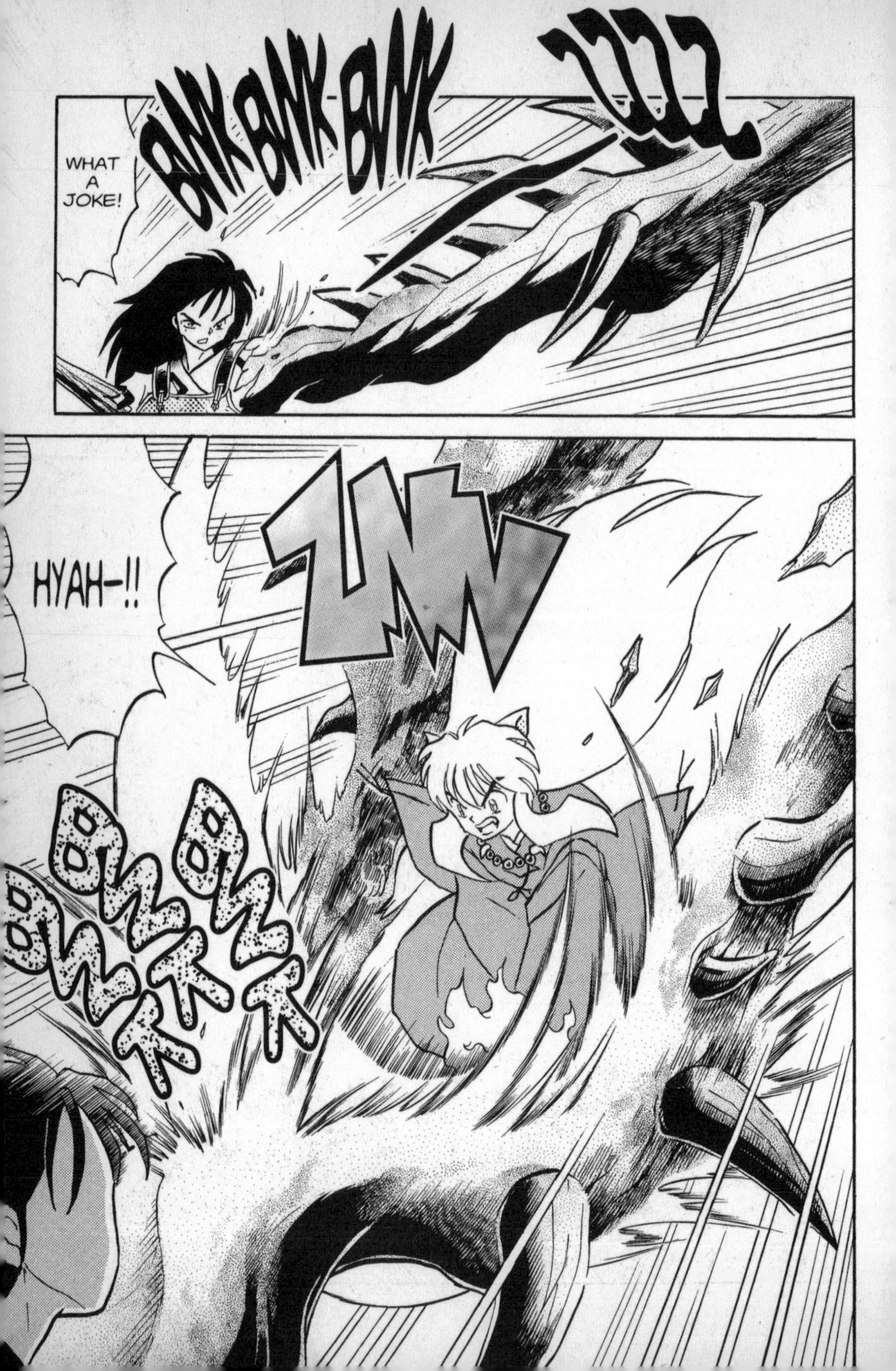
WHAT A JOKE!
HYAH-!!

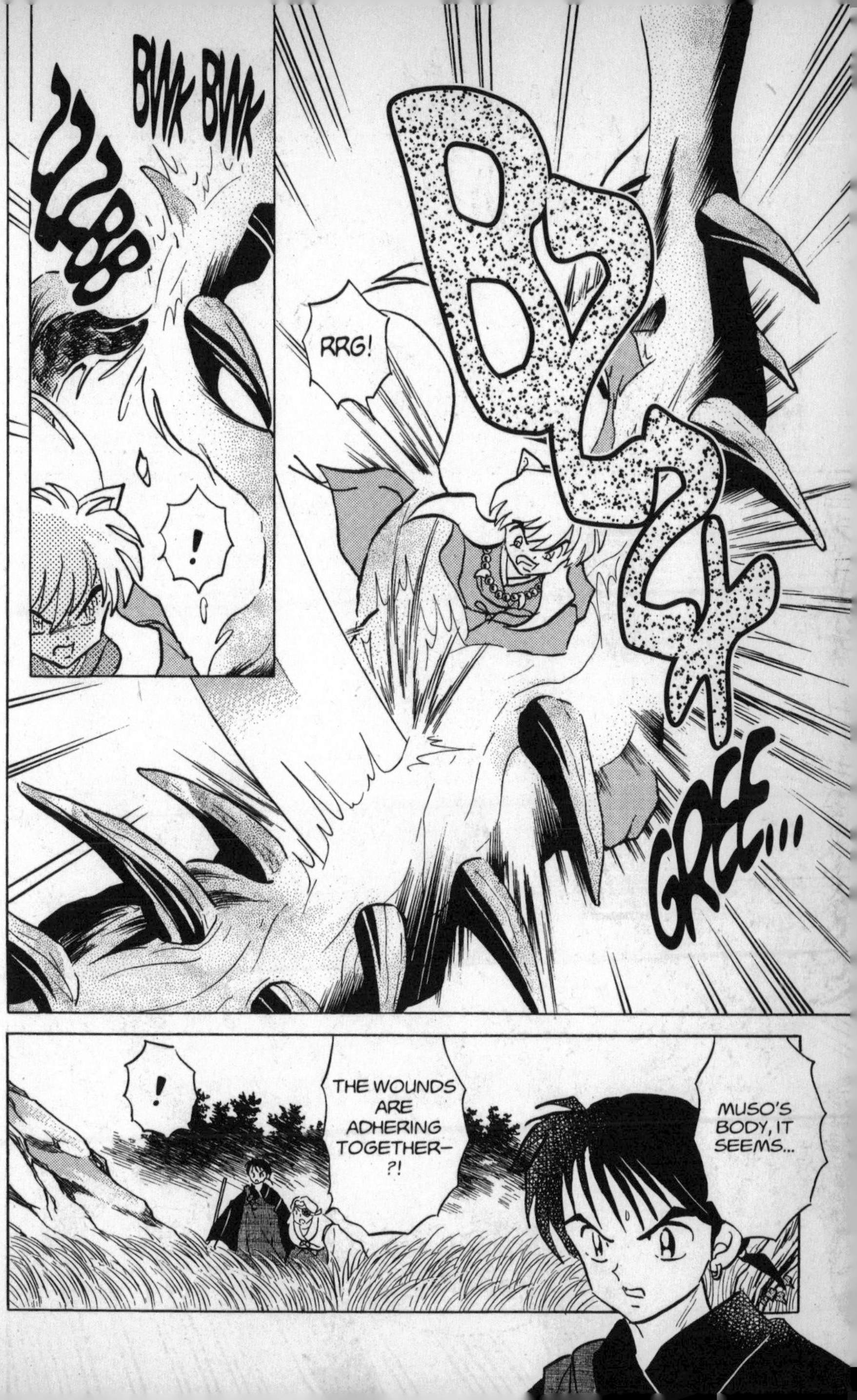
ZZRBB
BVVK BVVK
!
RRG!
BDZZK
GREE...
!
THE WOUNDS ARE ADHERING TOGETHER--?!
MUSO'S BODY, IT SEEMS...

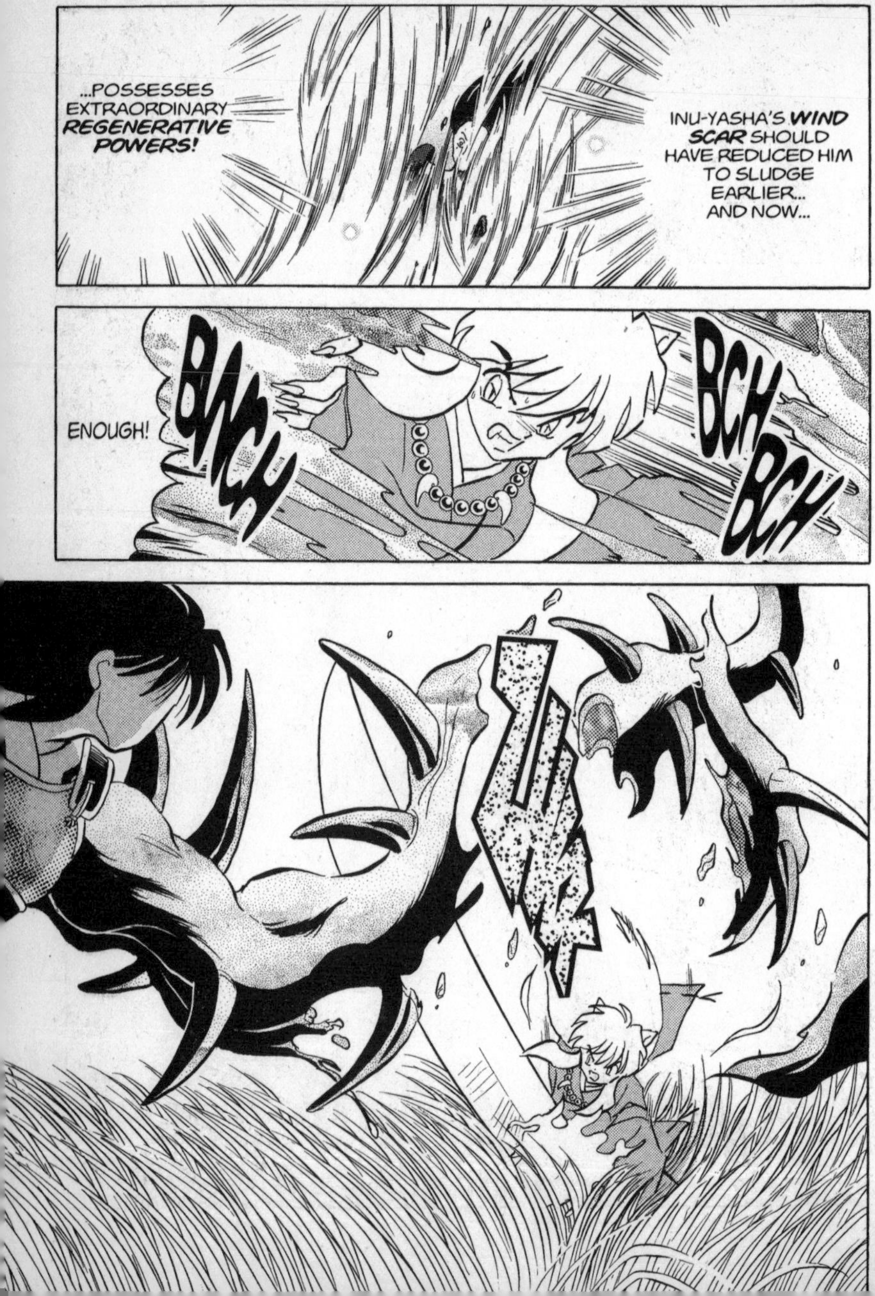
...POSSESSES EXTRAORDINARY REGENERATIVE POWERS!
INU-YASHA'S WIND SCAR SHOULD HAVE REDUCED HIM TO SLUDGE EARLIER... AND NOW...
ENOUGH!
BCH BCH BCH

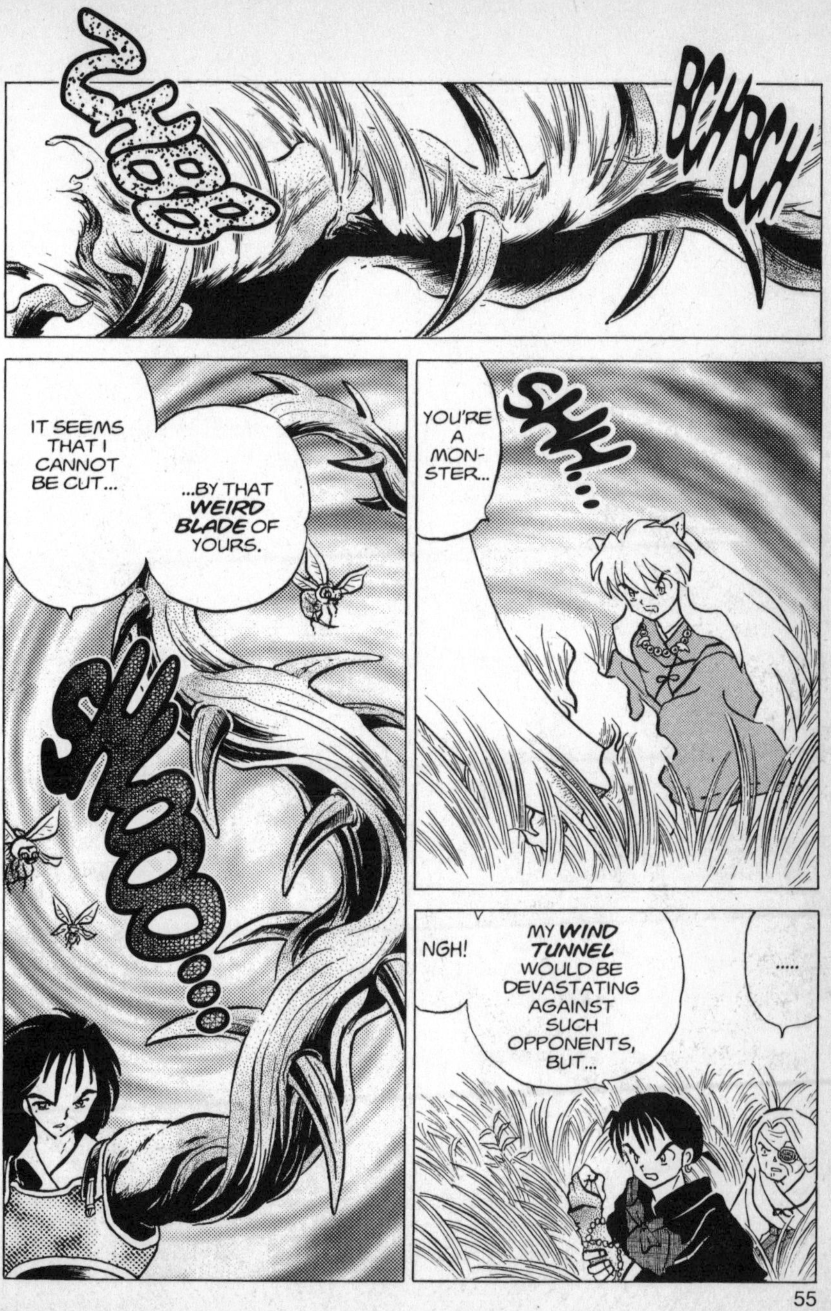
ZHBB
BCH BCH
IT SEEMS THAT I CANNOT BE CUT...
...BY THAT WEIRD BLADE OF YOURS.
SHOOO...
YOU'RE A MON-STER...
SHH...
NGH!
MY WIND TUNNEL WOULD BE DEVASTATING AGAINST SUCH OPPONENTS, BUT...
.....

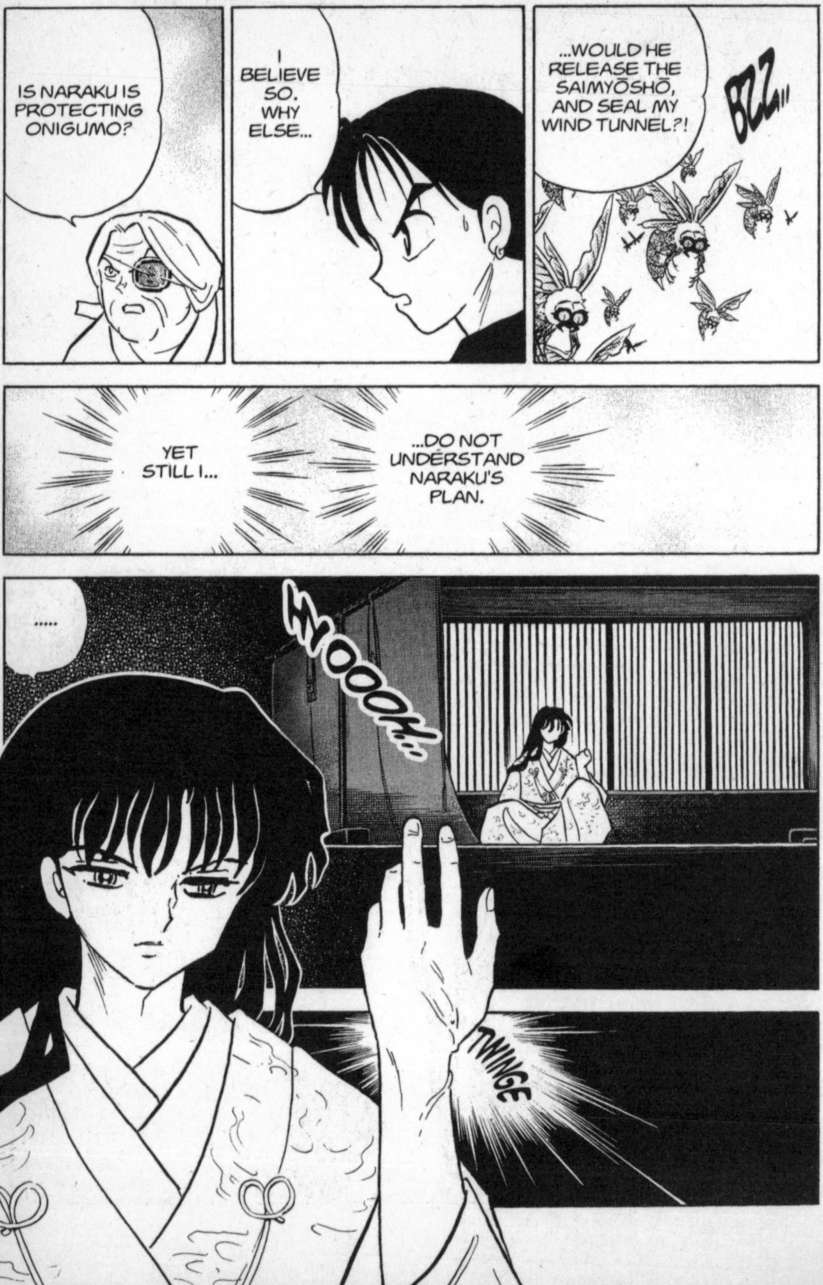
IS NARAKU IS PROTECTING ONIGUMO?
I BELIEVE SO. WHY ELSE...
...WOULD HE RELEASE THE SAIMYŌSHŌ, AND SEAL MY WIND TUNNEL?!
BZZ
YET STILL I...
...DO NOT UNDERSTAND NARAKU'S PLAN.
.....
WHOOOH
TWINGE

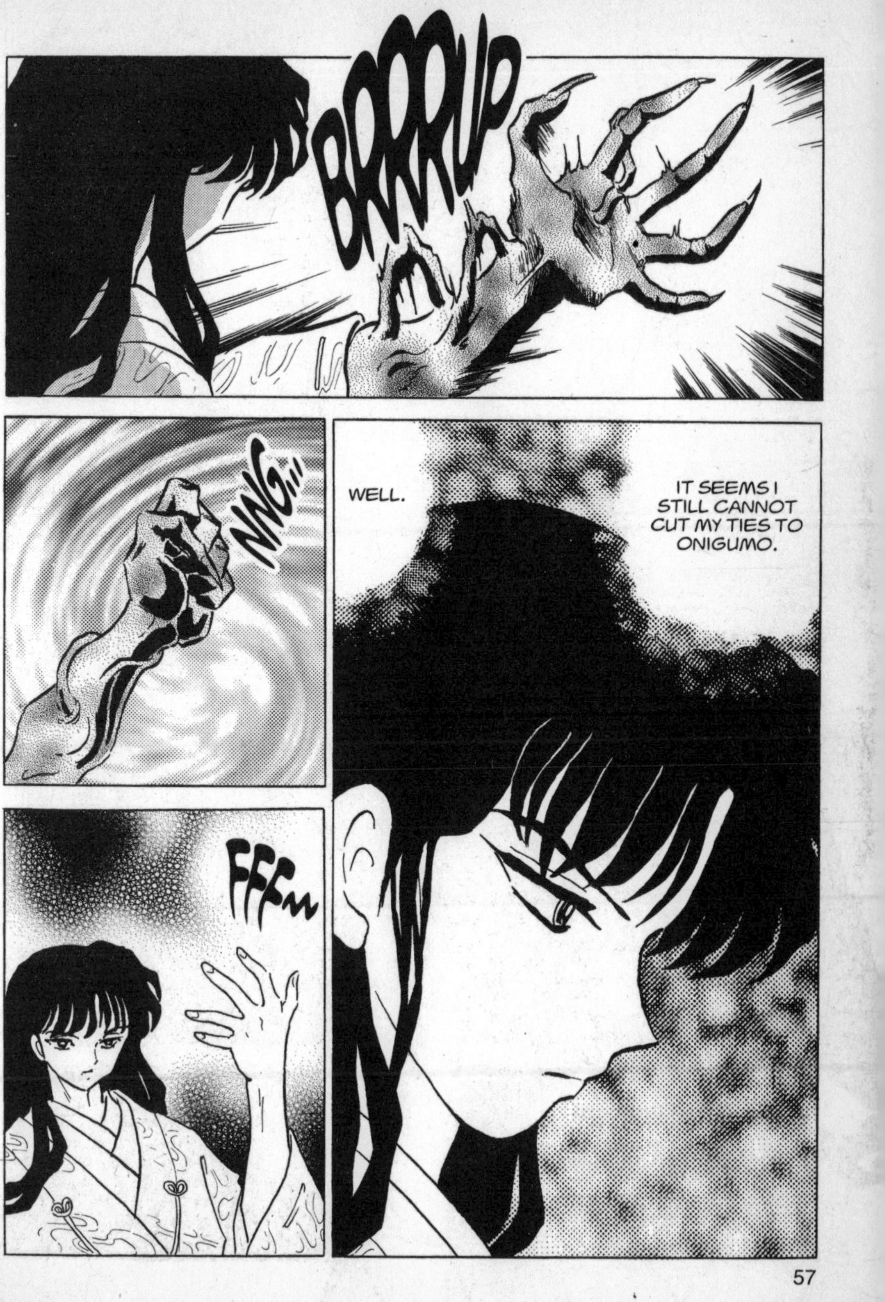
BRRRUP
NNG...
FFF
WELL.
IT SEEMS I STILL CANNOT CUT MY TIES TO ONIGUMO.

WIND
SCAR!

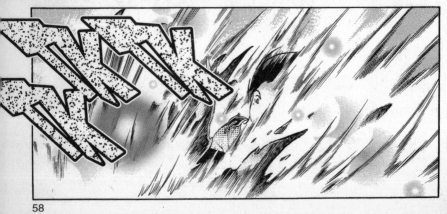

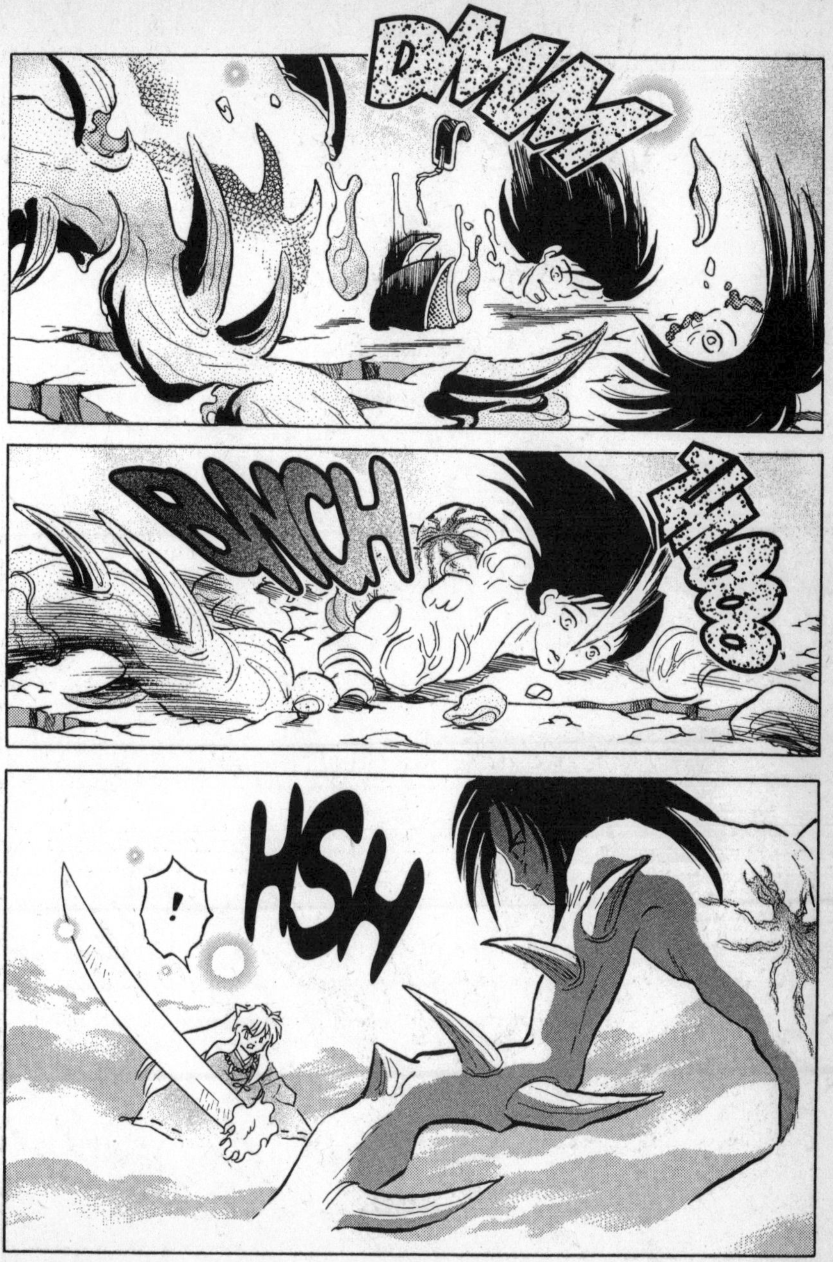
BWCH
THOOO
!
HSH

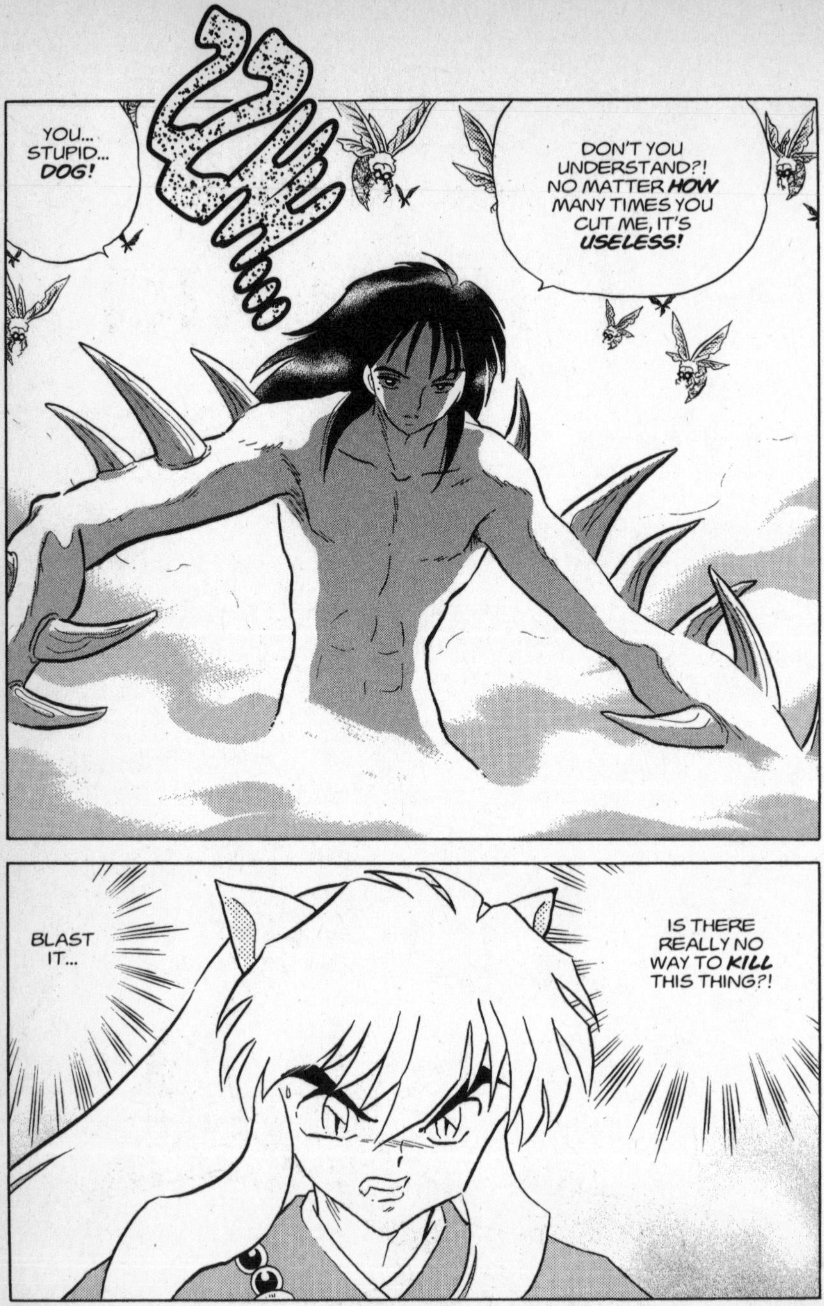
YOU... STUPID... DOG!
DON'T YOU UNDERSTAND?! NO MATTER HOW MANY TIMES YOU CUT ME, IT'S USELESS!
BLAST IT...
IS THERE REALLY NO WAY TO KILL THIS THING?!

SCROLL FOUR

THE HEART

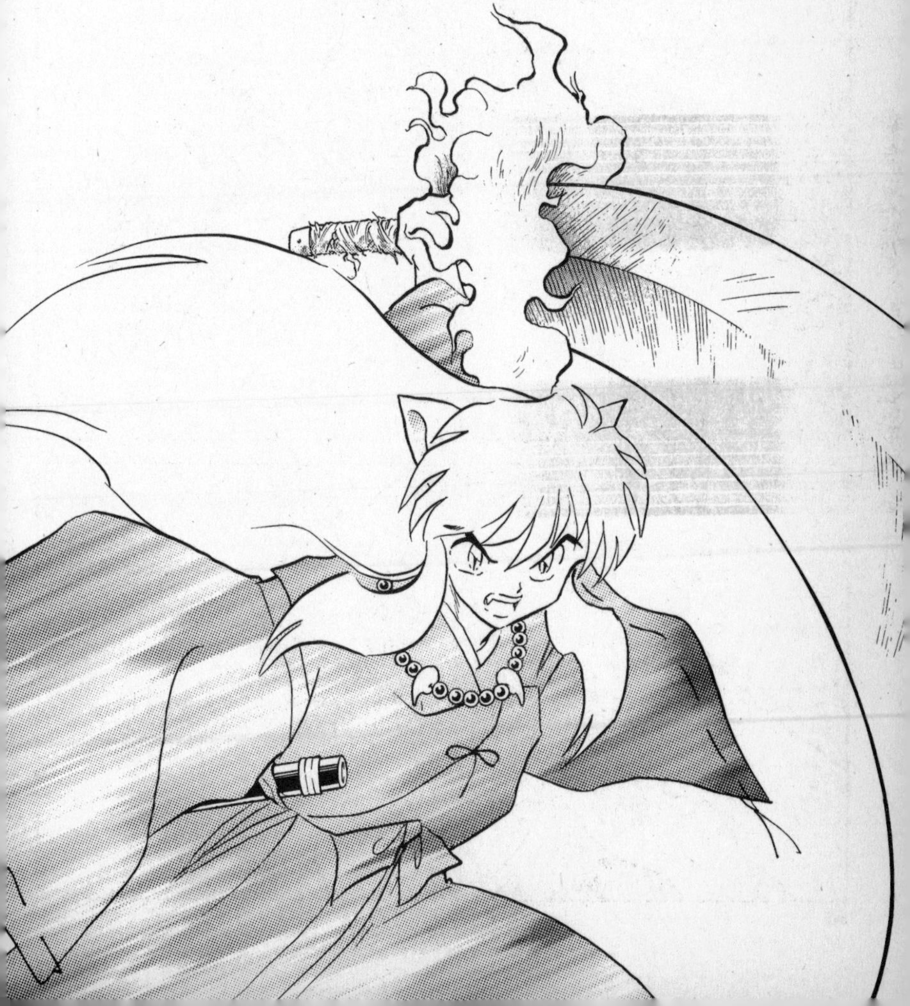

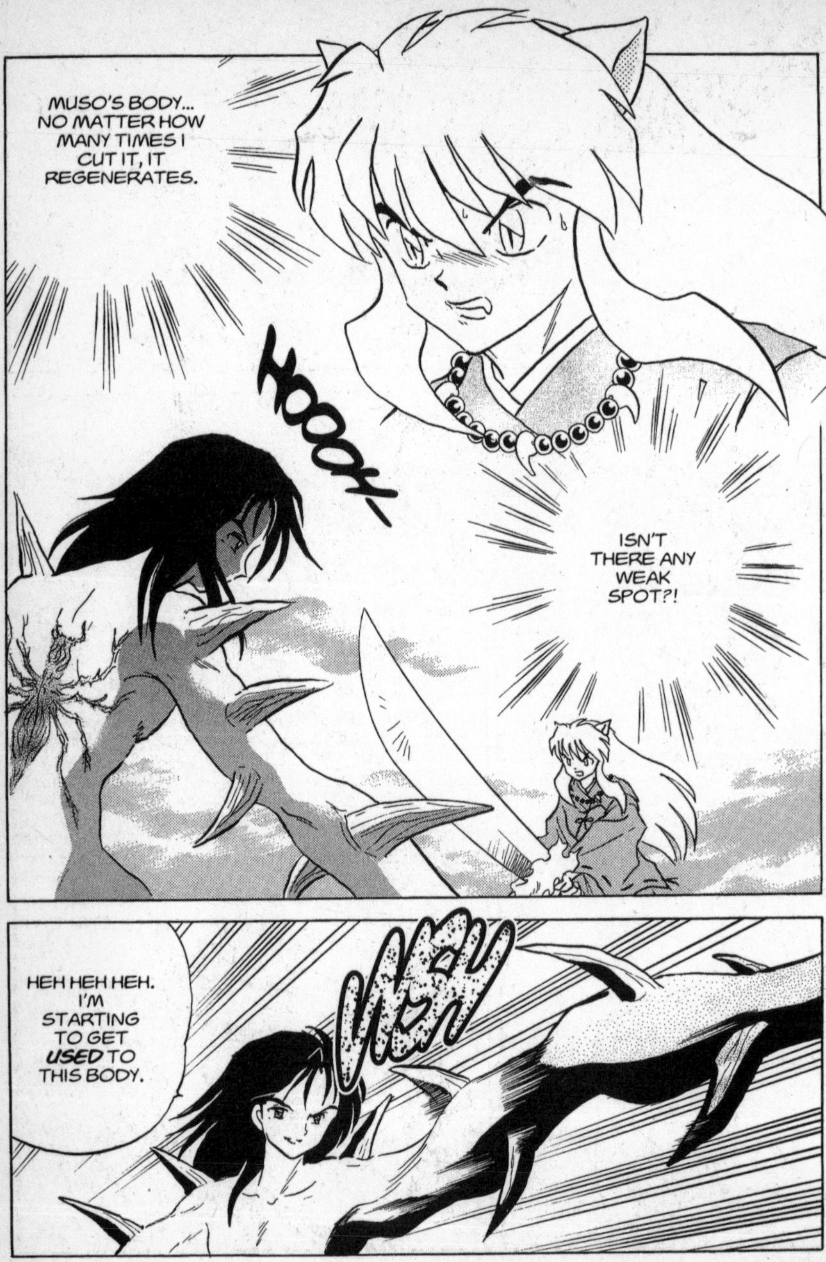
MUSO'S BODY... NO MATTER HOW MANY TIMES I CUT IT, IT REGENERATES.
HOOOH
ISN'T THERE ANY WEAK SPOT?!
HEH HEH HEH. I'M STARTING TO GET ***USED*** TO THIS BODY.

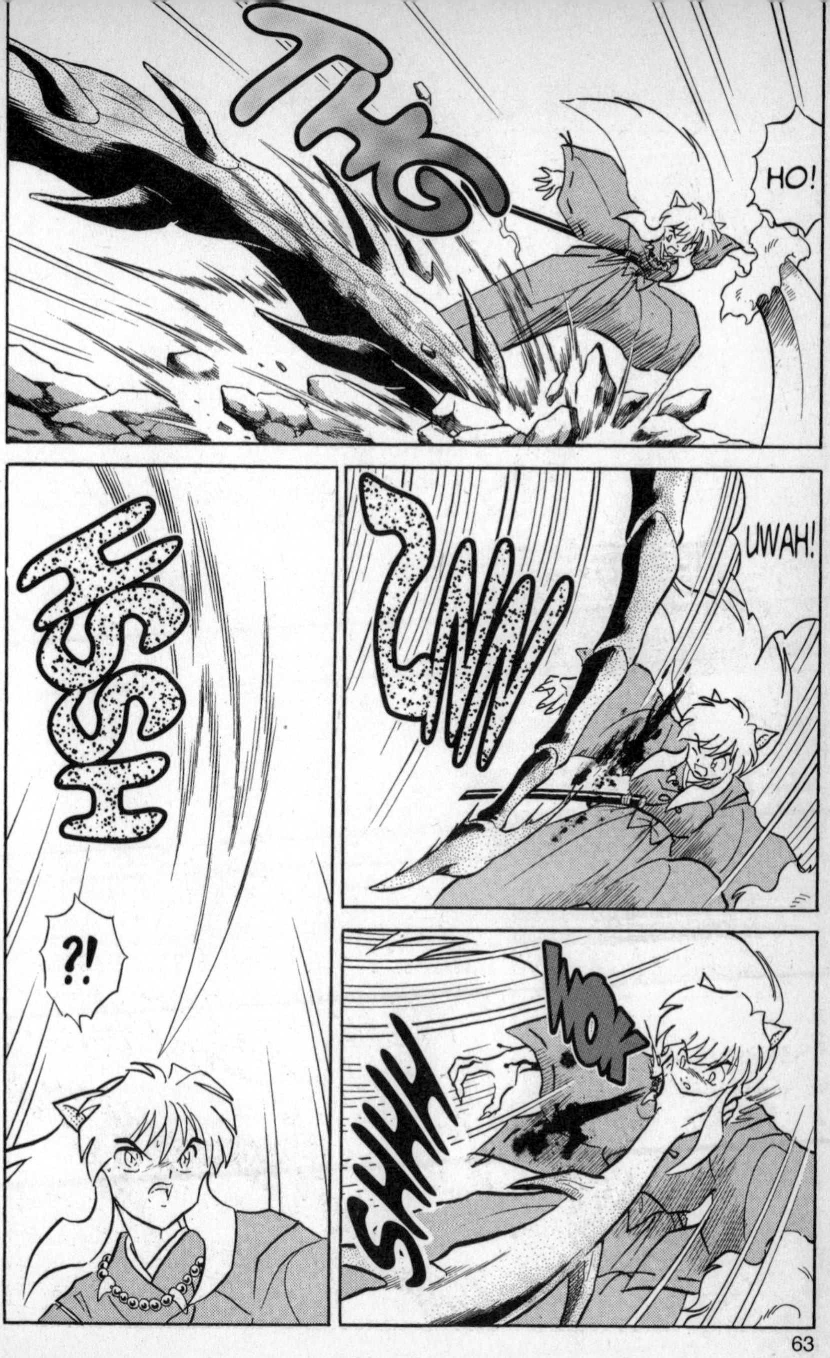
THG
HO!
WHSH
?!
UWAH!
SHHH
WOK

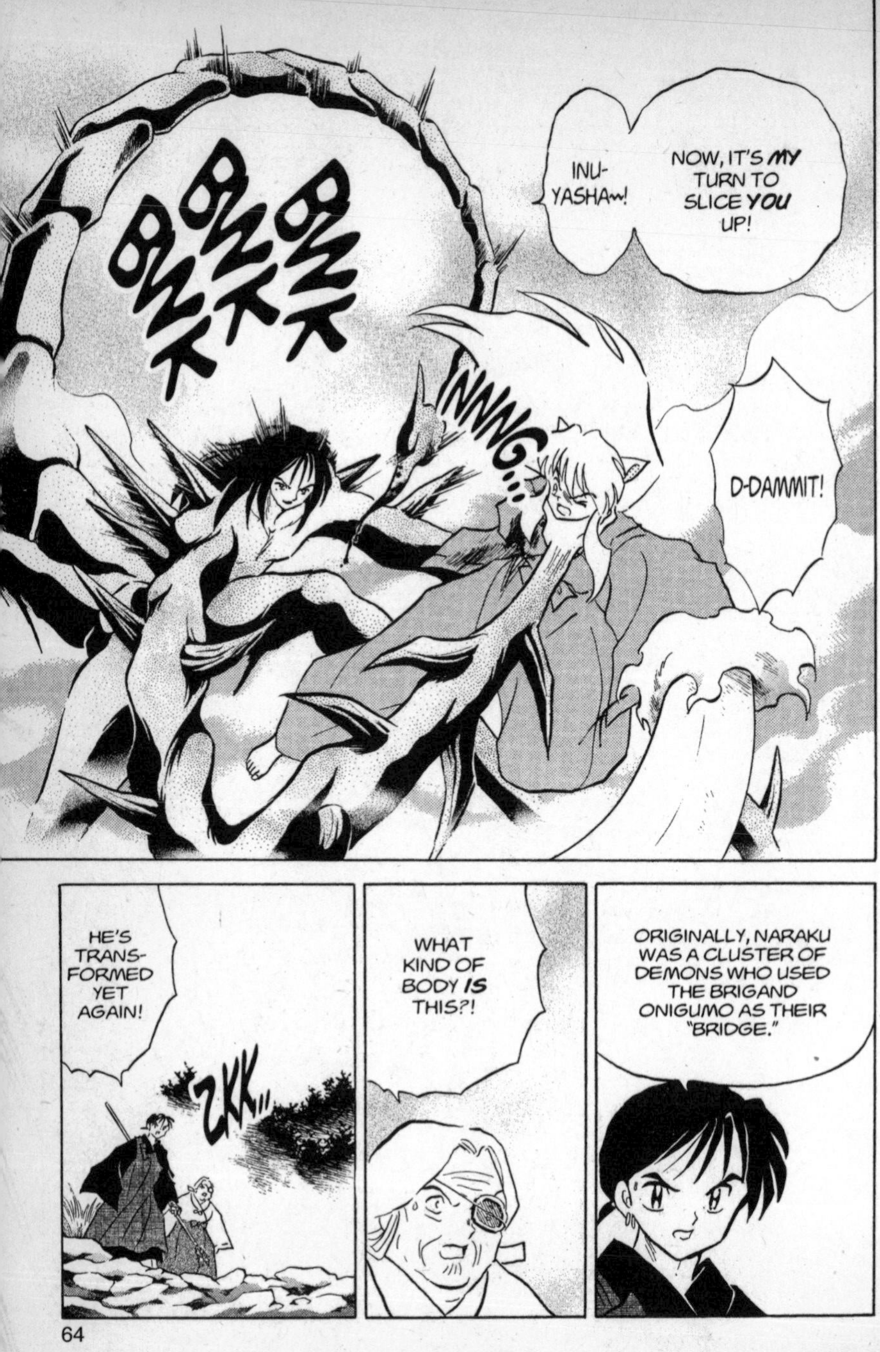
BWNK BWNK BWNK
INU-YASHA~!
NOW, IT'S *MY* TURN TO SLICE *YOU* UP!
INNNG...
D-DAMMIT!
HE'S TRANS-FORMED YET AGAIN!
ZKK...
WHAT KIND OF BODY *IS* THIS?!
ORIGINALLY, NARAKU WAS A CLUSTER OF DEMONS WHO USED THE BRIGAND ONIGUMO AS THEIR "BRIDGE."

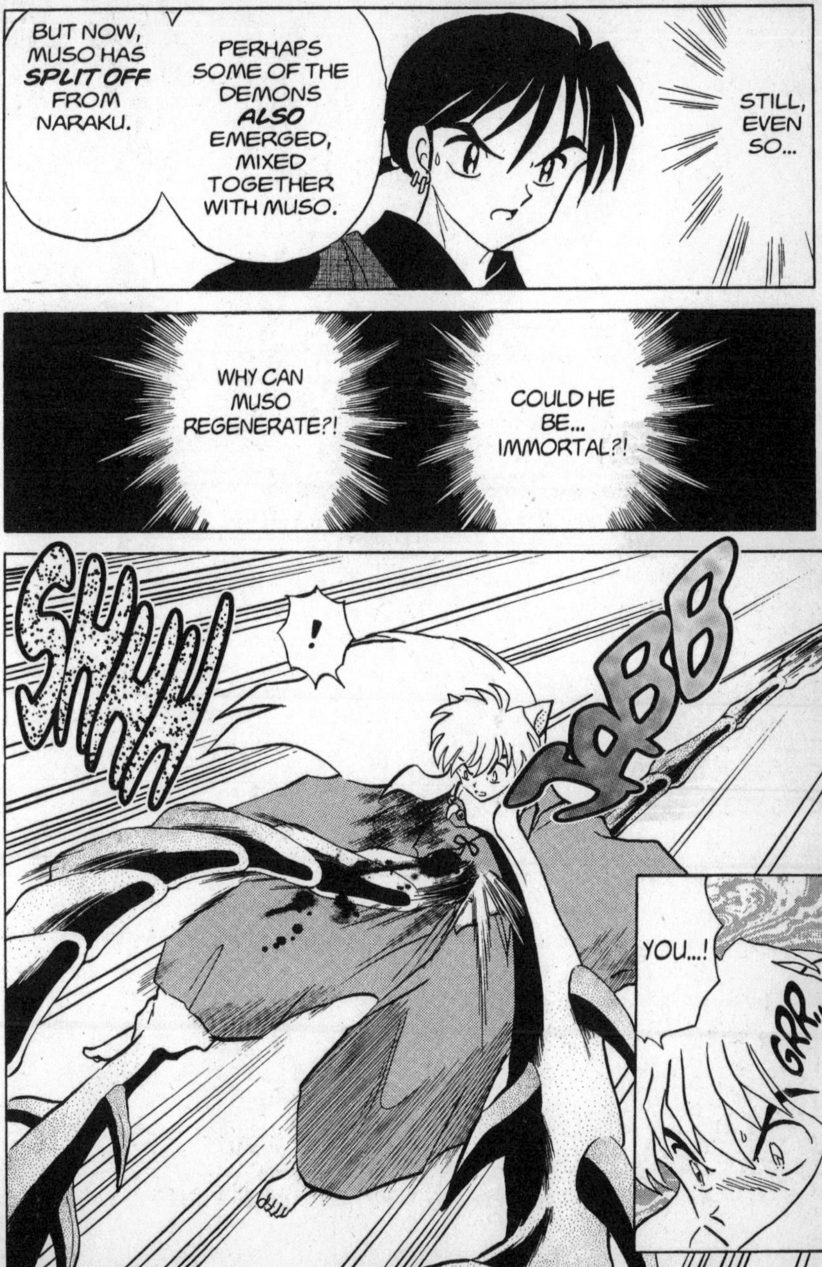
BUT NOW, MUSO HAS SPLIT OFF FROM NARAKU.
PERHAPS SOME OF THE DEMONS ALSO EMERGED, MIXED TOGETHER WITH MUSO.
STILL, EVEN SO...
WHY CAN MUSO REGENERATE?!
COULD HE BE... IMMORTAL?!
SHWW
!
YOU...!
GRR...

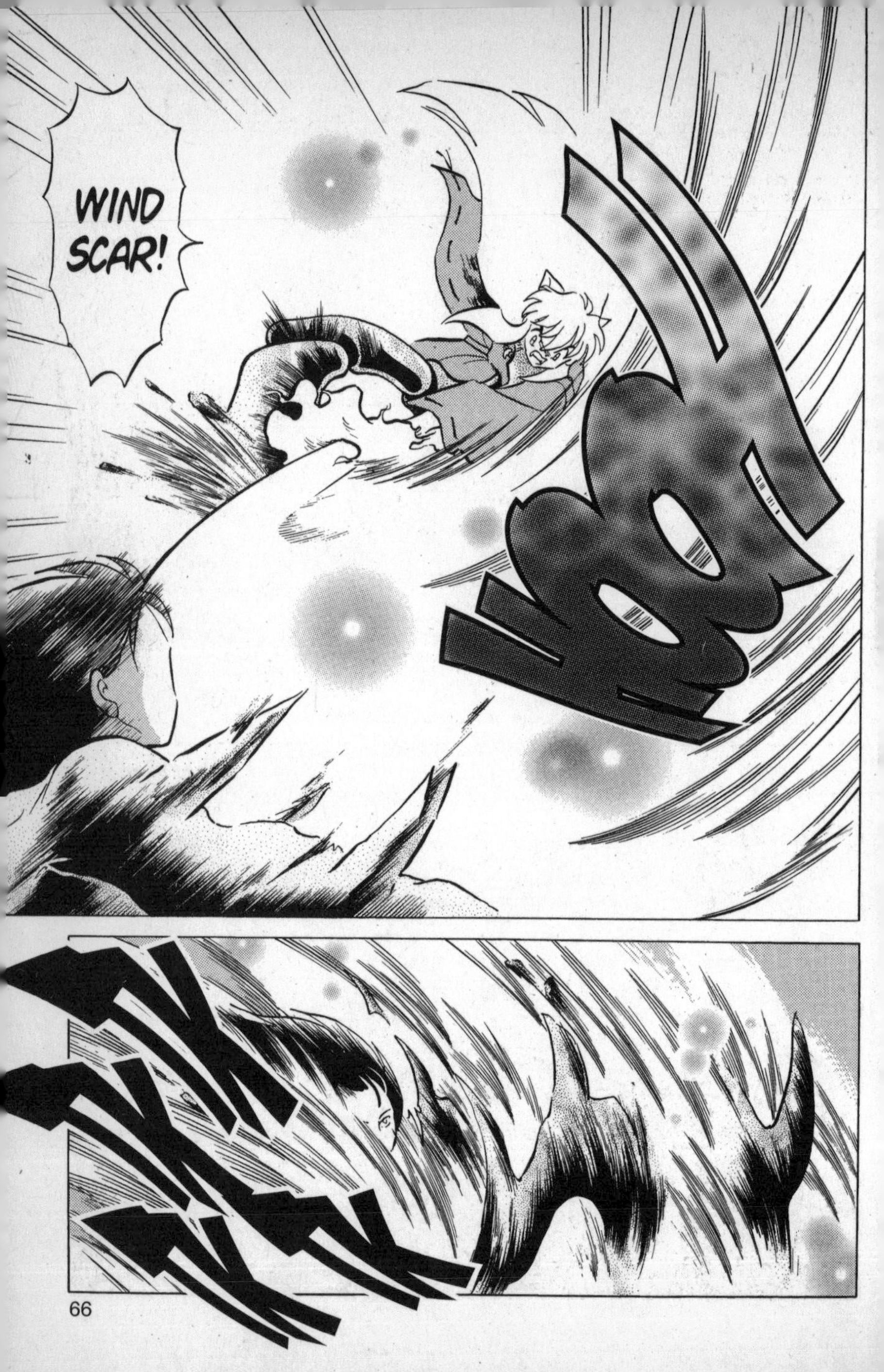
WIND
SCAR!

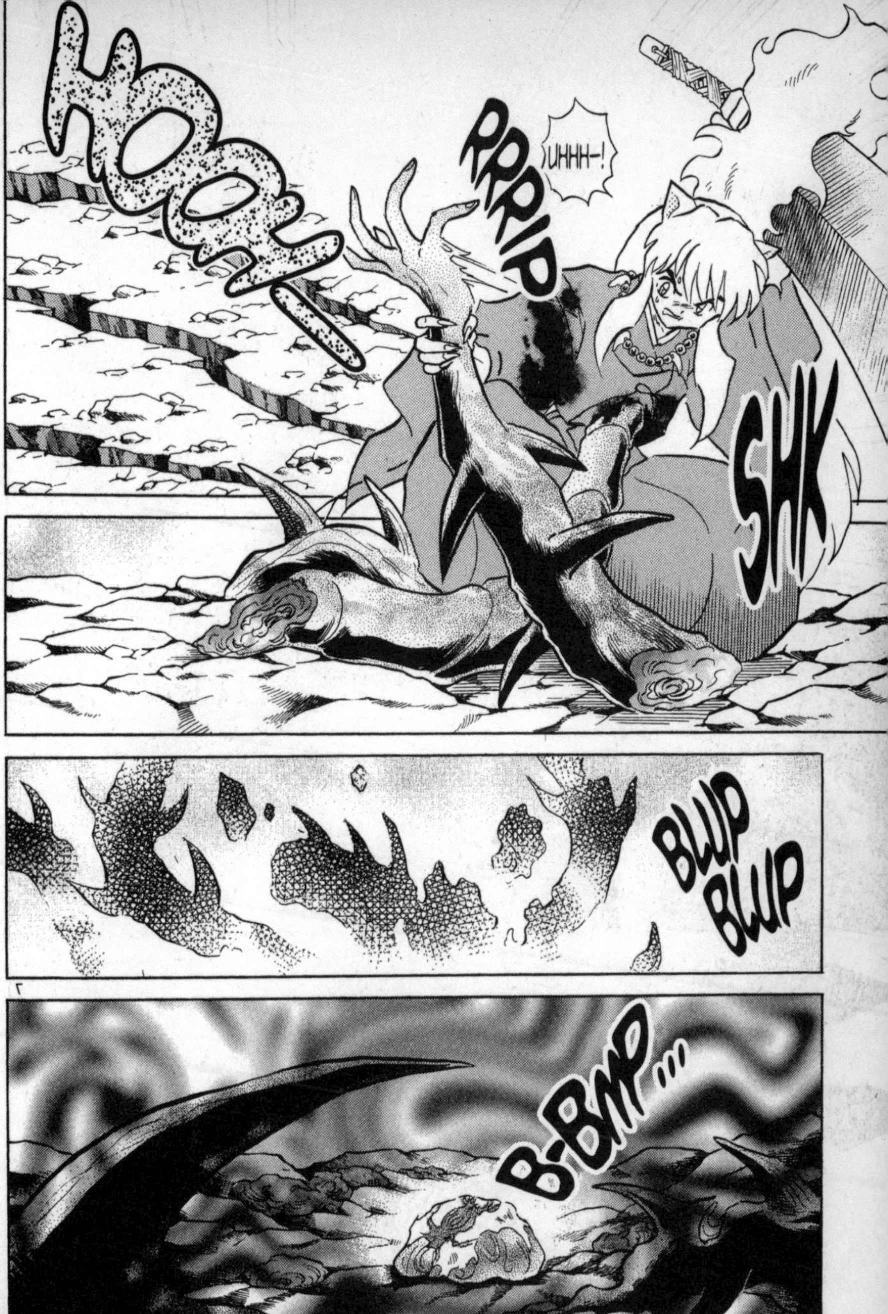
HOOOH!
RRRIP
UHHH-!
SHK
BLUP
BLUP
B-BMP...

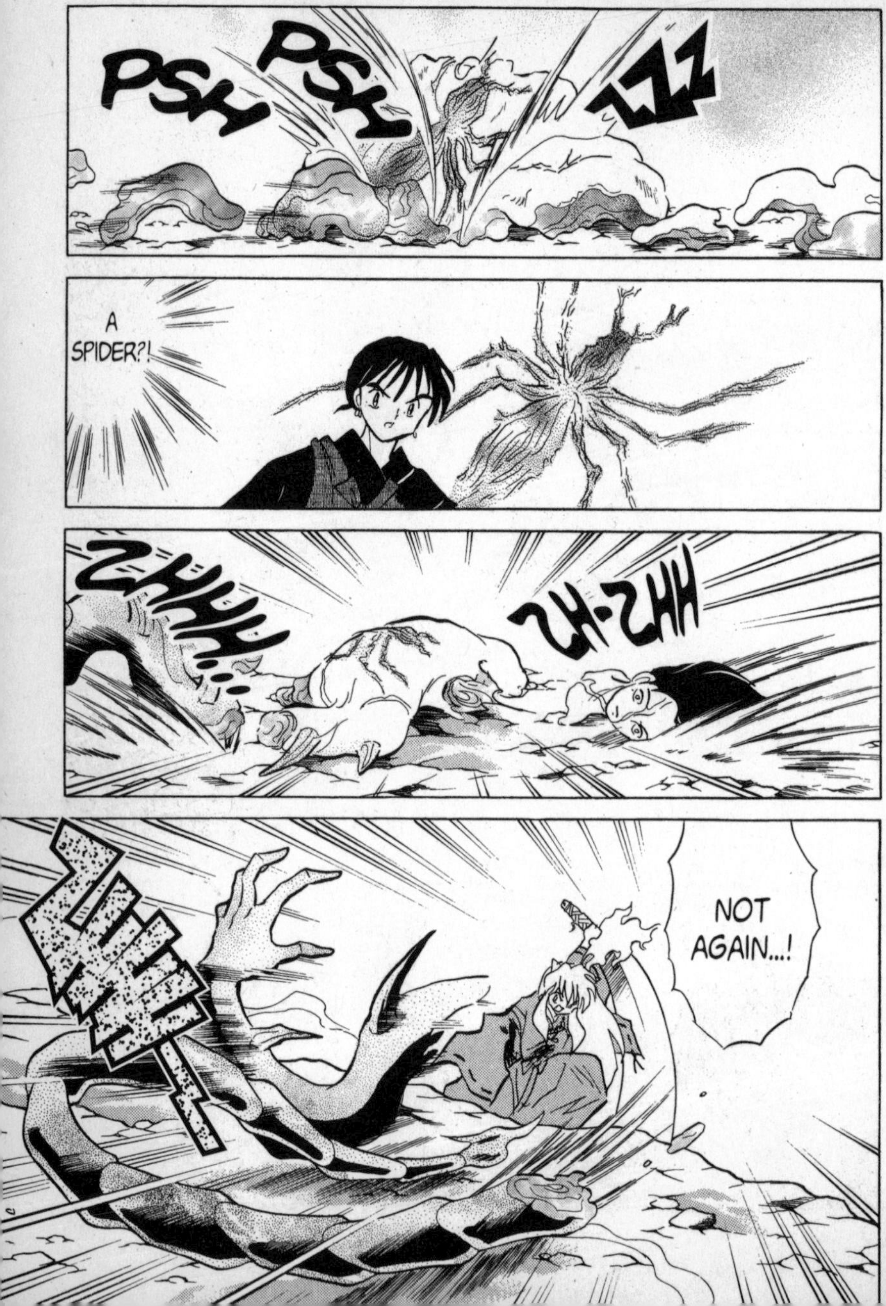
PSH
PSH
ZZZ
A SPIDER?!
ZHHHH...
ZH-ZHH
NOT AGAIN...!

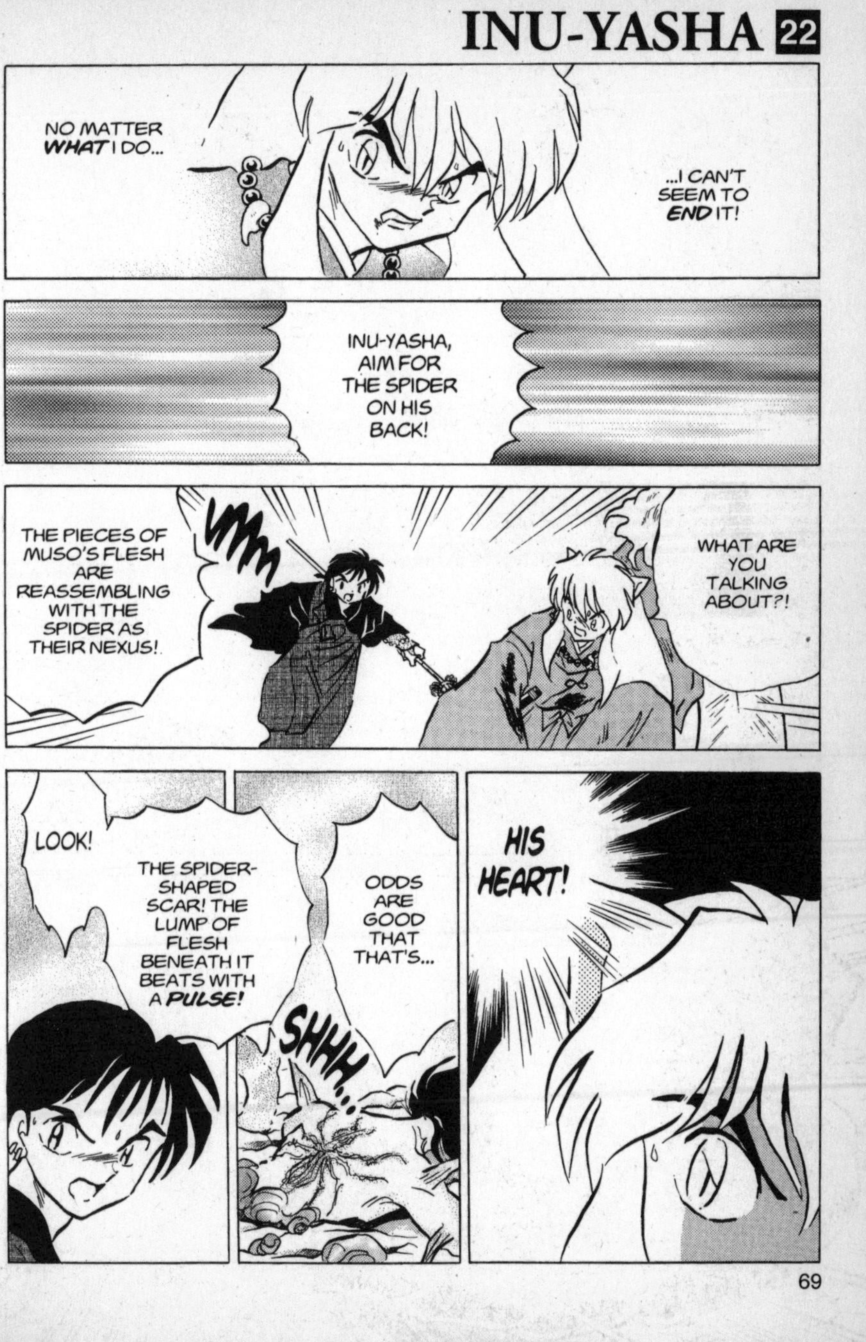
NO MATTER WHAT I DO...
...I CAN'T SEEM TO END IT!
INU-YASHA, AIM FOR THE SPIDER ON HIS BACK!
THE PIECES OF MUSO'S FLESH ARE REASSEMBLING WITH THE SPIDER AS THEIR NEXUS!
VMM
WHAT ARE YOU TALKING ABOUT?!
LOOK!
THE SPIDER-SHAPED SCAR! THE LUMP OF FLESH BENEATH IT BEATS WITH A PULSE!
ODDS ARE GOOD THAT THAT'S...
SHHH...
HIS HEART!

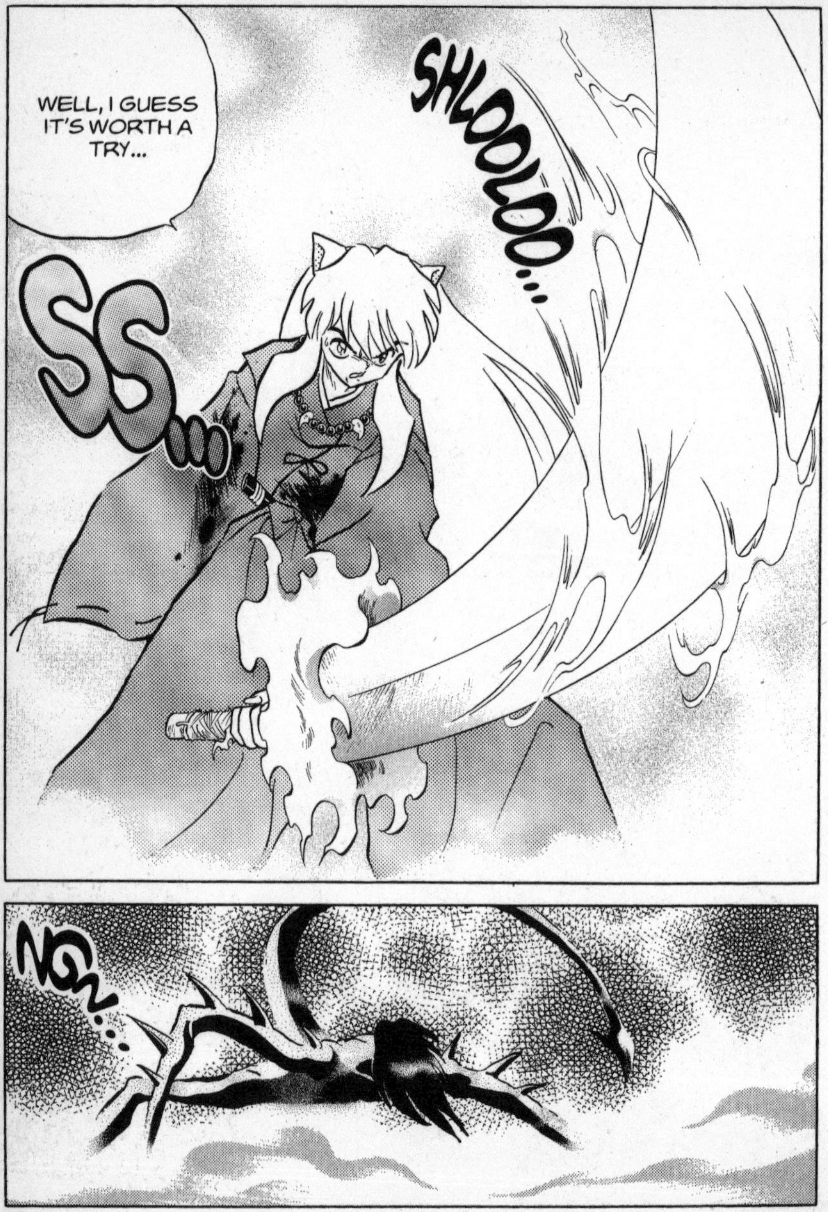
WELL, I GUESS IT'S WORTH A TRY...
SHLOOLOO...
SS...
NGN...

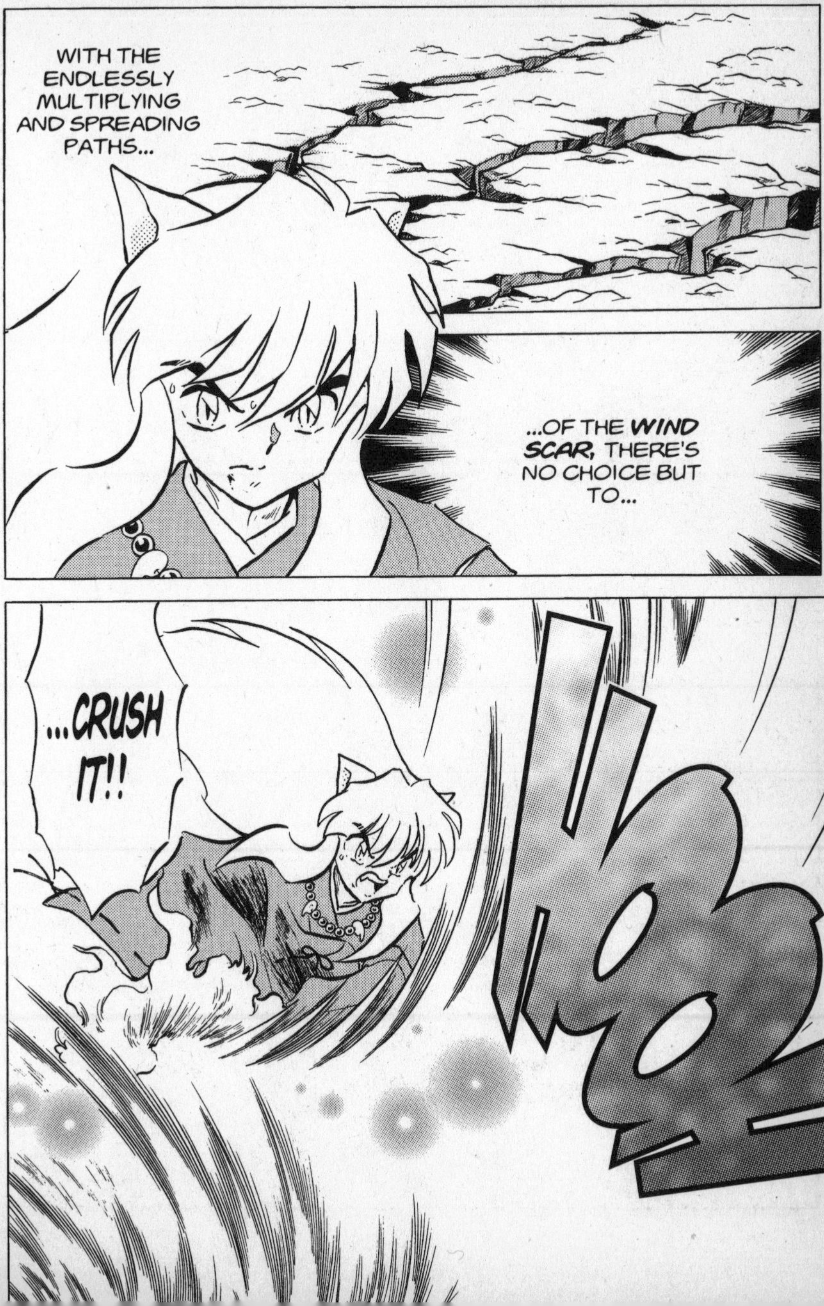
WITH THE ENDLESSLY MULTIPLYING AND SPREADING PATHS...
...OF THE *WIND SCAR,* THERE'S NO CHOICE BUT TO...
...CRUSH IT!!

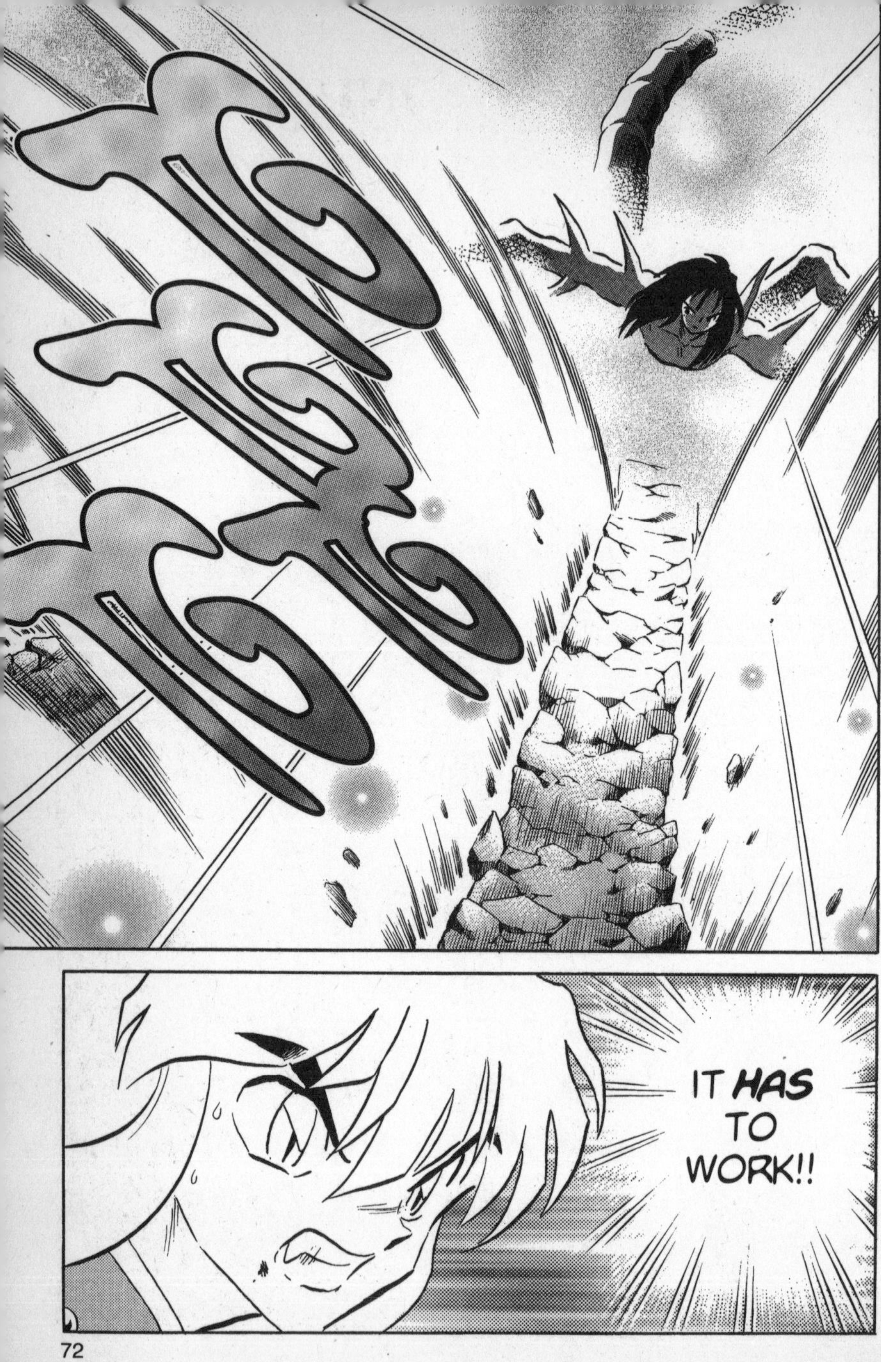
IT *HAS* TO WORK!!

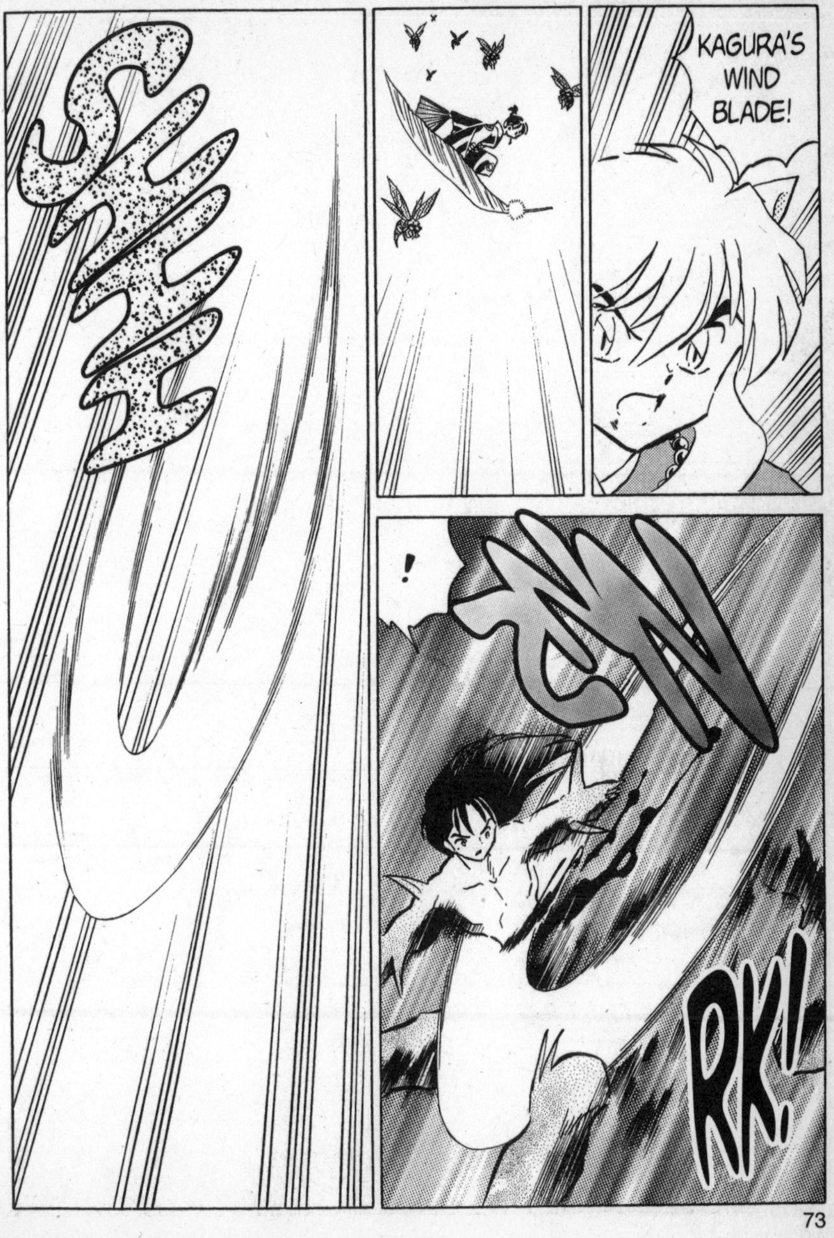
KAGURA'S
WIND
BLADE!
!
RK!

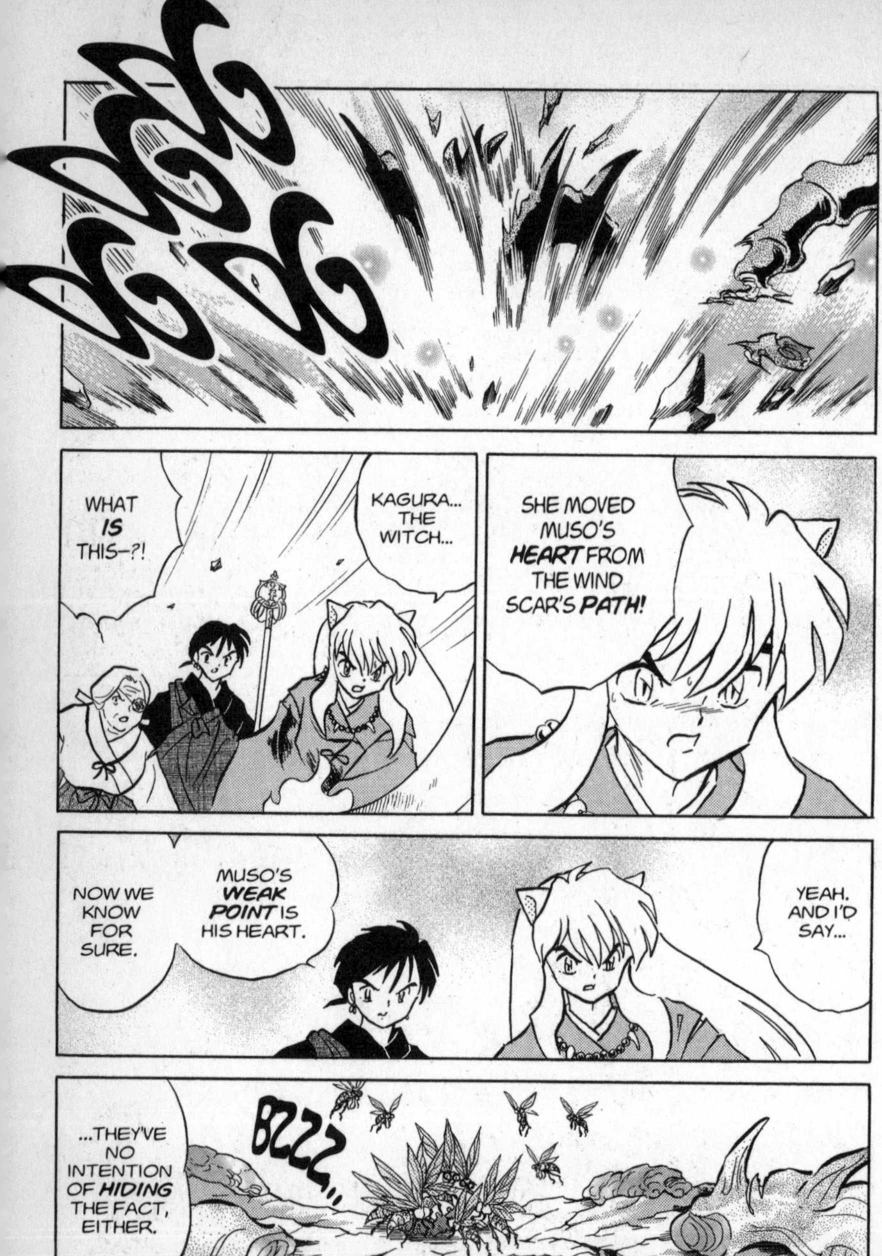
WHAT IS THIS–?!
KAGURA... THE WITCH...
SHE MOVED MUSO'S HEART FROM THE WIND SCAR'S PATH!
NOW WE KNOW FOR SURE.
MUSO'S WEAK POINT IS HIS HEART.
YEAH. AND I'D SAY...
...THEY'VE NO INTENTION OF HIDING THE FACT, EITHER.
BZZZ...

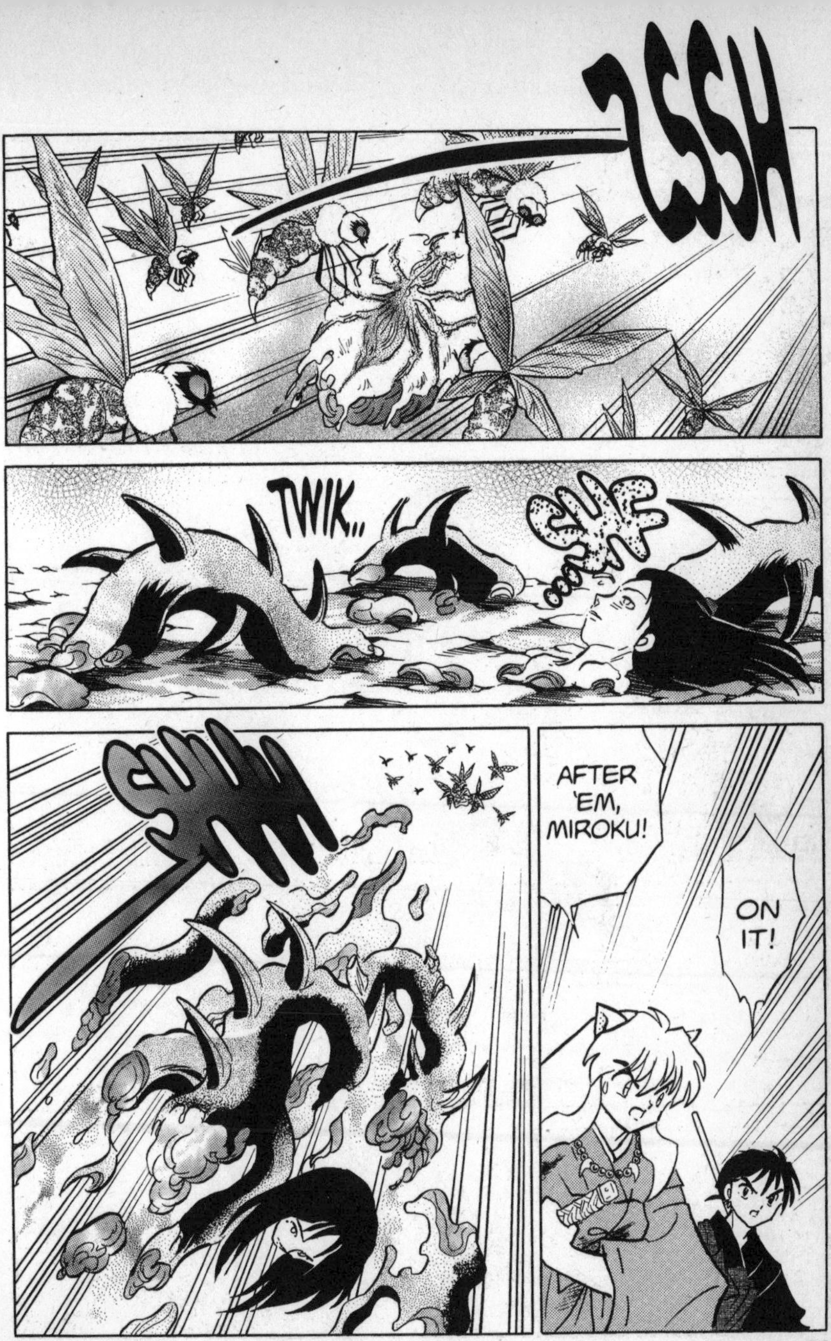
ZSSH
TWIK..
AFTER 'EM, MIROKU!
ON IT!

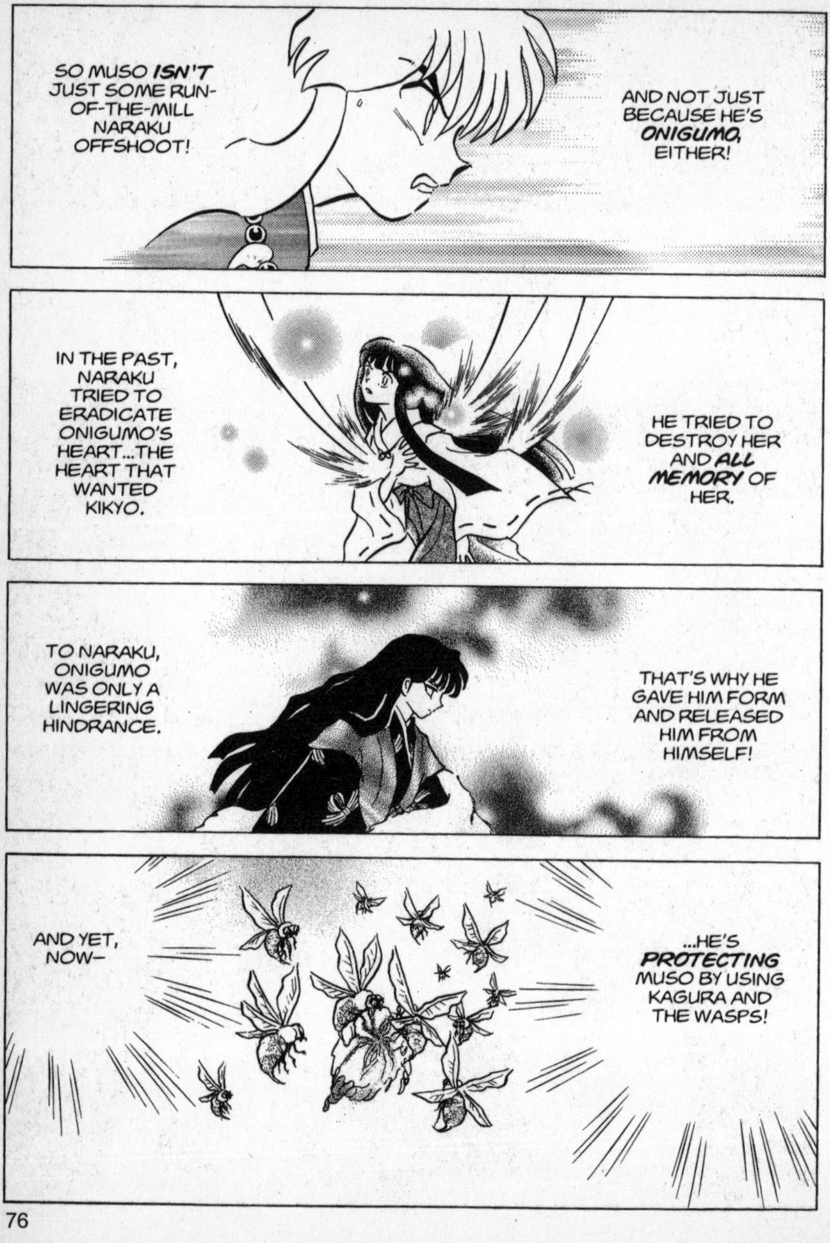
SO MUSO ISN'T JUST SOME RUN-OF-THE-MILL NARAKU OFFSHOOT!
AND NOT JUST BECAUSE HE'S ONIGUMO, EITHER!
IN THE PAST, NARAKU TRIED TO ERADICATE ONIGUMO'S HEART...THE HEART THAT WANTED KIKYO.
HE TRIED TO DESTROY HER AND ALL MEMORY OF HER.
TO NARAKU, ONIGUMO WAS ONLY A LINGERING HINDRANCE.
THAT'S WHY HE GAVE HIM FORM AND RELEASED HIM FROM HIMSELF!
AND YET, NOW–
...HE'S PROTECTING MUSO BY USING KAGURA AND THE WASPS!

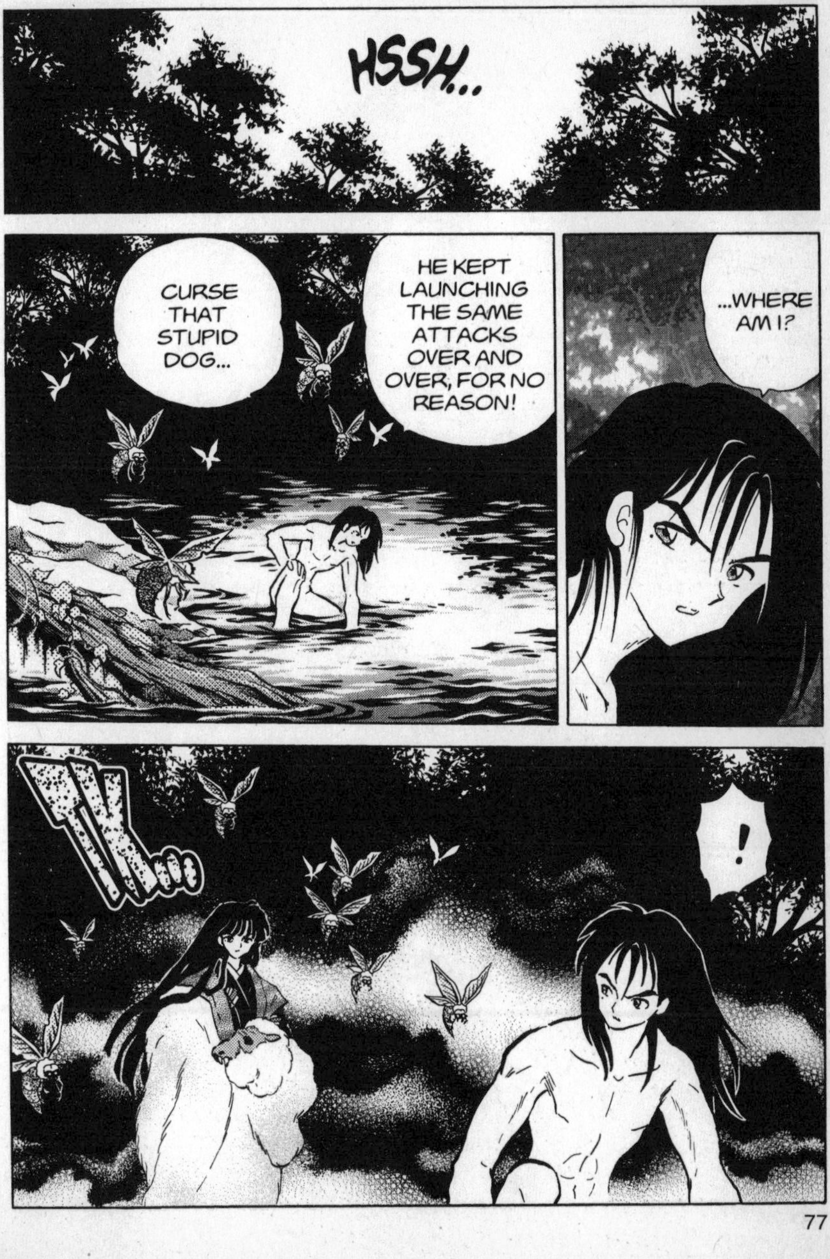
HSSH...
CURSE THAT STUPID DOG...
HE KEPT LAUNCHING THE SAME ATTACKS OVER AND OVER, FOR NO REASON!
...WHERE AM I?
!

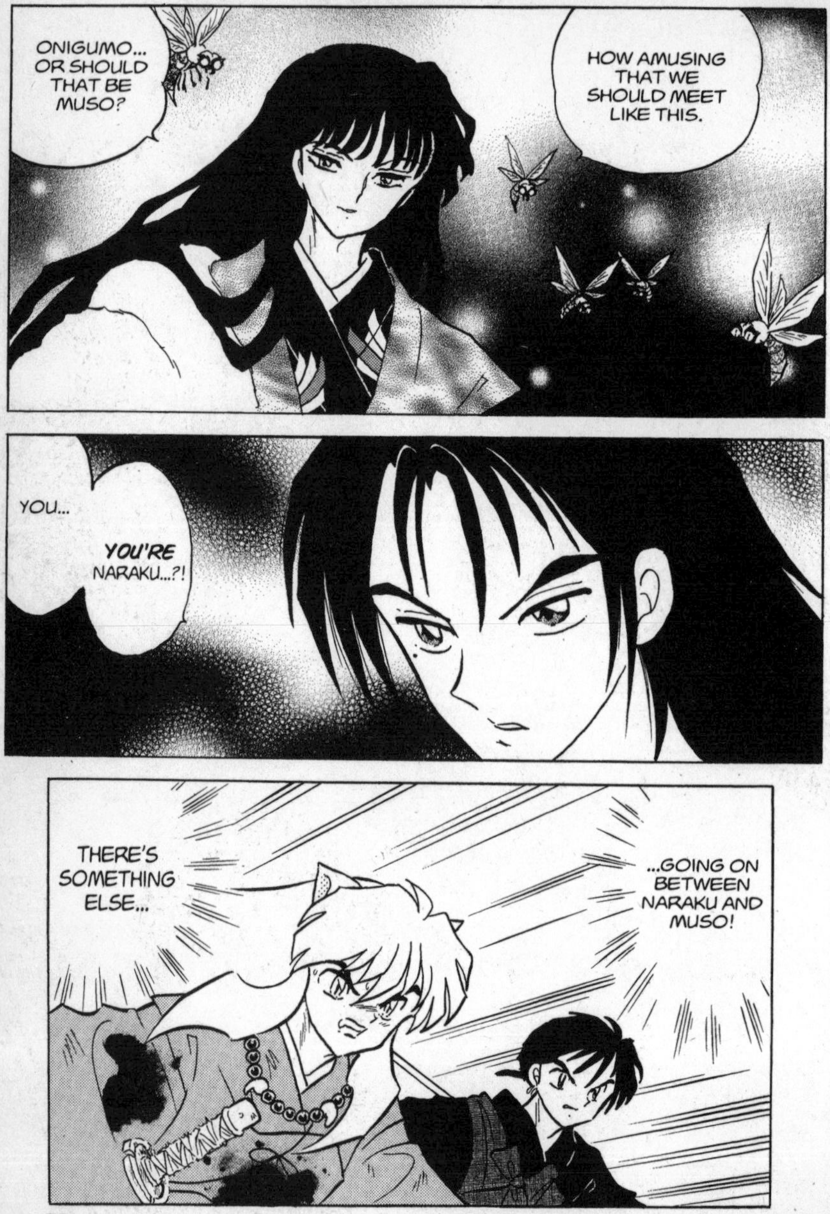
ONIGUMO... OR SHOULD THAT BE MUSO?
HOW AMUSING THAT WE SHOULD MEET LIKE THIS.
YOU...
YOU'RE NARAKU...?!
THERE'S SOMETHING ELSE...
...GOING ON BETWEEN NARAKU AND MUSO!

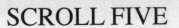

SCROLL FIVE

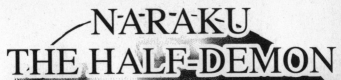

NARAKU THE HALF-DEMON

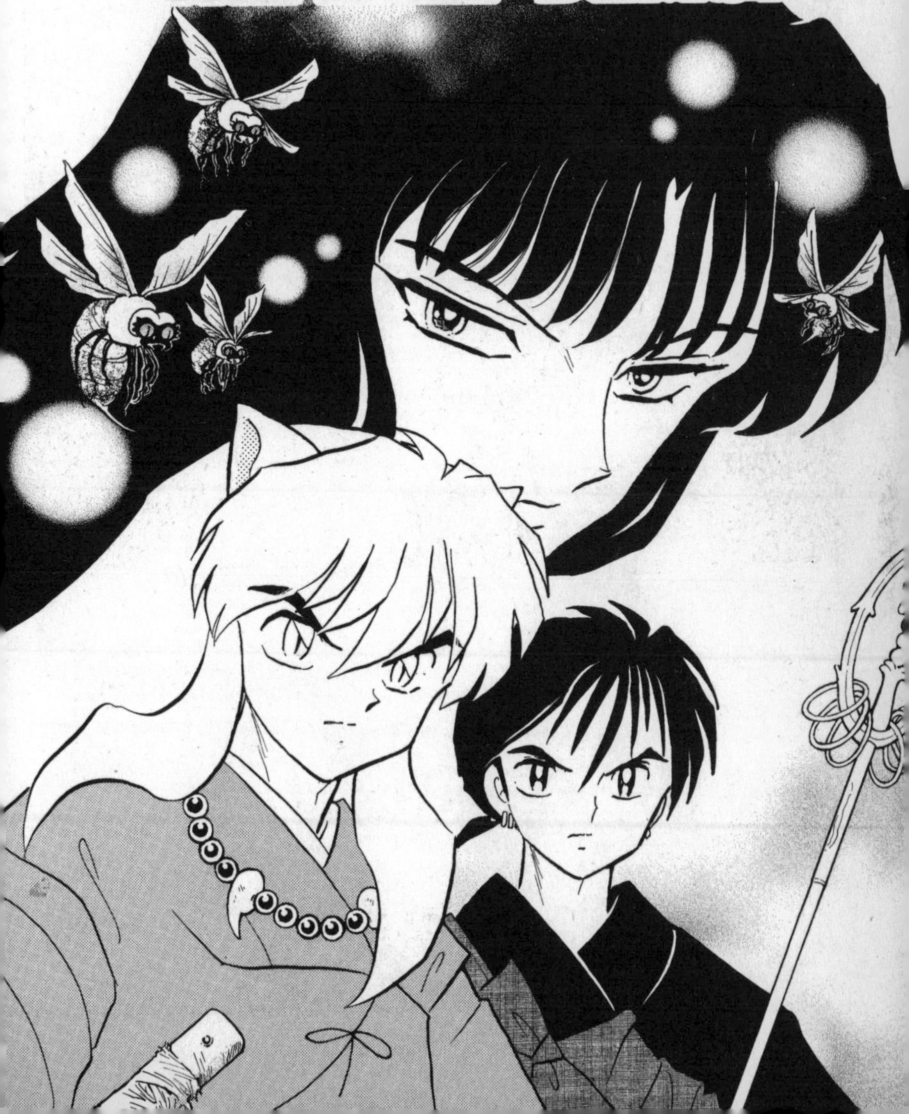

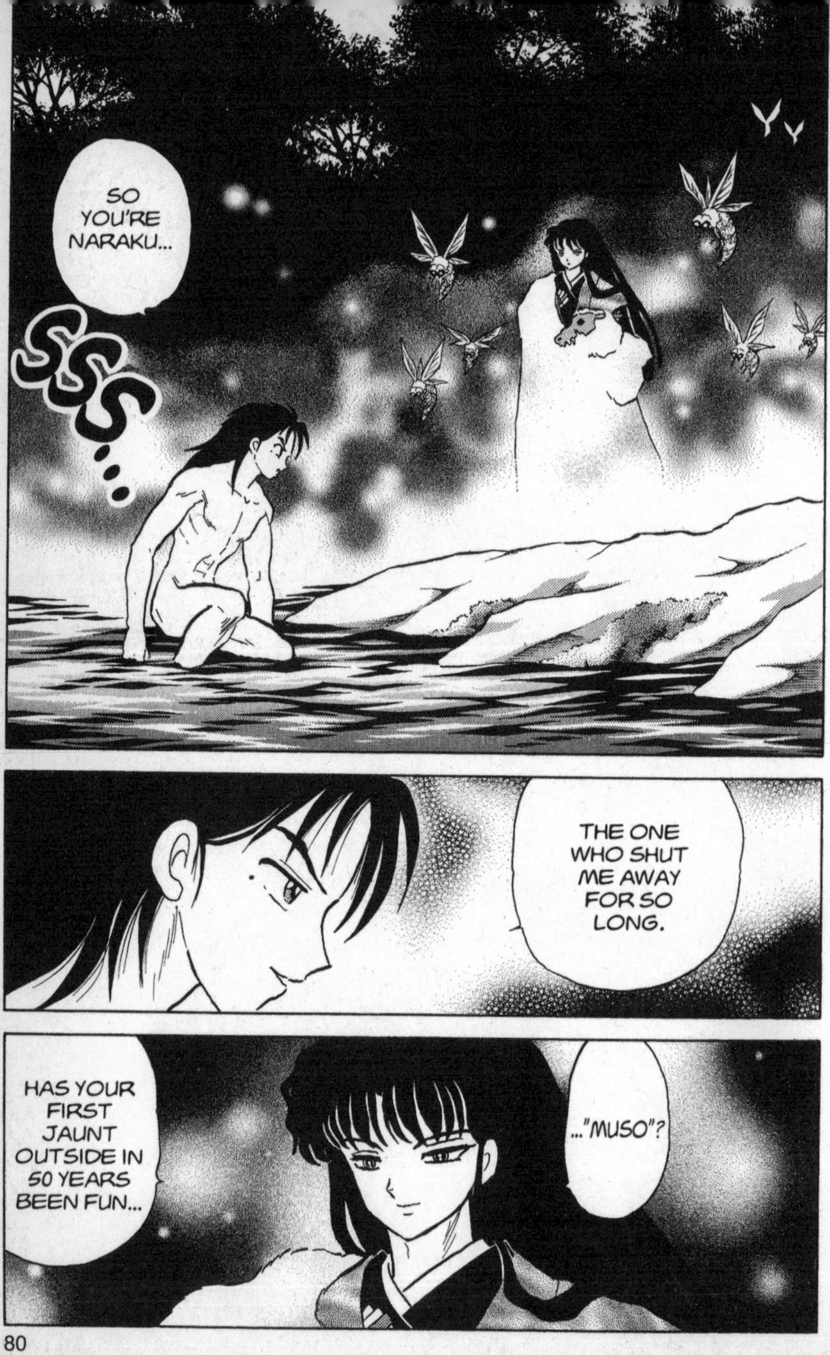
SO YOU'RE NARAKU...
SSS...
YY
THE ONE WHO SHUT ME AWAY FOR SO LONG.
HAS YOUR FIRST JAUNT OUTSIDE IN 50 YEARS BEEN FUN...
..."MUSO"?

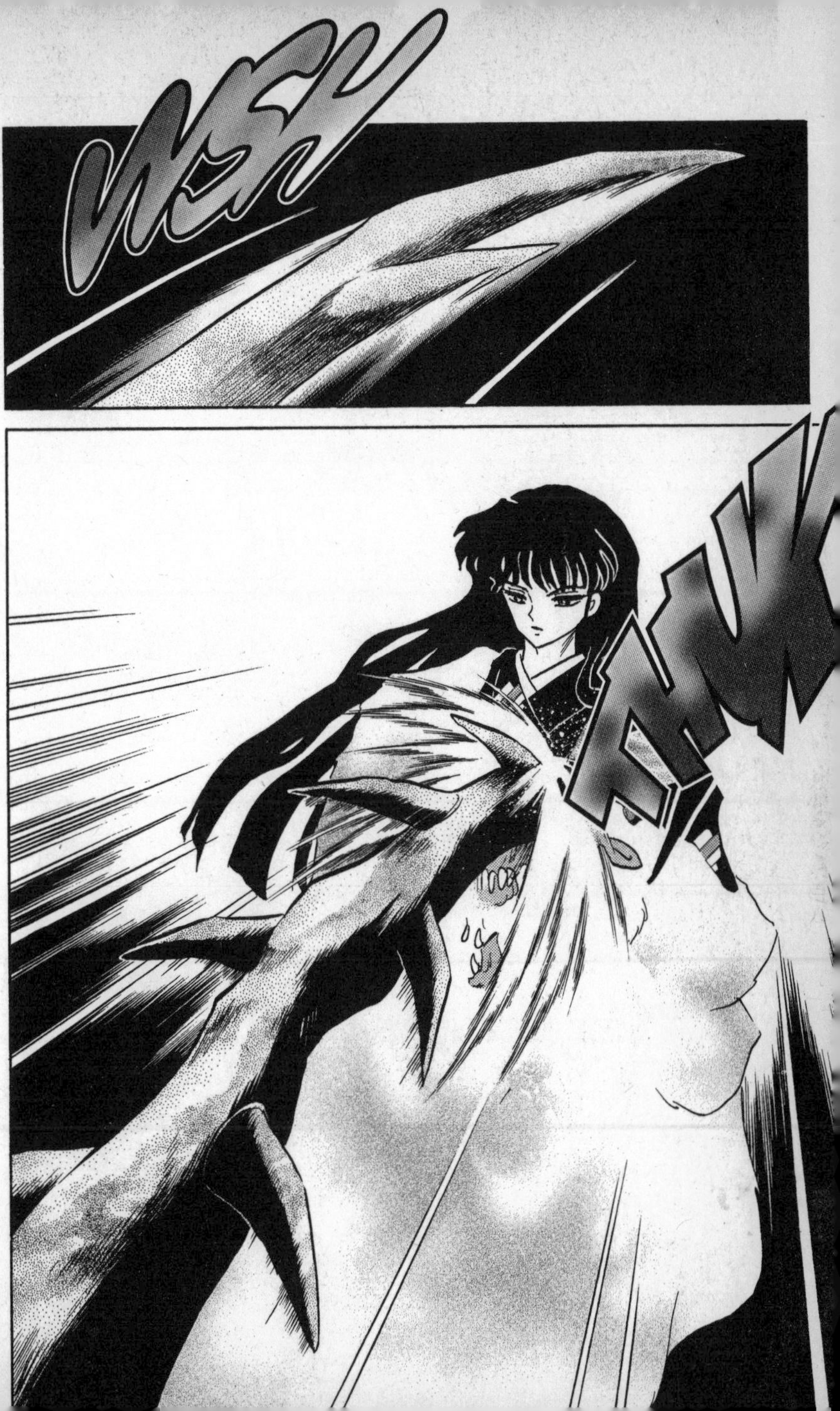
THUK

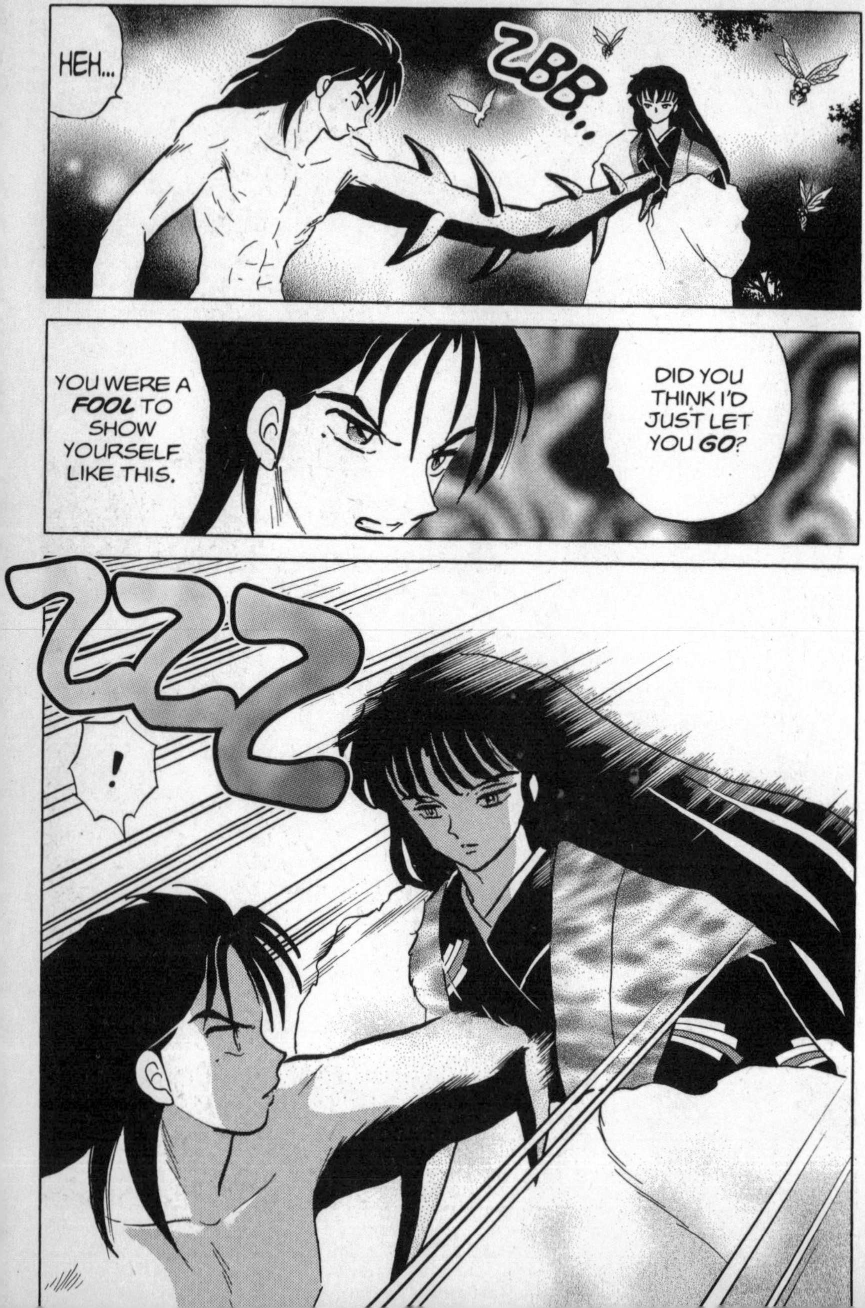
ZBB...
HEH...
DID YOU THINK I'D JUST LET YOU GO?
YOU WERE A FOOL TO SHOW YOURSELF LIKE THIS.
ZZZ
!

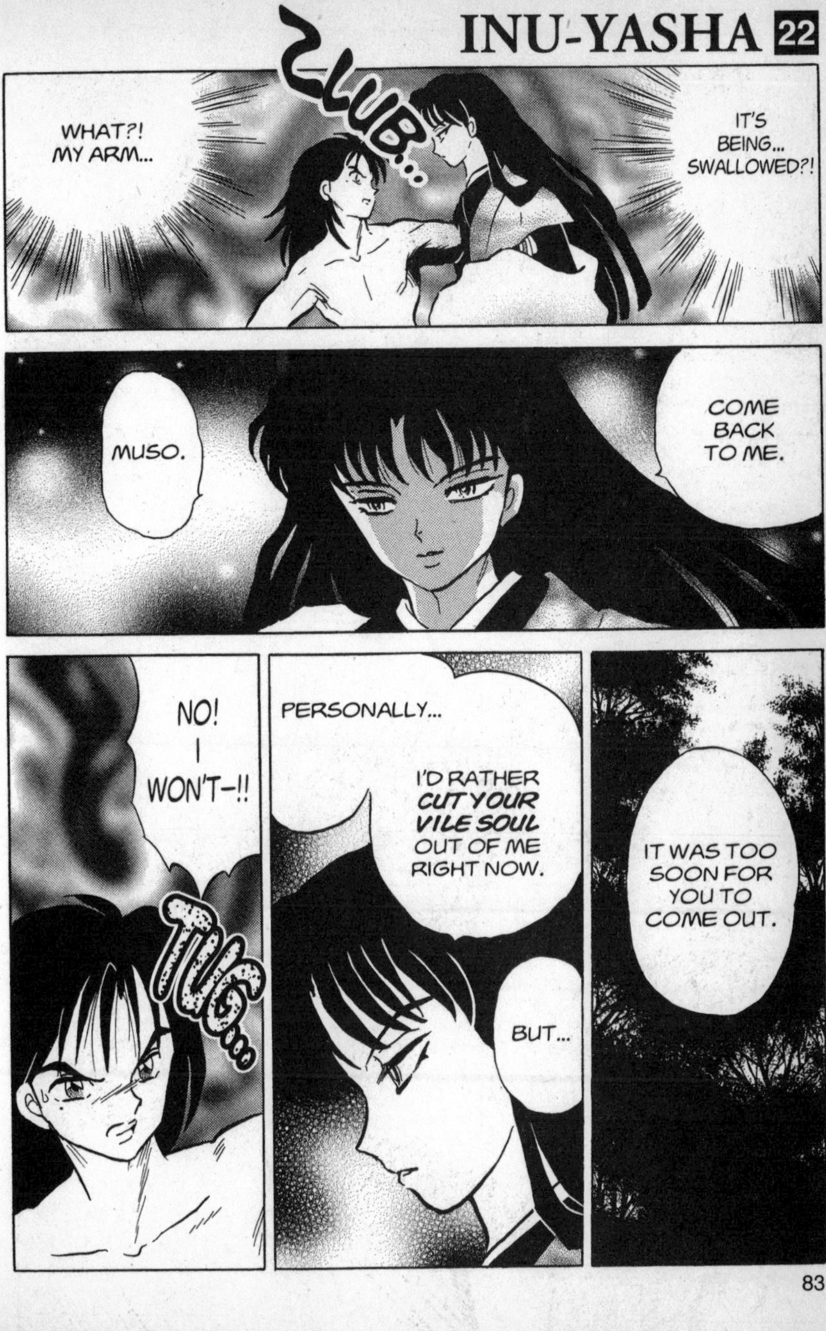
WHAT?! MY ARM...
GLUB...
IT'S BEING... SWALLOWED?!
MUSO.
COME BACK TO ME.
NO! I WON'T-!!
TUG...
PERSONALLY...
I'D RATHER CUT YOUR VILE SOUL OUT OF ME RIGHT NOW.
BUT...
IT WAS TOO SOON FOR YOU TO COME OUT.

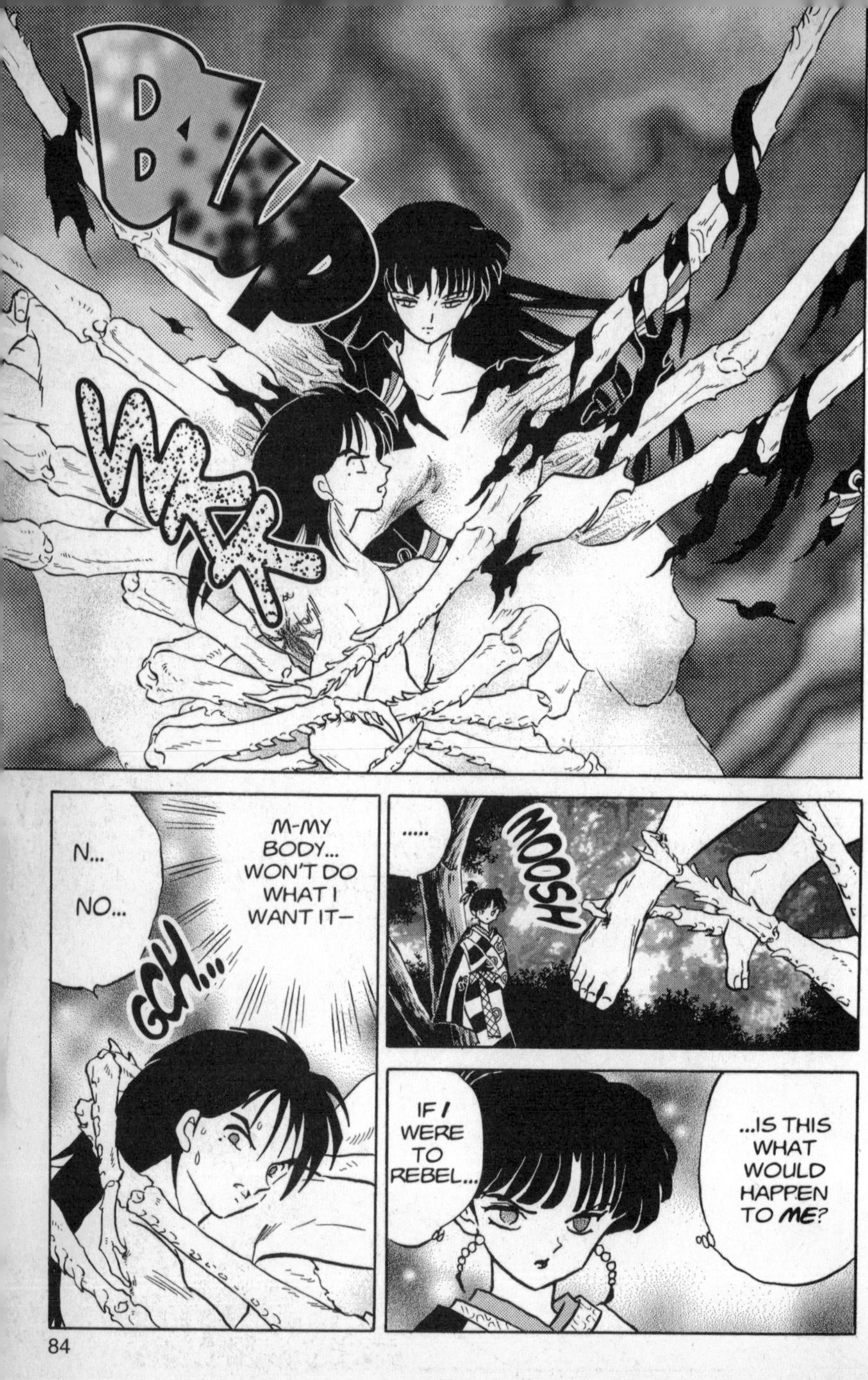
WHAK
N...
NO...
M-MY BODY... WON'T DO WHAT I WANT IT–
GCH...
.....
MOOSH
IF I WERE TO REBEL...
...IS THIS WHAT WOULD HAPPEN TO *ME*?

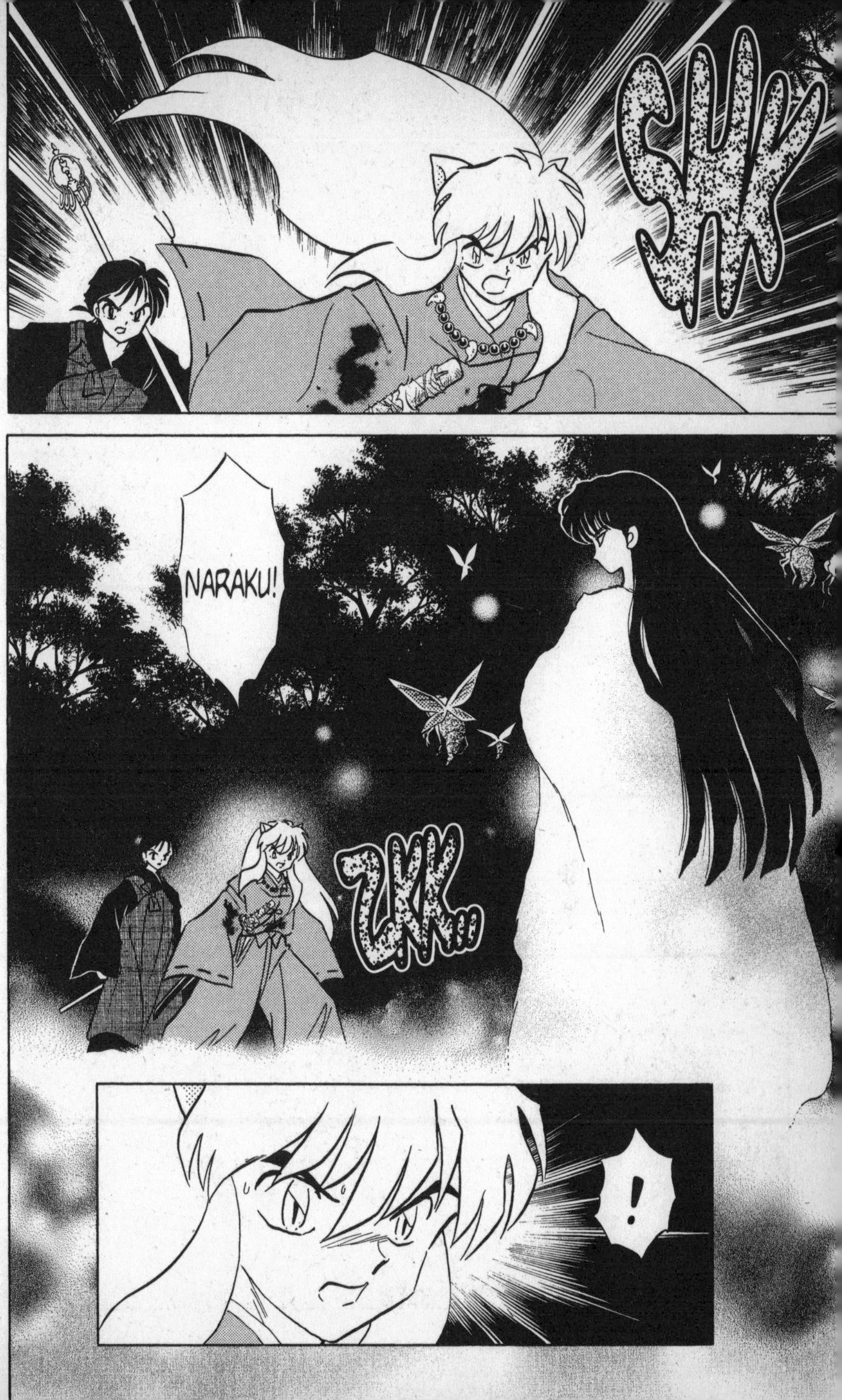
SHK
NARAKU!
ZKK...
!

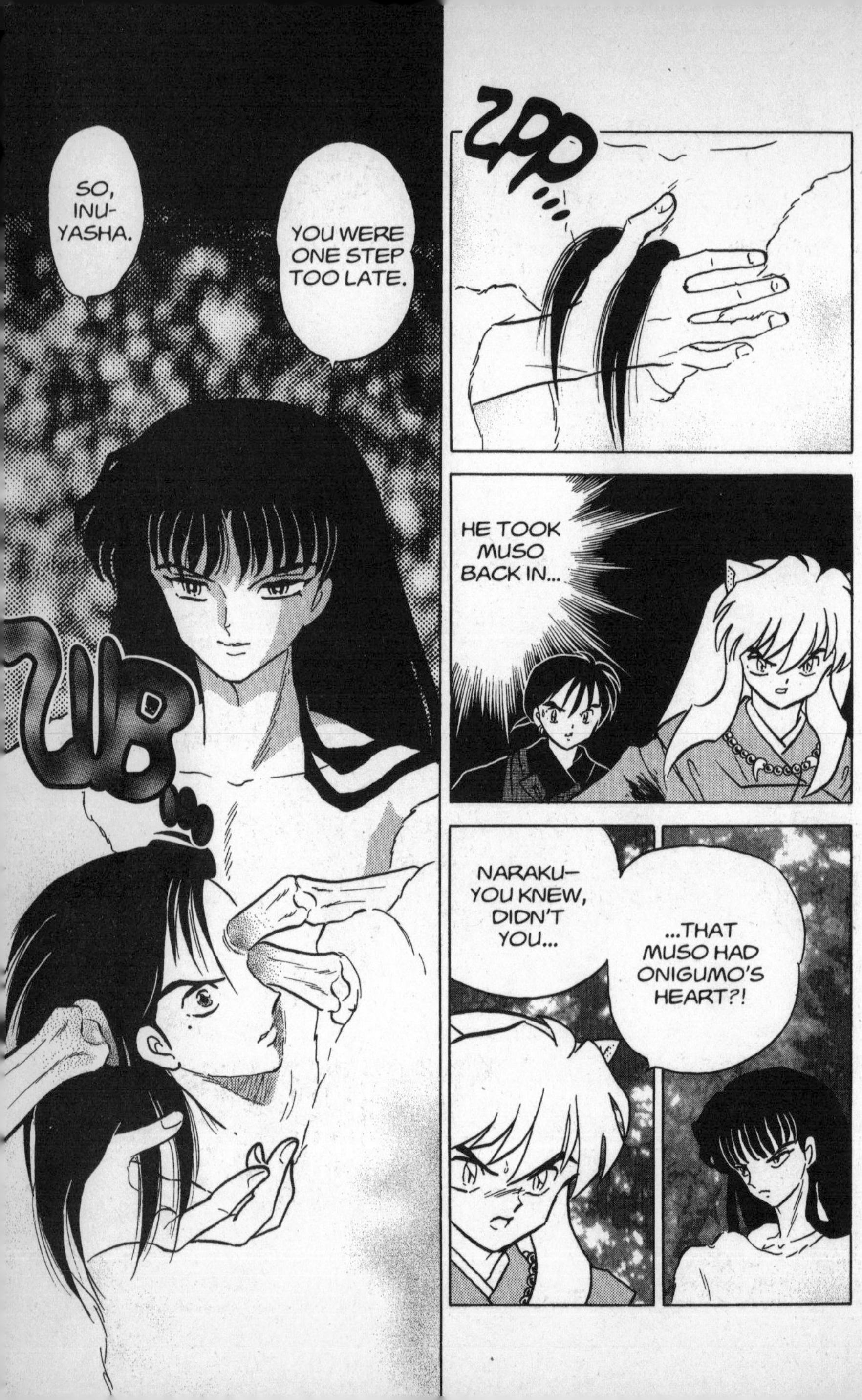
SO, INU-YASHA.
YOU WERE ONE STEP TOO LATE.
HE TOOK MUSO BACK IN...
NARAKU-YOU KNEW, DIDN'T YOU...
...THAT MUSO HAD ONIGUMO'S HEART?!

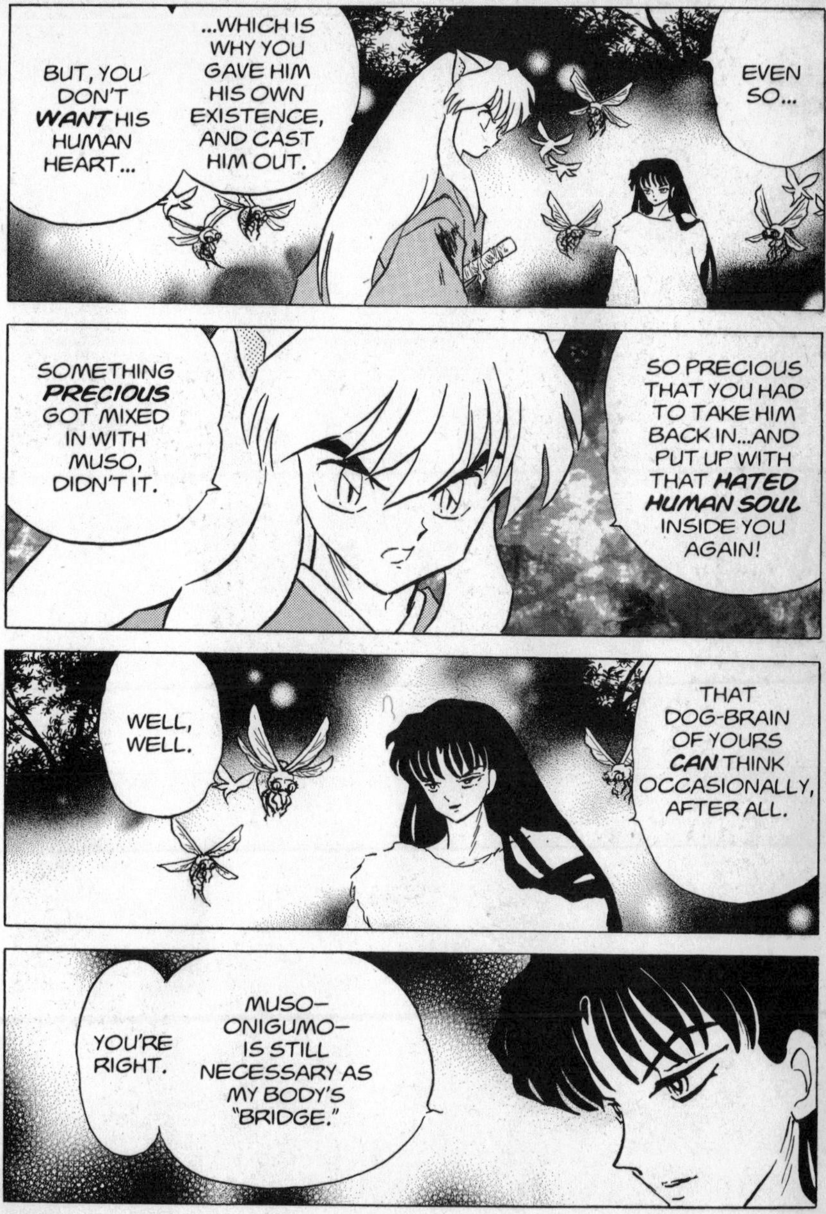
BUT, YOU DON'T *WANT* HIS HUMAN HEART...
...WHICH IS WHY YOU GAVE HIM HIS OWN EXISTENCE, AND CAST HIM OUT.
EVEN SO...
SOMETHING *PRECIOUS* GOT MIXED IN WITH MUSO, DIDN'T IT.
SO PRECIOUS THAT YOU HAD TO TAKE HIM BACK IN...AND PUT UP WITH THAT *HATED HUMAN SOUL* INSIDE YOU AGAIN!
WELL, WELL.
THAT DOG-BRAIN OF YOURS *CAN* THINK OCCASIONALLY, AFTER ALL.
YOU'RE RIGHT.
MUSO—ONIGUMO—IS STILL NECESSARY AS MY BODY'S "BRIDGE."

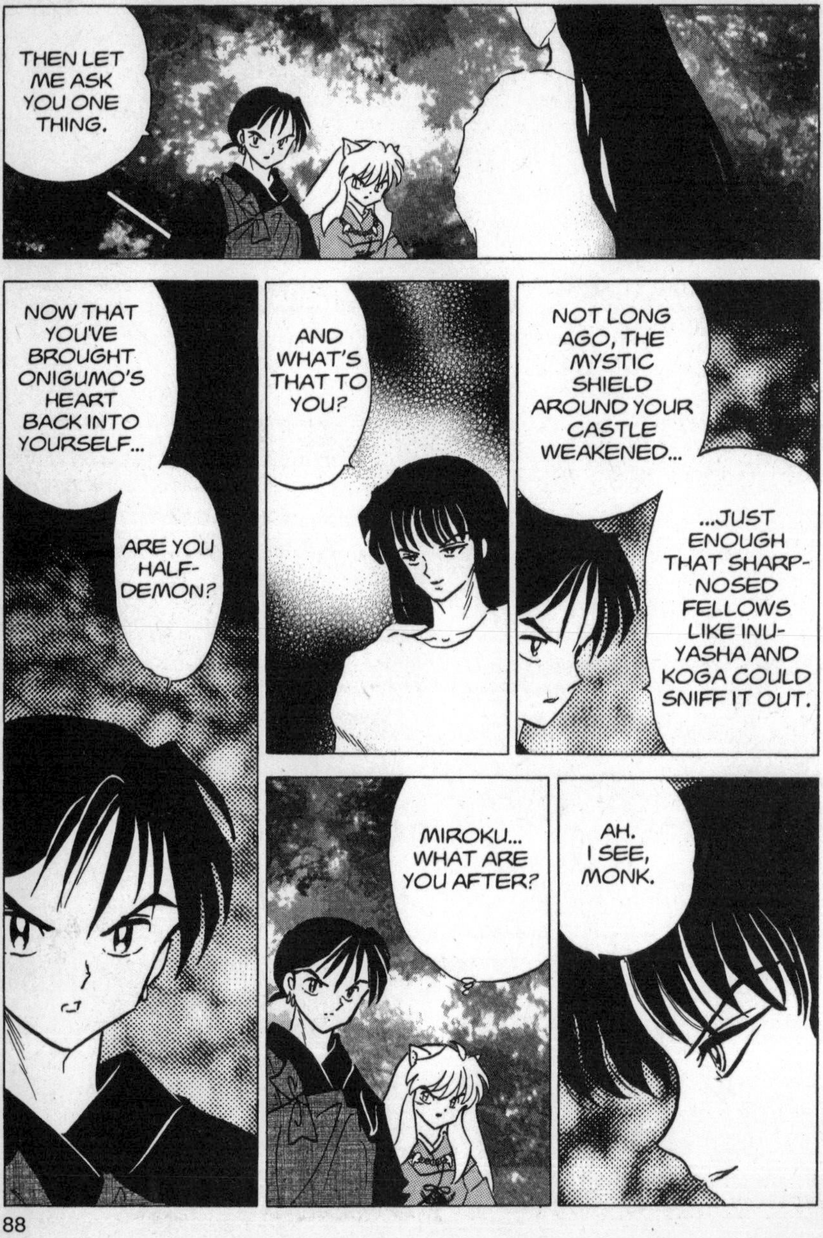
THEN LET ME ASK YOU ONE THING.
NOW THAT YOU'VE BROUGHT ONIGUMO'S HEART BACK INTO YOURSELF...
ARE YOU HALF-DEMON?
AND WHAT'S THAT TO YOU?
NOT LONG AGO, THE MYSTIC SHIELD AROUND YOUR CASTLE WEAKENED...
...JUST ENOUGH THAT SHARP-NOSED FELLOWS LIKE INU-YASHA AND KOGA COULD SNIFF IT OUT.
MIROKU... WHAT ARE YOU AFTER?
AH. I SEE, MONK.

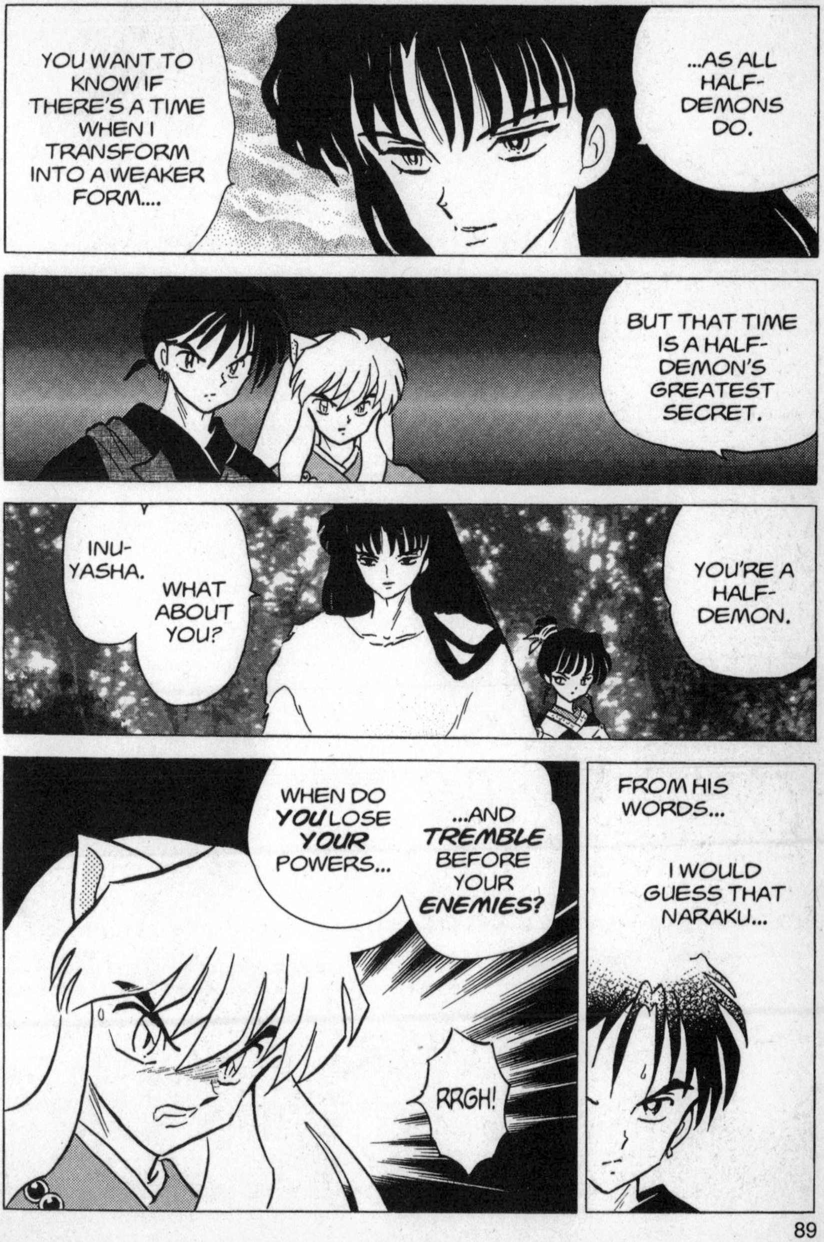
YOU WANT TO KNOW IF THERE'S A TIME WHEN I TRANSFORM INTO A WEAKER FORM....
...AS ALL HALF-DEMONS DO.
BUT THAT TIME IS A HALF-DEMON'S GREATEST SECRET.
INU-YASHA.
WHAT ABOUT YOU?
YOU'RE A HALF-DEMON.
WHEN DO ***YOU*** LOSE ***YOUR*** POWERS...
...AND ***TREMBLE*** BEFORE YOUR ***ENEMIES?***
RRGH!
FROM HIS WORDS...
I WOULD GUESS THAT NARAKU...

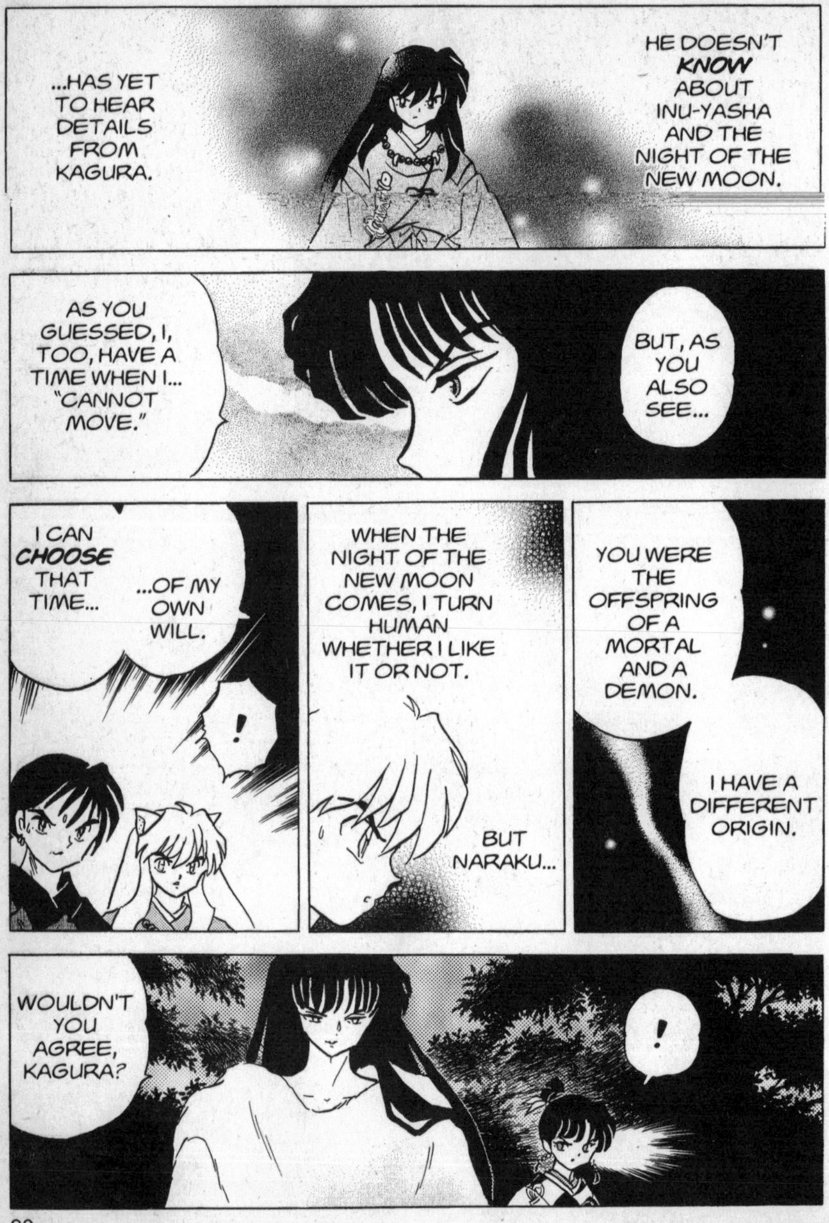
...HAS YET TO HEAR DETAILS FROM KAGURA.
HE DOESN'T KNOW ABOUT INU-YASHA AND THE NIGHT OF THE NEW MOON.
AS YOU GUESSED, I, TOO, HAVE A TIME WHEN I... "CANNOT MOVE."
BUT, AS YOU ALSO SEE...
I CAN CHOOSE THAT TIME...
...OF MY OWN WILL.
!
WHEN THE NIGHT OF THE NEW MOON COMES, I TURN HUMAN WHETHER I LIKE IT OR NOT.
BUT NARAKU...
YOU WERE THE OFFSPRING OF A MORTAL AND A DEMON.
I HAVE A DIFFERENT ORIGIN.
WOULDN'T YOU AGREE, KAGURA?
!

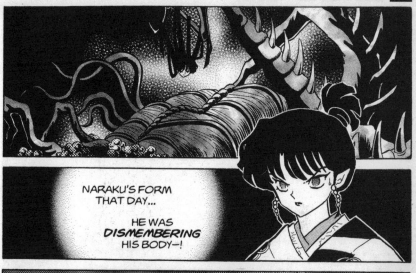

NARAKU'S FORM THAT DAY...

HE WAS *DISMEMBERING* HIS BODY—!

AS FOR ME, "THAT TIME" IS FOR *EXPERIMENT.*

REARRANGING MYSELF MOST EFFECTIVELY.

THROWING AWAY THAT WHICH DOES NOT HELP ME.

EMERGING MORE POWERFUL THAN EVER.

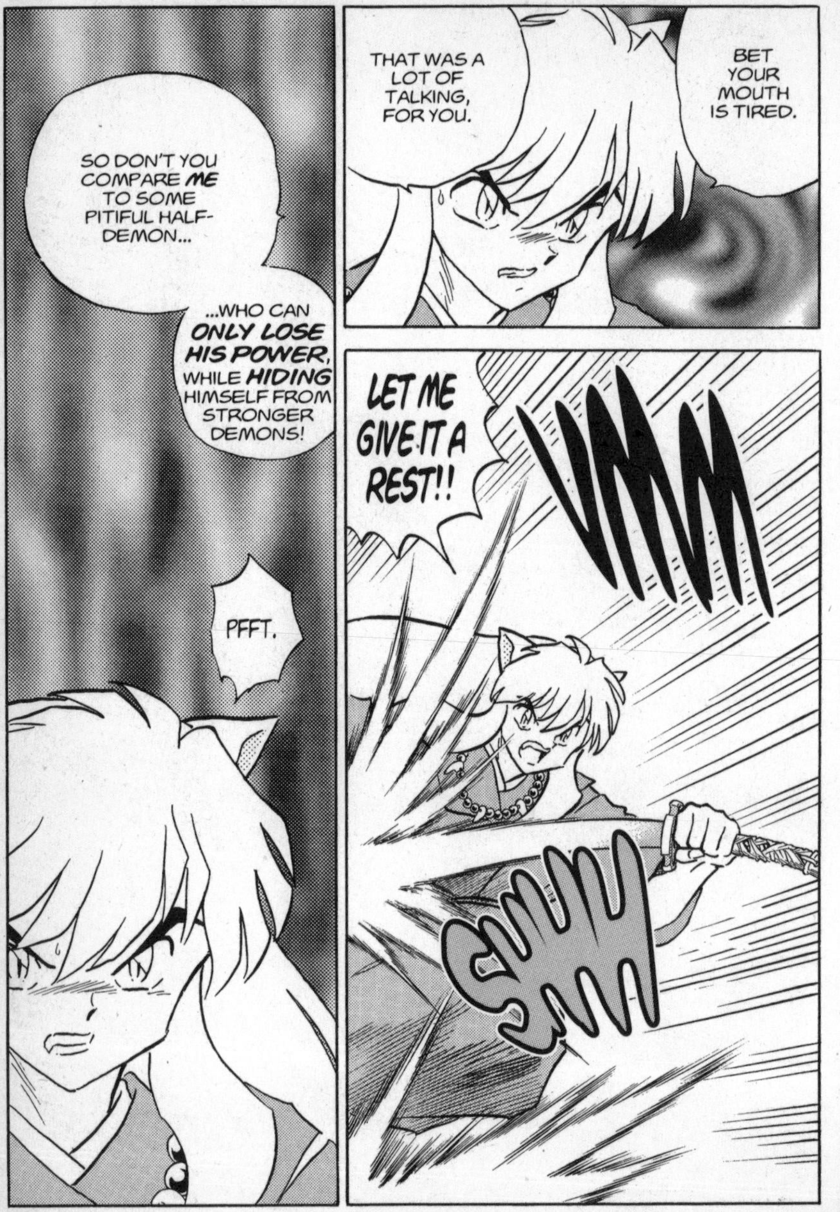
SO DON'T YOU COMPARE **ME** TO SOME PITIFUL HALF-DEMON...
...WHO CAN **ONLY LOSE HIS POWER**, WHILE **HIDING** HIMSELF FROM STRONGER DEMONS!
PFFT.
THAT WAS A LOT OF TALKING, FOR YOU.
BET YOUR MOUTH IS TIRED.
LET ME GIVE IT A REST!!

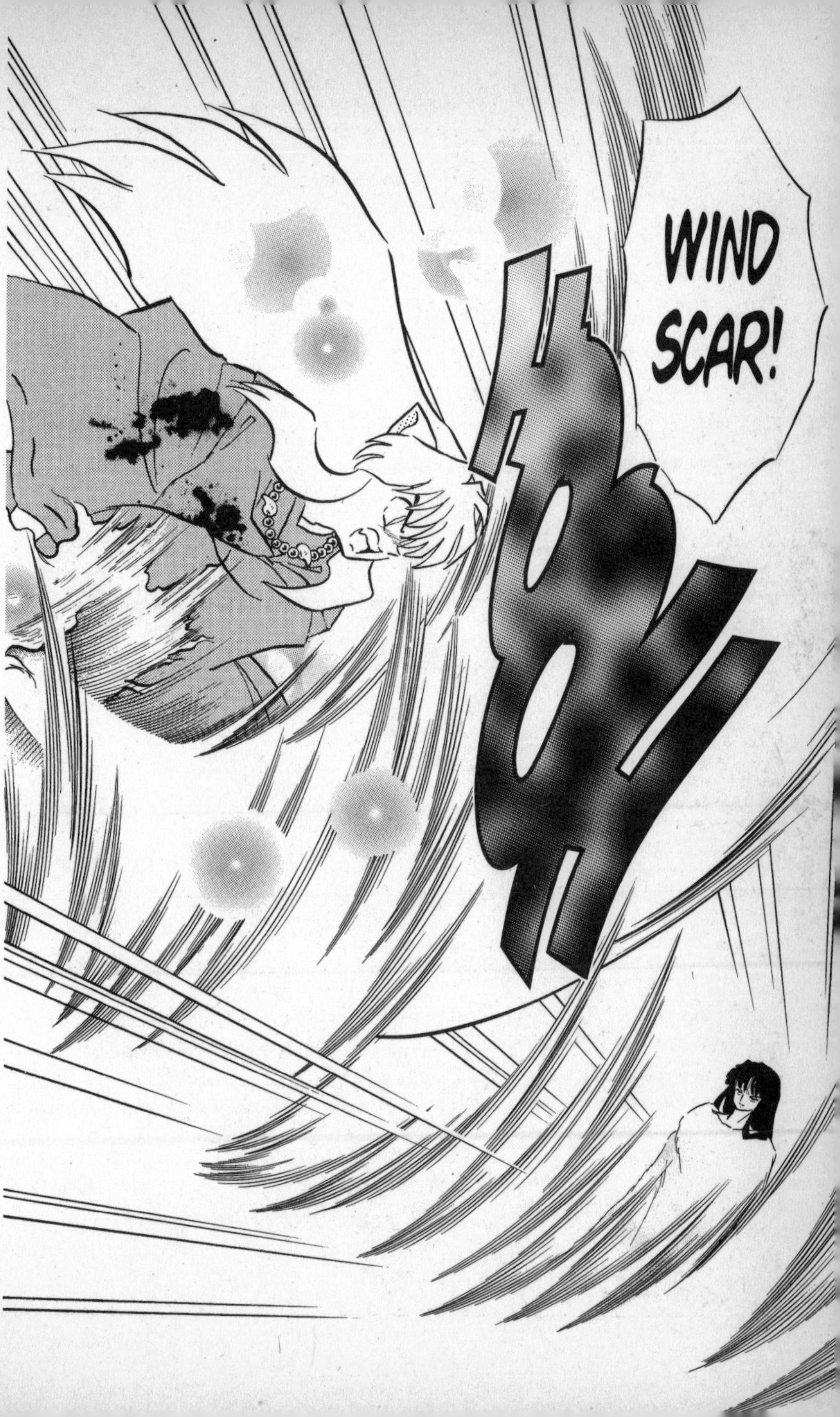
WIND SCAR!

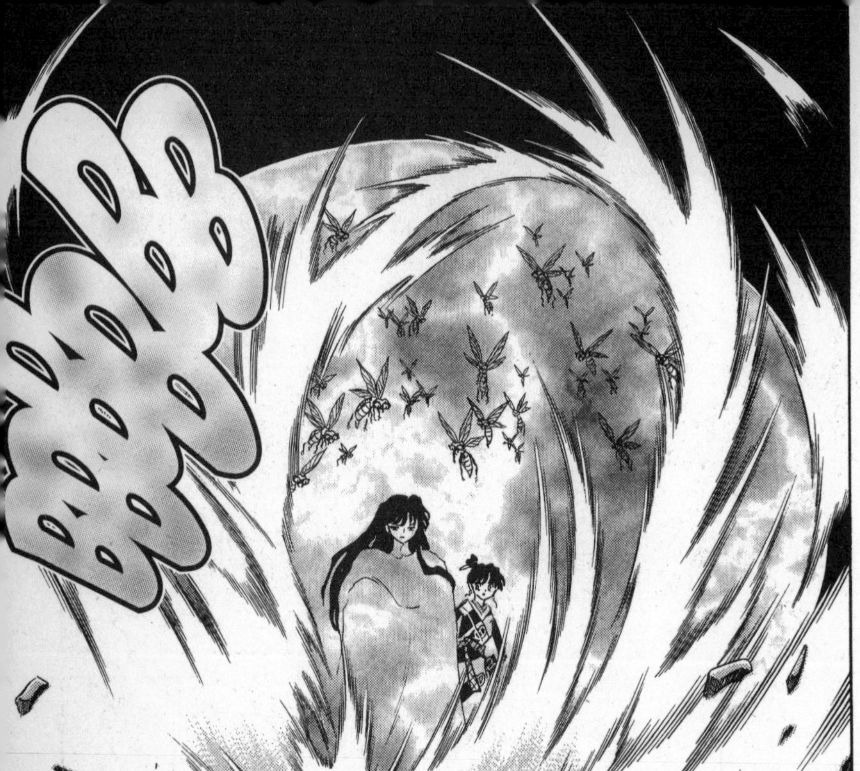

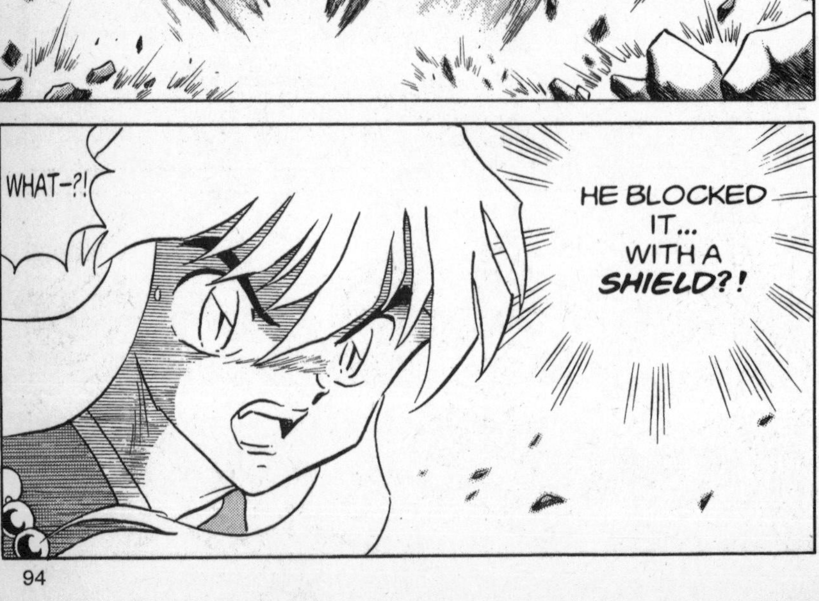
WHAT-?!
HE BLOCKED IT... WITH A SHIELD?!

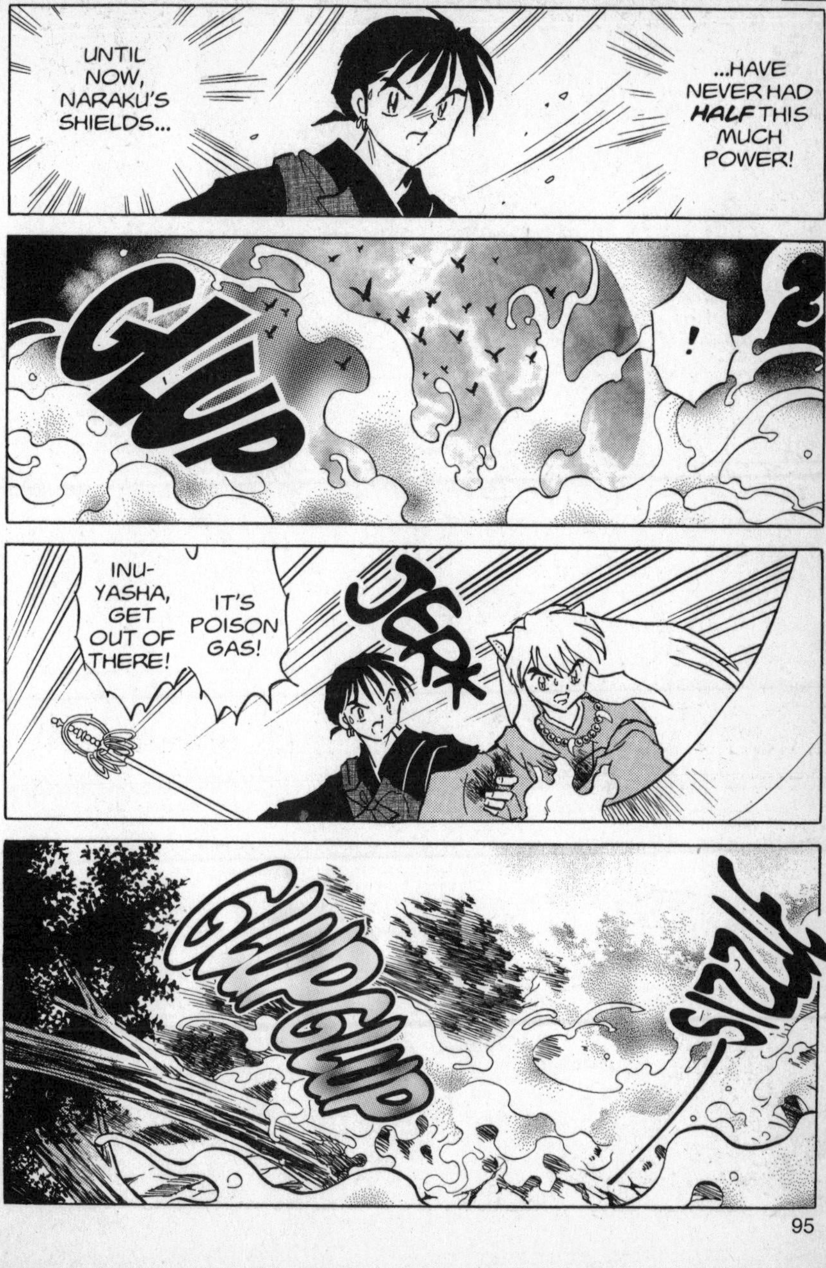
UNTIL NOW, NARAKU'S SHIELDS...
...HAVE NEVER HAD *HALF* THIS MUCH POWER!
!
GLUP
INU-YASHA, GET OUT OF THERE!
IT'S POISON GAS!
JERK
SIZZLE
GLUPGLUP

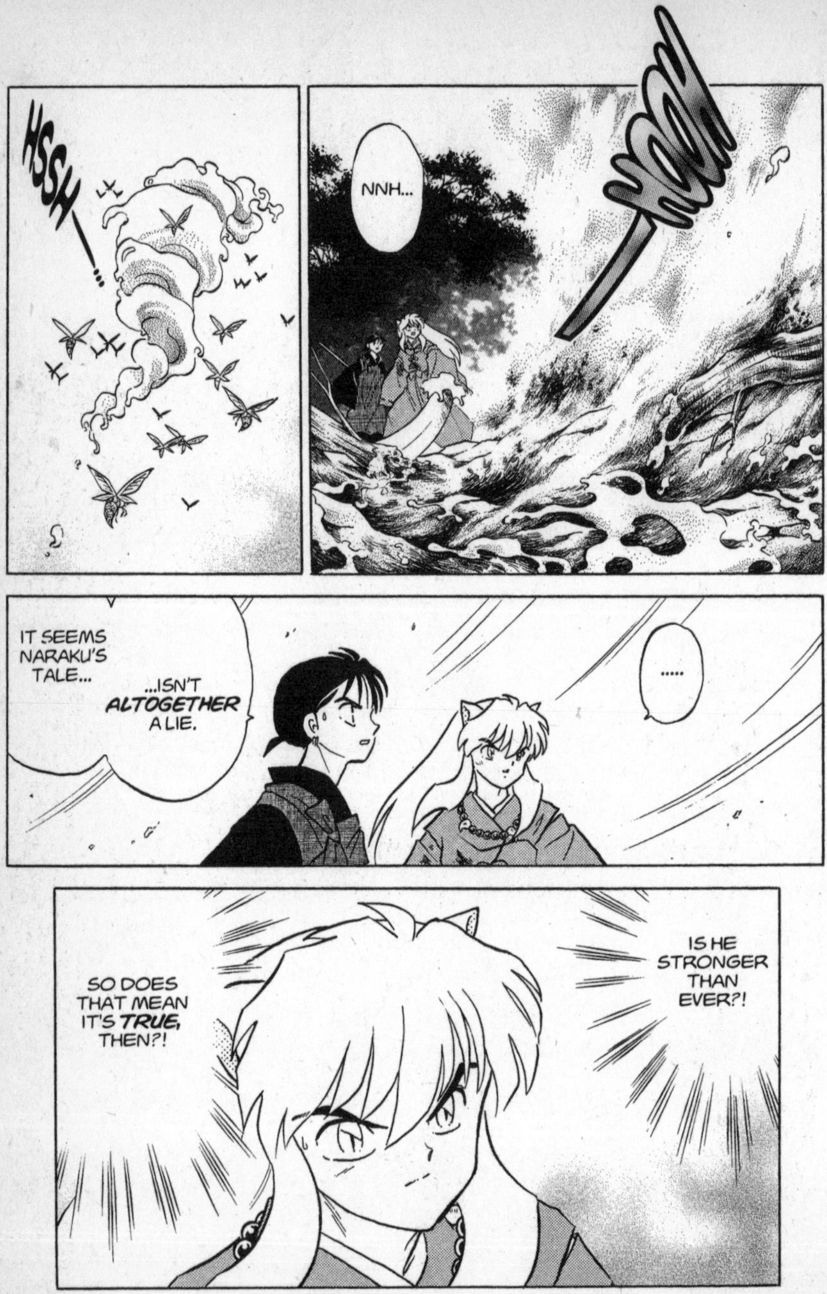
HSSH—!!
NNH...
WOOSH
IT SEEMS NARAKU'S TALE...
...ISN'T ALTOGETHER A LIE.
.....
SO DOES THAT MEAN IT'S TRUE, THEN?!
IS HE STRONGER THAN EVER?!

SCROLL SIX

THE OGRE BATS

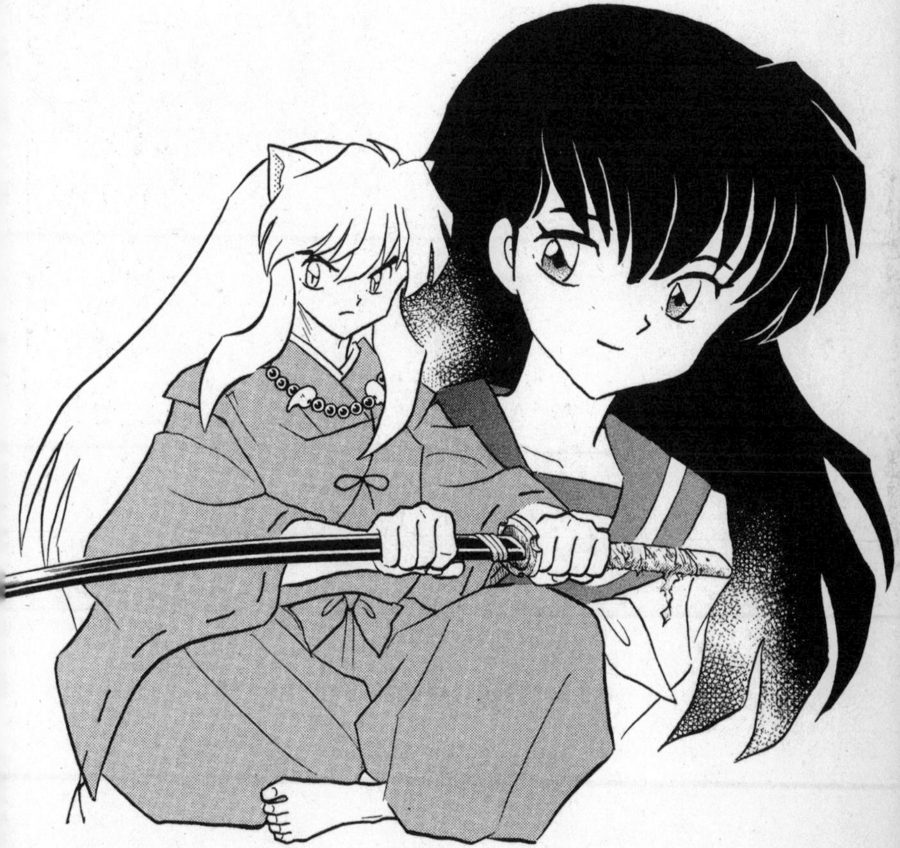

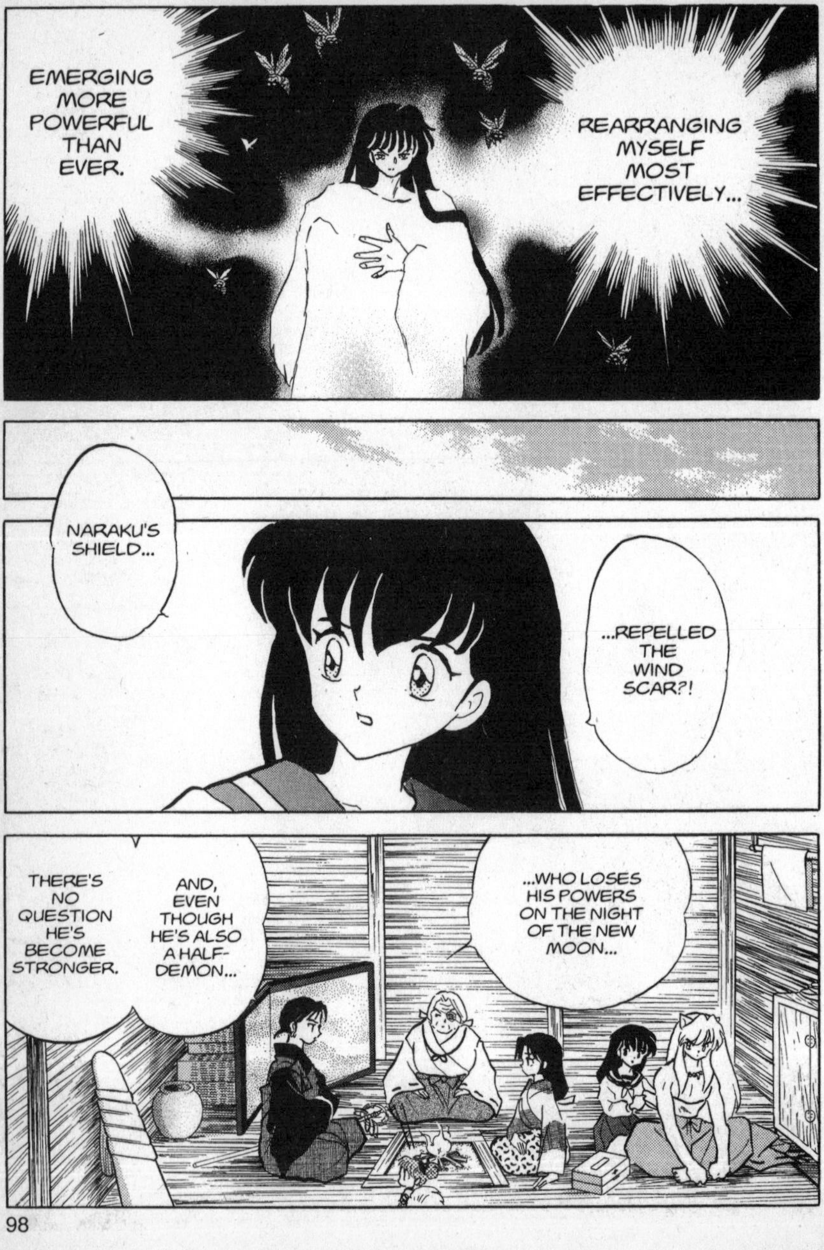
EMERGING MORE POWERFUL THAN EVER.
REARRANGING MYSELF MOST EFFECTIVELY...
NARAKU'S SHIELD...
...REPELLED THE WIND SCAR?!
THERE'S NO QUESTION HE'S BECOME STRONGER.
AND, EVEN THOUGH HE'S ALSO A HALF-DEMON...
...WHO LOSES HIS POWERS ON THE NIGHT OF THE NEW MOON...

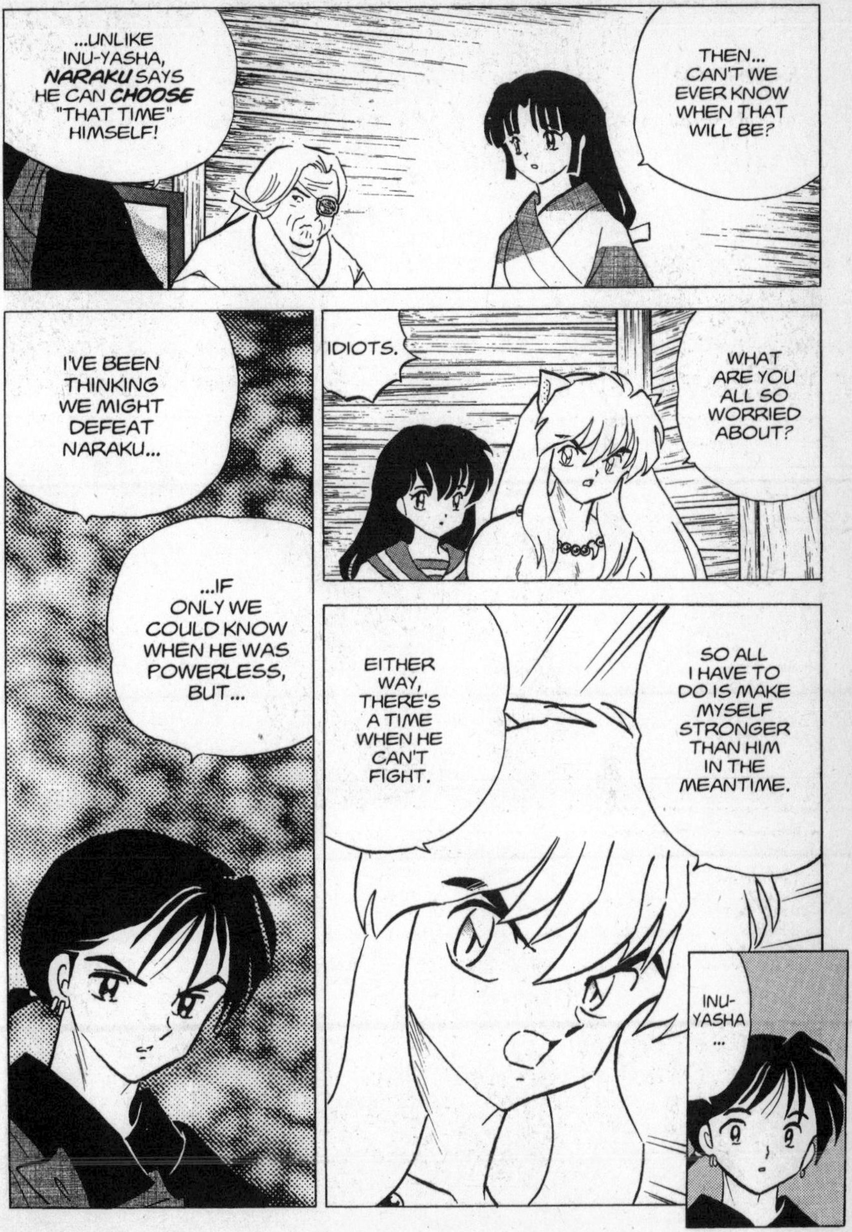
...UNLIKE INU-YASHA, NARAKU SAYS HE CAN CHOOSE "THAT TIME" HIMSELF!
THEN... CAN'T WE EVER KNOW WHEN THAT WILL BE?
I'VE BEEN THINKING WE MIGHT DEFEAT NARAKU...
...IF ONLY WE COULD KNOW WHEN HE WAS POWERLESS, BUT...
IDIOTS.
WHAT ARE YOU ALL SO WORRIED ABOUT?
EITHER WAY, THERE'S A TIME WHEN HE CAN'T FIGHT.
SO ALL I HAVE TO DO IS MAKE MYSELF STRONGER THAN HIM IN THE MEANTIME.
INU-YASHA...

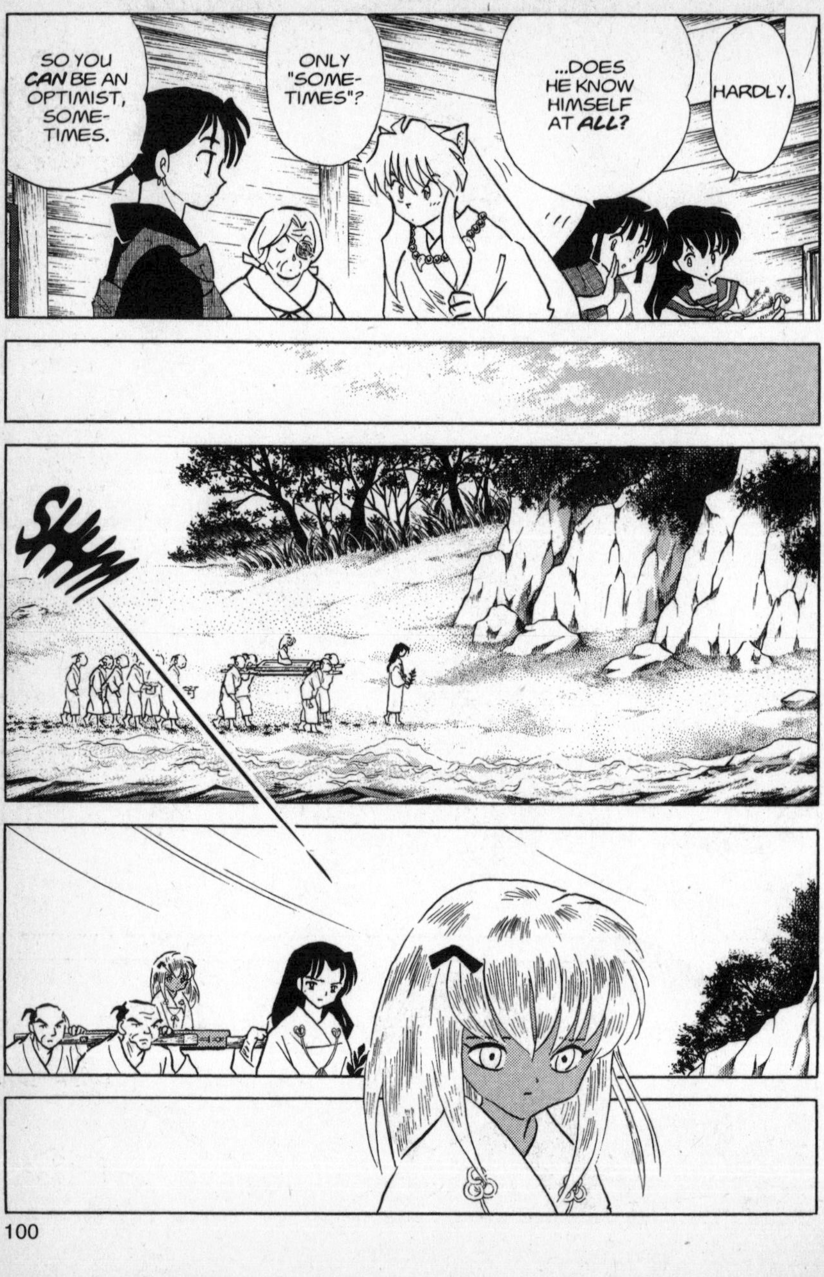
SO YOU CAN BE AN OPTIMIST, SOME-TIMES.
ONLY "SOME-TIMES"?
...DOES HE KNOW HIMSELF AT ALL?
HARDLY.
SHWW

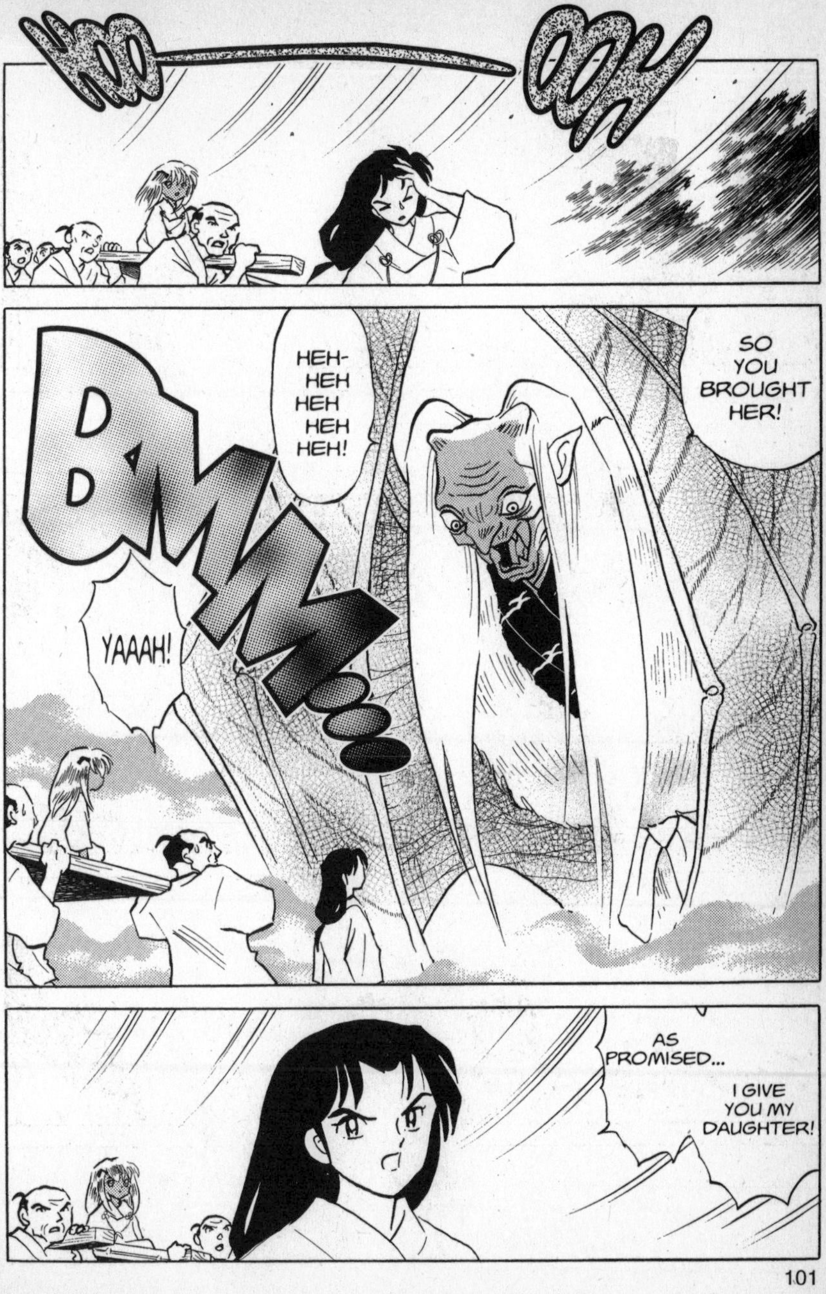
HOO—OOH
HEH-HEH HEH HEH HEH!
SO YOU BROUGHT HER!
BMM...
YAAAH!
AS PROMISED...
I GIVE YOU MY DAUGHTER!

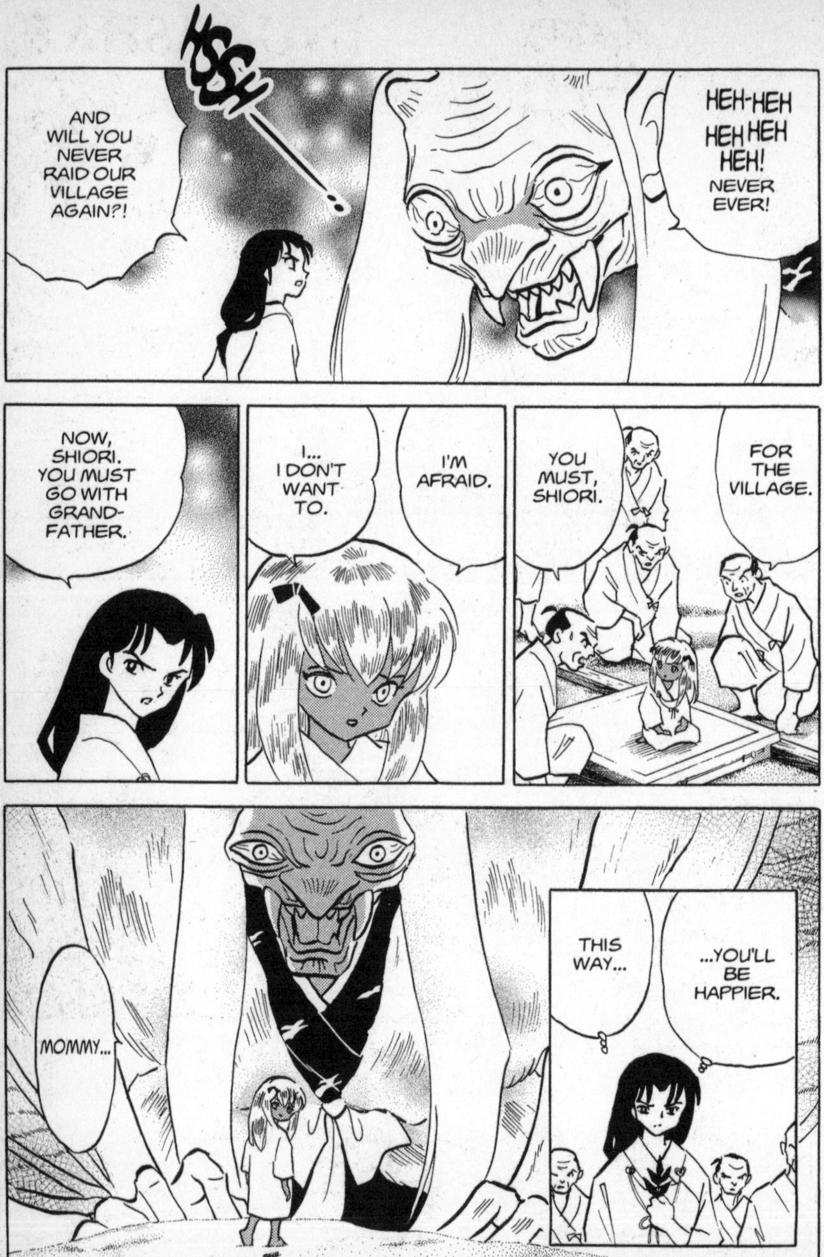
AND WILL YOU NEVER RAID OUR VILLAGE AGAIN?!
HSSH
HEH-HEH HEH HEH HEH! NEVER EVER!
NOW, SHIORI. YOU MUST GO WITH GRAND-FATHER.
I... I DON'T WANT TO.
I'M AFRAID.
YOU MUST, SHIORI.
FOR THE VILLAGE.
MOMMY...
THIS WAY...
...YOU'LL BE HAPPIER.

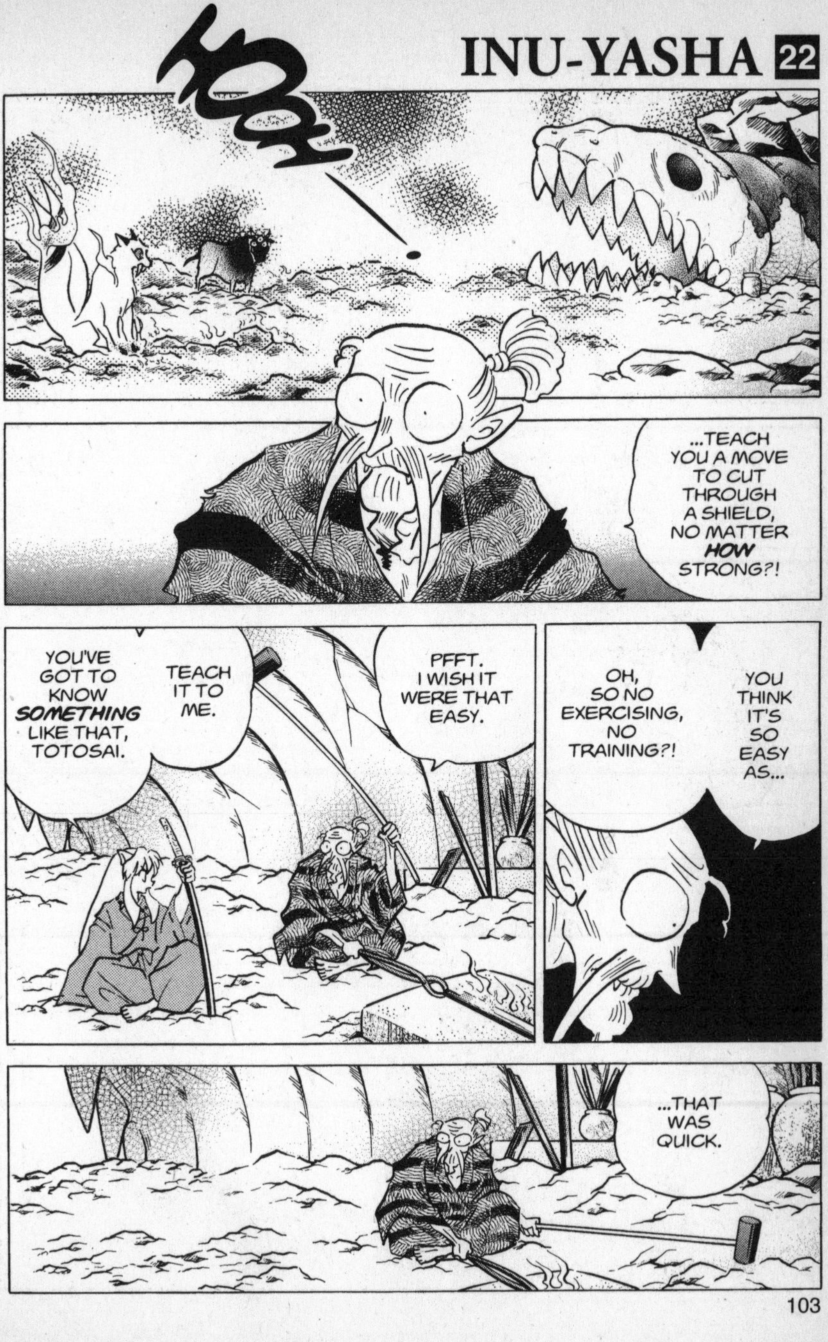
HOOH!
...TEACH YOU A MOVE TO CUT THROUGH A SHIELD, NO MATTER **HOW** STRONG?!
YOU'VE GOT TO KNOW **SOMETHING** LIKE THAT, TOTOSAI.
TEACH IT TO ME.
PFFT. I WISH IT WERE THAT EASY.
OH, SO NO EXERCISING, NO TRAINING?!
YOU THINK IT'S SO EASY AS...
...THAT WAS QUICK.

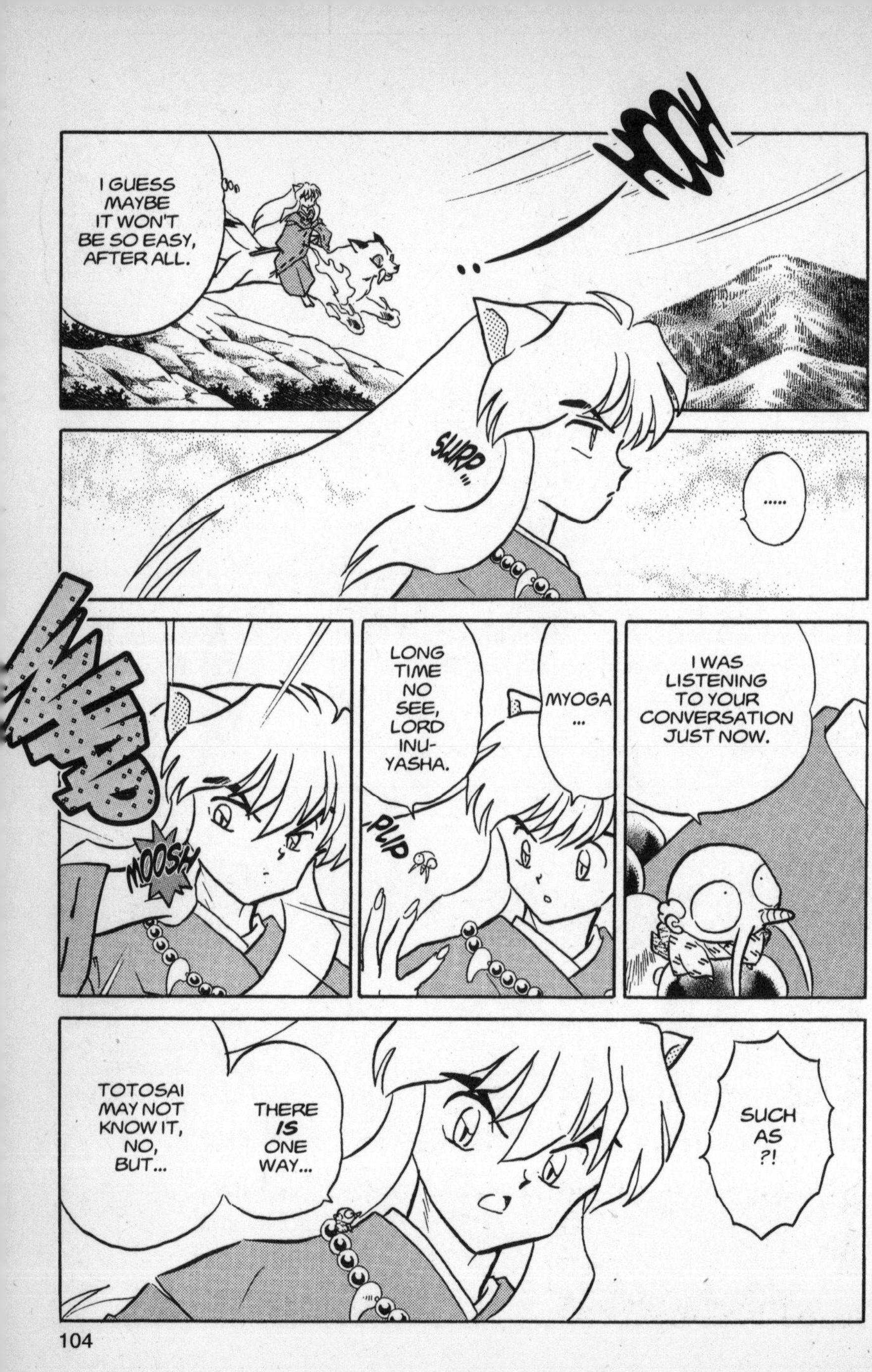

I GUESS MAYBE IT WON'T BE SO EASY, AFTER ALL.
HOOH
..
SLURP
.....
WHAP
MOOSH
LONG TIME NO SEE, LORD INU-YASHA.
PLIP
MYOGA...
I WAS LISTENING TO YOUR CONVERSATION JUST NOW.
TOTOSAI MAY NOT KNOW IT, NO, BUT...
THERE *IS* ONE WAY...
SUCH AS ?!

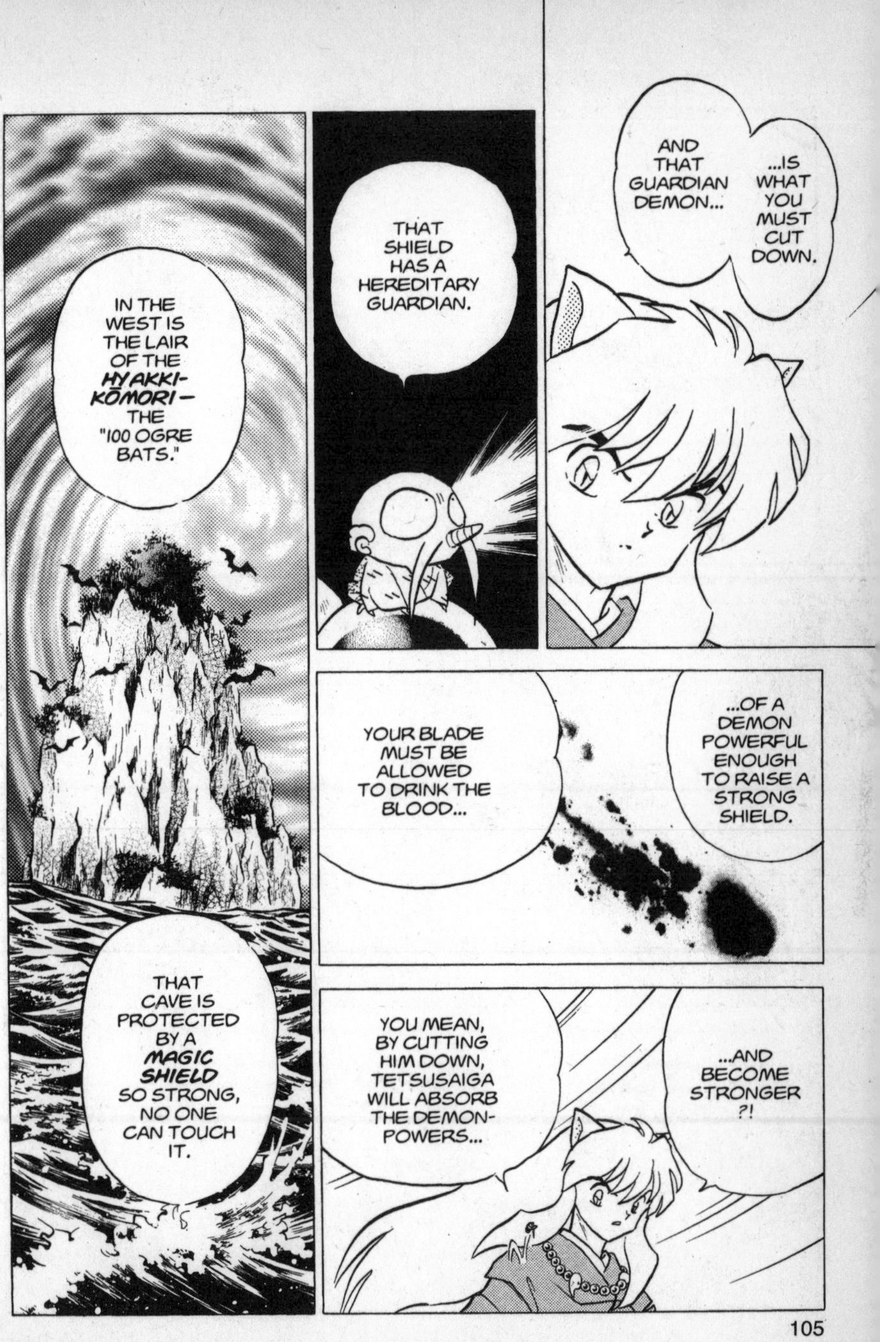
IN THE WEST IS THE LAIR OF THE ***HYAKKI-KŌMORI*** — THE "100 OGRE BATS."
THAT CAVE IS PROTECTED BY A ***MAGIC SHIELD*** SO STRONG, NO ONE CAN TOUCH IT.
THAT SHIELD HAS A HEREDITARY GUARDIAN.
AND THAT GUARDIAN DEMON...
...IS WHAT YOU MUST CUT DOWN.
YOUR BLADE MUST BE ALLOWED TO DRINK THE BLOOD...
...OF A DEMON POWERFUL ENOUGH TO RAISE A STRONG SHIELD.
YOU MEAN, BY CUTTING HIM DOWN, TETSUSAIGA WILL ABSORB THE DEMON-POWERS...
...AND BECOME STRONGER ?!

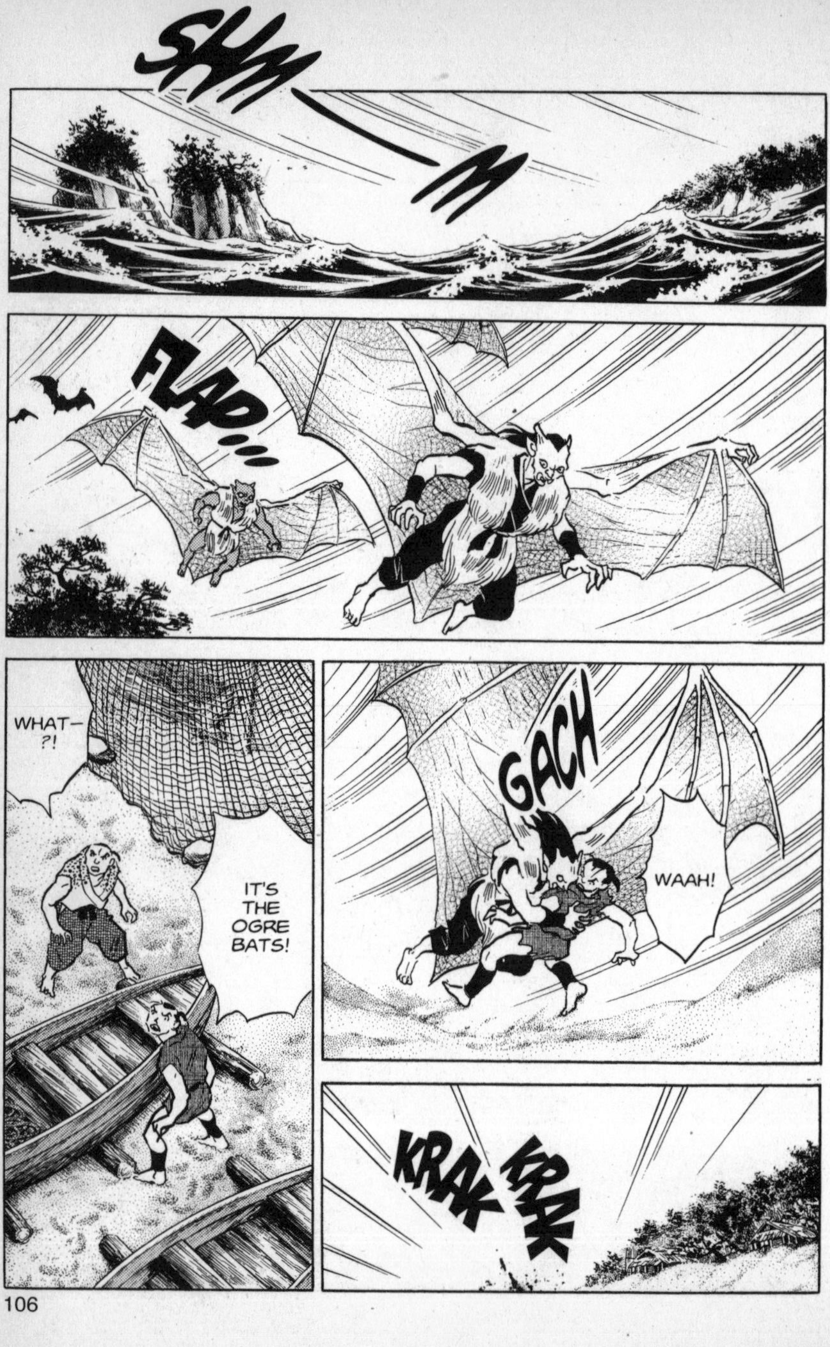
SHM—M
FLAP
WHAT—?!
IT'S THE OGRE BATS!
GACH
WAAH!
KRAK
KRAK

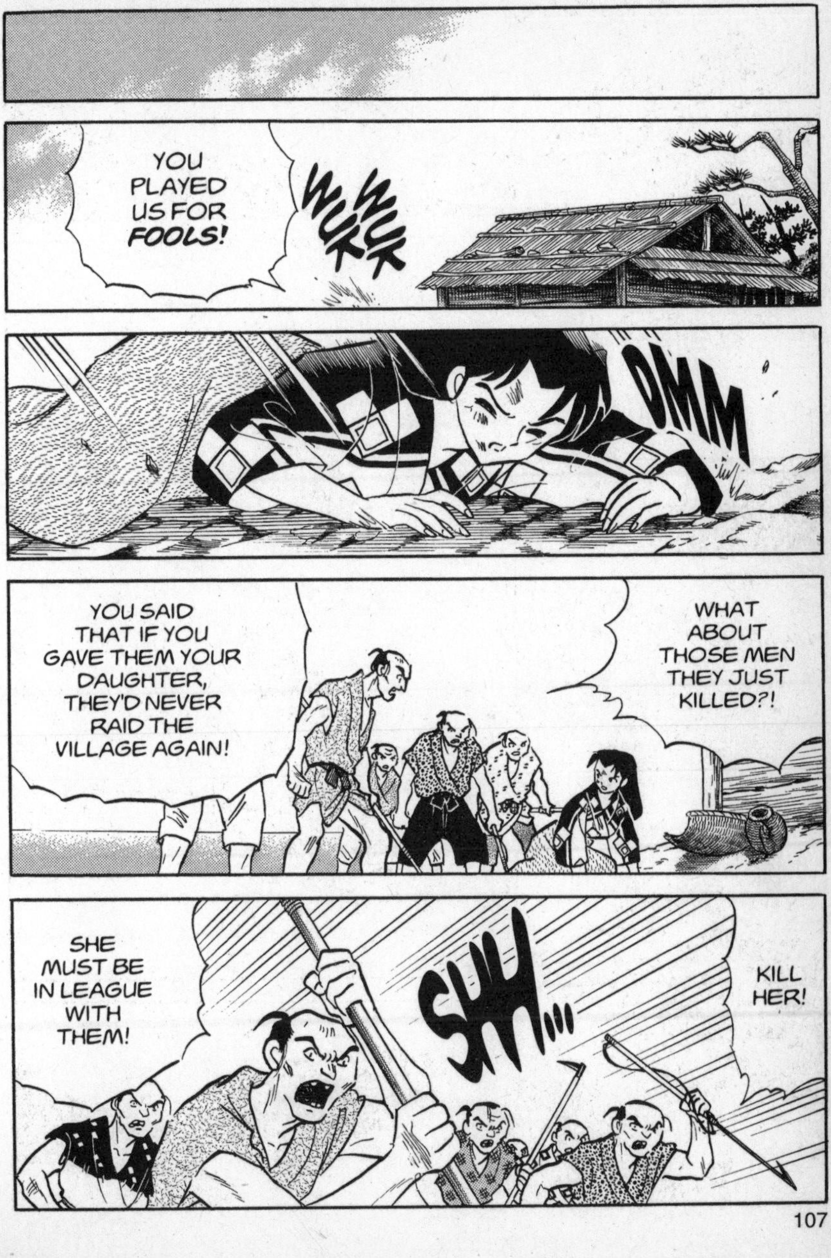

YOU PLAYED US FOR FOOLS!
WUK
WUK
OMM
YOU SAID THAT IF YOU GAVE THEM YOUR DAUGHTER, THEY'D NEVER RAID THE VILLAGE AGAIN!
WHAT ABOUT THOSE MEN THEY JUST KILLED?!
SHE MUST BE IN LEAGUE WITH THEM!
SHH...
KILL HER!

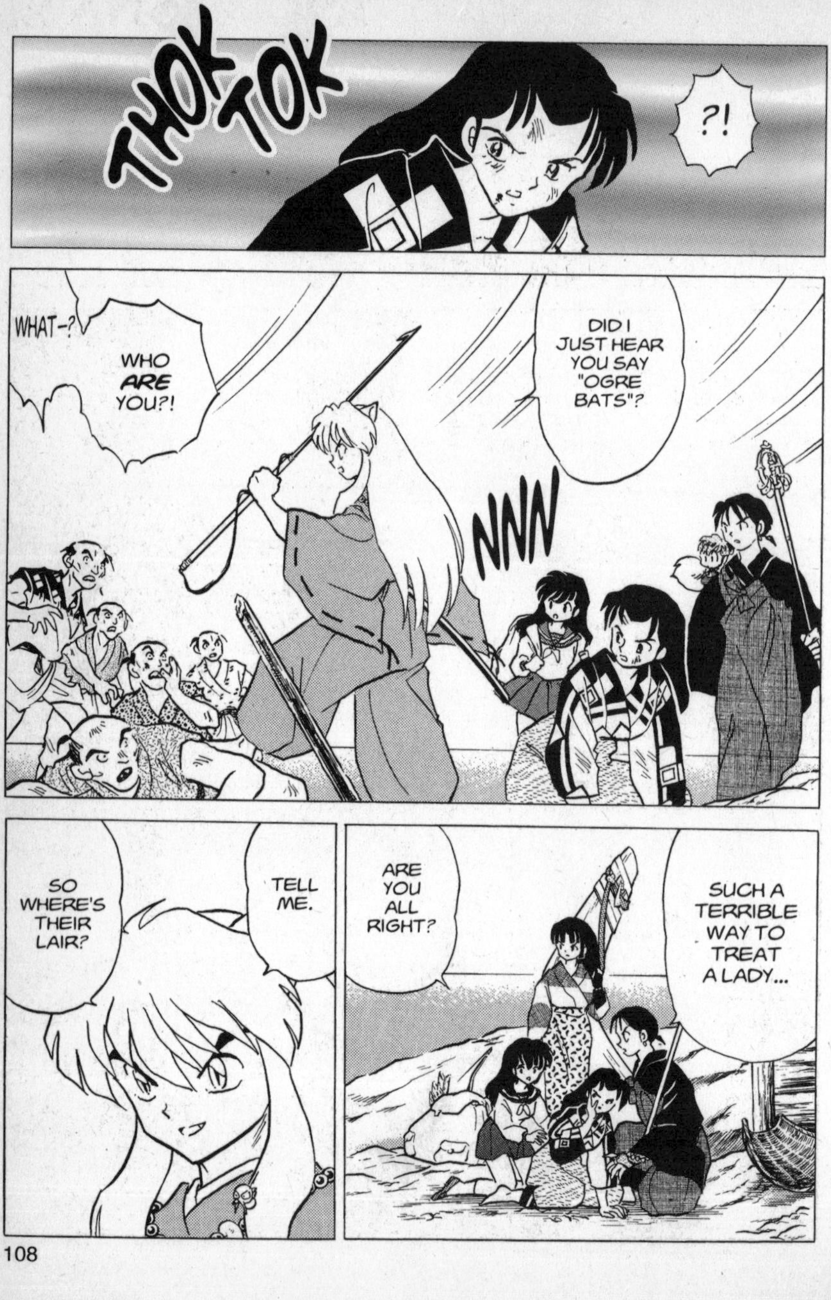

THOK TOK
?!
WHAT-?
WHO ARE YOU?!
DID I JUST HEAR YOU SAY "OGRE BATS"?
NNN
SO WHERE'S THEIR LAIR?
TELL ME.
ARE YOU ALL RIGHT?
SUCH A TERRIBLE WAY TO TREAT A LADY...

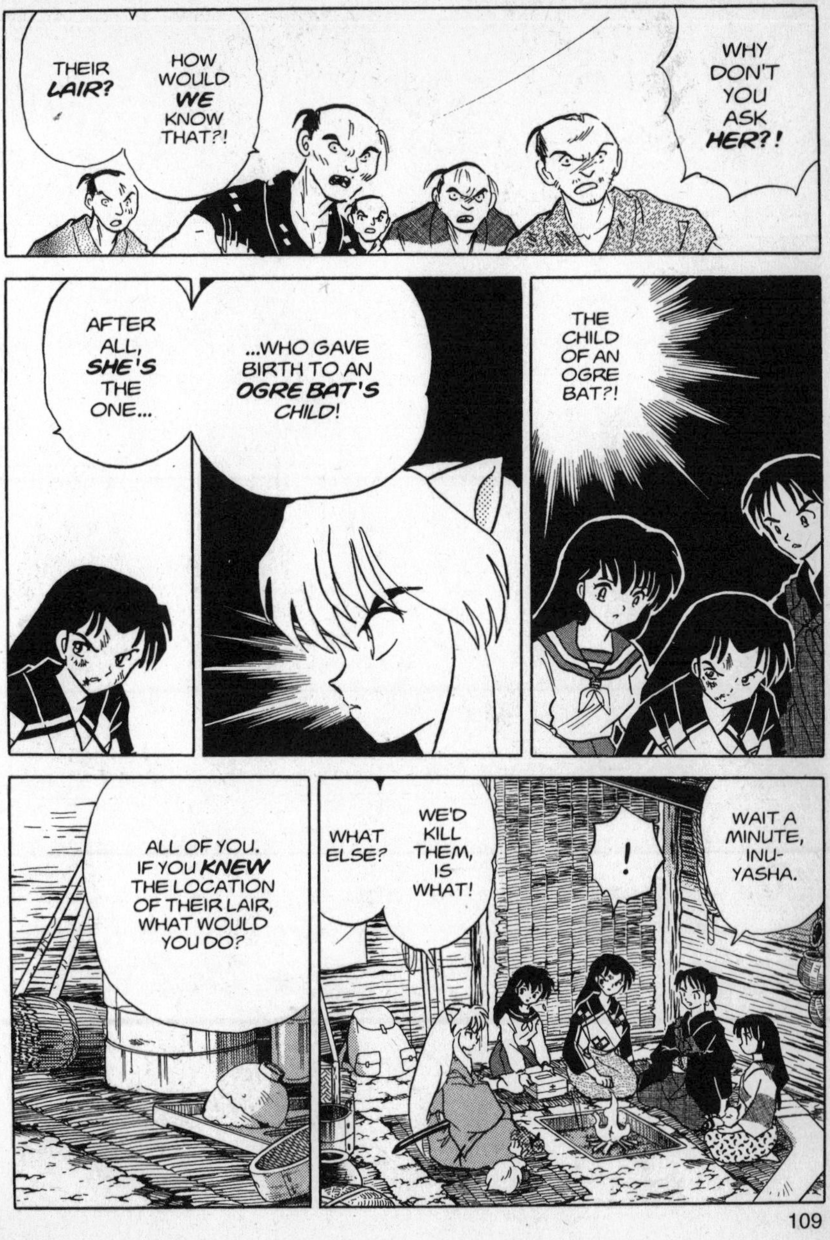
THEIR LAIR?
HOW WOULD WE KNOW THAT?!
WHY DON'T YOU ASK HER?!
AFTER ALL, SHE'S THE ONE...
...WHO GAVE BIRTH TO AN OGRE BAT'S CHILD!
THE CHILD OF AN OGRE BAT?!
ALL OF YOU. IF YOU KNEW THE LOCATION OF THEIR LAIR, WHAT WOULD YOU DO?
WHAT ELSE?
WE'D KILL THEM, IS WHAT!
!
WAIT A MINUTE, INU-YASHA.

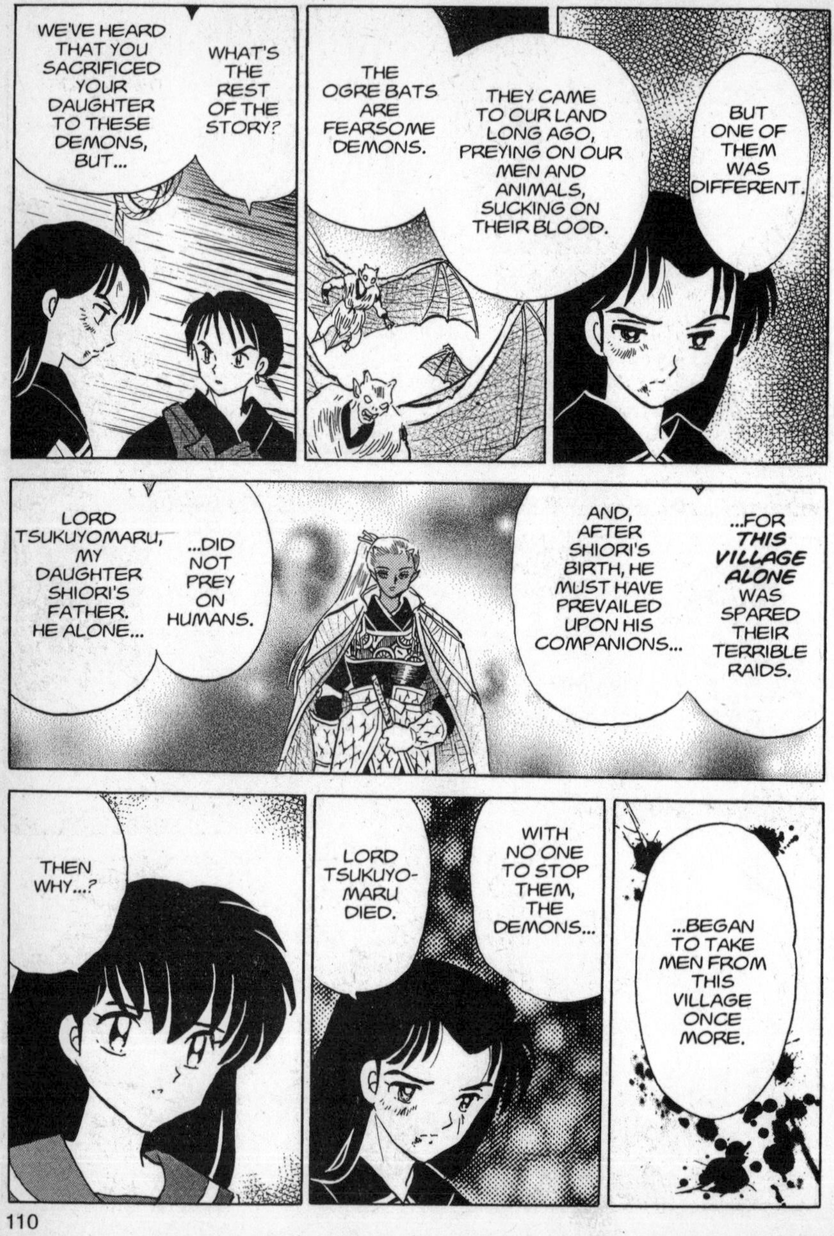

WE'VE HEARD THAT YOU SACRIFICED YOUR DAUGHTER TO THESE DEMONS, BUT...
WHAT'S THE REST OF THE STORY?
THE OGRE BATS ARE FEARSOME DEMONS.
THEY CAME TO OUR LAND LONG AGO, PREYING ON OUR MEN AND ANIMALS, SUCKING ON THEIR BLOOD.
BUT ONE OF THEM WAS DIFFERENT.
LORD TSUKUYOMARU, MY DAUGHTER SHIORI'S FATHER. HE ALONE...
...DID NOT PREY ON HUMANS.
AND, AFTER SHIORI'S BIRTH, HE MUST HAVE PREVAILED UPON HIS COMPANIONS...
...FOR *THIS VILLAGE ALONE* WAS SPARED THEIR TERRIBLE RAIDS.
THEN WHY...?
LORD TSUKUYO-MARU DIED.
WITH NO ONE TO STOP THEM, THE DEMONS...
...BEGAN TO TAKE MEN FROM THIS VILLAGE ONCE MORE.

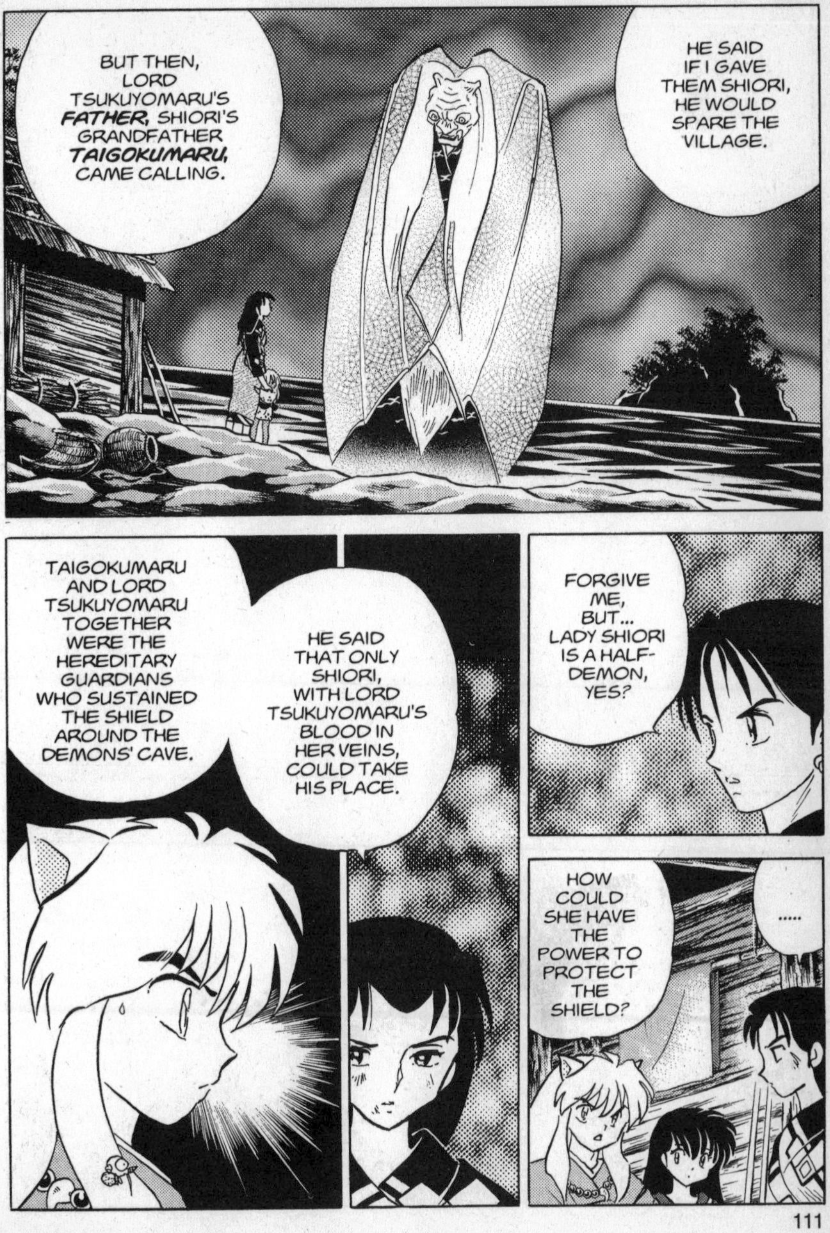
BUT THEN, LORD TSUKUYOMARU'S **FATHER**, SHIORI'S GRANDFATHER **TAIGOKUMARU**, CAME CALLING.
HE SAID IF I GAVE THEM SHIORI, HE WOULD SPARE THE VILLAGE.
TAIGOKUMARU AND LORD TSUKUYOMARU TOGETHER WERE THE HEREDITARY GUARDIANS WHO SUSTAINED THE SHIELD AROUND THE DEMONS' CAVE.
HE SAID THAT ONLY SHIORI, WITH LORD TSUKUYOMARU'S BLOOD IN HER VEINS, COULD TAKE HIS PLACE.
FORGIVE ME, BUT... LADY SHIORI IS A HALF-DEMON, YES?
HOW COULD SHE HAVE THE POWER TO PROTECT THE SHIELD?
.....

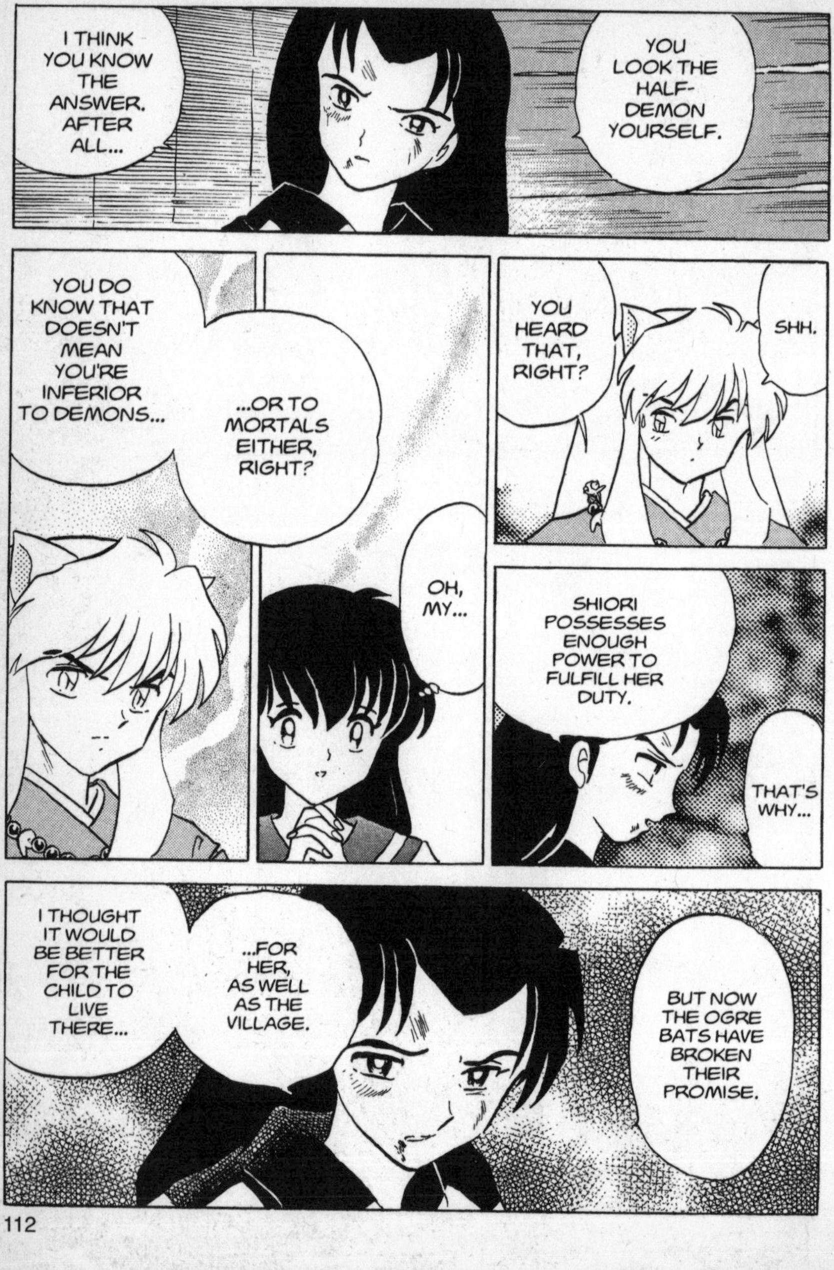
I THINK YOU KNOW THE ANSWER. AFTER ALL...
YOU LOOK THE HALF-DEMON YOURSELF.
YOU DO KNOW THAT DOESN'T MEAN YOU'RE INFERIOR TO DEMONS...
...OR TO MORTALS EITHER, RIGHT?
OH, MY...
YOU HEARD THAT, RIGHT?
SHH.
SHIORI POSSESSES ENOUGH POWER TO FULFILL HER DUTY.
THAT'S WHY...
I THOUGHT IT WOULD BE BETTER FOR THE CHILD TO LIVE THERE...
...FOR HER, AS WELL AS THE VILLAGE.
BUT NOW THE OGRE BATS HAVE BROKEN THEIR PROMISE.

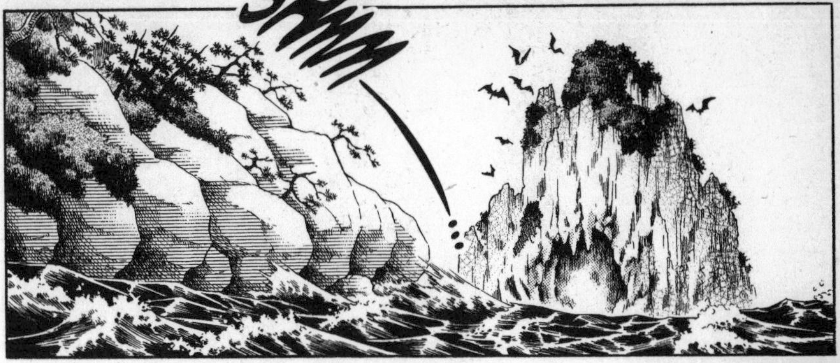
SHMM

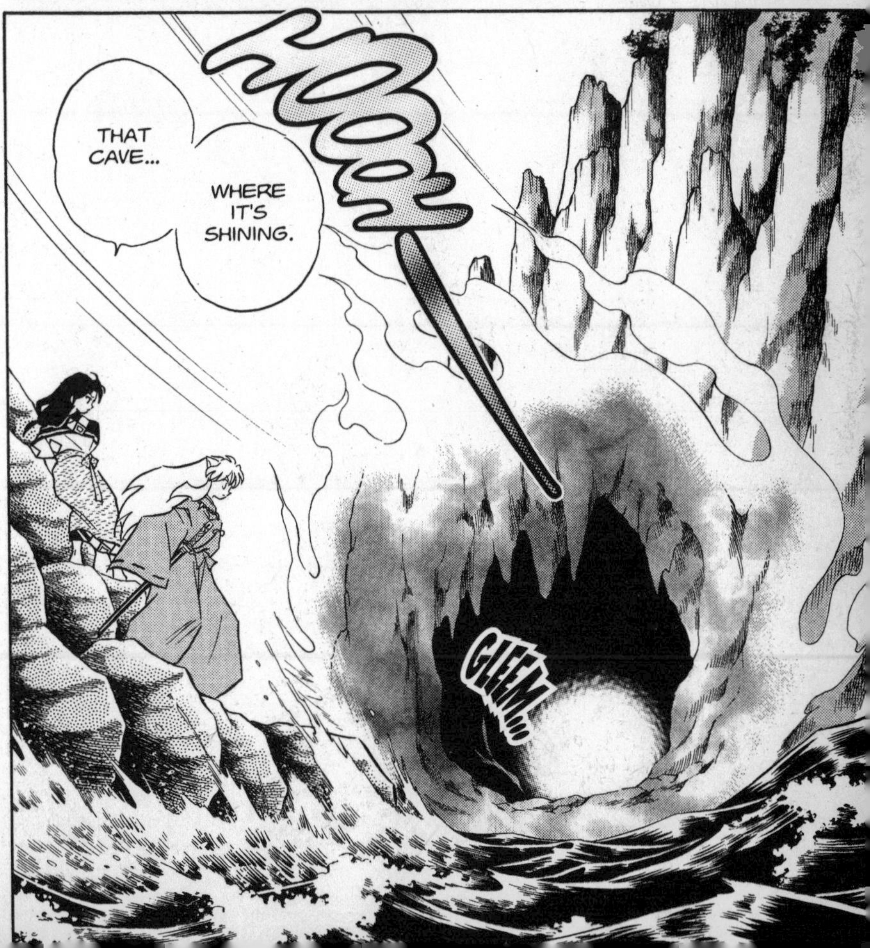
HOOOH
THAT CAVE...
WHERE IT'S SHINING.
GLEEM...

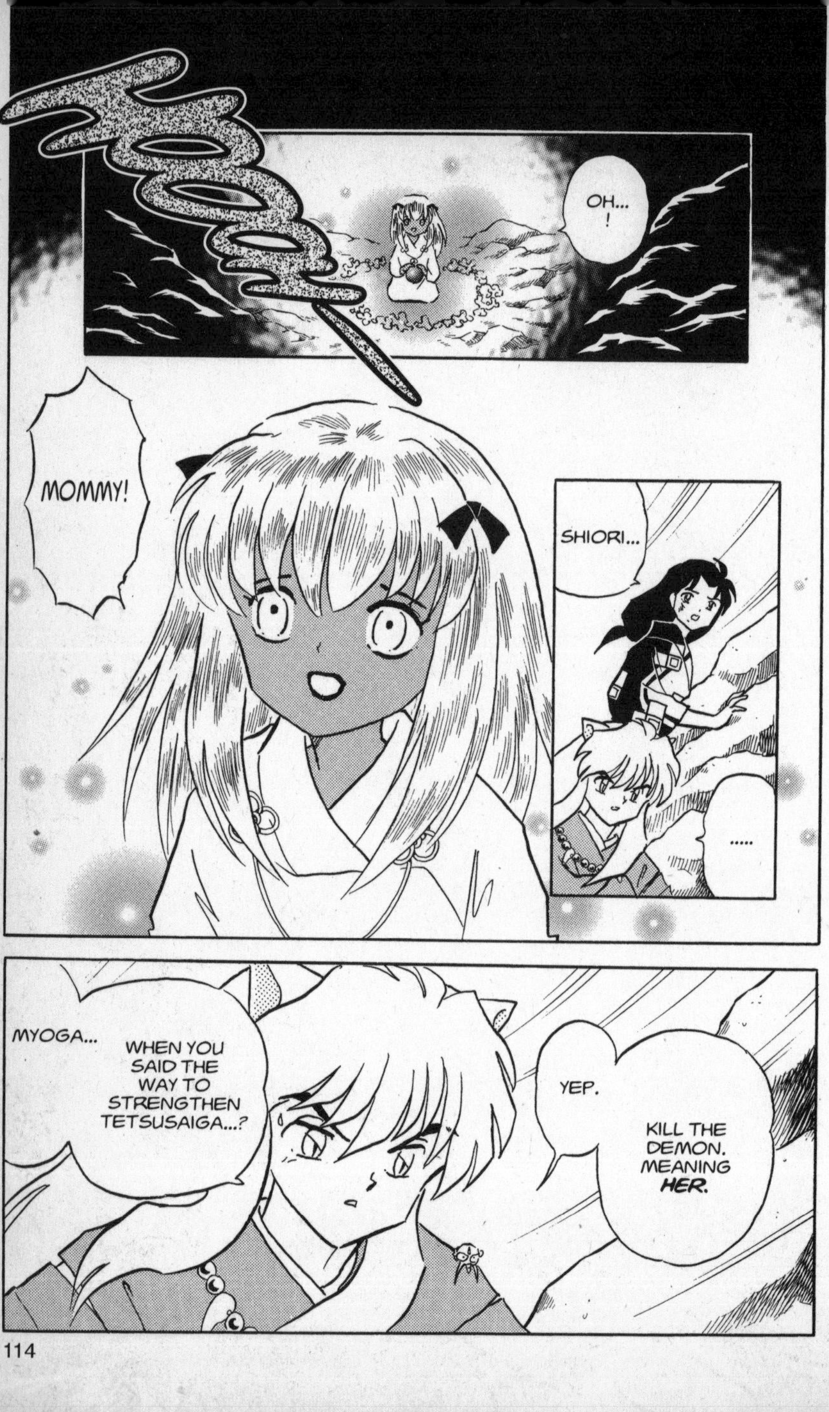
OH... !
MOMMY!
SHIORI...
.....
MYOGA...
WHEN YOU SAID THE WAY TO STRENGTHEN TETSUSAIGA...?
YEP.
KILL THE DEMON. MEANING **HER.**

SCROLL SEVEN

SHIORI'S SHIELD

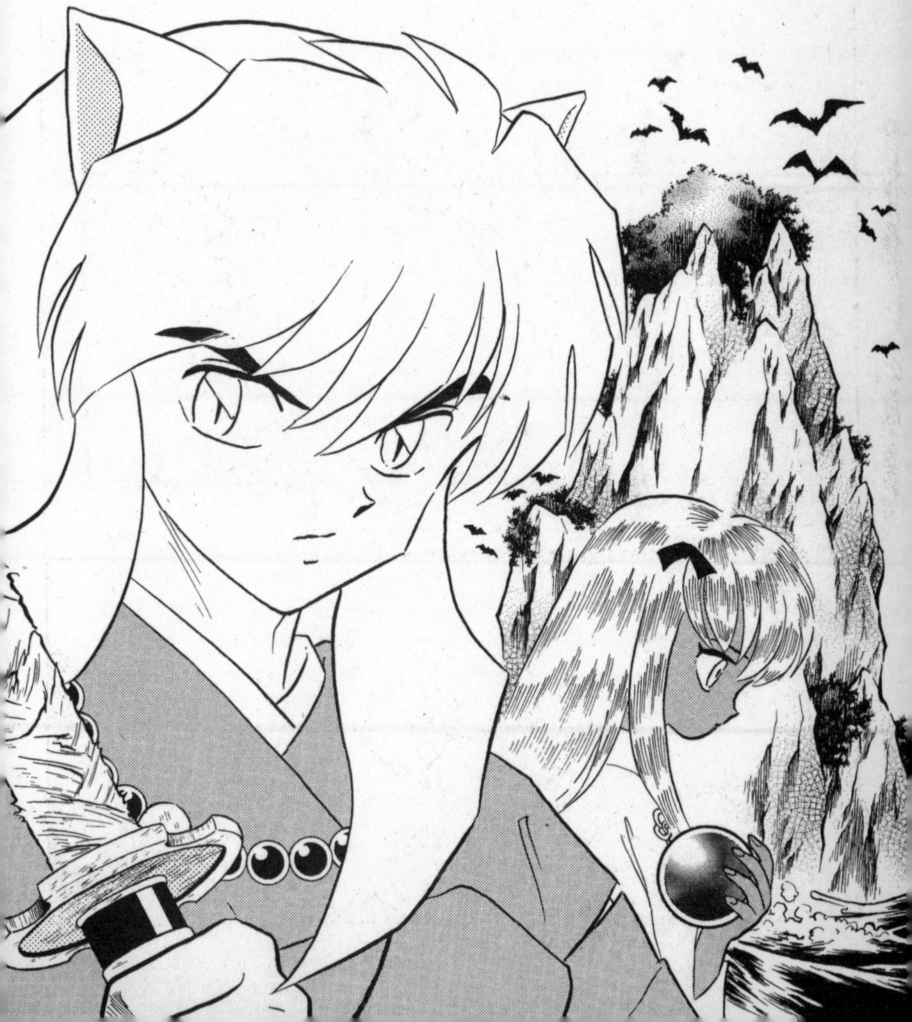

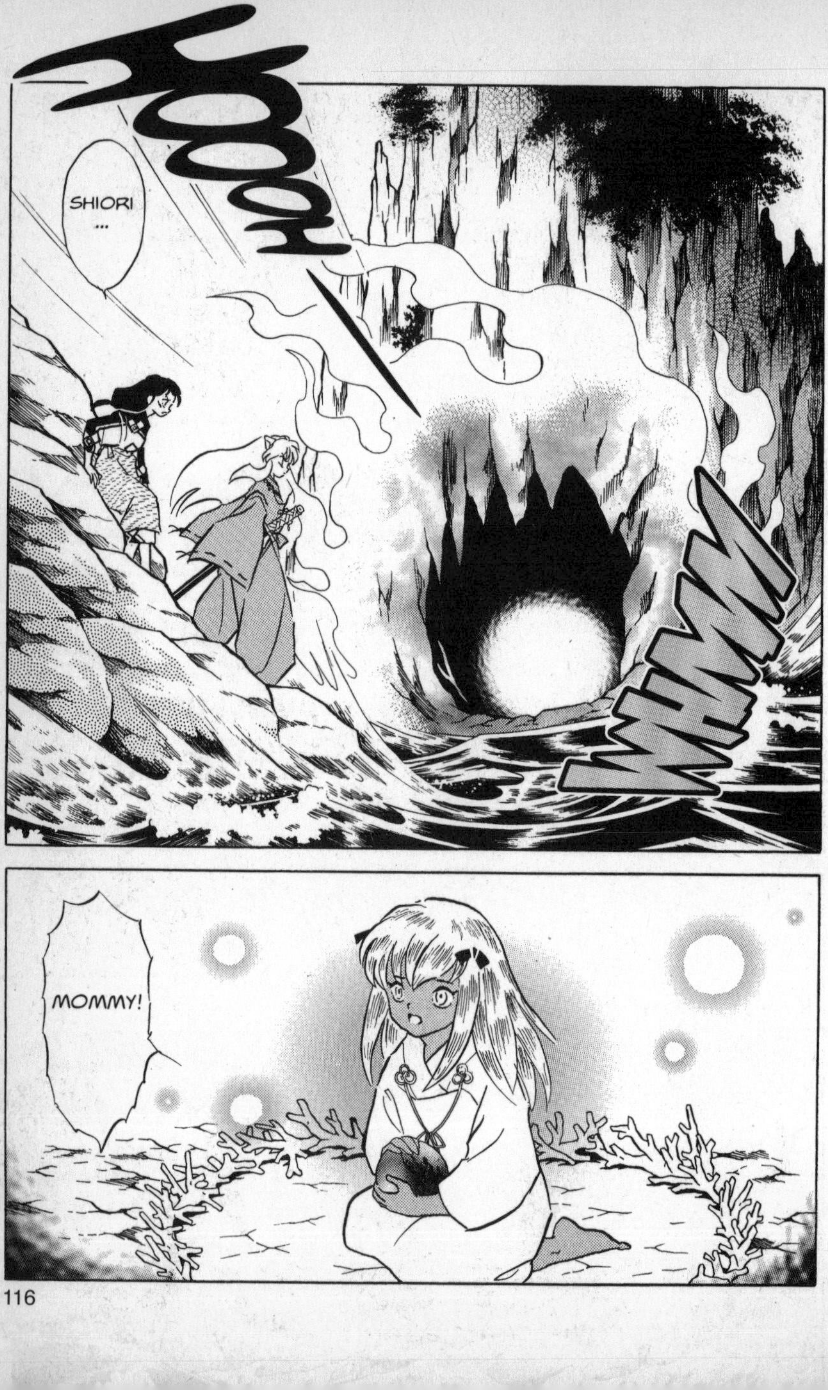
HOOOH!
SHIORI ...
WHMMMM!
MOMMY!

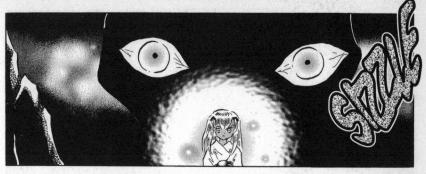

SPIZZLE

!

HEH-HEH HEH HEH... I *THOUGHT* I'D HEARD NOISE.

TAIGO-KUMARU!

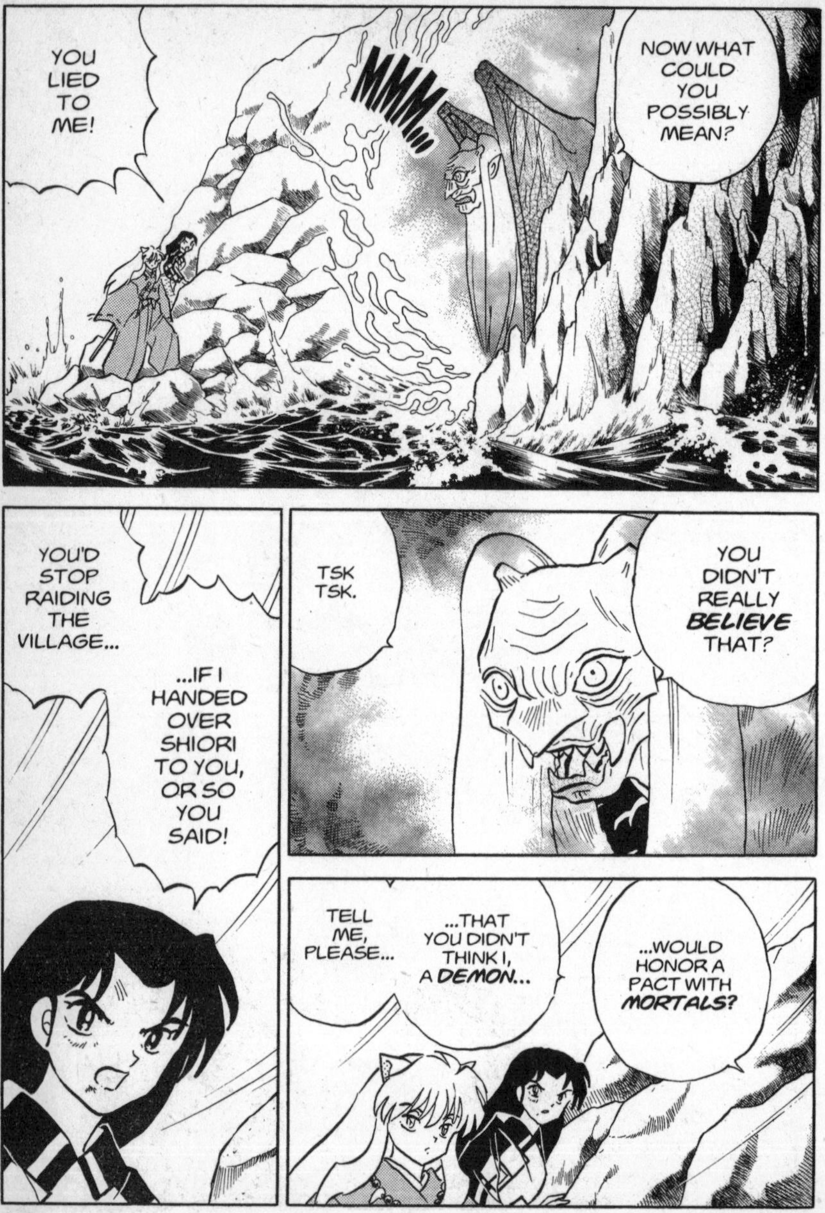
YOU LIED TO ME!
MMM...
NOW WHAT COULD YOU POSSIBLY MEAN?
YOU'D STOP RAIDING THE VILLAGE...
...IF I HANDED OVER SHIORI TO YOU, OR SO YOU SAID!
TSK TSK.
YOU DIDN'T REALLY BELIEVE THAT?
TELL ME, PLEASE...
...THAT YOU DIDN'T THINK I, A DEMON...
...WOULD HONOR A PACT WITH MORTALS?

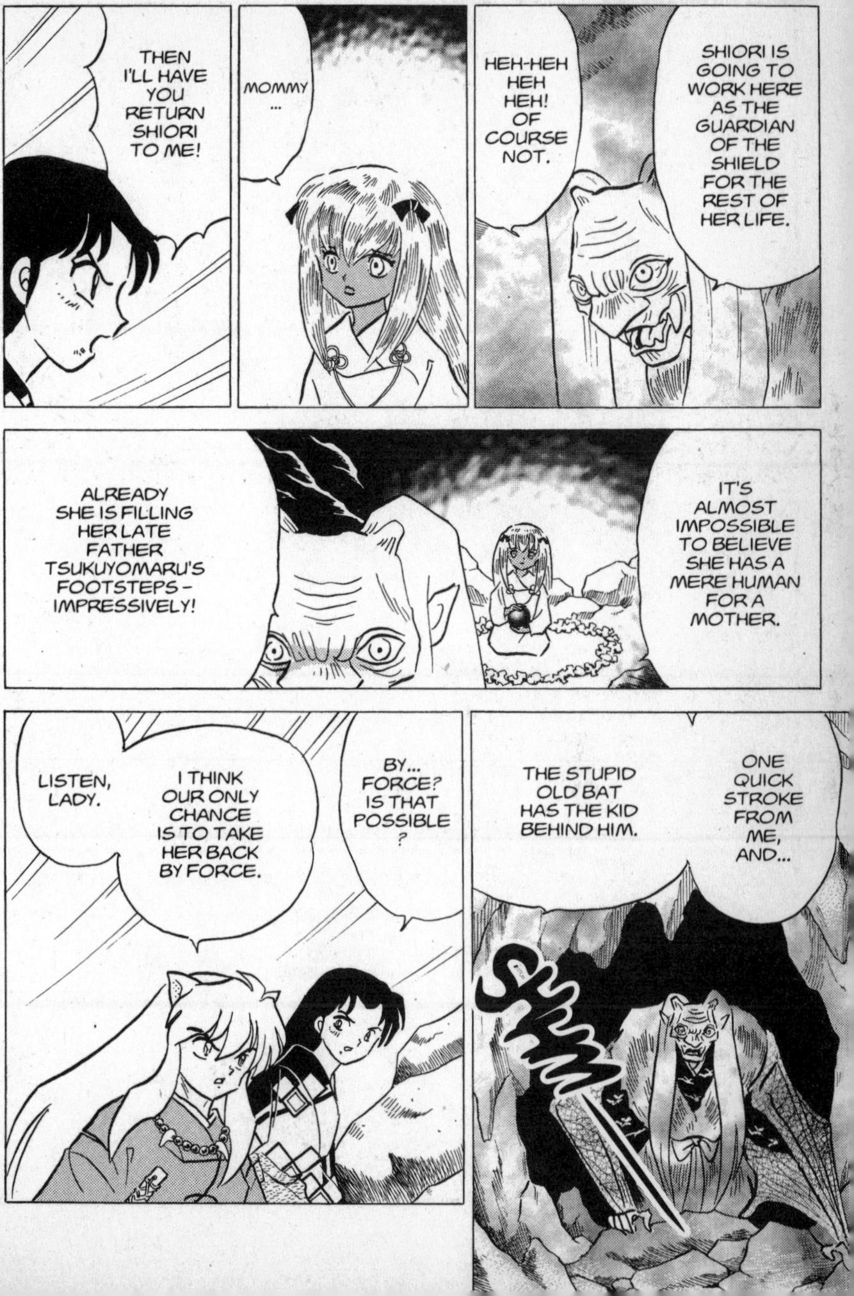
THEN I'LL HAVE YOU RETURN SHIORI TO ME!
MOMMY ...
HEH-HEH HEH HEH! OF COURSE NOT.
SHIORI IS GOING TO WORK HERE AS THE GUARDIAN OF THE SHIELD FOR THE REST OF HER LIFE.
ALREADY SHE IS FILLING HER LATE FATHER TSUKUYOMARU'S FOOTSTEPS - IMPRESSIVELY!
IT'S ALMOST IMPOSSIBLE TO BELIEVE SHE HAS A MERE HUMAN FOR A MOTHER.
LISTEN, LADY.
I THINK OUR ONLY CHANCE IS TO TAKE HER BACK BY FORCE.
BY... FORCE? IS THAT POSSIBLE ?
THE STUPID OLD BAT HAS THE KID BEHIND HIM.
ONE QUICK STROKE FROM ME, AND...

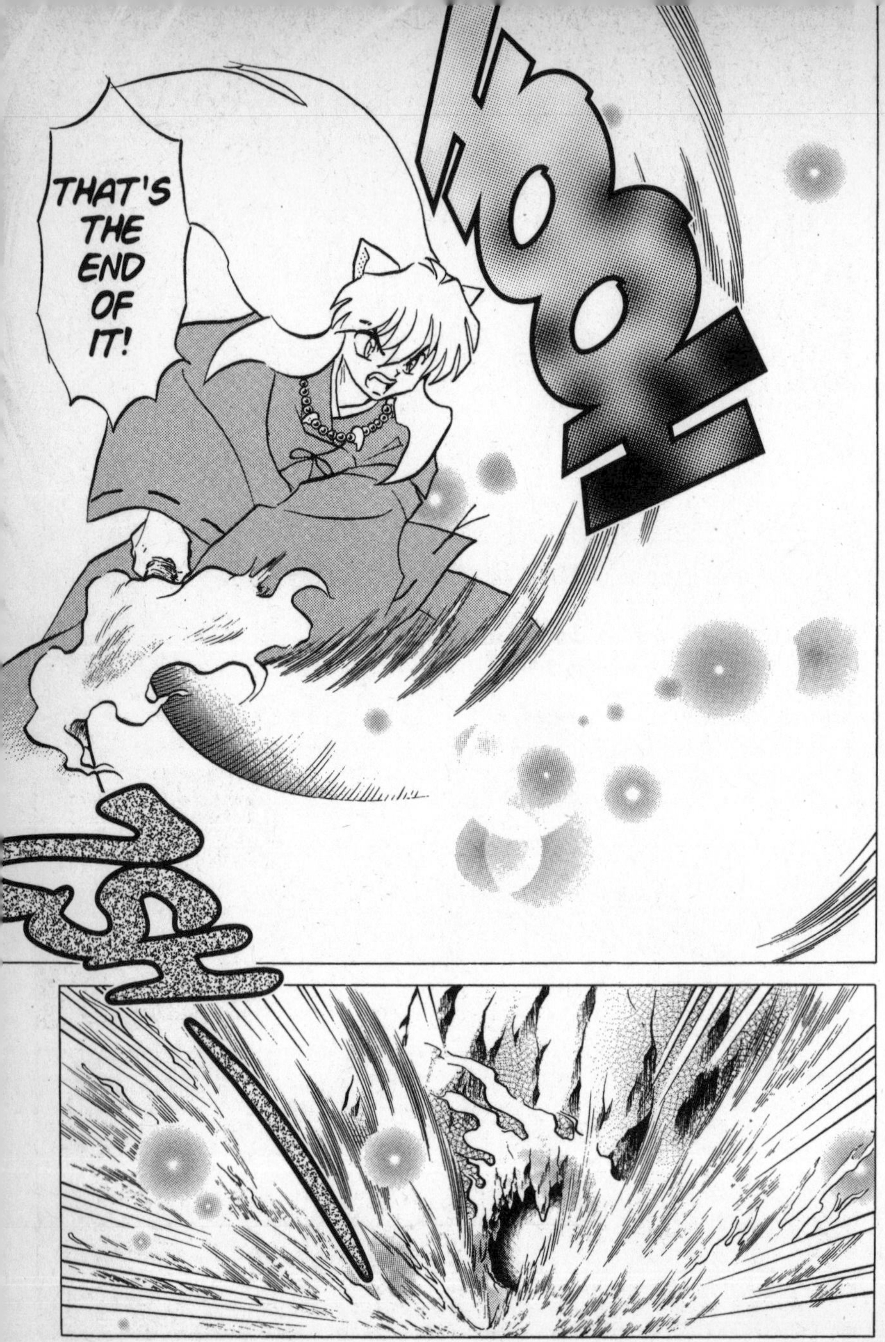
THAT'S THE END OF IT!

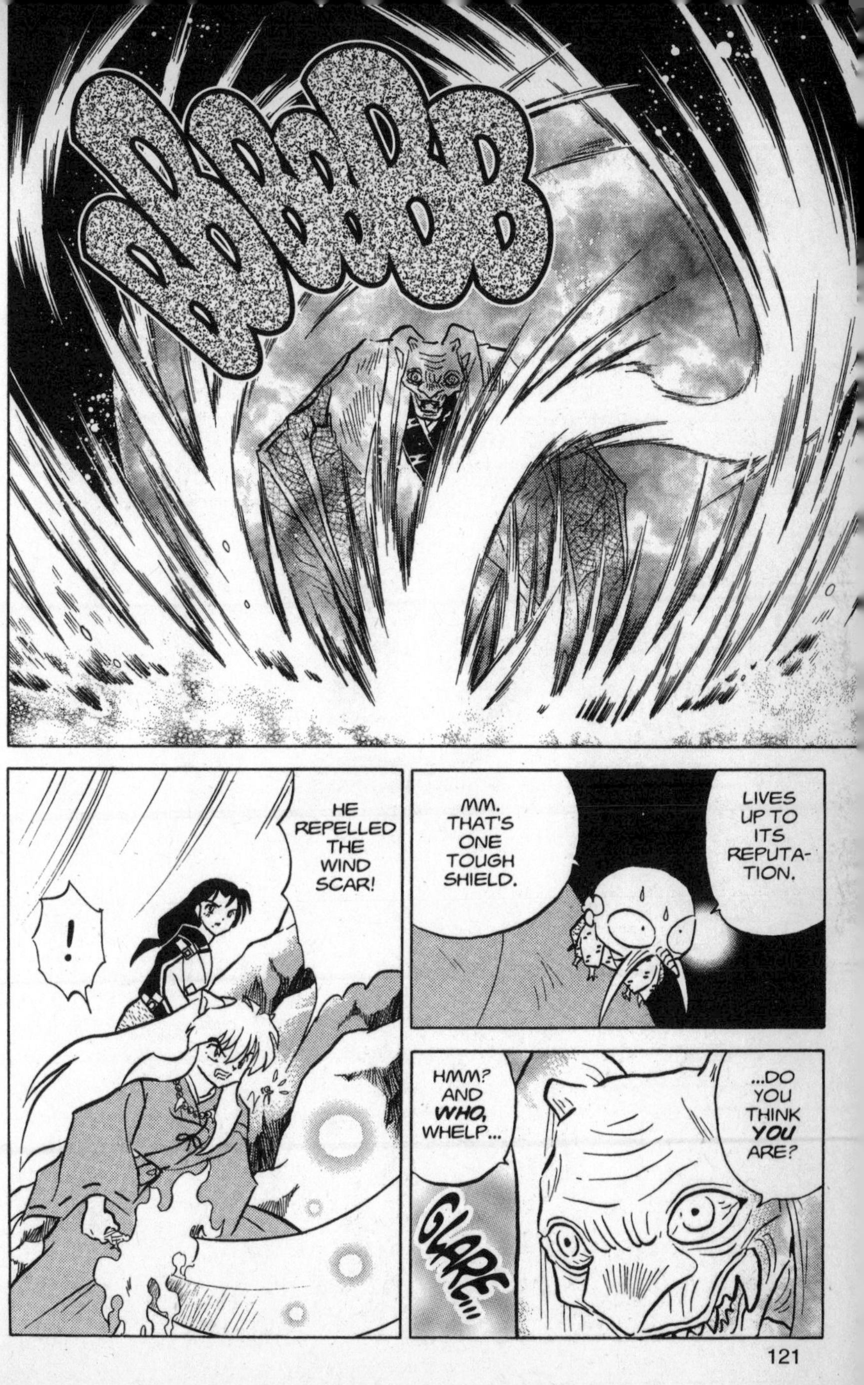
HE REPELLED THE WIND SCAR!
!
MM. THAT'S ONE TOUGH SHIELD.
LIVES UP TO ITS REPUTA-TION.
HMM? AND **WHO,** WHELP...
...DO YOU THINK **YOU** ARE?
GLARE...

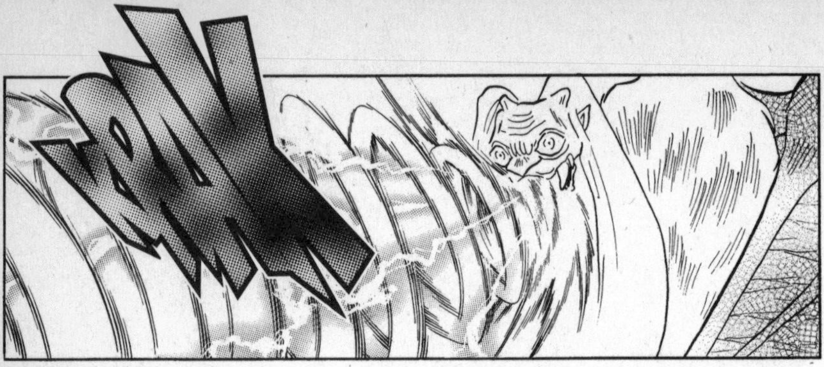

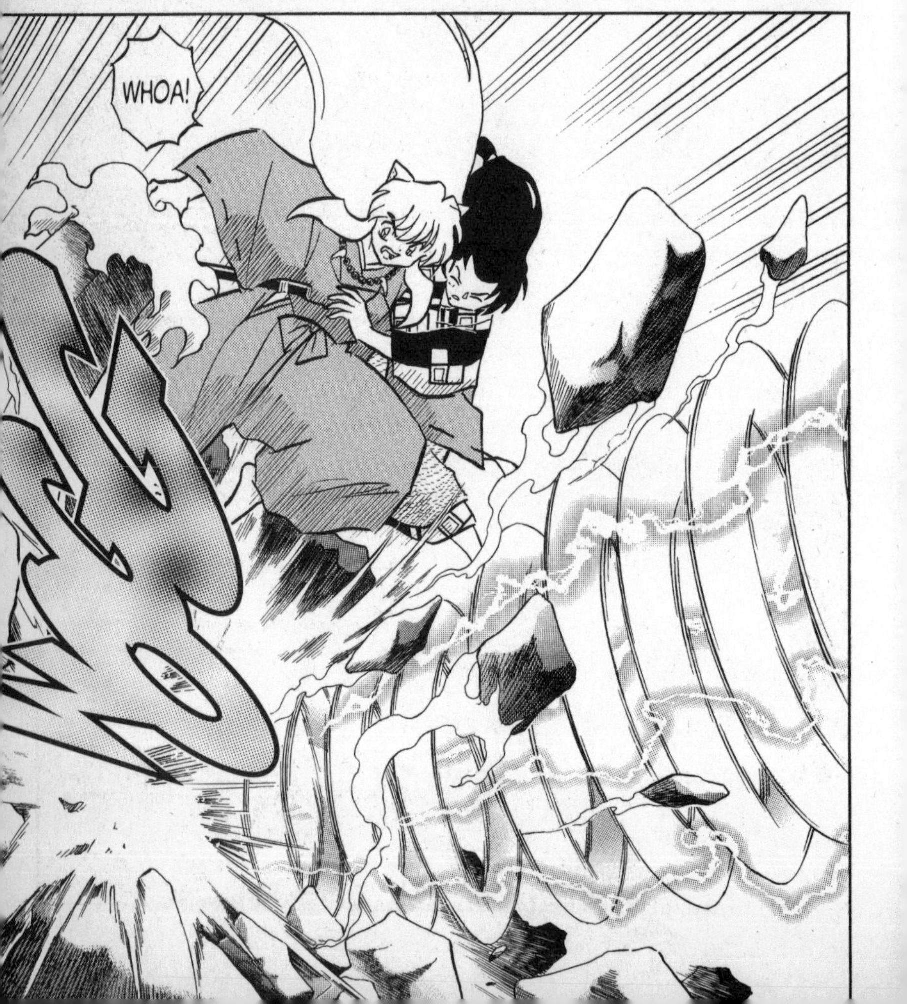
WHOA!

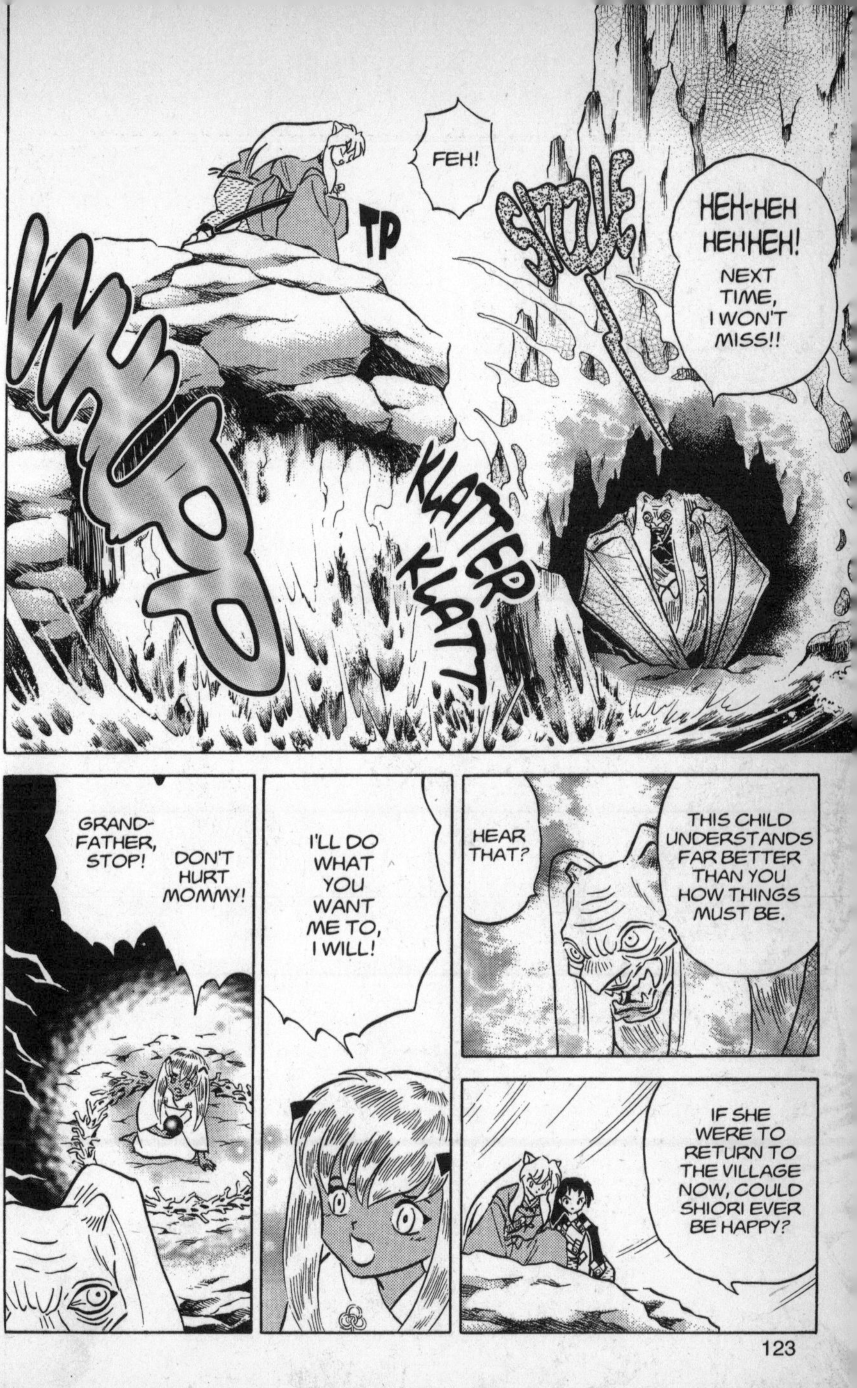
FEH!
TP
SIZZLE
HEH-HEH HEHHEH!
NEXT TIME, I WON'T MISS!!
KLATTER KLATT
GRAND-FATHER, STOP!
DON'T HURT MOMMY!
I'LL DO WHAT YOU WANT ME TO, I WILL!
HEAR THAT?
THIS CHILD UNDERSTANDS FAR BETTER THAN YOU HOW THINGS MUST BE.
IF SHE WERE TO RETURN TO THE VILLAGE NOW, COULD SHIORI EVER BE HAPPY?

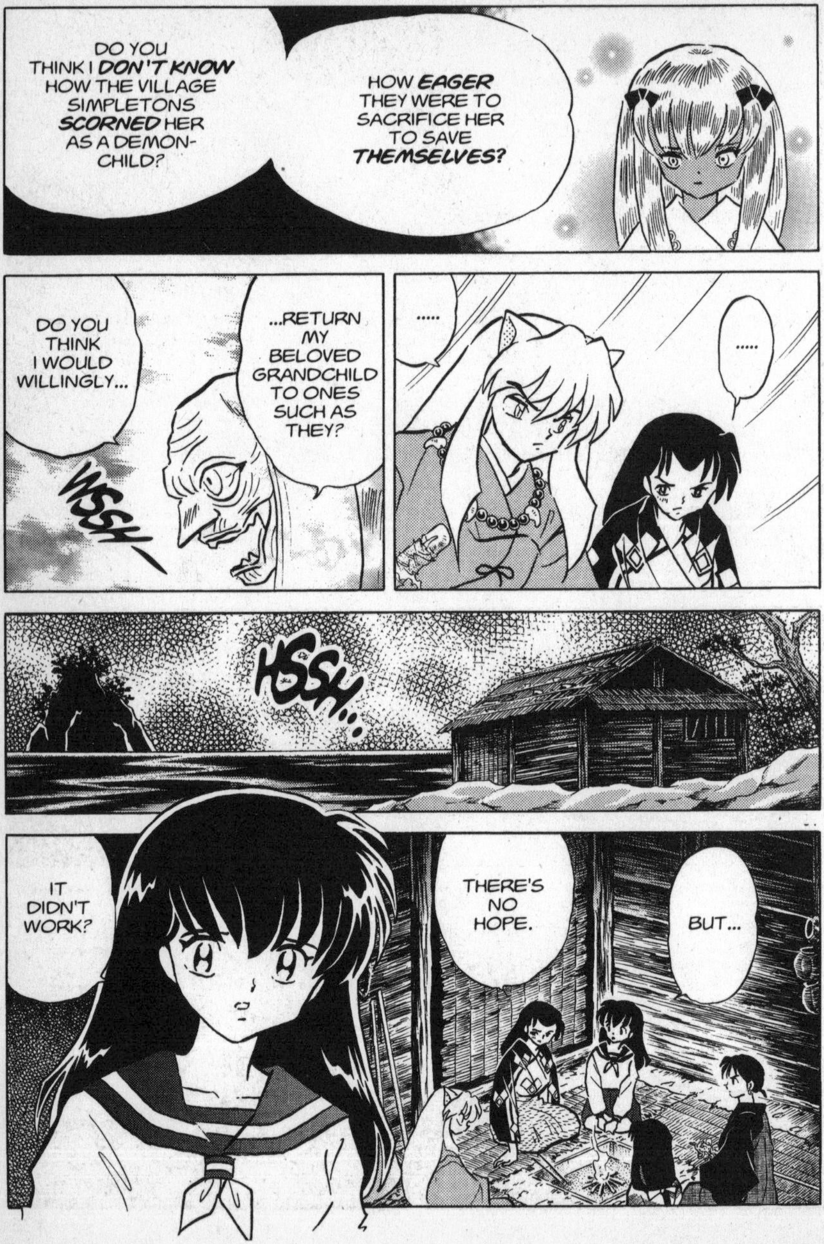
DO YOU THINK I DON'T KNOW HOW THE VILLAGE SIMPLETONS SCORNED HER AS A DEMON-CHILD?
HOW EAGER THEY WERE TO SACRIFICE HER TO SAVE THEMSELVES?
DO YOU THINK I WOULD WILLINGLY...
...RETURN MY BELOVED GRANDCHILD TO ONES SUCH AS THEY?
WSSH
.....
.....
HSSH...
IT DIDN'T WORK?
THERE'S NO HOPE.
BUT...

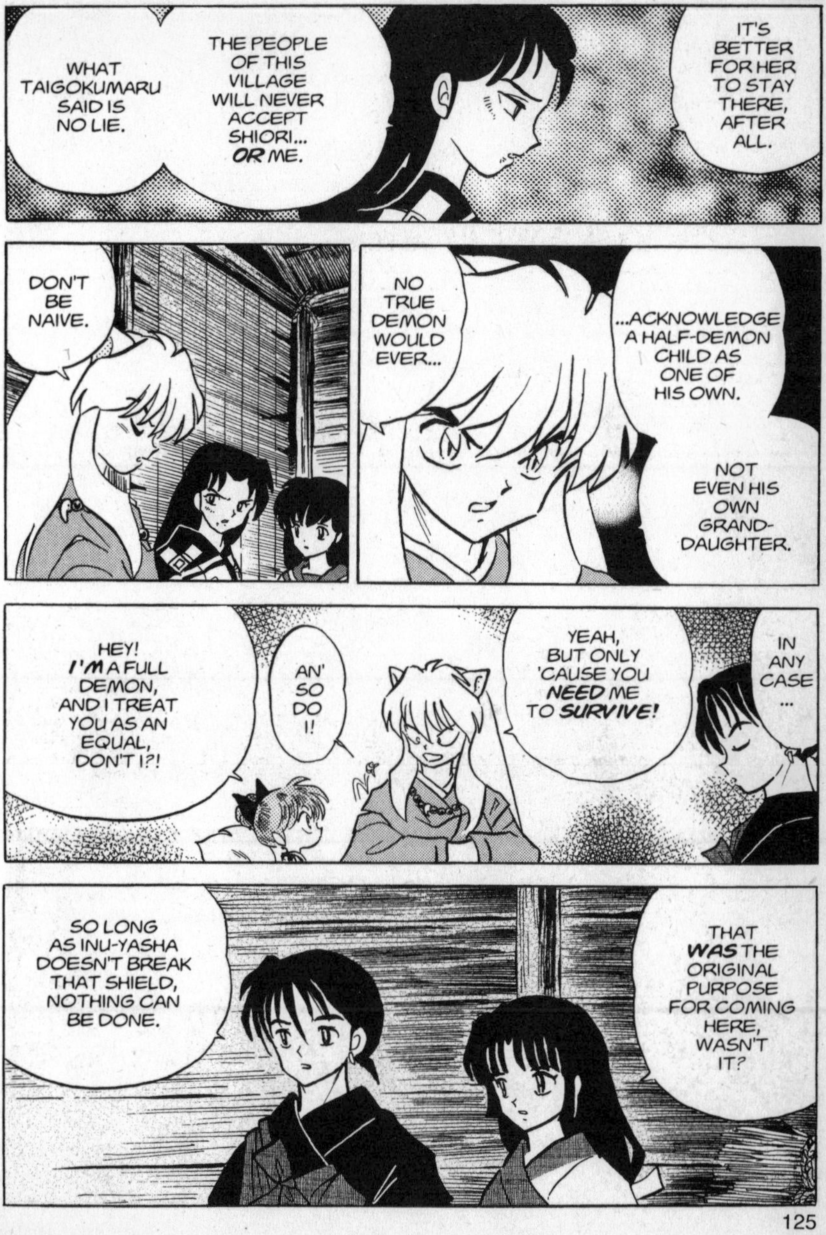
WHAT TAIGOKUMARU SAID IS NO LIE.
THE PEOPLE OF THIS VILLAGE WILL NEVER ACCEPT SHIORI... **OR** ME.
IT'S BETTER FOR HER TO STAY THERE, AFTER ALL.
DON'T BE NAIVE.
NO TRUE DEMON WOULD EVER...
...ACKNOWLEDGE A HALF-DEMON CHILD AS ONE OF HIS OWN.
NOT EVEN HIS OWN GRAND-DAUGHTER.
HEY! ***I'M*** A FULL DEMON, AND I TREAT YOU AS AN EQUAL, DON'T I?!
AN' SO DO I!
YEAH, BUT ONLY 'CAUSE YOU ***NEED*** ME TO ***SURVIVE!***
IN ANY CASE ...
SO LONG AS INU-YASHA DOESN'T BREAK THAT SHIELD, NOTHING CAN BE DONE.
THAT ***WAS*** THE ORIGINAL PURPOSE FOR COMING HERE, WASN'T IT?

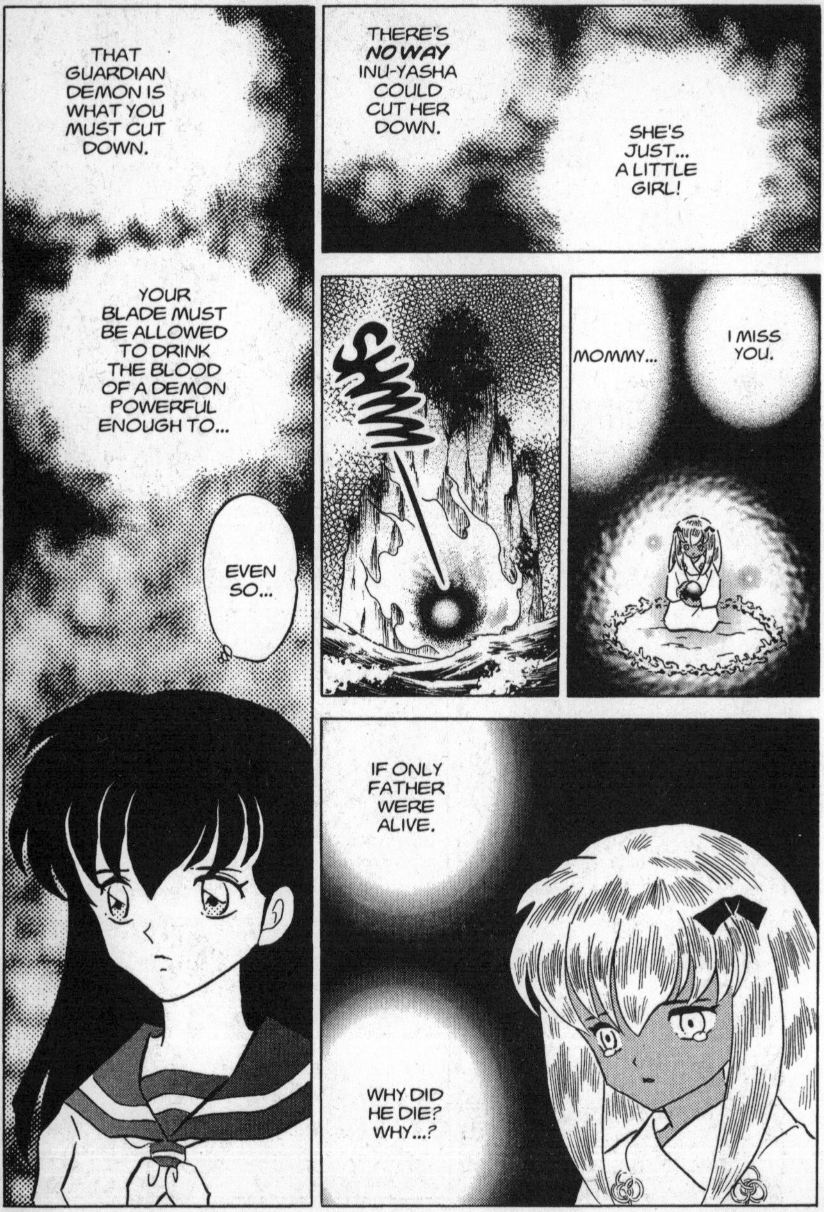
THAT GUARDIAN DEMON IS WHAT YOU MUST CUT DOWN.
YOUR BLADE MUST BE ALLOWED TO DRINK THE BLOOD OF A DEMON POWERFUL ENOUGH TO...
EVEN SO...
THERE'S **NO WAY** INU-YASHA COULD CUT HER DOWN.
SHE'S JUST... A LITTLE GIRL!
SHMM
MOMMY...
I MISS YOU.
IF ONLY FATHER WERE ALIVE.
WHY DID HE DIE? WHY...?

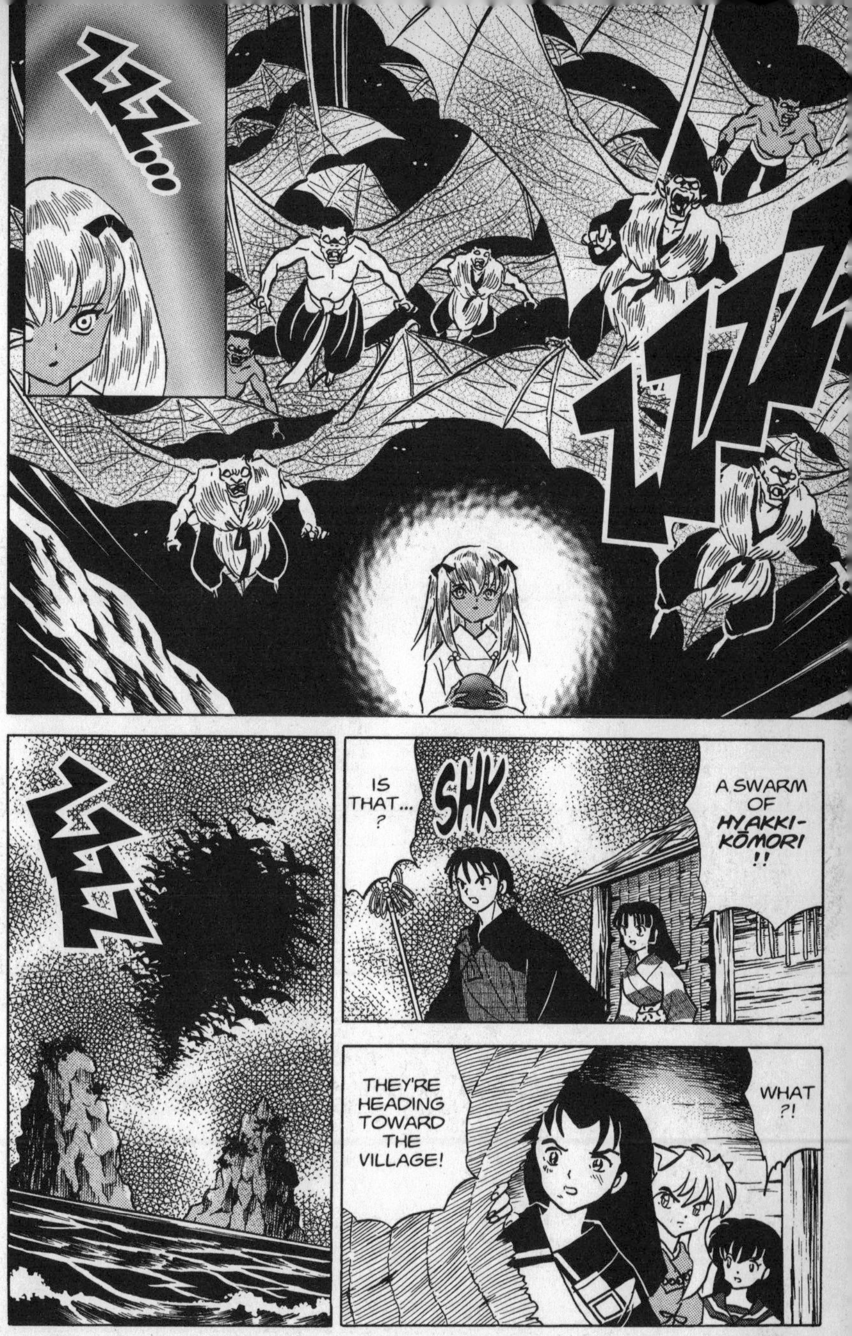
ZZZ...
IS THAT... ?
SHK
A SWARM OF HYAKKI-KŌMORI !!
THEY'RE HEADING TOWARD THE VILLAGE!
WHAT ?!

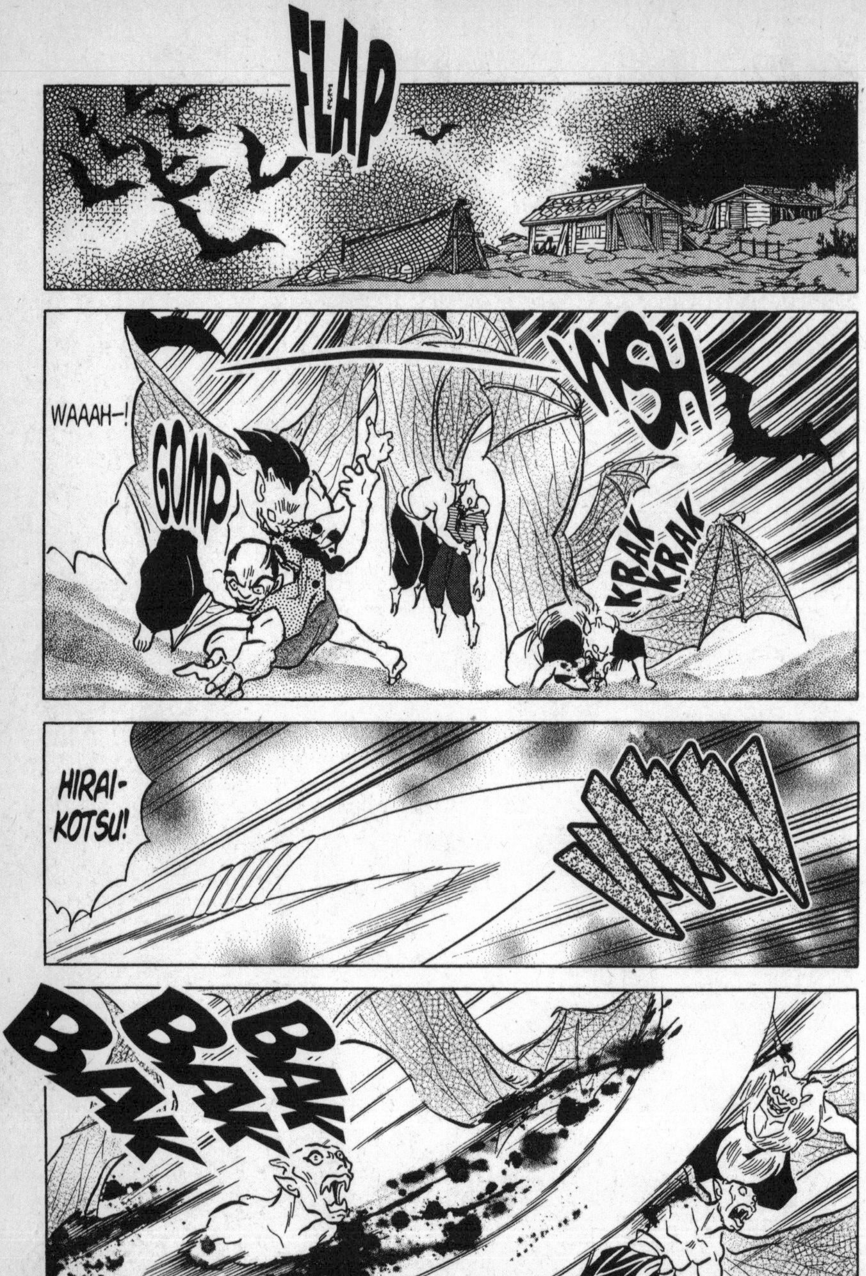
FLAP
WAAAH-!
GOMP
WSH
KRAK KRAK
HIRAI-KOTSU!
BAK BAK BAK

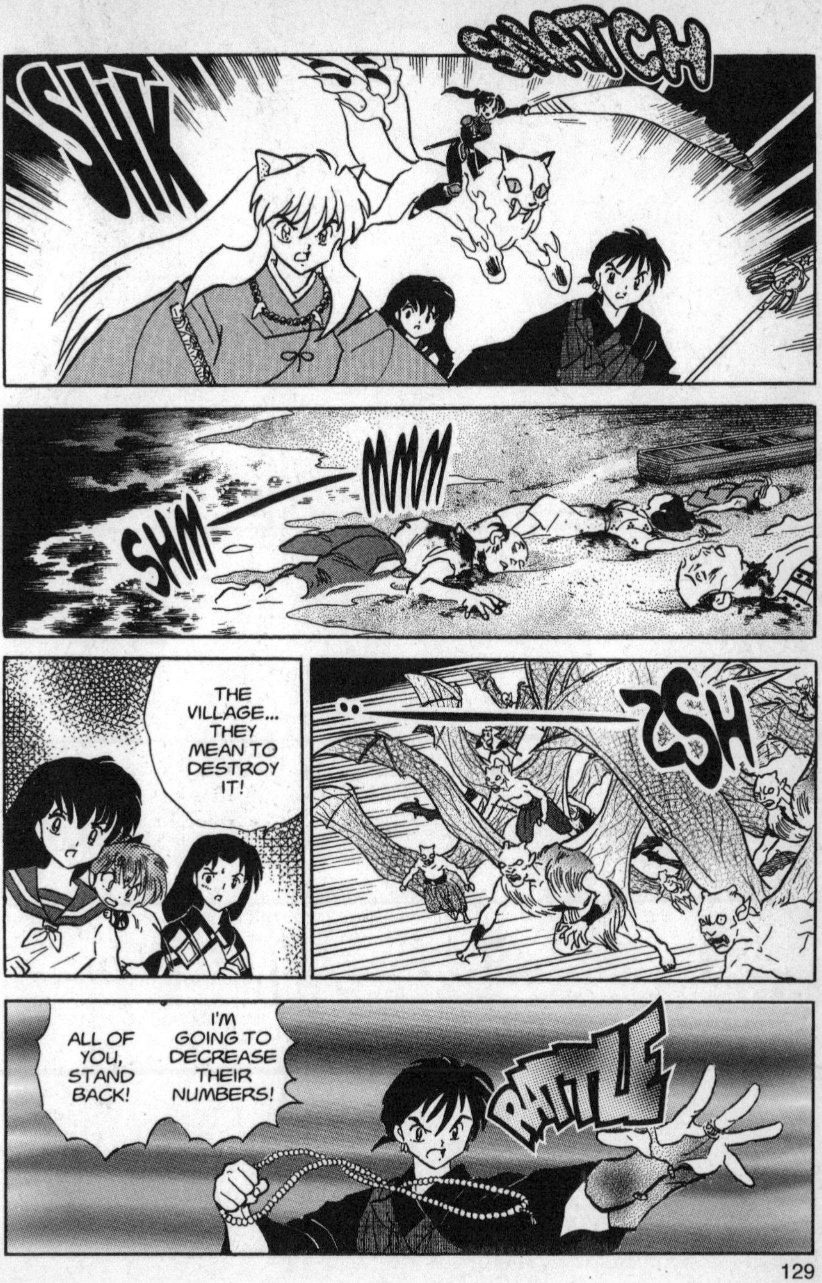
SHATCH
SHK
SHM
MMM
THE VILLAGE... THEY MEAN TO DESTROY IT!
ZSH
ALL OF YOU, STAND BACK!
I'M GOING TO DECREASE THEIR NUMBERS!
BHTTLE

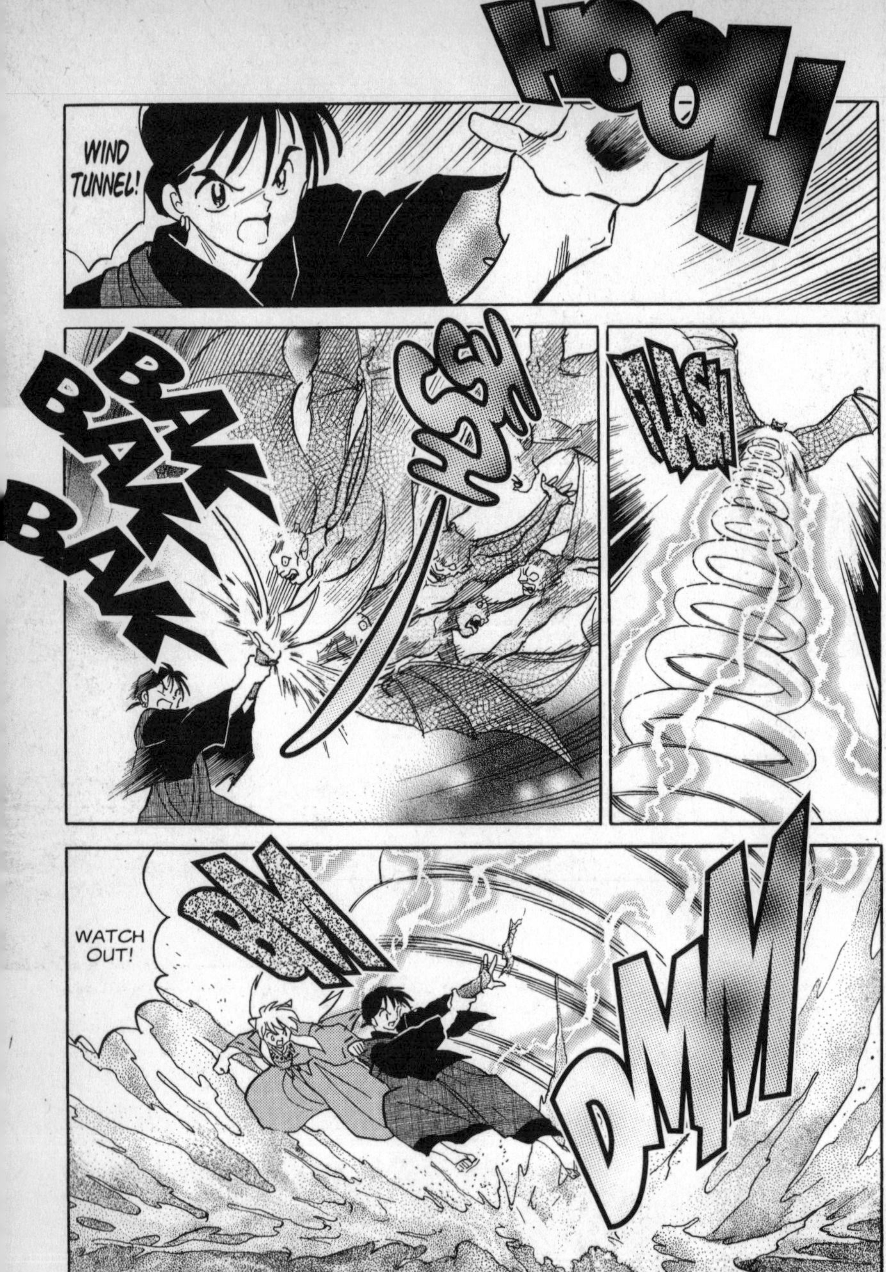
WIND TUNNEL!
BAK BAK BAK
WATCH OUT!

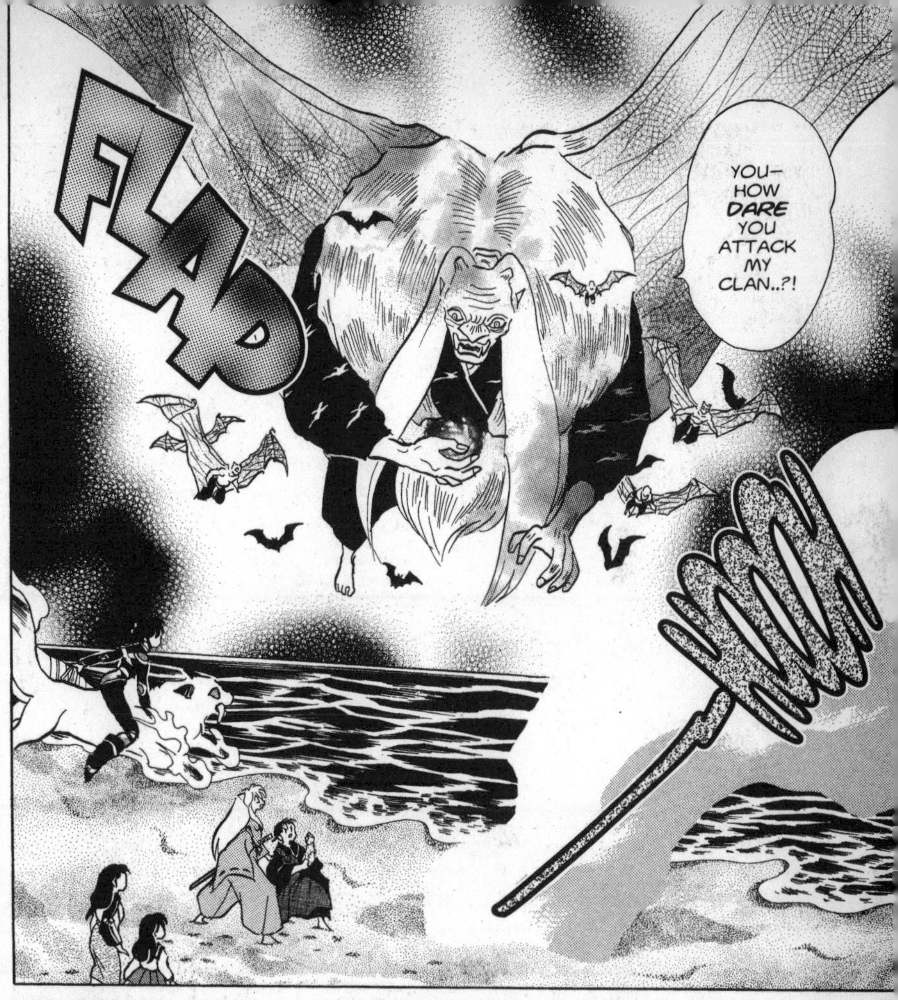
FLAP
YOU— HOW DARE YOU ATTACK MY CLAN..?!
WOOSH
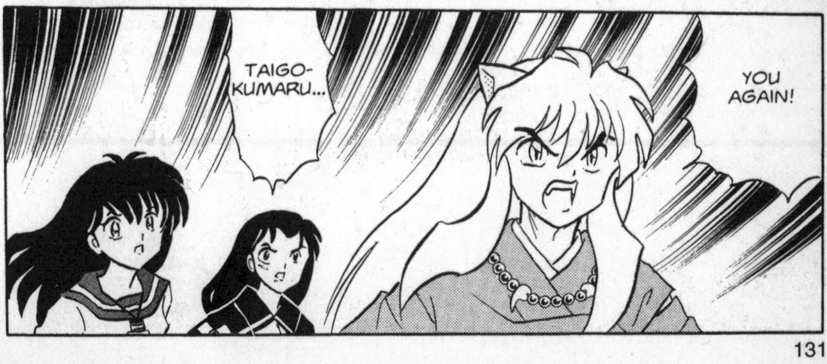
TAIGO-KUMARU...
YOU AGAIN!

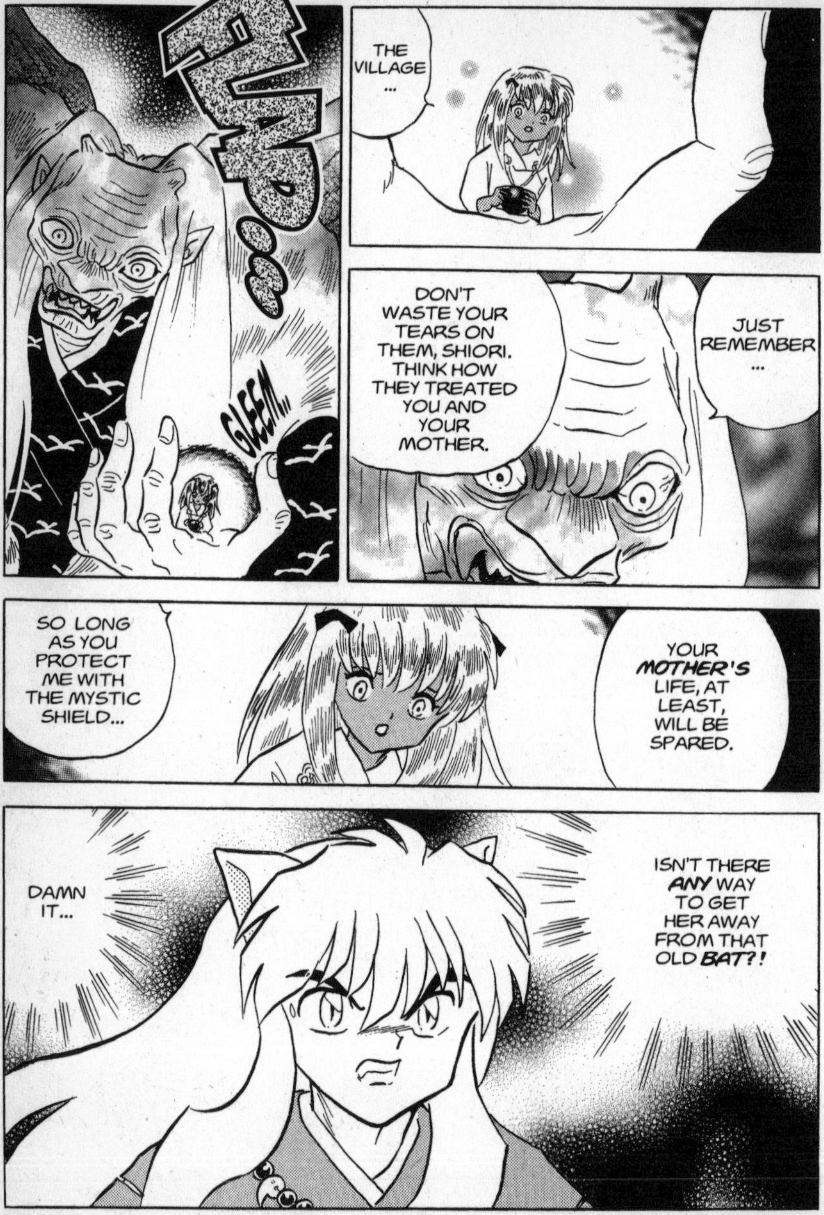

FLAPOOO
GLEEM...
THE VILLAGE ...
DON'T WASTE YOUR TEARS ON THEM, SHIORI. THINK HOW THEY TREATED YOU AND YOUR MOTHER.
JUST REMEMBER ...
SO LONG AS YOU PROTECT ME WITH THE MYSTIC SHIELD...
YOUR MOTHER'S LIFE, AT LEAST, WILL BE SPARED.
DAMN IT...
ISN'T THERE ANY WAY TO GET HER AWAY FROM THAT OLD BAT?!

SCROLL EIGHT

A FATHER'S WISH

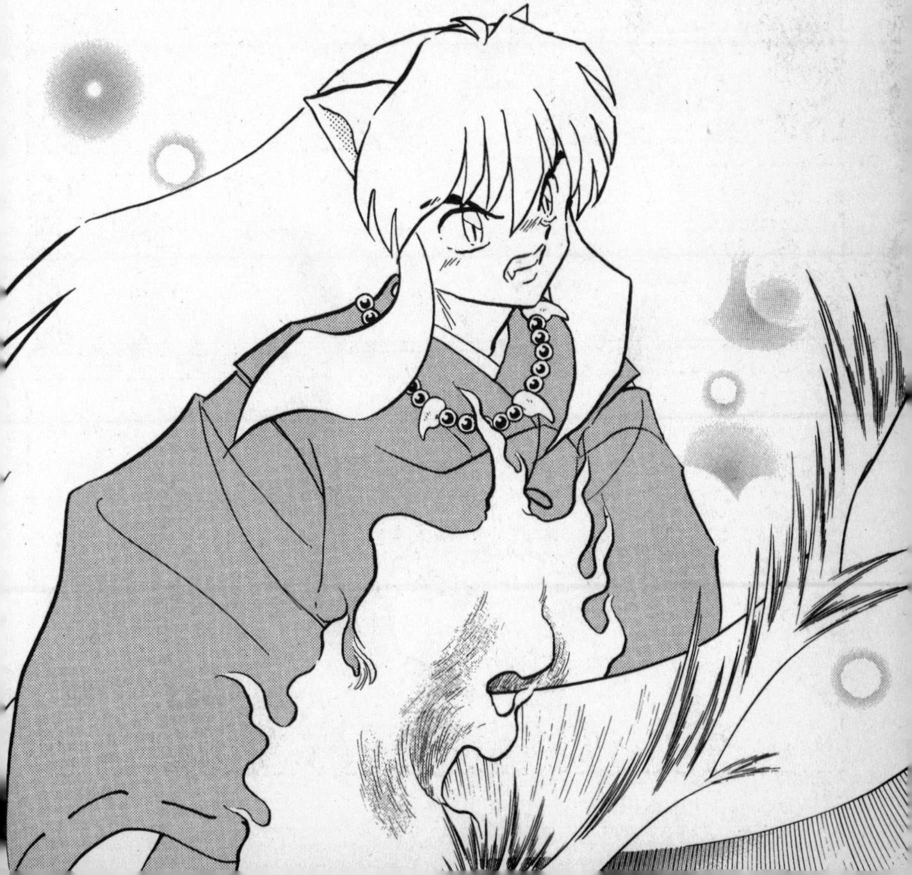

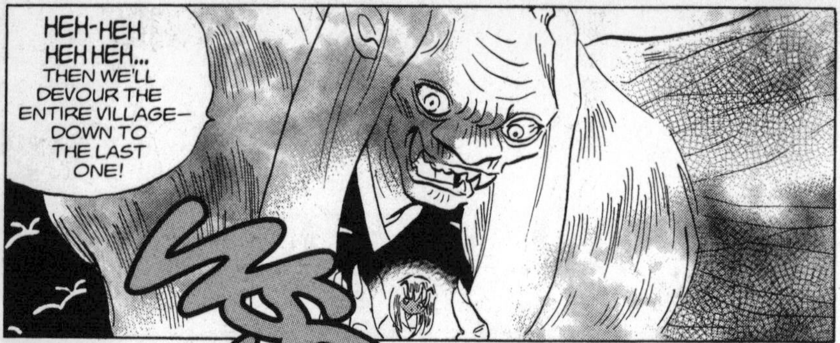
HEH-HEH HEH HEH... THEN WE'LL DEVOUR THE ENTIRE VILLAGE—DOWN TO THE LAST ONE!
VSSH...

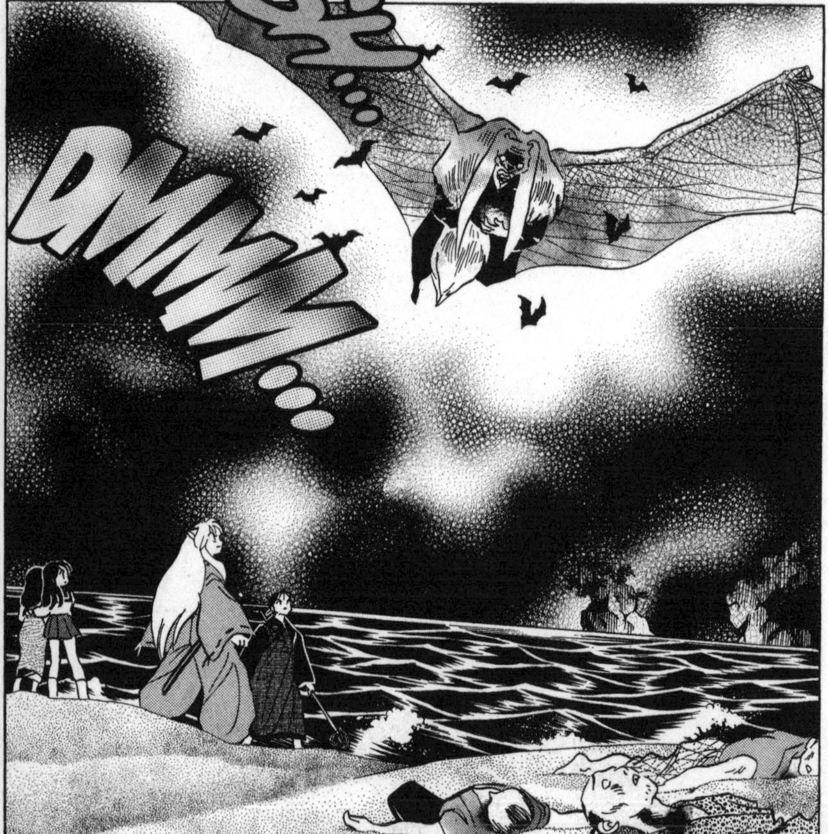
DMMM...

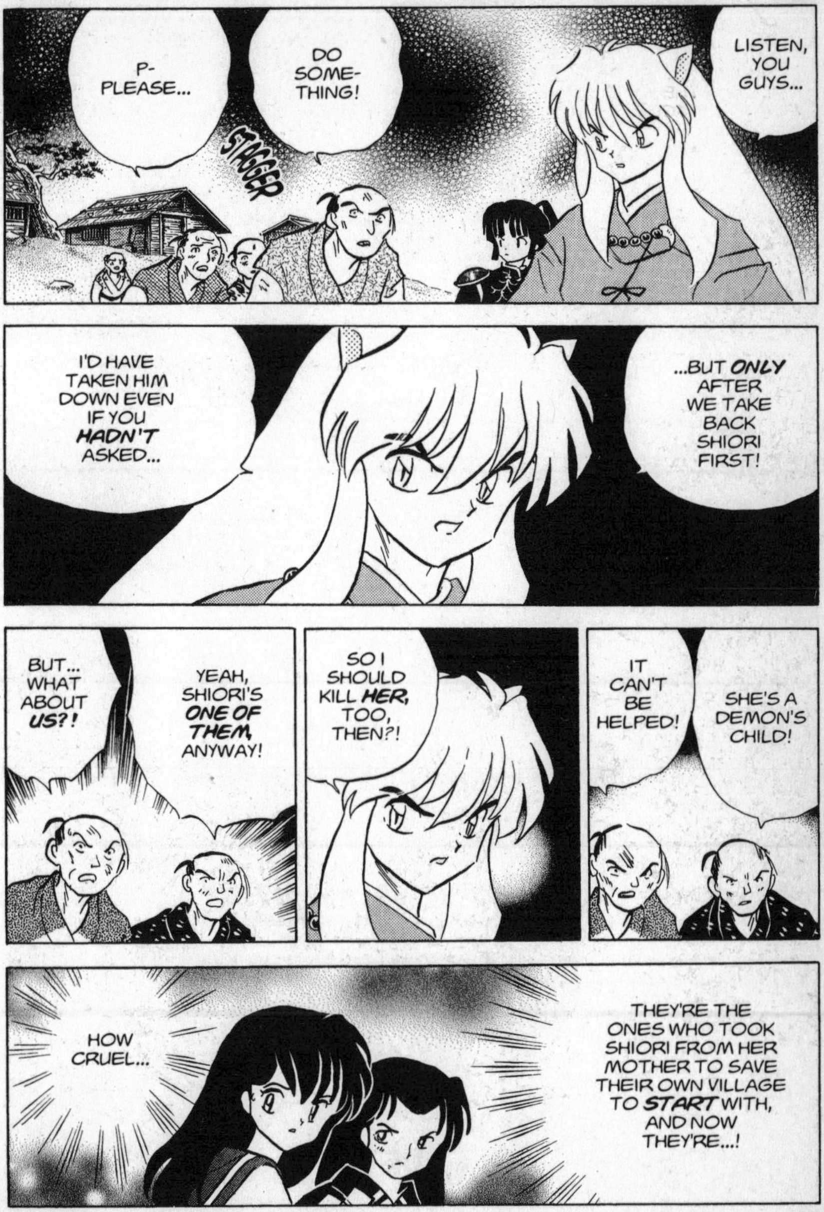
P-PLEASE...
DO SOME-THING!
STAGGER
LISTEN, YOU GUYS...
I'D HAVE TAKEN HIM DOWN EVEN IF YOU HADN'T ASKED...
...BUT ONLY AFTER WE TAKE BACK SHIORI FIRST!
BUT... WHAT ABOUT US?!
YEAH, SHIORI'S ONE OF THEM, ANYWAY!
SO I SHOULD KILL HER, TOO, THEN?!
IT CAN'T BE HELPED!
SHE'S A DEMON'S CHILD!
HOW CRUEL...
THEY'RE THE ONES WHO TOOK SHIORI FROM HER MOTHER TO SAVE THEIR OWN VILLAGE TO START WITH, AND NOW THEY'RE...!

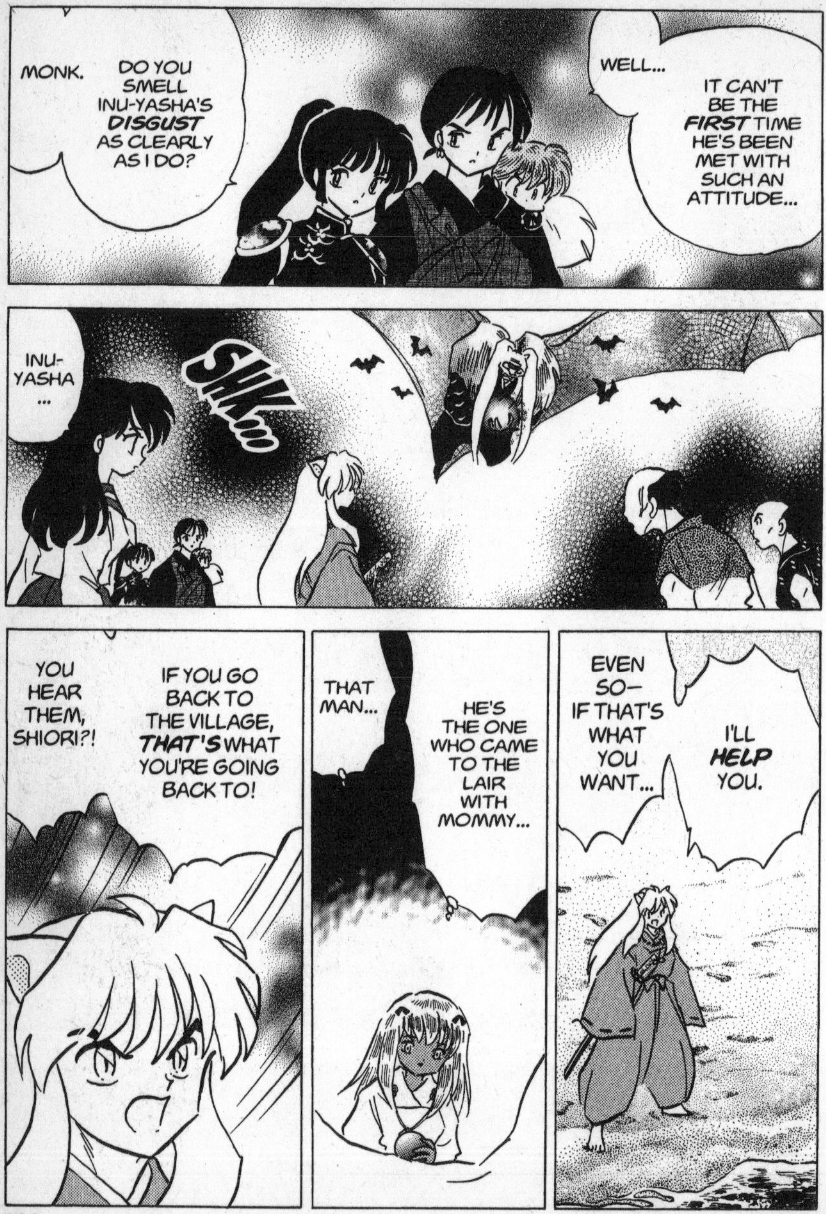
MONK.
DO YOU SMELL INU-YASHA'S **DISGUST** AS CLEARLY AS I DO?
WELL...
IT CAN'T BE THE **FIRST** TIME HE'S BEEN MET WITH SUCH AN ATTITUDE...
INU-YASHA...
SHK...
YOU HEAR THEM, SHIORI?!
IF YOU GO BACK TO THE VILLAGE, **THAT'S** WHAT YOU'RE GOING BACK TO!
THAT MAN...
HE'S THE ONE WHO CAME TO THE LAIR WITH MOMMY...
EVEN SO— IF THAT'S WHAT YOU WANT...
I'LL **HELP** YOU.

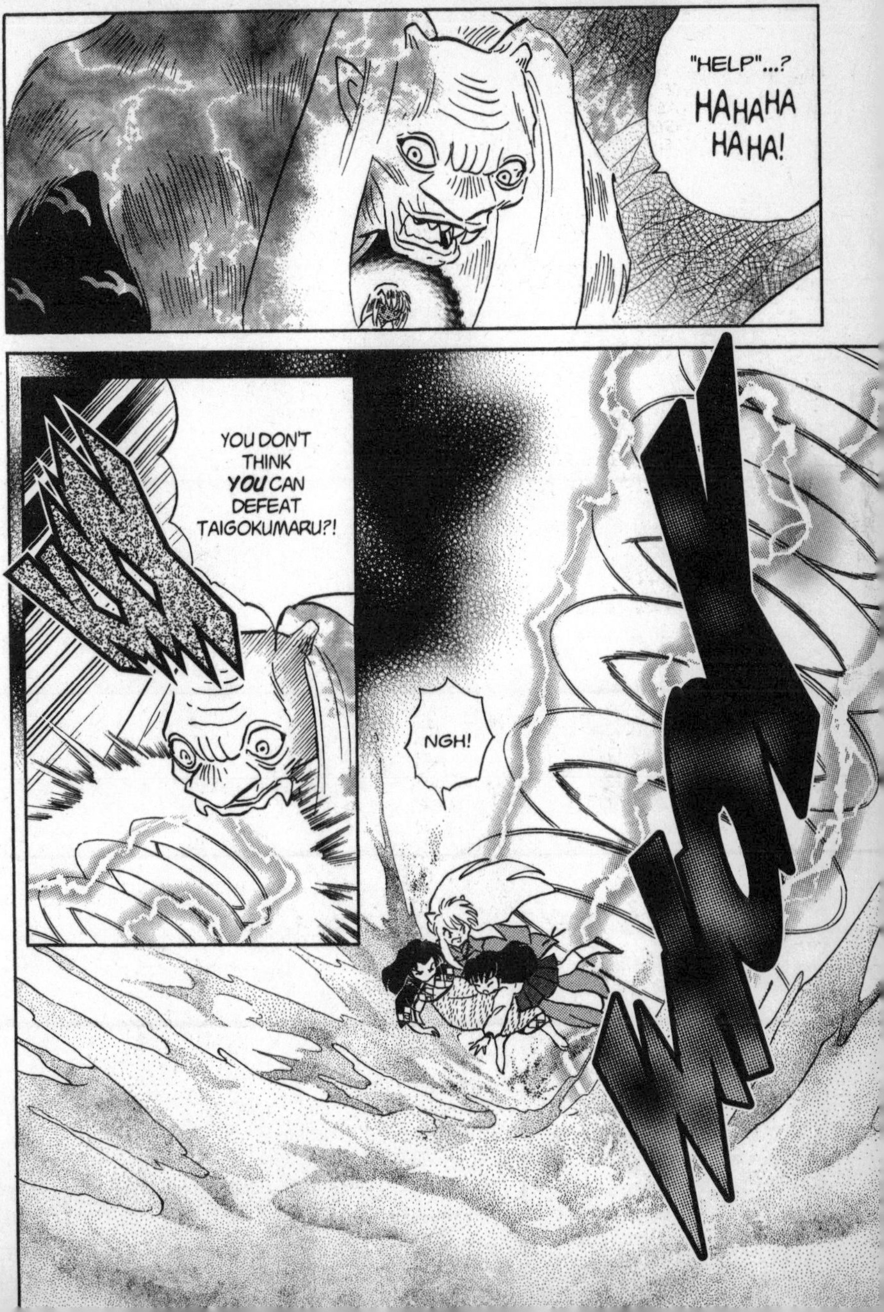
"HELP"...?
HAHAHA HAHA!
YOU DON'T THINK YOU CAN DEFEAT TAIGOKUMARU?!
NGH!

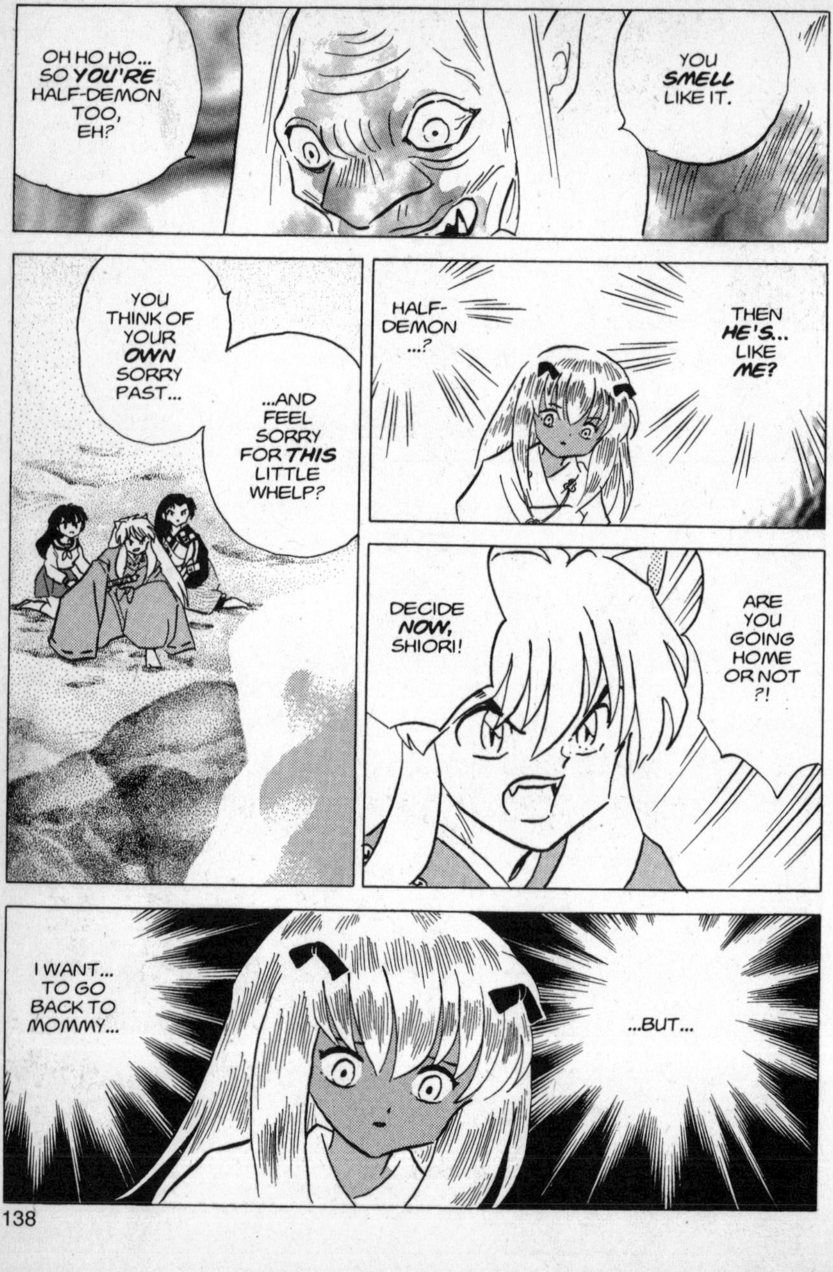
OH HO HO... SO YOU'RE HALF-DEMON TOO, EH?
YOU SMELL LIKE IT.
YOU THINK OF YOUR OWN SORRY PAST...
...AND FEEL SORRY FOR THIS LITTLE WHELP?
HALF-DEMON ...?
THEN HE'S... LIKE ME?
DECIDE NOW, SHIORI!
ARE YOU GOING HOME OR NOT ?!
I WANT... TO GO BACK TO MOMMY...
...BUT...

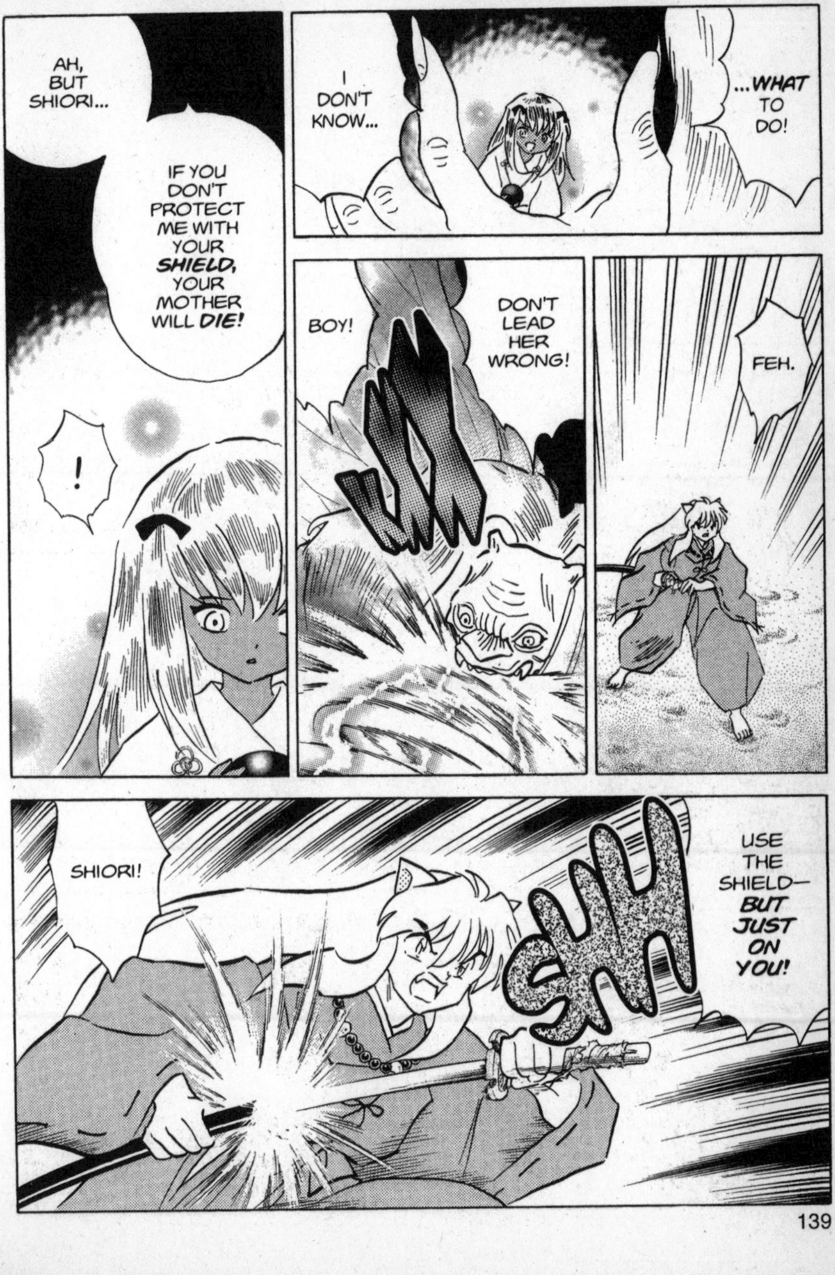
AH, BUT SHIORI...
IF YOU DON'T PROTECT ME WITH YOUR SHIELD, YOUR MOTHER WILL DIE!
!
I DON'T KNOW...
...WHAT TO DO!
BOY!
DON'T LEAD HER WRONG!
FEH.
SHIORI!
SHH
USE THE SHIELD— BUT JUST ON YOU!

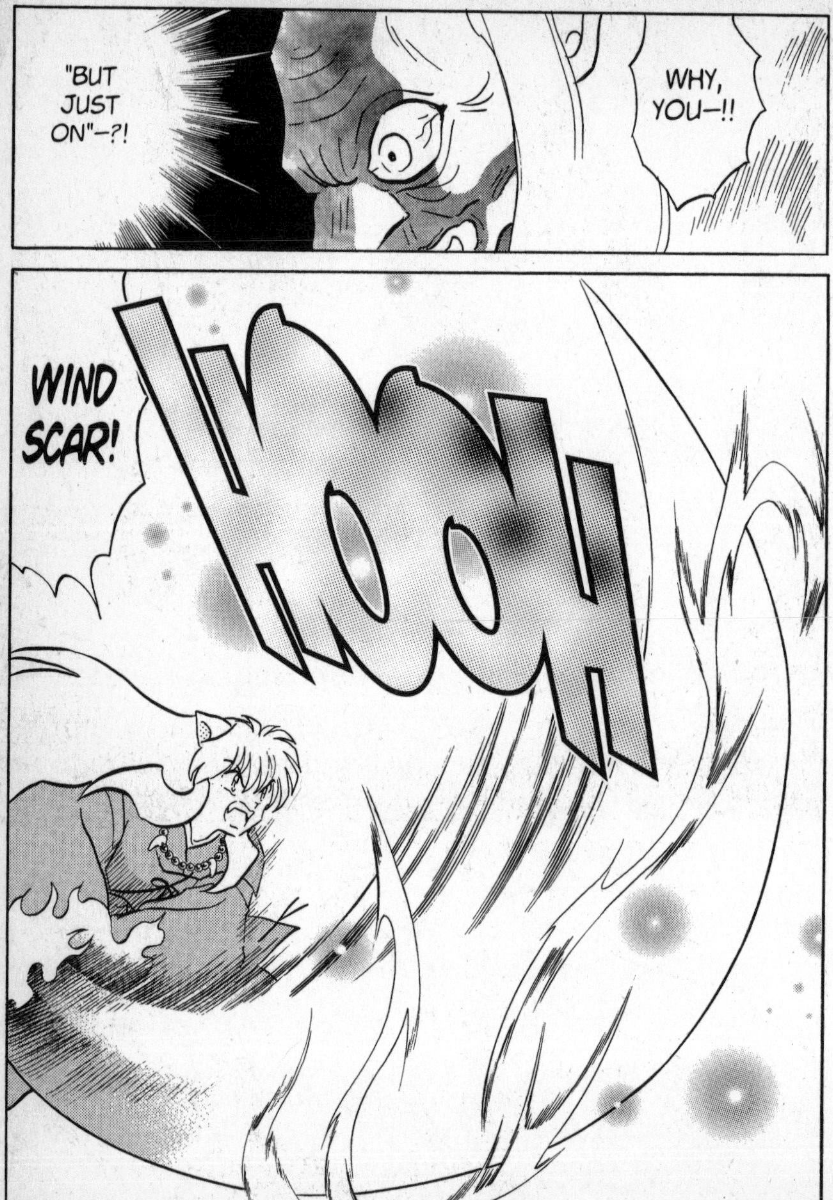
"BUT
JUST
ON"–?!
WHY,
YOU–!!
WIND
SCAR!
WOOH

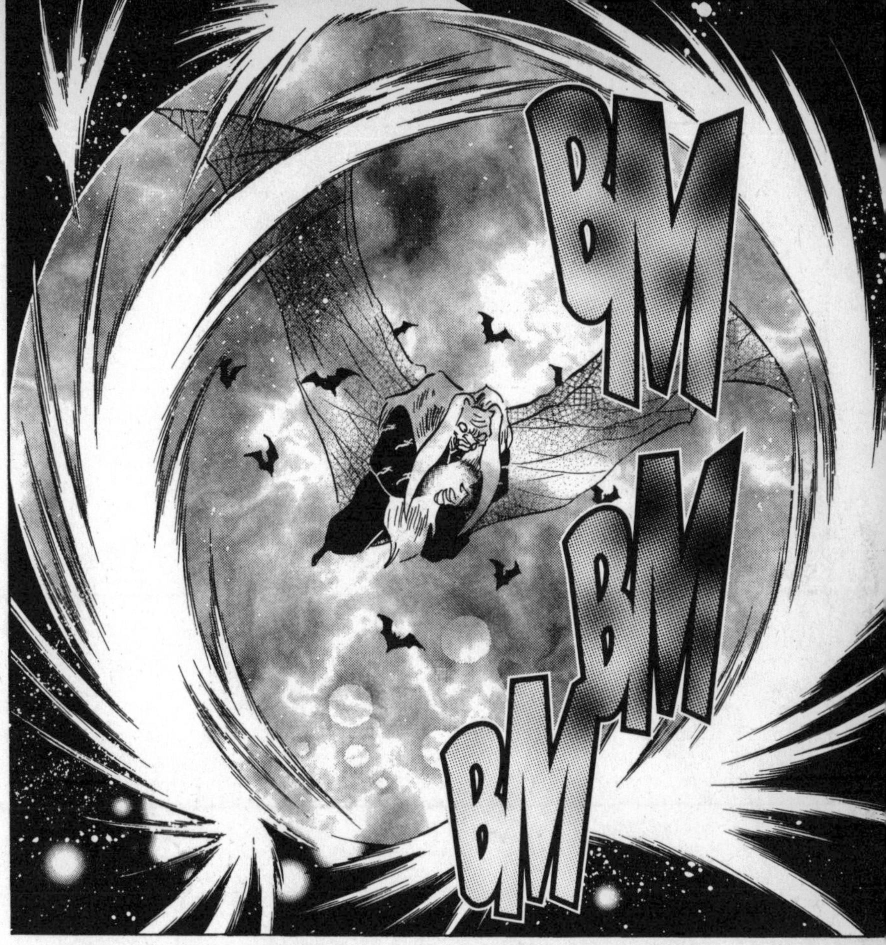
BM
BM
BM

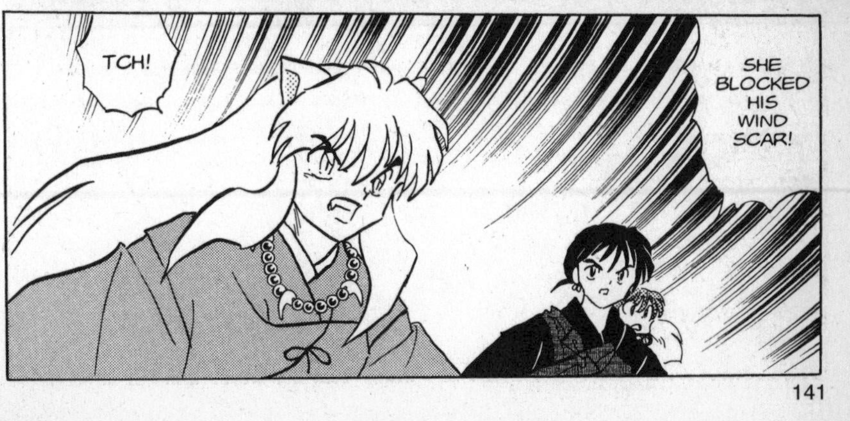
TCH!
SHE BLOCKED HIS WIND SCAR!

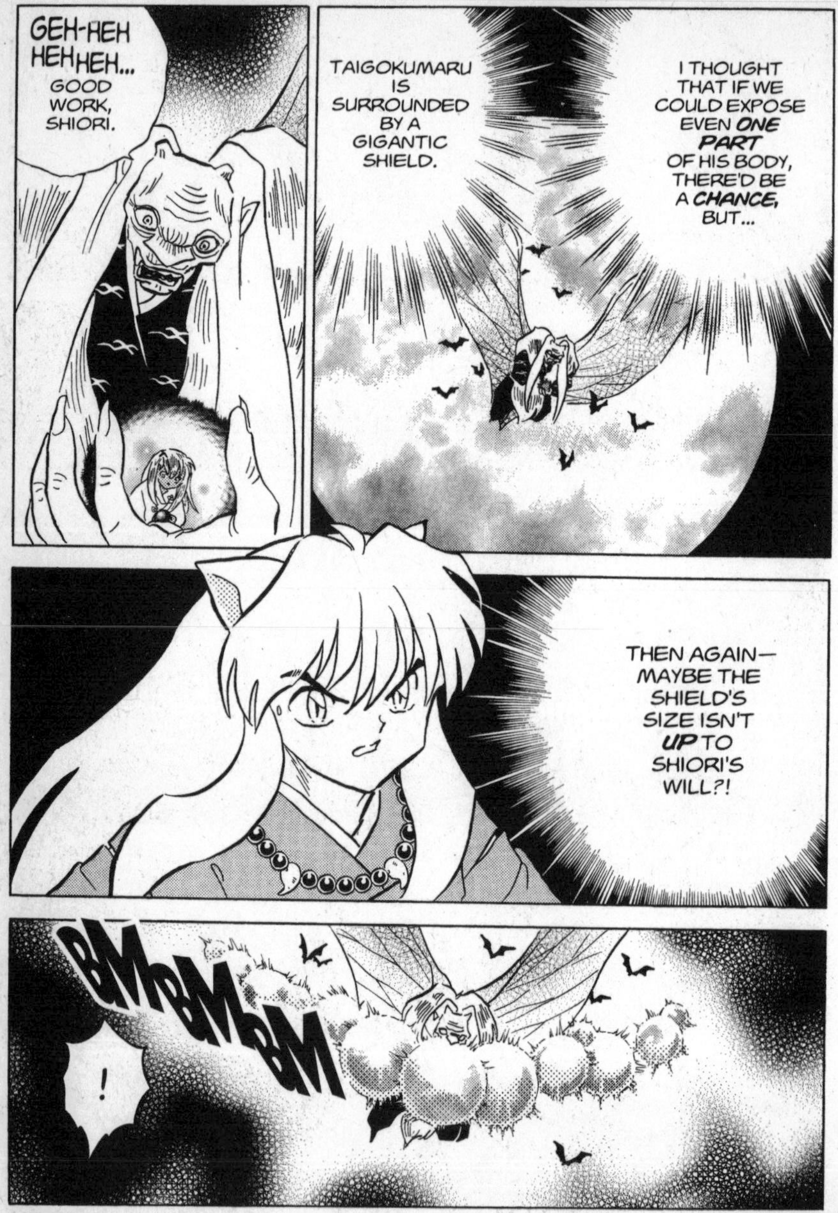
GEH-HEH HEH HEH... GOOD WORK, SHIORI.
TAIGOKUMARU IS SURROUNDED BY A GIGANTIC SHIELD.
I THOUGHT THAT IF WE COULD EXPOSE EVEN ONE PART OF HIS BODY, THERE'D BE A CHANCE, BUT...
THEN AGAIN— MAYBE THE SHIELD'S SIZE ISN'T UP TO SHIORI'S WILL?!
!

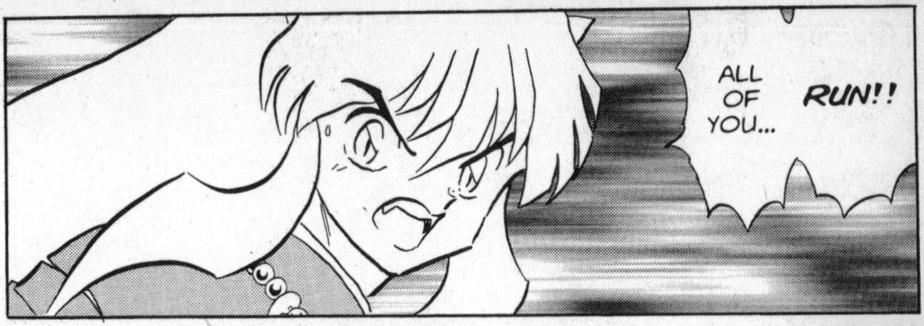
ALL OF YOU...
RUN!!

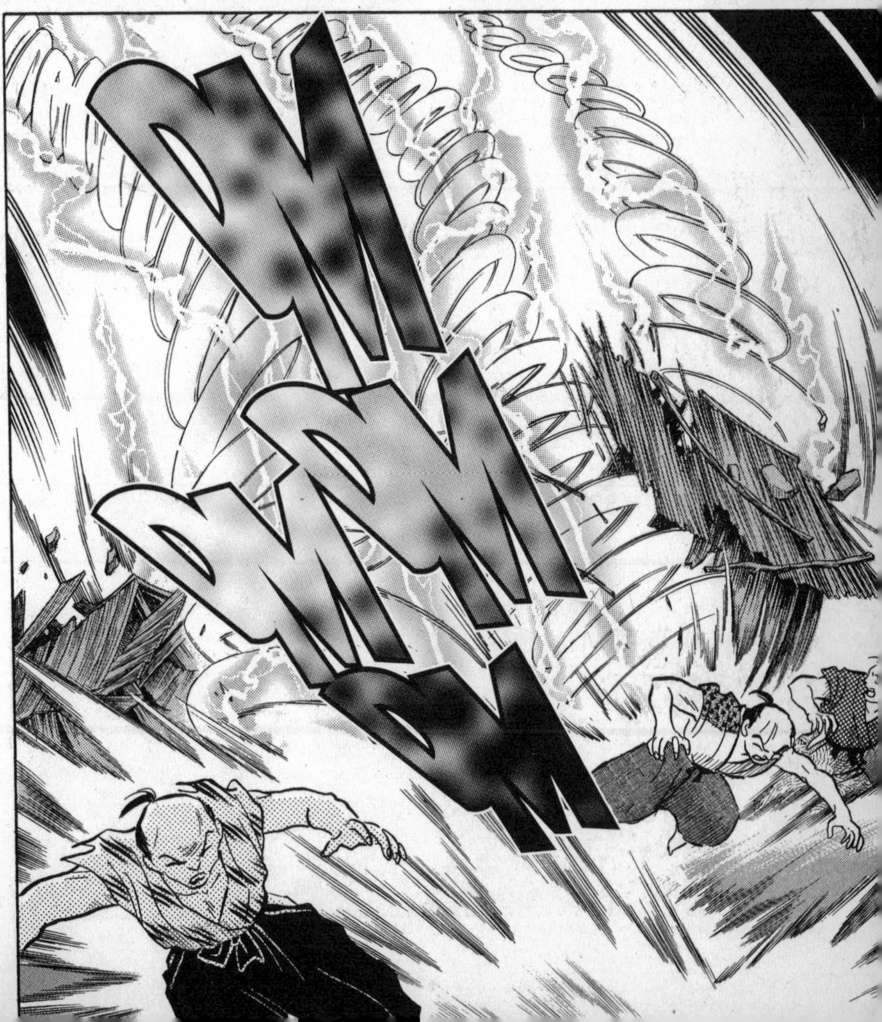

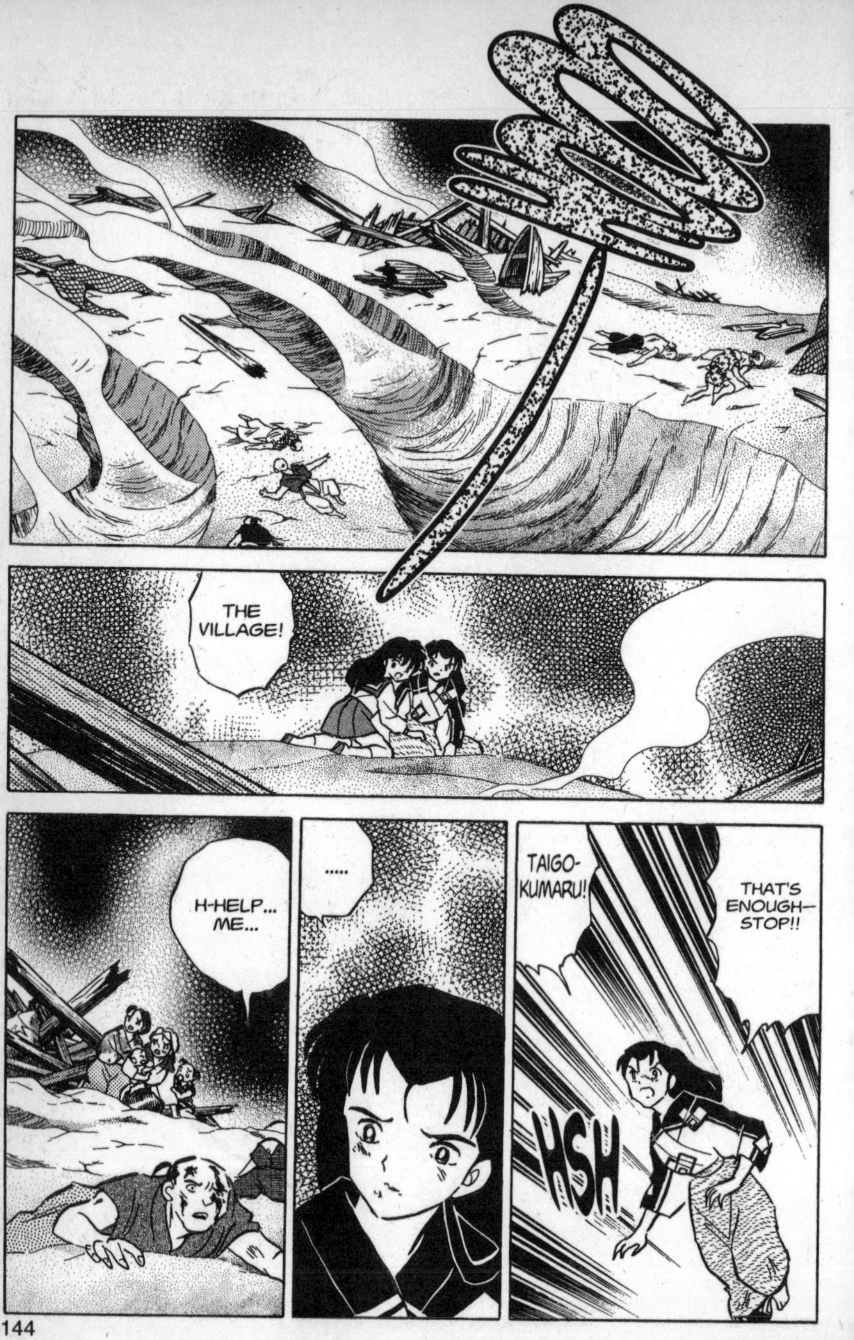
THE VILLAGE!
H-HELP... ME...
.....
TAIGO-KUMARU!
THAT'S ENOUGH—STOP!!
HSH

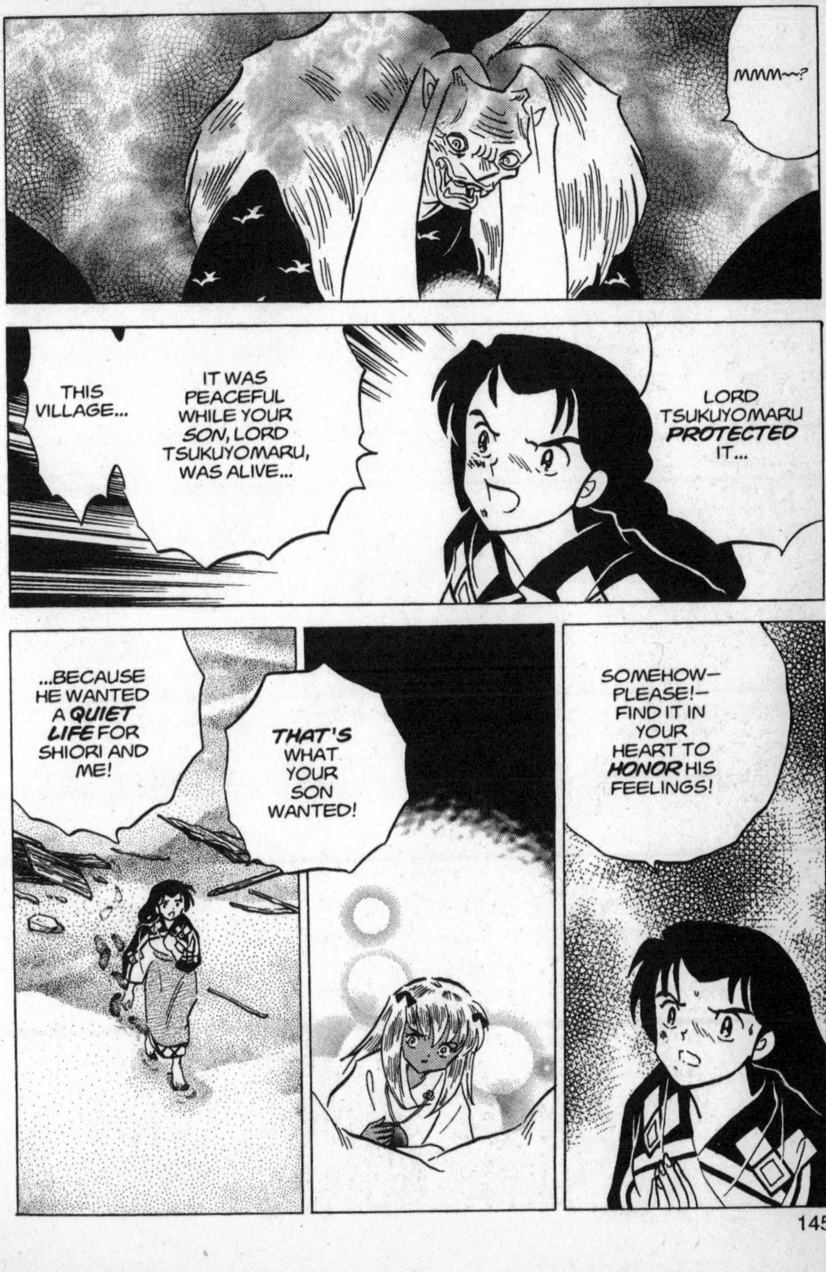
MMM~~?
THIS VILLAGE...
IT WAS PEACEFUL WHILE YOUR *SON*, LORD TSUKUYOMARU, WAS ALIVE...
LORD TSUKUYOMARU ***PROTECTED*** IT...
...BECAUSE HE WANTED A ***QUIET LIFE*** FOR SHIORI AND ME!
THAT'S WHAT YOUR SON WANTED!
SOMEHOW—PLEASE!—FIND IT IN YOUR HEART TO ***HONOR*** HIS FEELINGS!

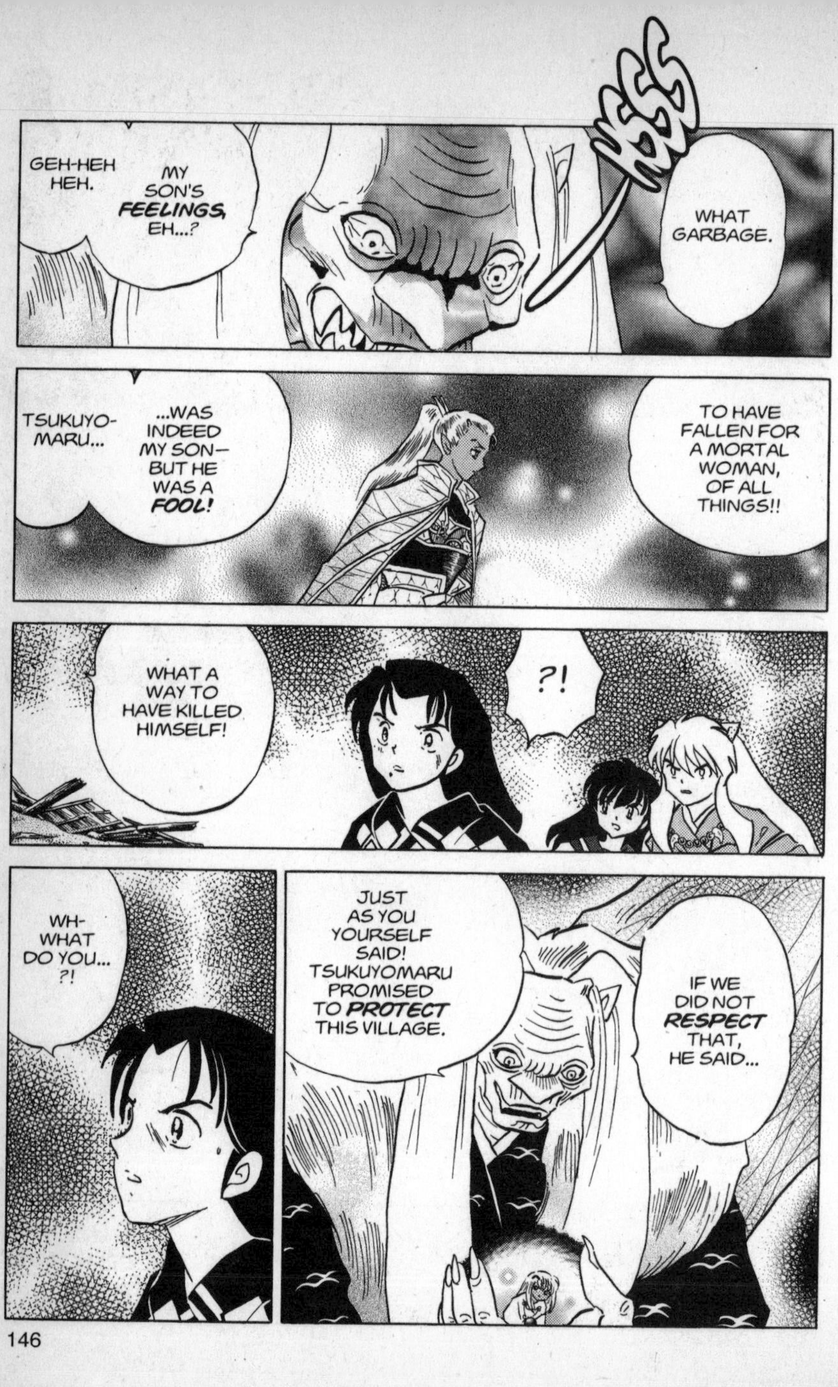
GEH-HEH HEH.
MY SON'S FEELINGS, EH...?
HSSS
WHAT GARBAGE.
TSUKUYOMARU...
...WAS INDEED MY SON—BUT HE WAS A FOOL!
TO HAVE FALLEN FOR A MORTAL WOMAN, OF ALL THINGS!!
WHAT A WAY TO HAVE KILLED HIMSELF!
?!
WH-WHAT DO YOU...?!
JUST AS YOU YOURSELF SAID! TSUKUYOMARU PROMISED TO PROTECT THIS VILLAGE.
IF WE DID NOT RESPECT THAT, HE SAID...

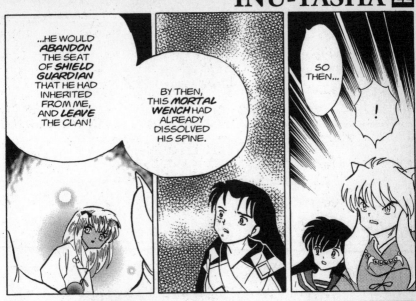

...HE WOULD **ABANDON** THE SEAT OF **SHIELD GUARDIAN** THAT HE HAD INHERITED FROM ME, AND **LEAVE** THE CLAN!

BY THEN, THIS **MORTAL WENCH** HAD ALREADY DISSOLVED HIS SPINE.

SO THEN...

!

"SO THEN" **WHAT?!**

DON'T TELL ME... YOUR OWN SON... YOUR FLESH AND BLOOD...!

GEH-HEH HEH HEH... WHAT **ELSE?**

I MYSELF...

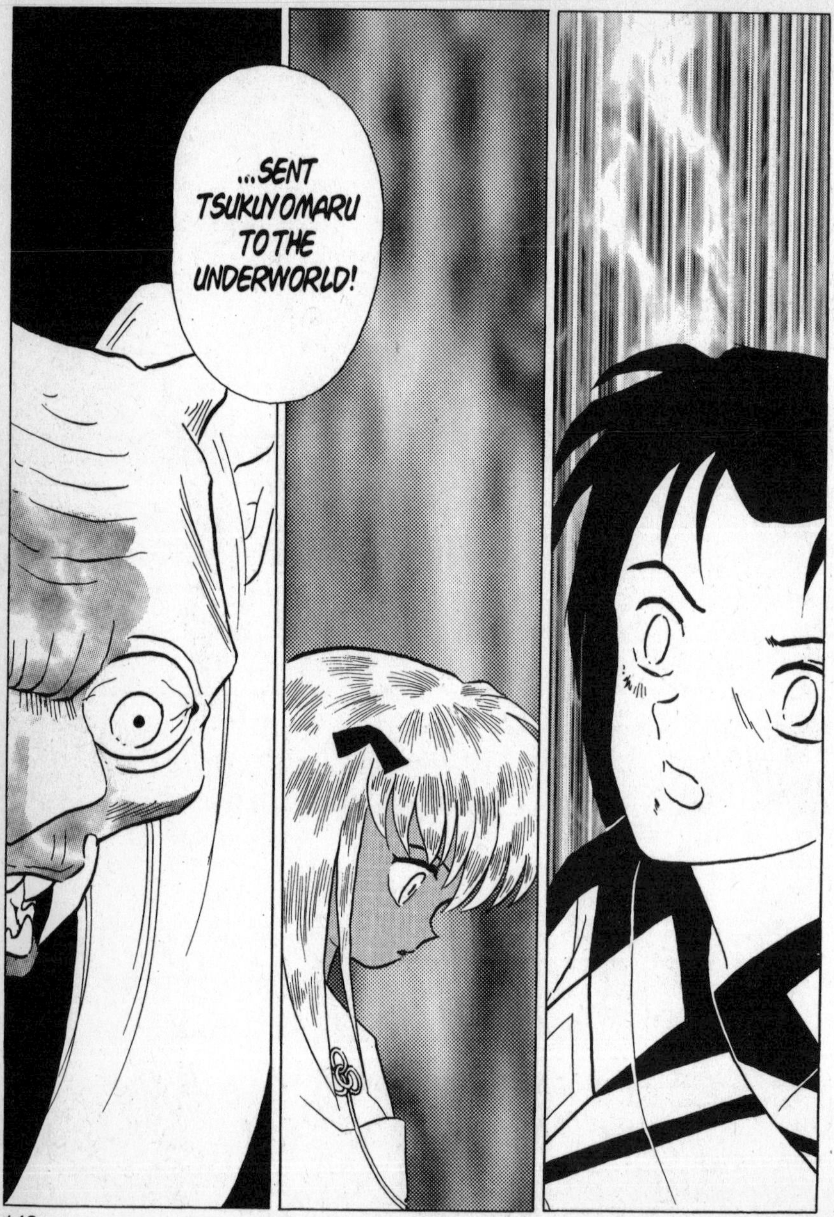
...SENT TSUKUYOMARU TO THE UNDERWORLD!

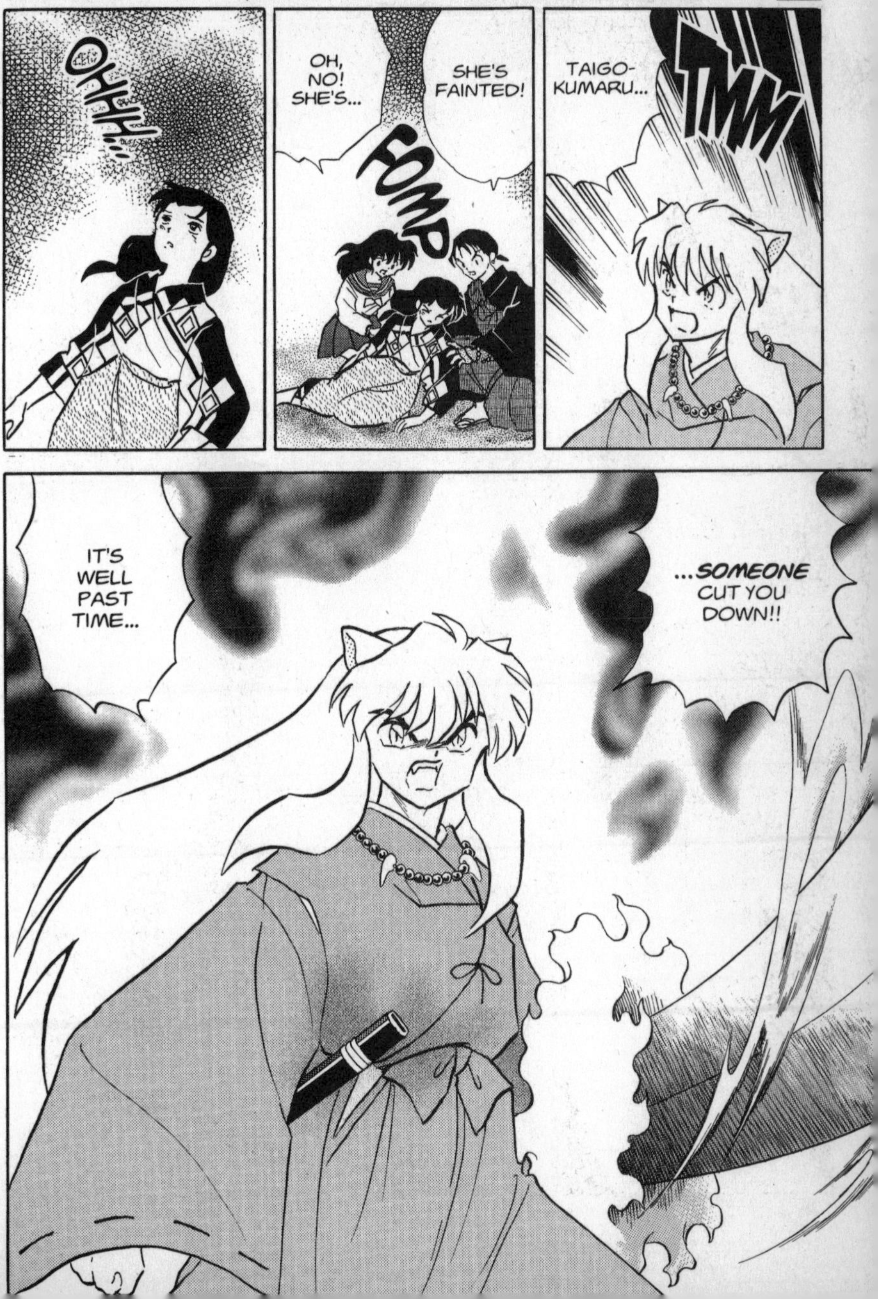
OHHH...
OH, NO! SHE'S...
SHE'S FAINTED!
FOMP
TAIGO-KUMARU...
TMM
IT'S WELL PAST TIME...
...SOMEONE CUT YOU DOWN!!

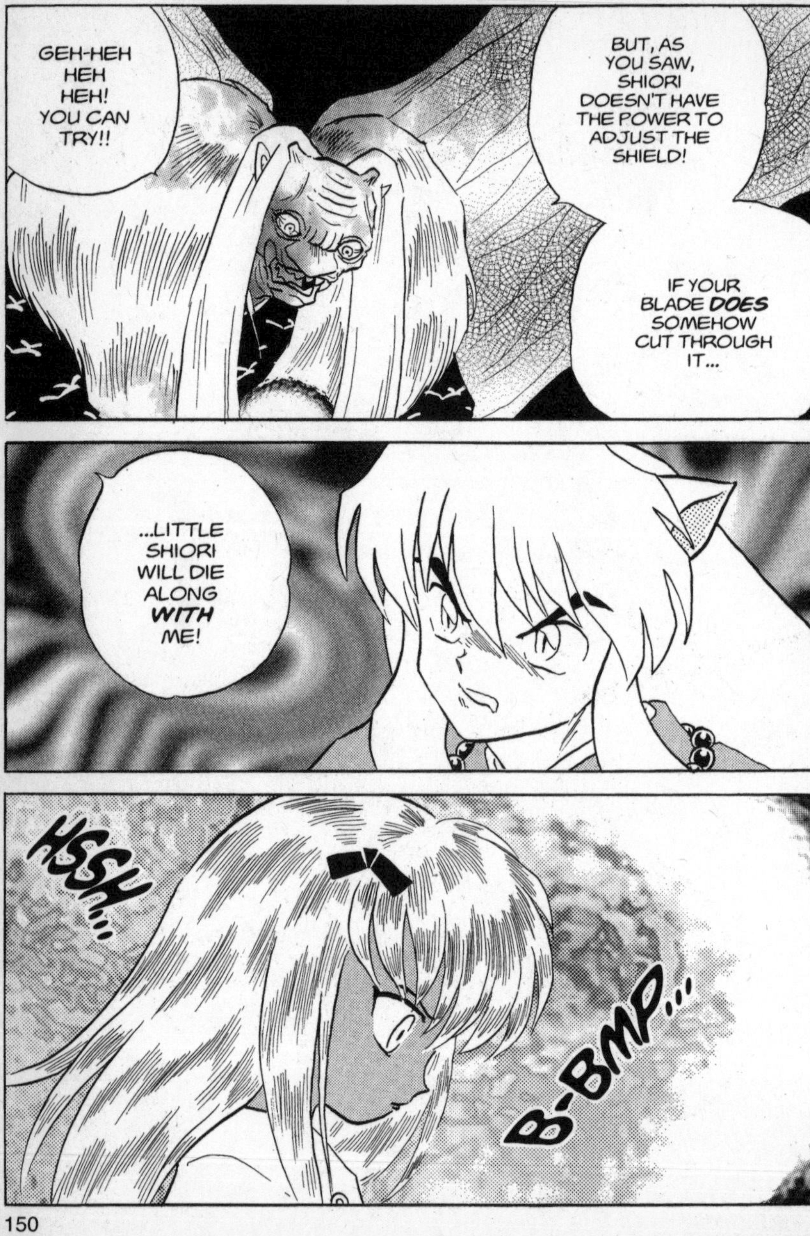
GEH-HEH HEH HEH! YOU CAN TRY!!
BUT, AS YOU SAW, SHIORI DOESN'T HAVE THE POWER TO ADJUST THE SHIELD!
IF YOUR BLADE **DOES** SOMEHOW CUT THROUGH IT...
...LITTLE SHIORI WILL DIE ALONG **WITH** ME!
HSSH...
B-BMP...

SCROLL NINE

SHIORI'S POWER

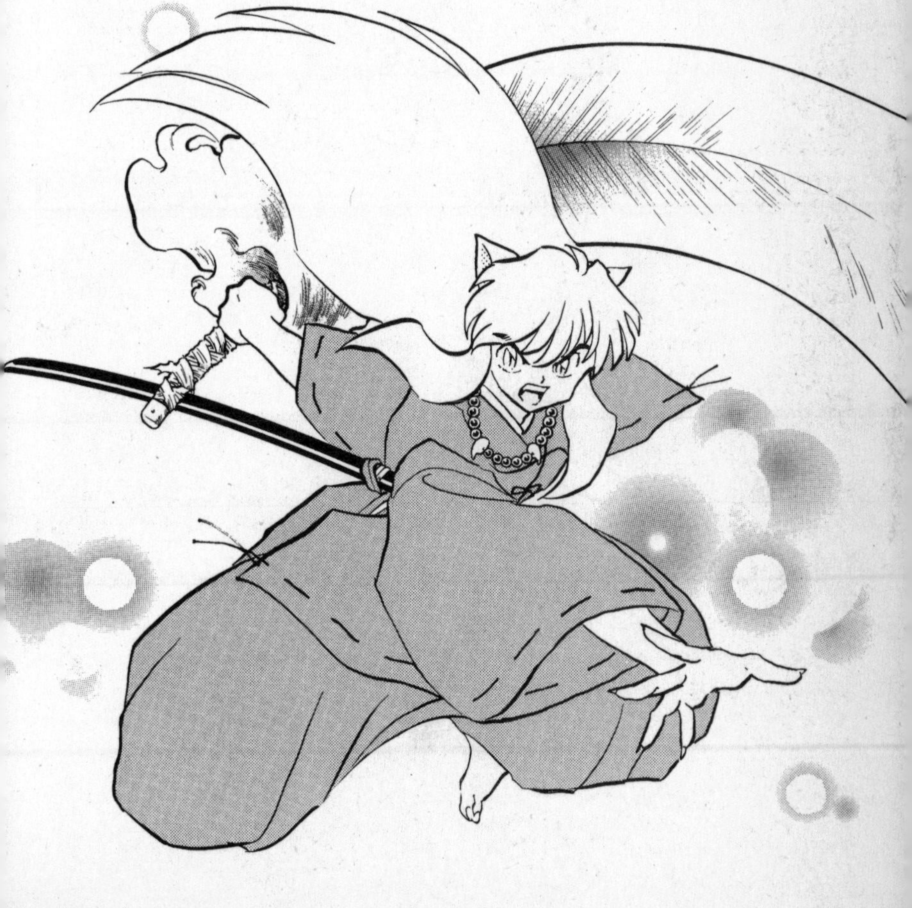

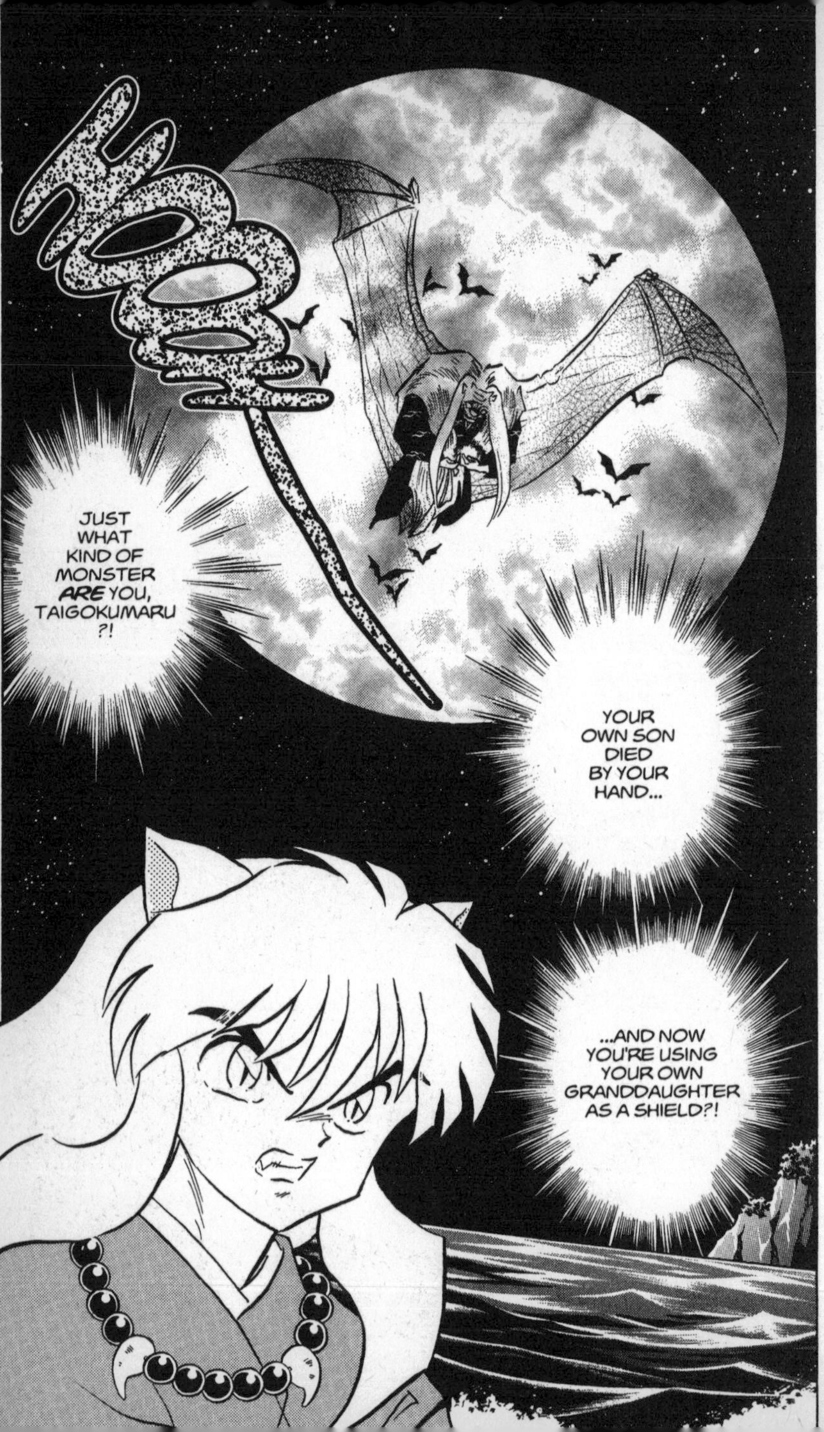

JUST WHAT KIND OF MONSTER ARE YOU, TAIGOKUMARU ?!
YOUR OWN SON DIED BY YOUR HAND...
...AND NOW YOU'RE USING YOUR OWN GRANDDAUGHTER AS A SHIELD?!

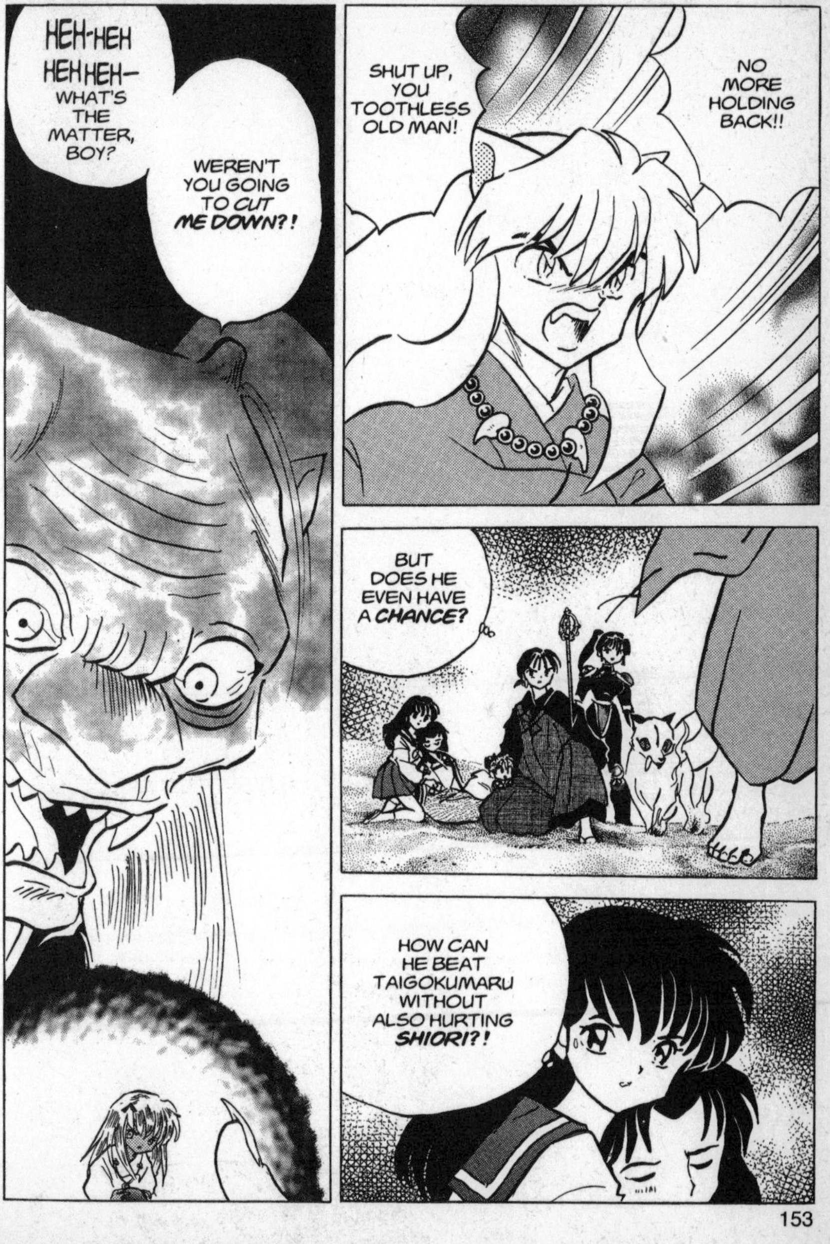
HEH-HEH HEH HEH– WHAT'S THE MATTER, BOY?
WEREN'T YOU GOING TO CUT ME DOWN?!
SHUT UP, YOU TOOTHLESS OLD MAN!
NO MORE HOLDING BACK!!
BUT DOES HE EVEN HAVE A CHANCE?
HOW CAN HE BEAT TAIGOKUMARU WITHOUT ALSO HURTING SHIORI?!

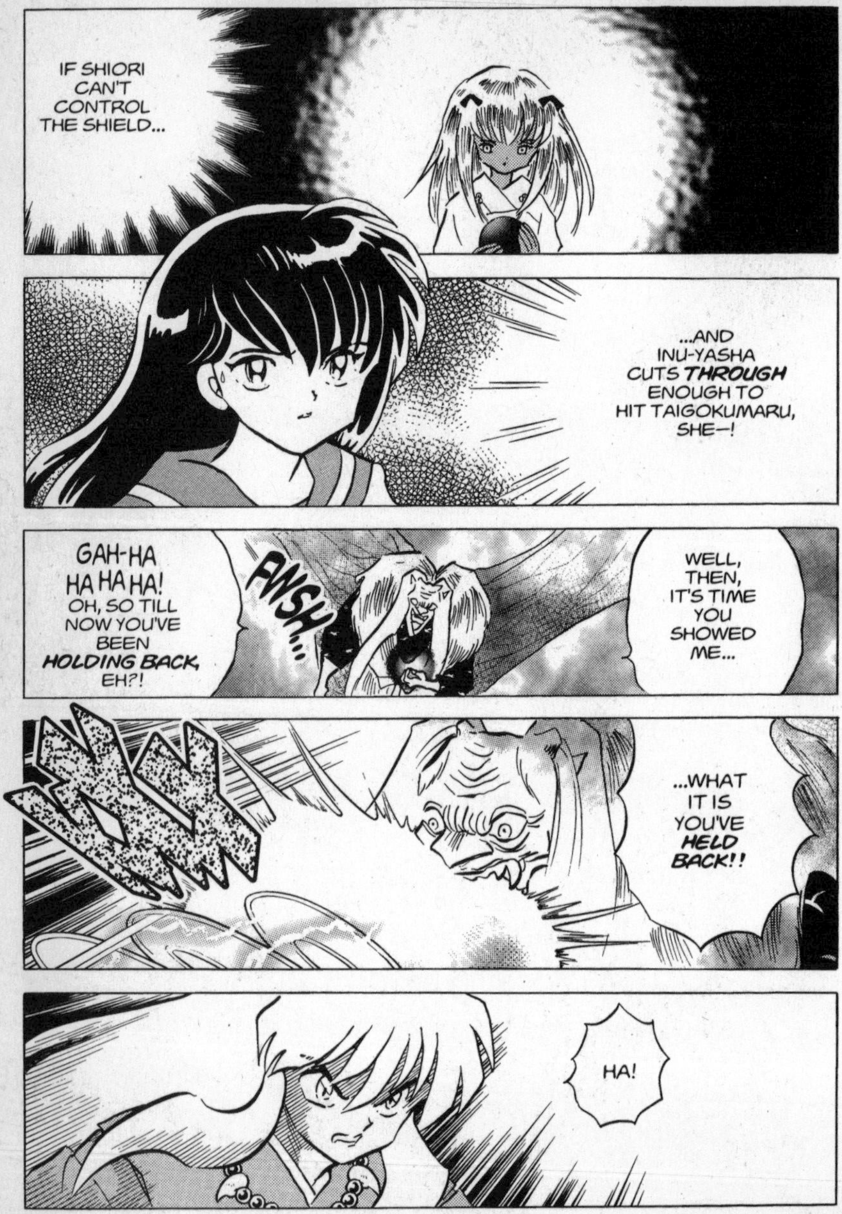

IF SHIORI CAN'T CONTROL THE SHIELD...
...AND INU-YASHA CUTS **THROUGH** ENOUGH TO HIT TAIGOKUMARU, SHE—!
GAH-HA HA HA HA! OH, SO TILL NOW YOU'VE BEEN ***HOLDING BACK,*** EH?!
FWSH...
WELL, THEN, IT'S TIME YOU SHOWED ME...
...WHAT IT IS YOU'VE ***HELD BACK!!***
HA!

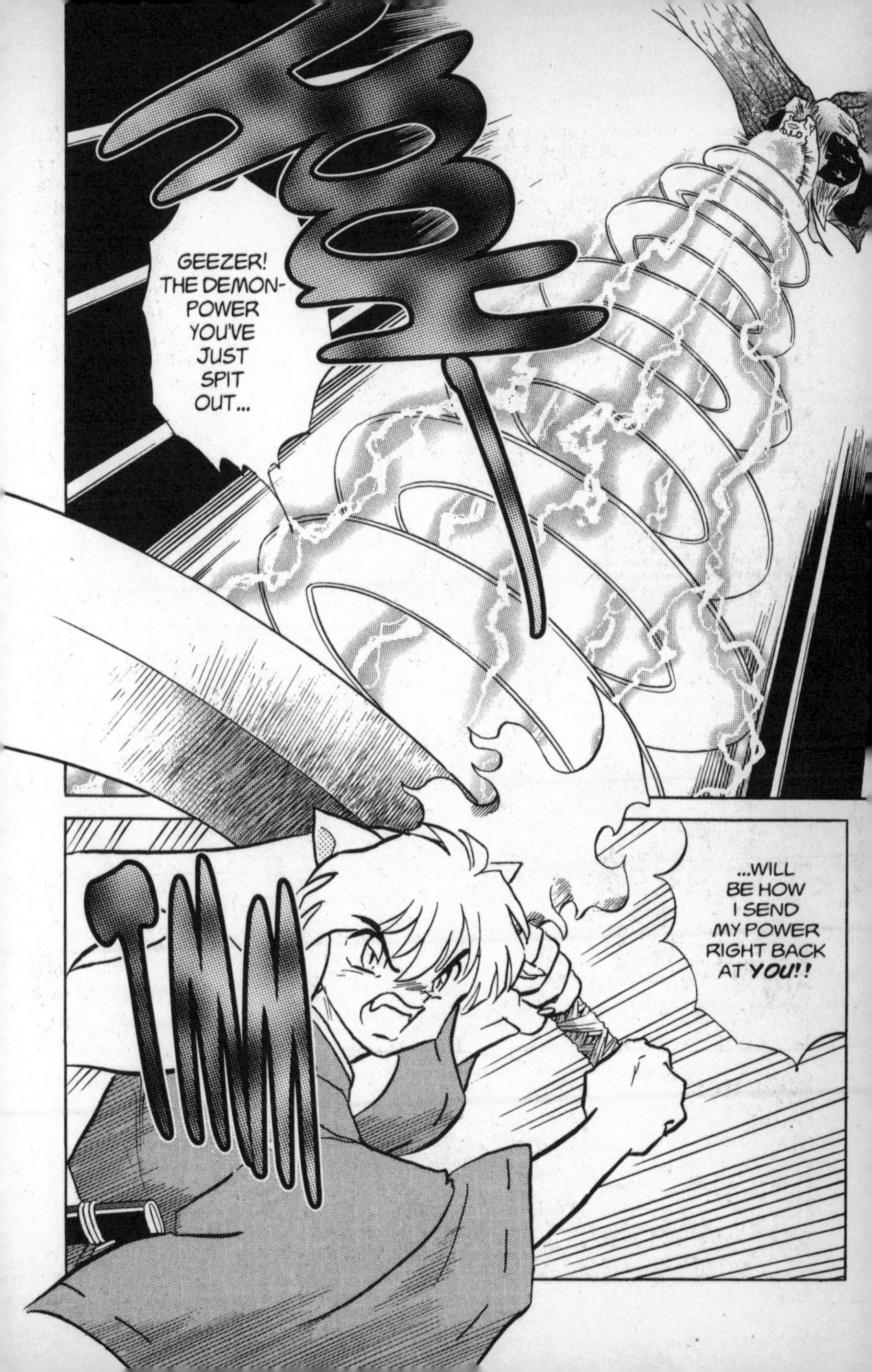
GEEZER! THE DEMON-POWER YOU'VE JUST SPIT OUT...
...WILL BE HOW I SEND MY POWER RIGHT BACK AT **YOU!!**

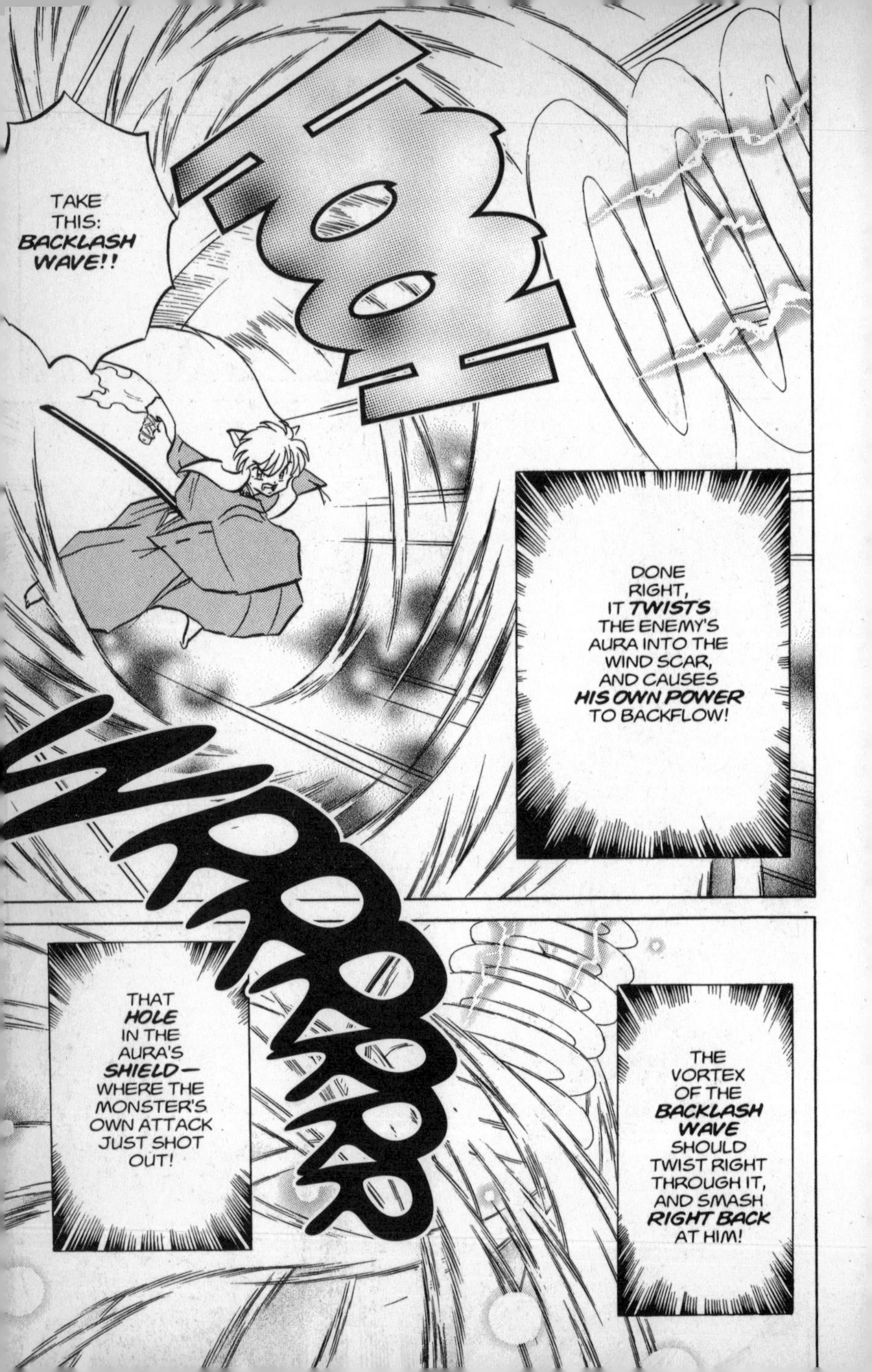
TAKE THIS: BACKLASH WAVE!!
DONE RIGHT, IT TWISTS THE ENEMY'S AURA INTO THE WIND SCAR, AND CAUSES HIS OWN POWER TO BACKFLOW!
THAT HOLE IN THE AURA'S SHIELD— WHERE THE MONSTER'S OWN ATTACK JUST SHOT OUT!
THE VORTEX OF THE BACKLASH WAVE SHOULD TWIST RIGHT THROUGH IT, AND SMASH RIGHT BACK AT HIM!

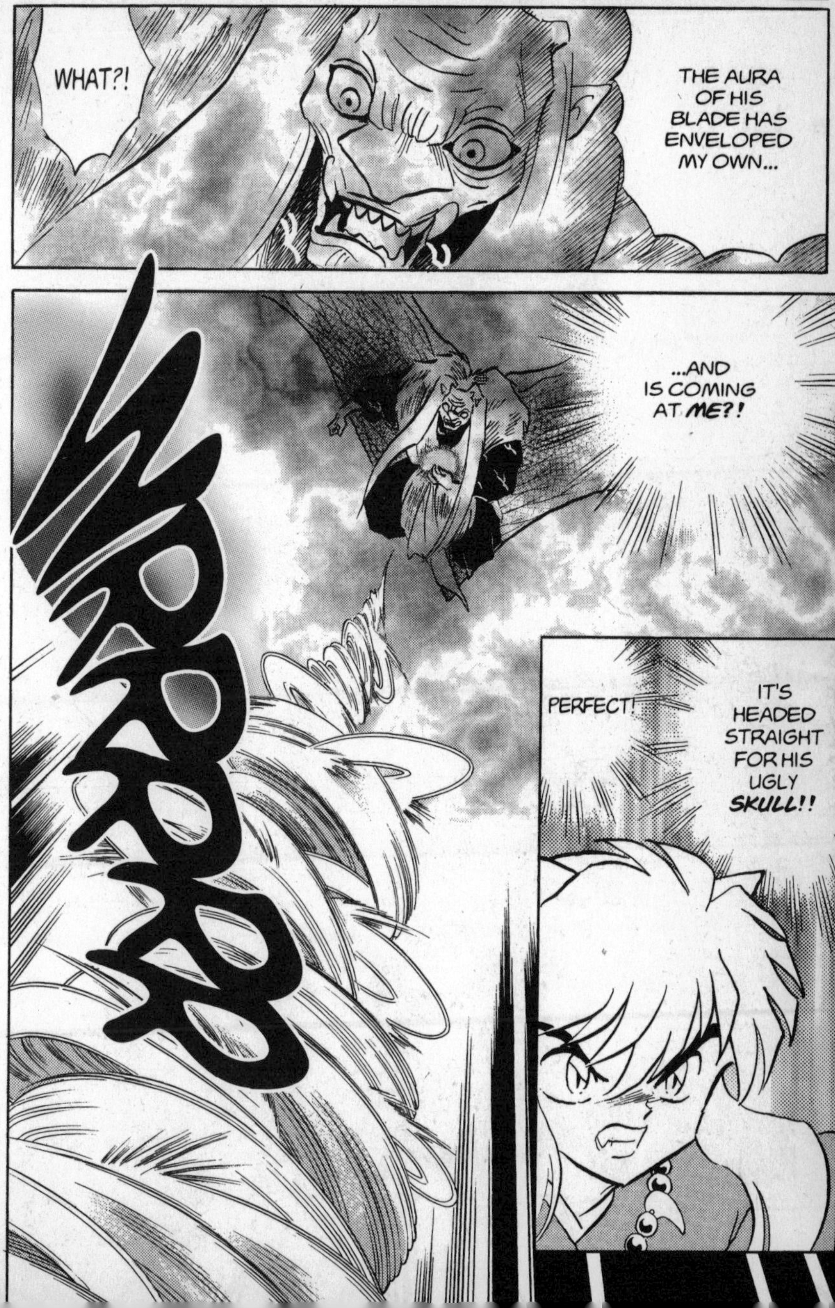
WHAT?!
THE AURA OF HIS BLADE HAS ENVELOPED MY OWN...
...AND IS COMING AT ME?!
PERFECT!
IT'S HEADED STRAIGHT FOR HIS UGLY SKULL!!

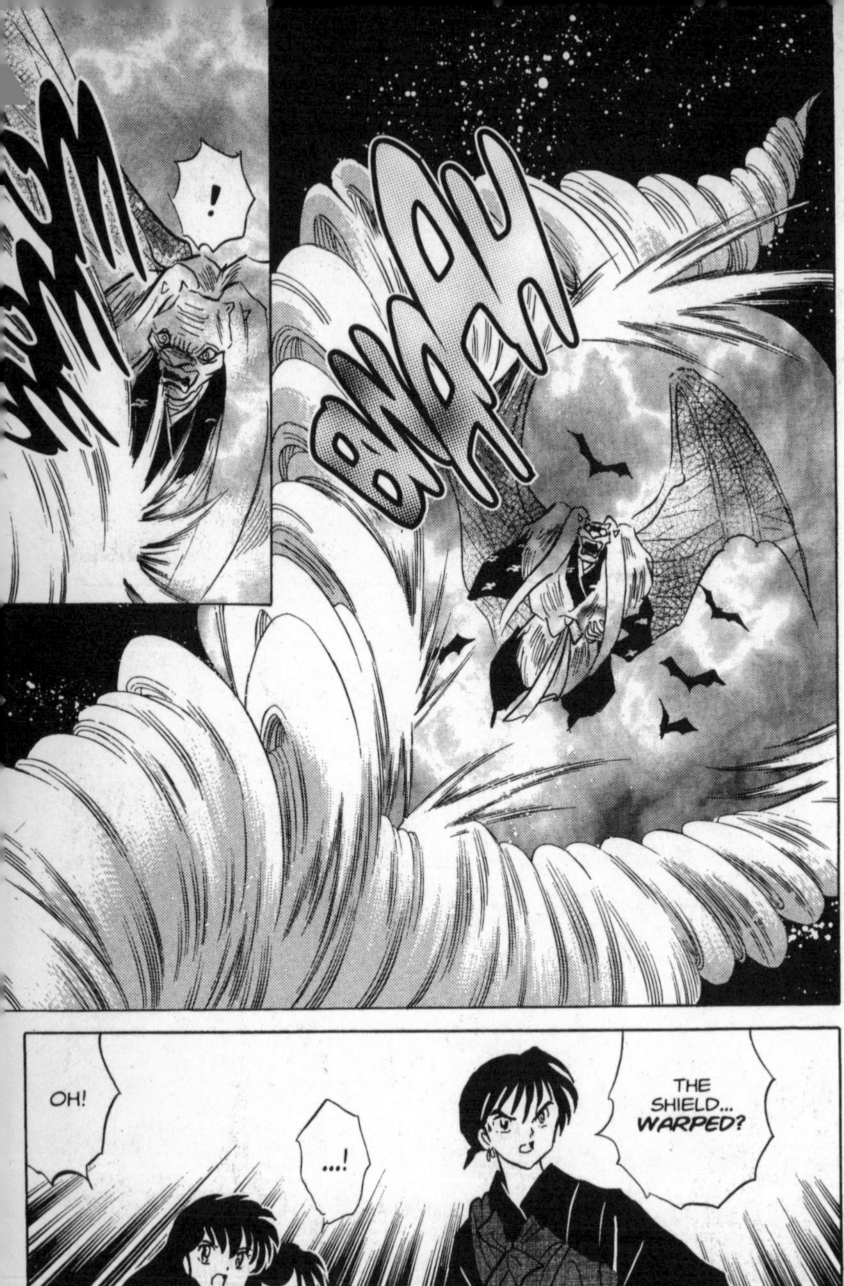
!
OH!
...!
THE SHIELD... **WARPED?**

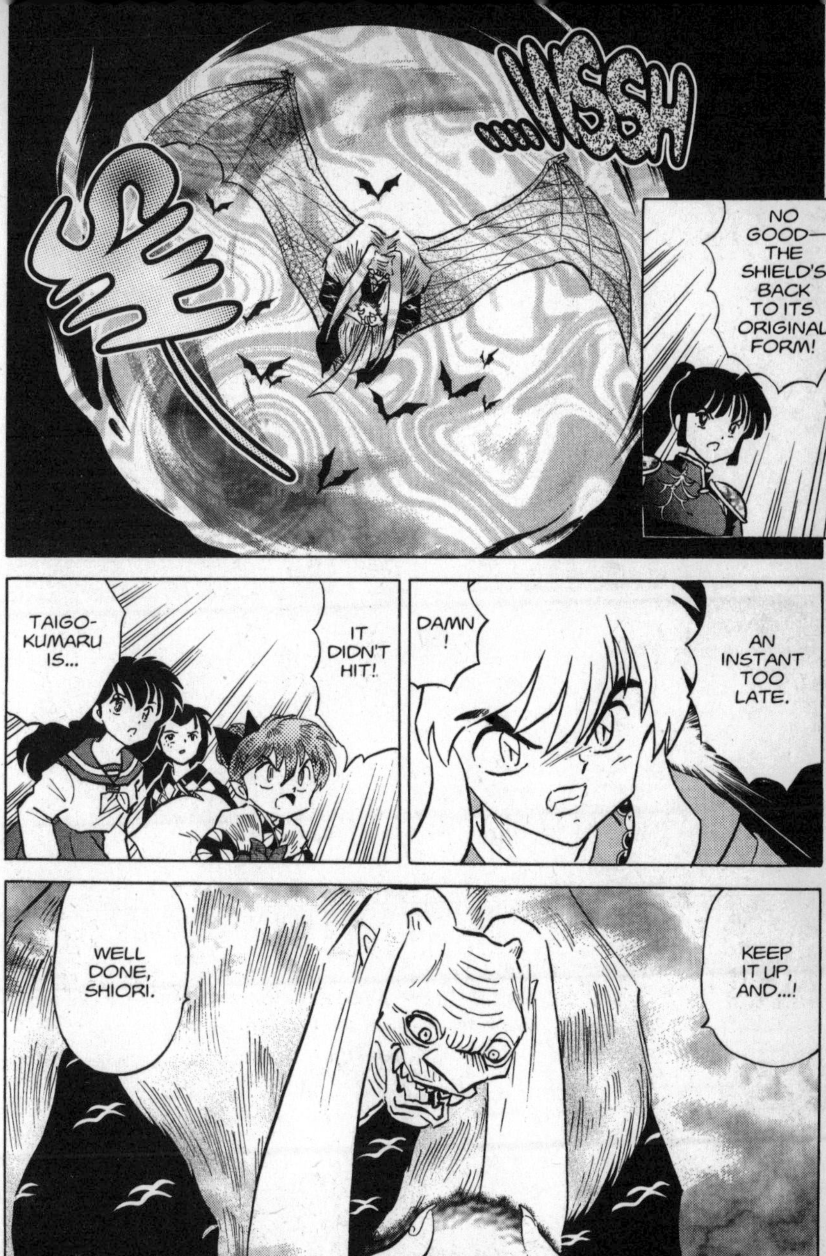
...WSSH
NO GOOD—THE SHIELD'S BACK TO ITS ORIGINAL FORM!
TAIGO-KUMARU IS...
IT DIDN'T HIT!
DAMN!
AN INSTANT TOO LATE.
WELL DONE, SHIORI.
KEEP IT UP, AND...!

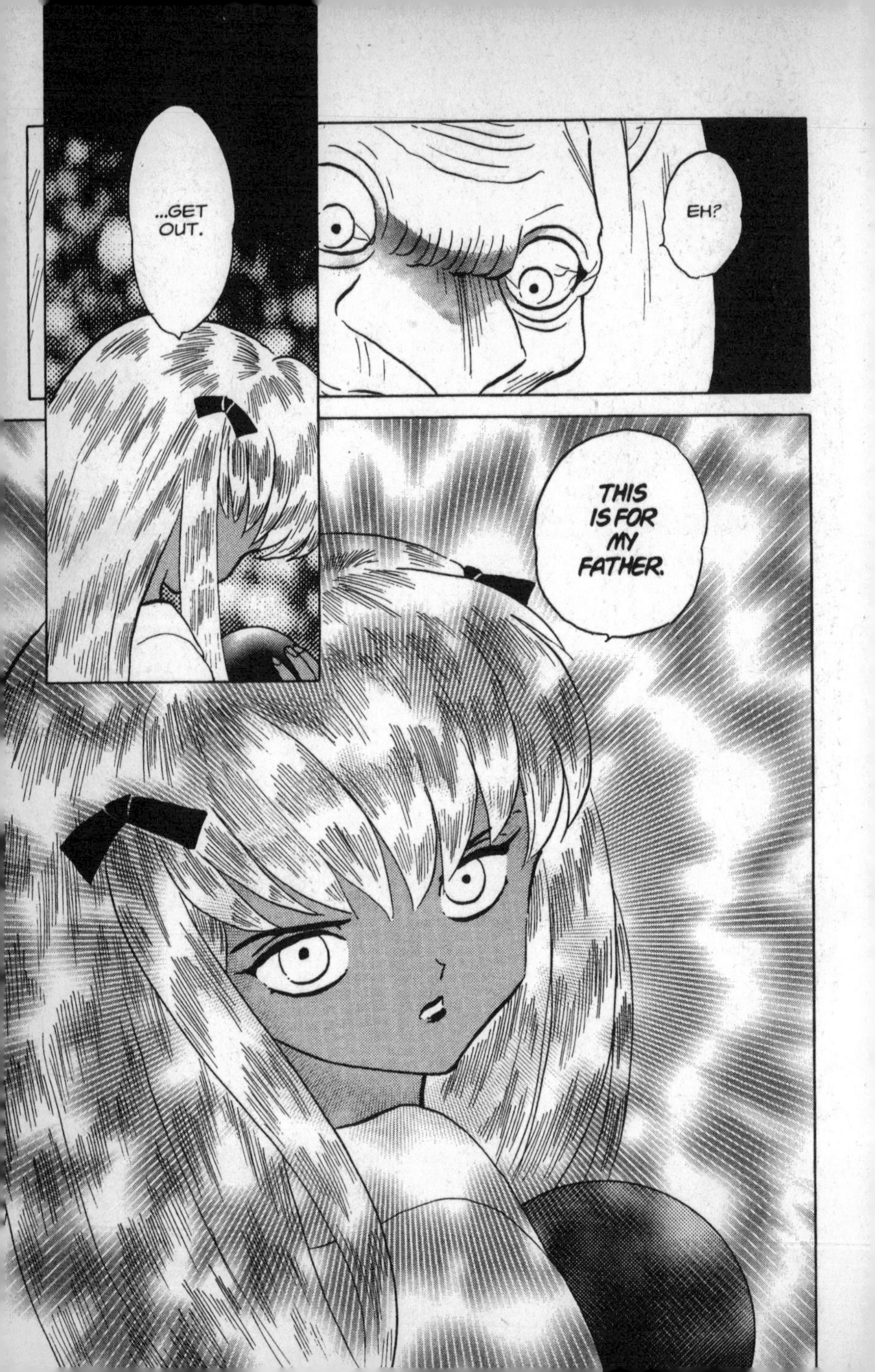
...GET OUT.
EH?
THIS IS FOR MY FATHER.

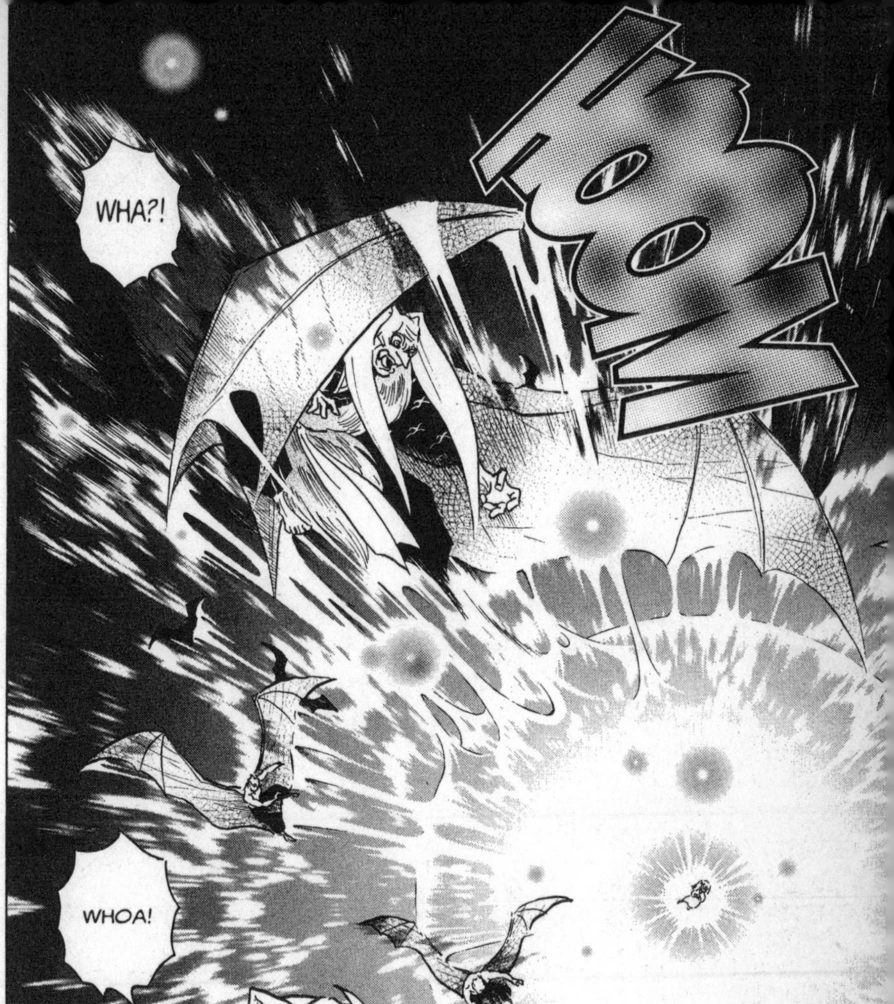
WHA?!
FOOM
WHOA!

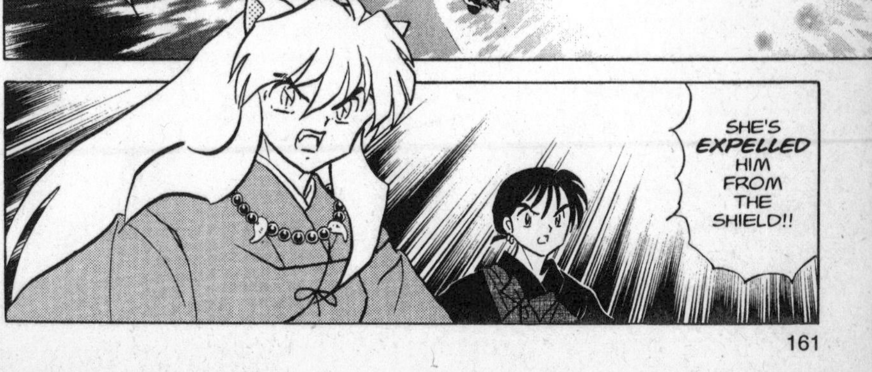
SHE'S EXPELLED HIM FROM THE SHIELD!!

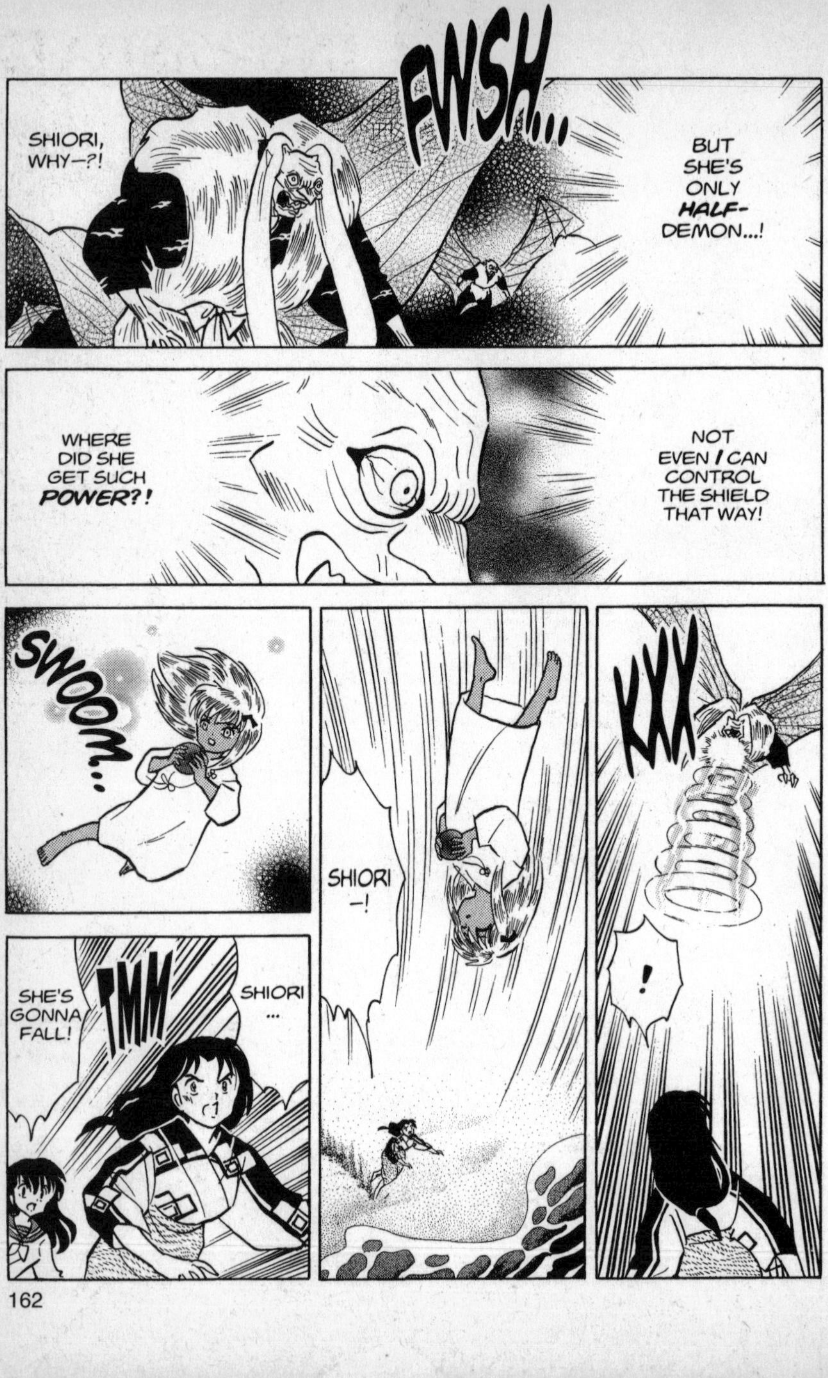
SHIORI, WHY—?!
FWSH...
BUT SHE'S ONLY HALF-DEMON...!
WHERE DID SHE GET SUCH POWER?!
NOT EVEN I CAN CONTROL THE SHIELD THAT WAY!
SWOOM...
SHE'S GONNA FALL!
TMM
SHIORI ...
SHIORI —!
KXX
!

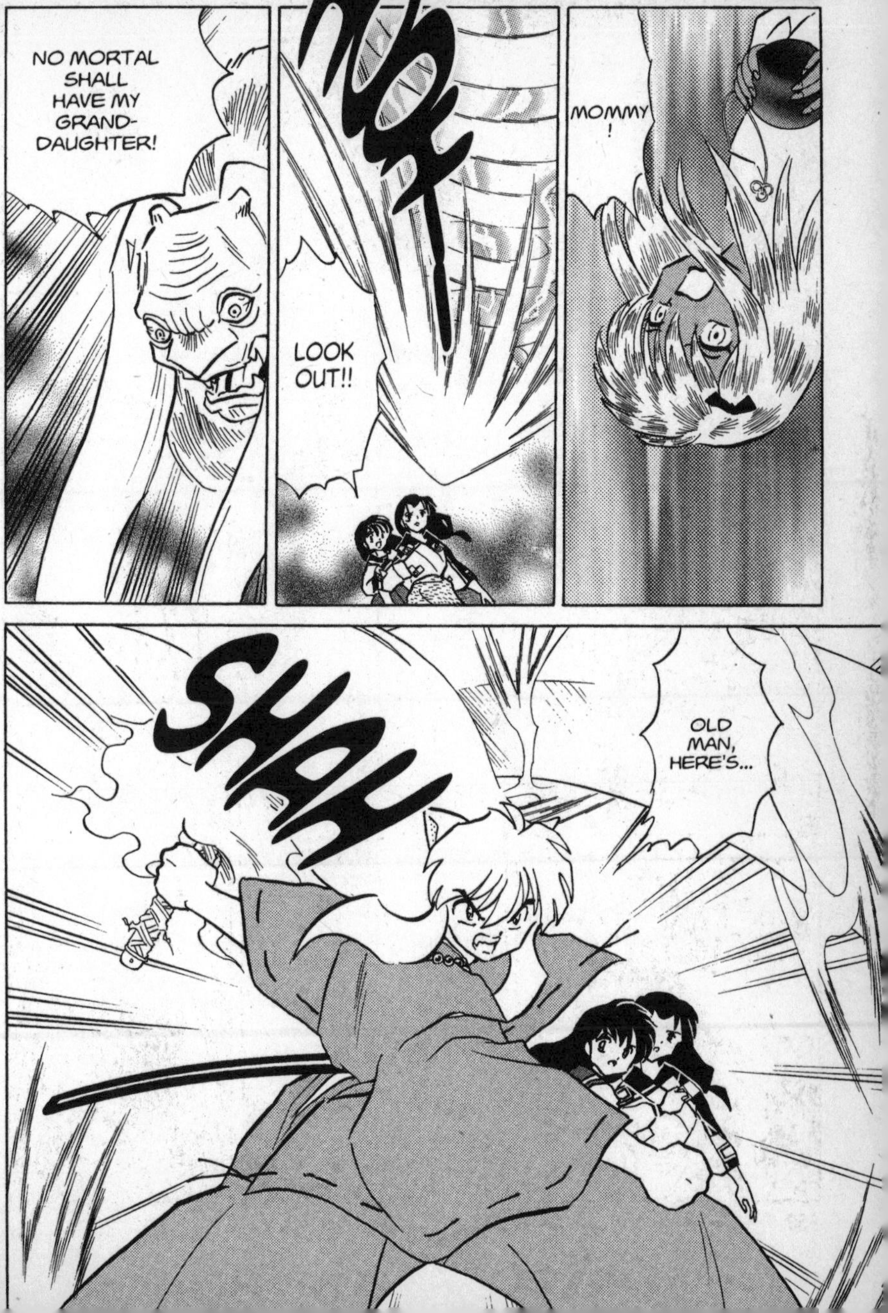
NO MORTAL SHALL HAVE MY GRAND-DAUGHTER!
HOOH
LOOK OUT!!
MOMMY!
SHAH
OLD MAN, HERE'S...

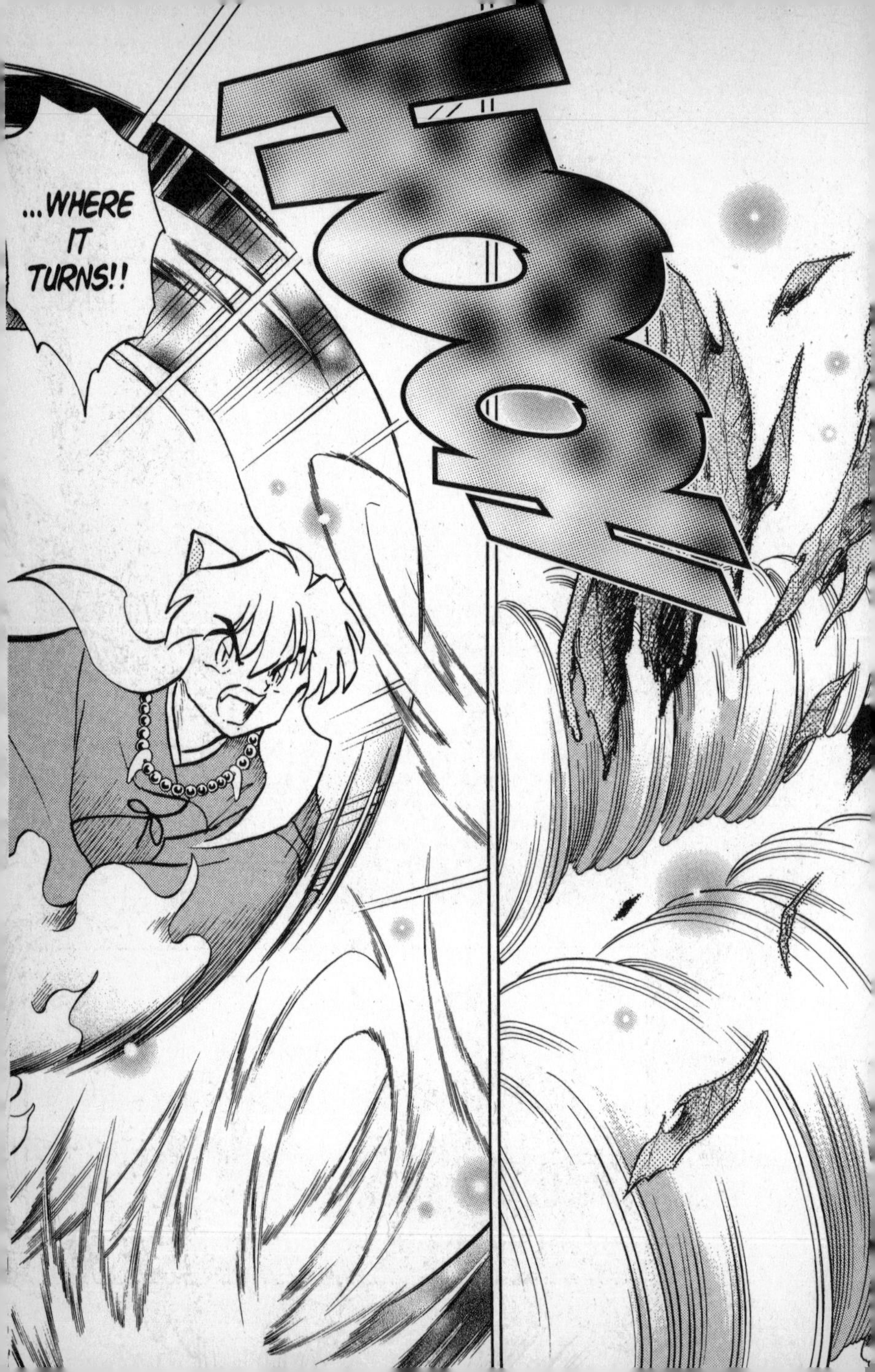
...WHERE IT TURNS!!
WOOM

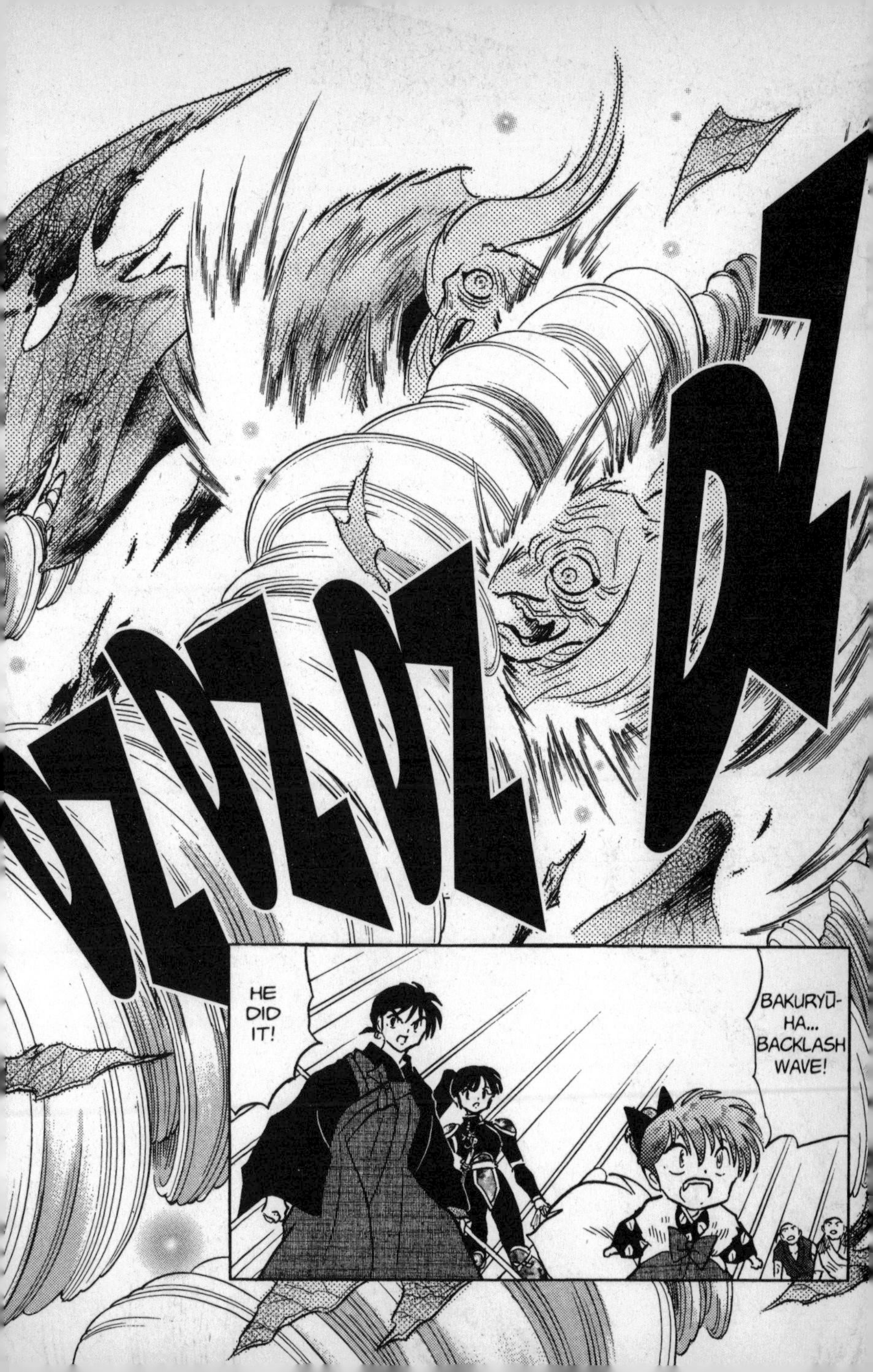
HE DID IT!
BAKURYŪ-HA... BACKLASH WAVE!

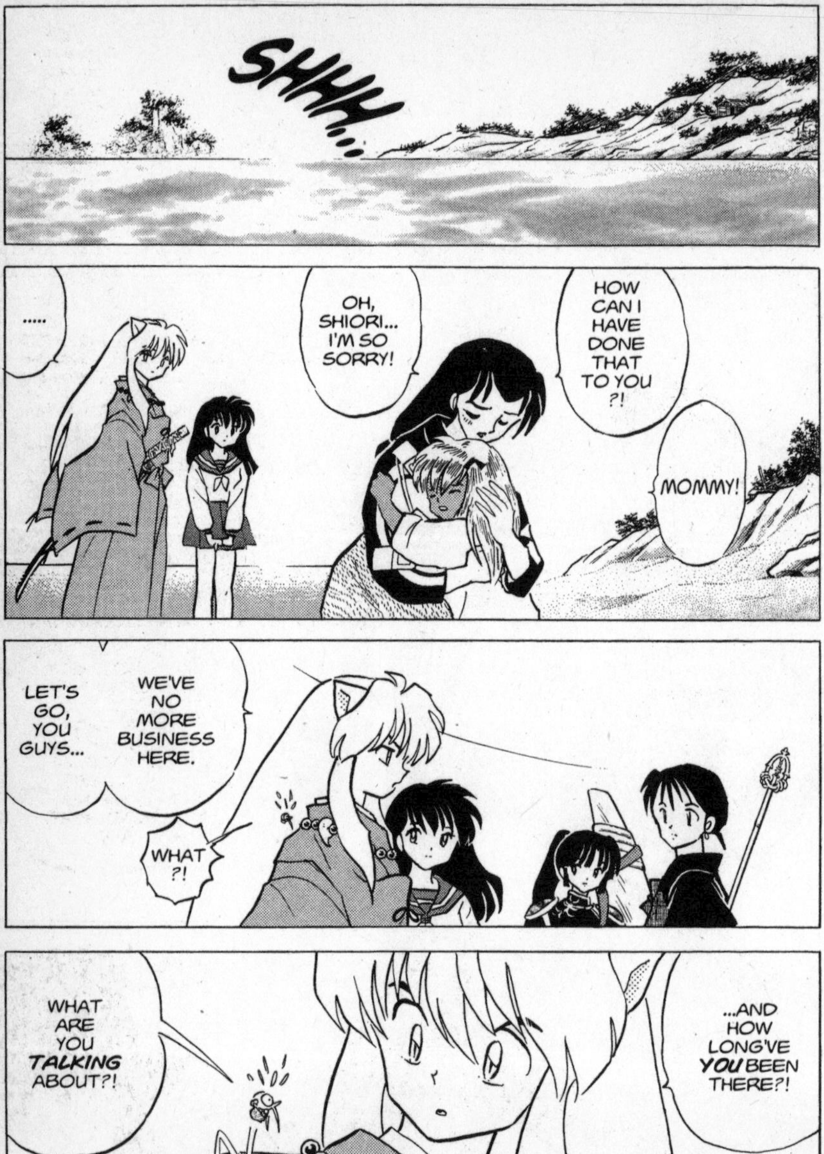
SHHH...
.....
OH, SHIORI... I'M SO SORRY!
HOW CAN I HAVE DONE THAT TO YOU ?!
MOMMY!
LET'S GO, YOU GUYS...
WE'VE NO MORE BUSINESS HERE.
WHAT ?!
WHAT ARE YOU TALKING ABOUT?!
...AND HOW LONG'VE YOU BEEN THERE?!

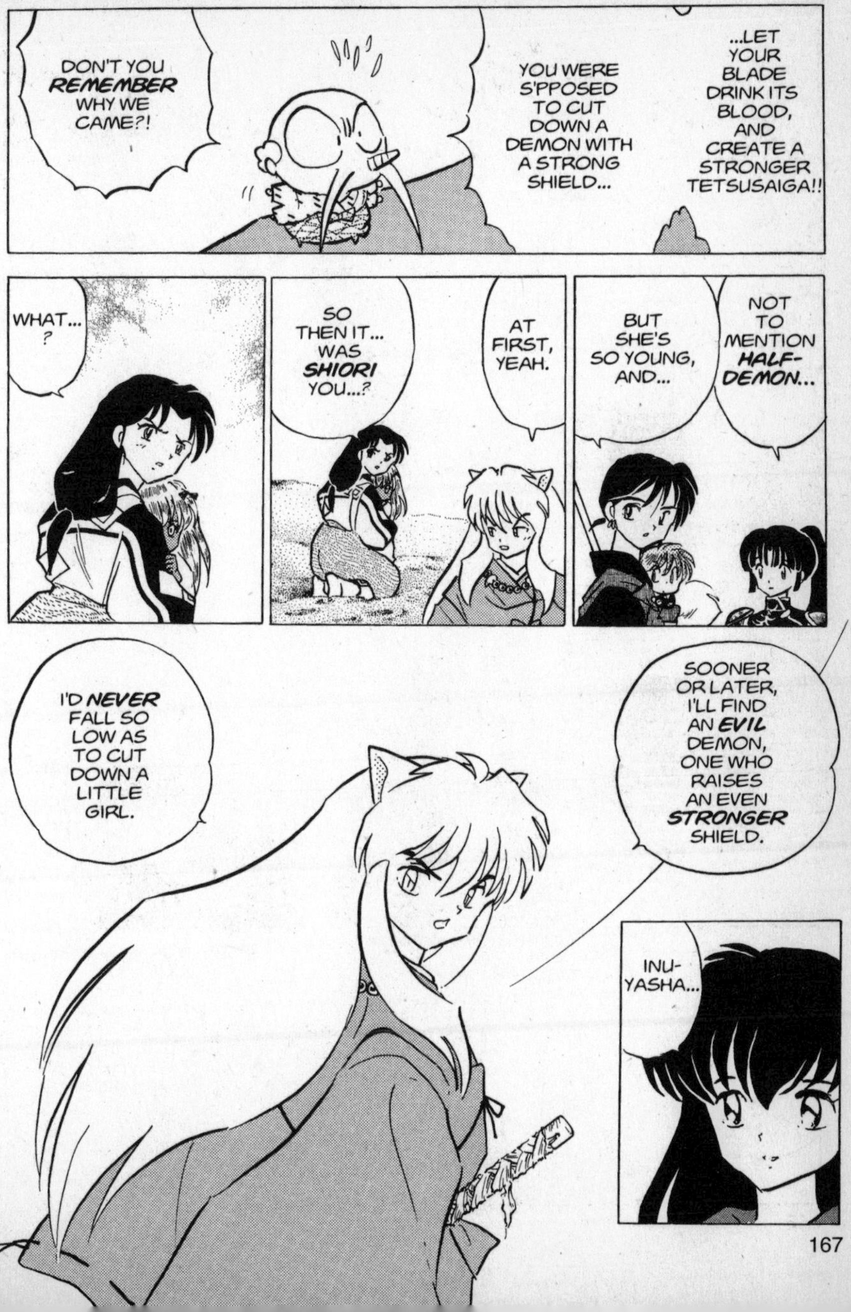
DON'T YOU *REMEMBER* WHY WE CAME?!
YOU WERE S'PPOSED TO CUT DOWN A DEMON WITH A STRONG SHIELD...
...LET YOUR BLADE DRINK ITS BLOOD, AND CREATE A STRONGER TETSUSAIGA!!
WHAT... ?
SO THEN IT... WAS *SHIORI* YOU...?
AT FIRST, YEAH.
BUT SHE'S SO YOUNG, AND...
NOT TO MENTION *HALF-DEMON*...
I'D *NEVER* FALL SO LOW AS TO CUT DOWN A LITTLE GIRL.
SOONER OR LATER, I'LL FIND AN *EVIL* DEMON, ONE WHO RAISES AN EVEN *STRONGER* SHIELD.
INU-YASHA...

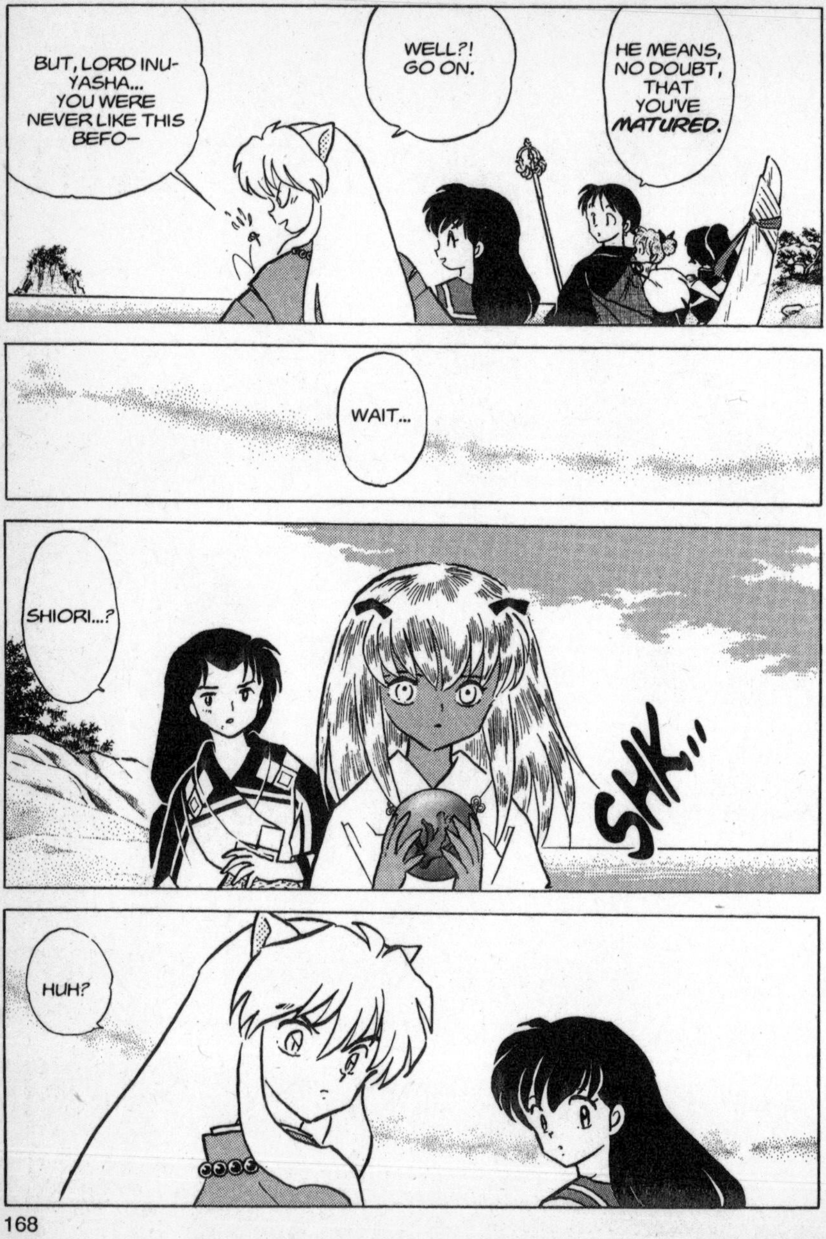
BUT, LORD INU-YASHA... YOU WERE NEVER LIKE THIS BEFO—
WELL?! GO ON.
HE MEANS, NO DOUBT, THAT YOU'VE MATURED.
WAIT...
SHIORI...?
SHK...
HUH?

SCROLL TEN

THE SCARLET BLADE

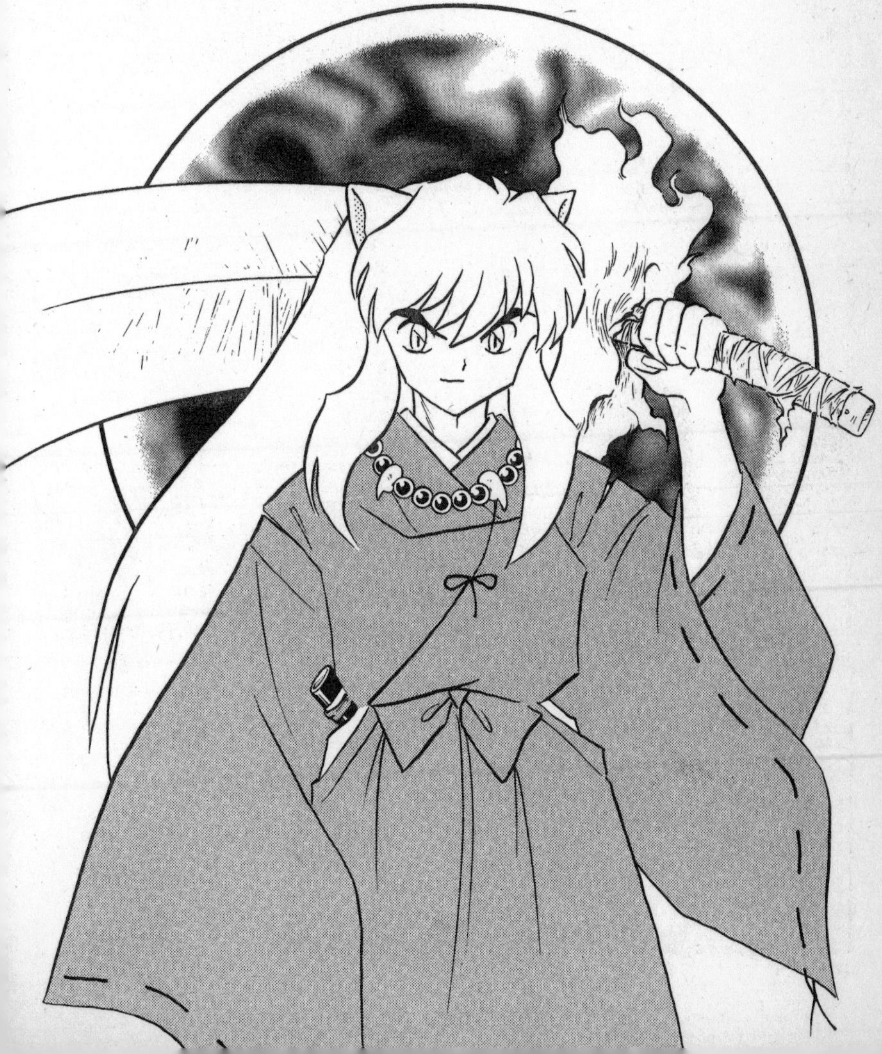

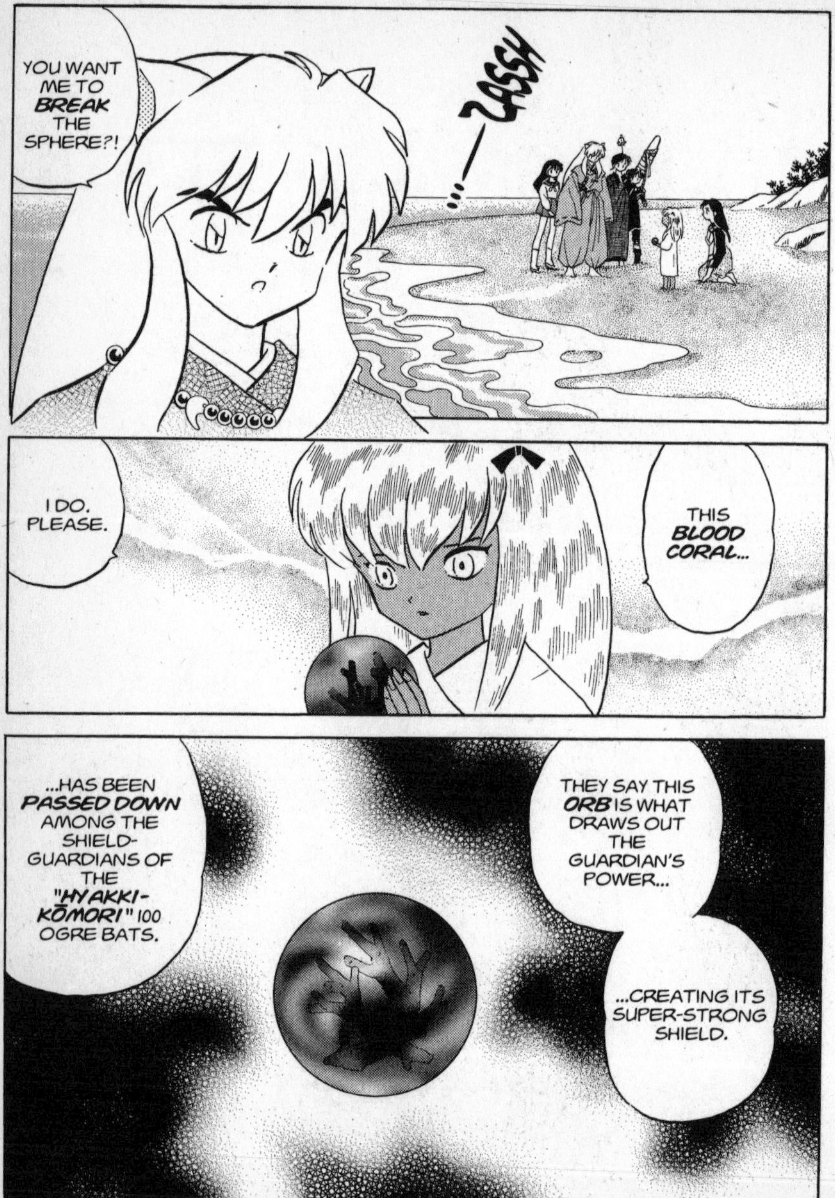
YOU WANT ME TO BREAK THE SPHERE?!
ZASSH
!!
I DO. PLEASE.
THIS BLOOD CORAL...
...HAS BEEN PASSED DOWN AMONG THE SHIELD-GUARDIANS OF THE "HYAKKI-KŌMORI" 100 OGRE BATS.
THEY SAY THIS ORB IS WHAT DRAWS OUT THE GUARDIAN'S POWER...
...CREATING ITS SUPER-STRONG SHIELD.

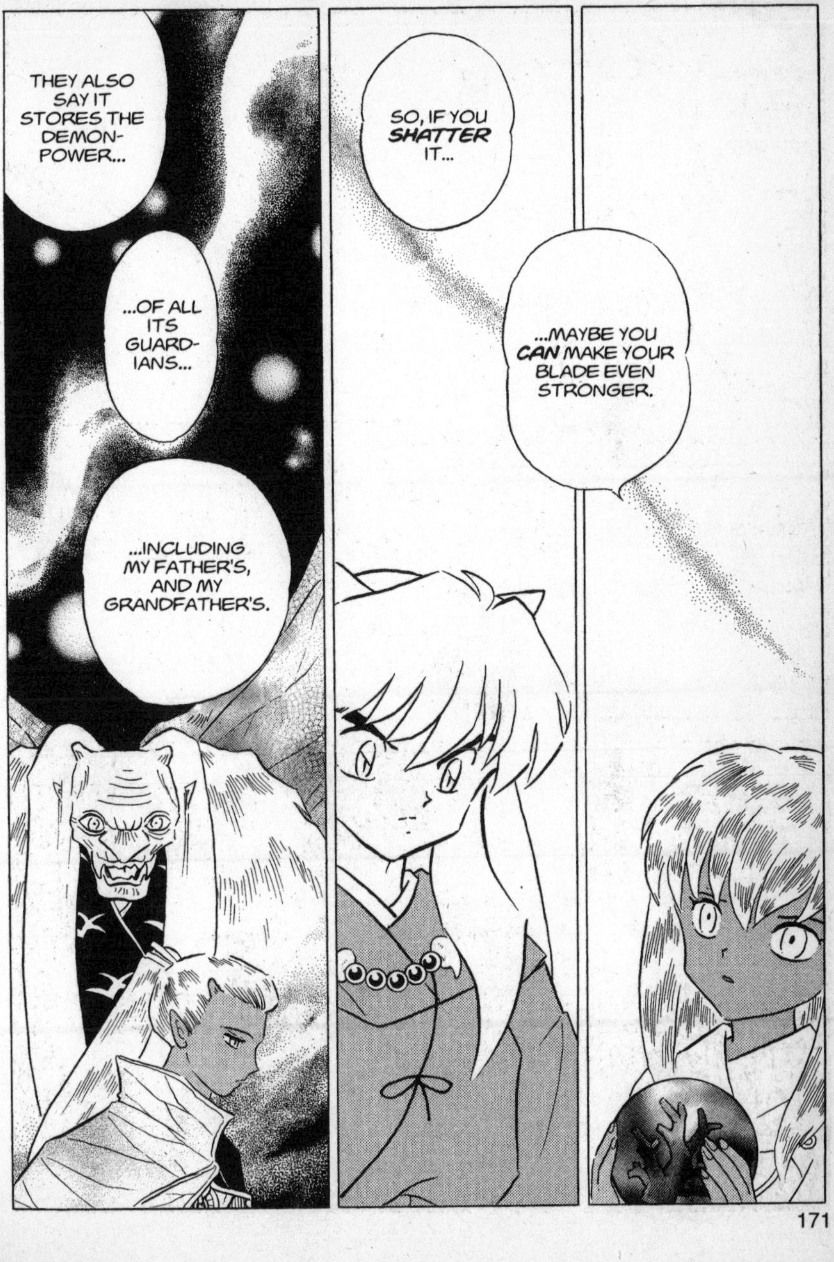
THEY ALSO SAY IT STORES THE DEMON-POWER...
...OF ALL ITS GUARD-IANS...
...INCLUDING MY FATHER'S, AND MY GRANDFATHER'S.
SO, IF YOU SHATTER IT...
...MAYBE YOU CAN MAKE YOUR BLADE EVEN STRONGER.

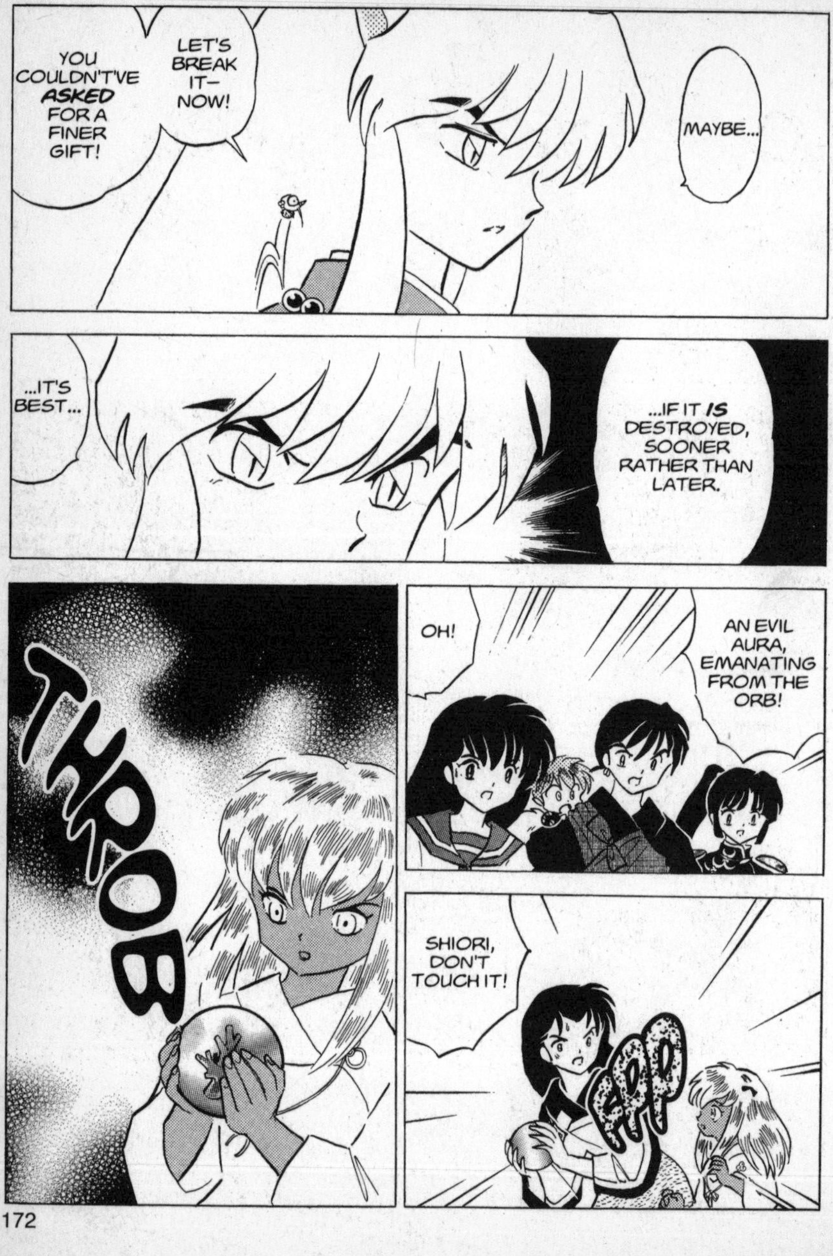

YOU COULDN'T'VE ASKED FOR A FINER GIFT!
LET'S BREAK IT— NOW!
MAYBE...
...IT'S BEST...
...IF IT IS DESTROYED, SOONER RATHER THAN LATER.
THROB
OH!
AN EVIL AURA, EMANATING FROM THE ORB!
SHIORI, DON'T TOUCH IT!
FOP

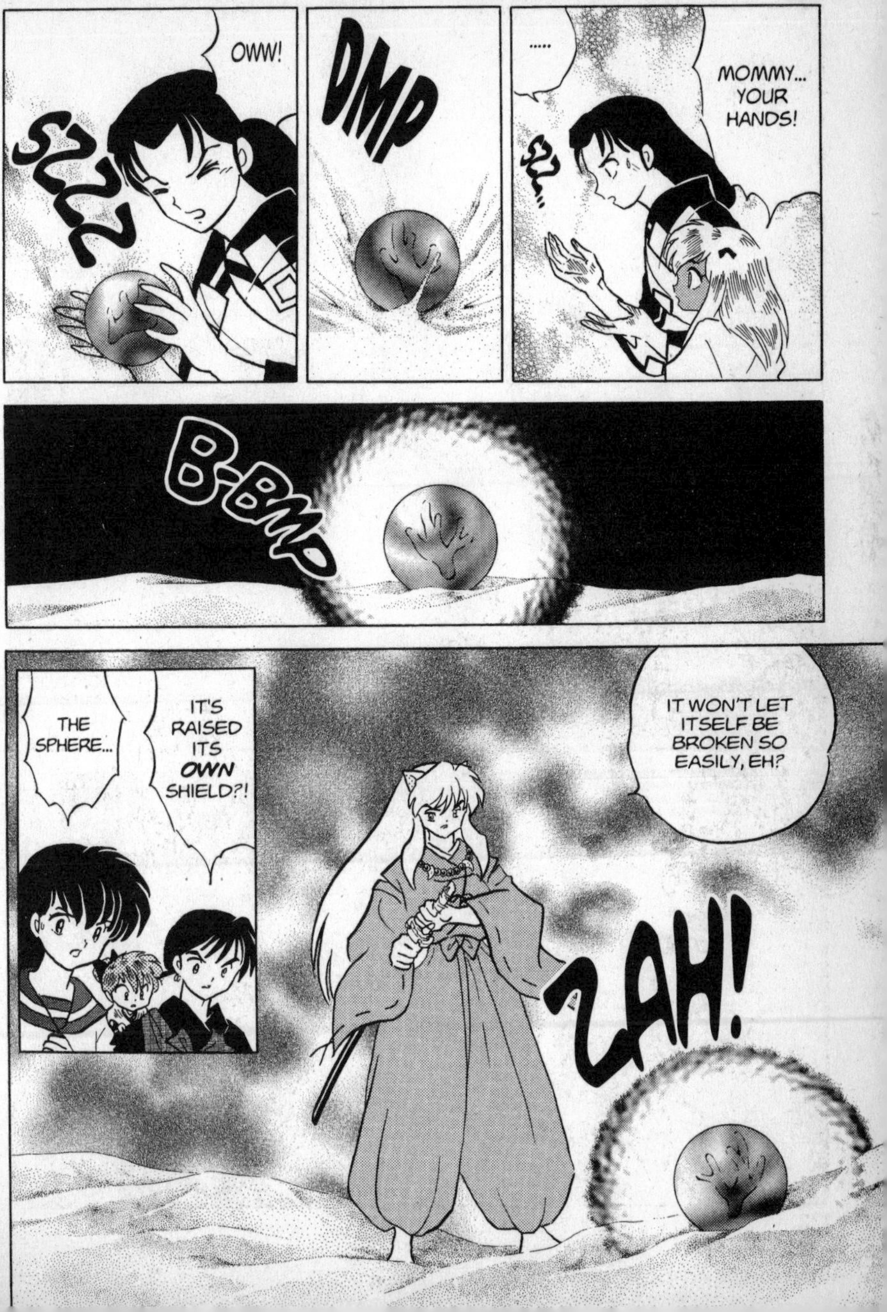
OWW!
SZZZ
DMP
.....
SZZ...
MOMMY... YOUR HANDS!
B-BMP
THE SPHERE...
IT'S RAISED ITS OWN SHIELD?!
IT WON'T LET ITSELF BE BROKEN SO EASILY, EH?
ZAH!

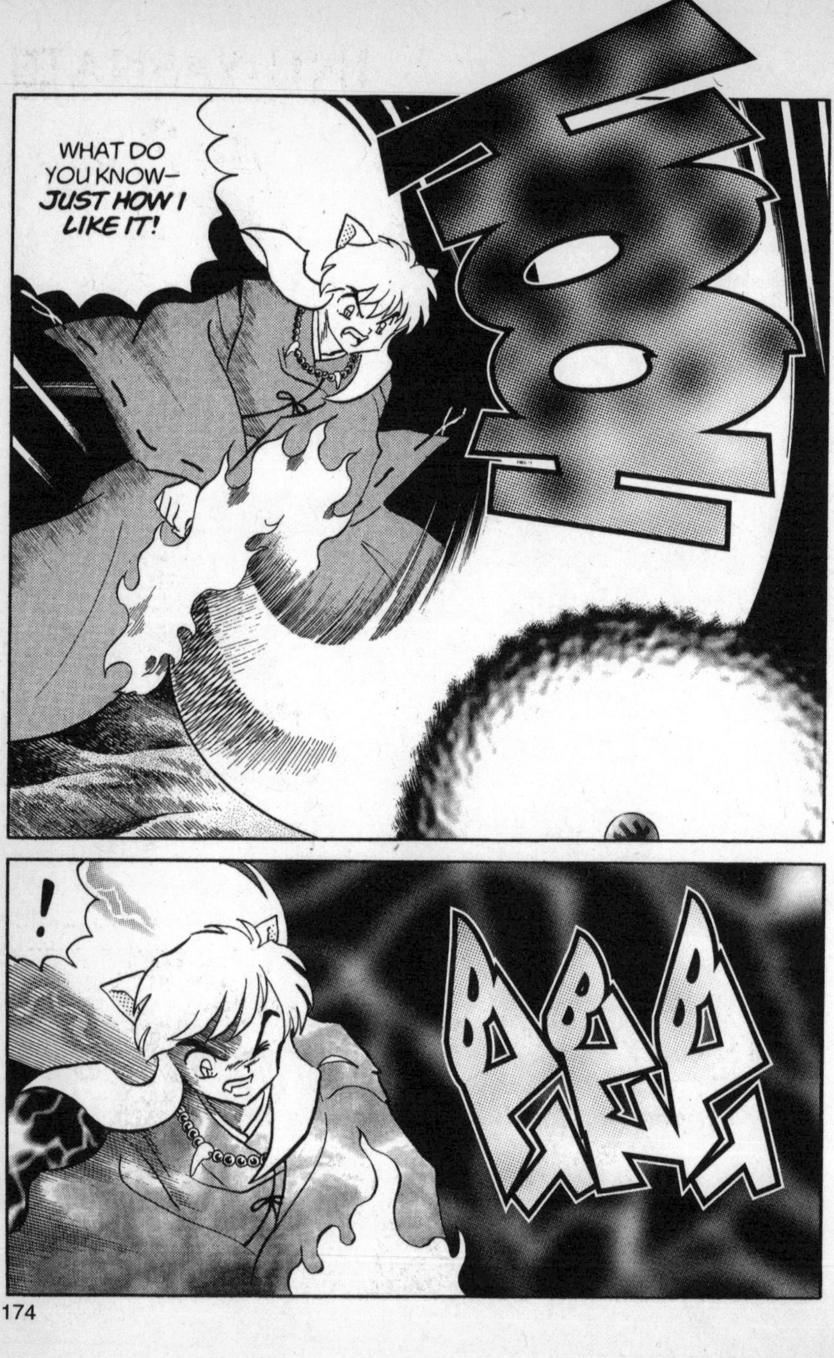
WHAT DO YOU KNOW— JUST HOW I LIKE IT!
!

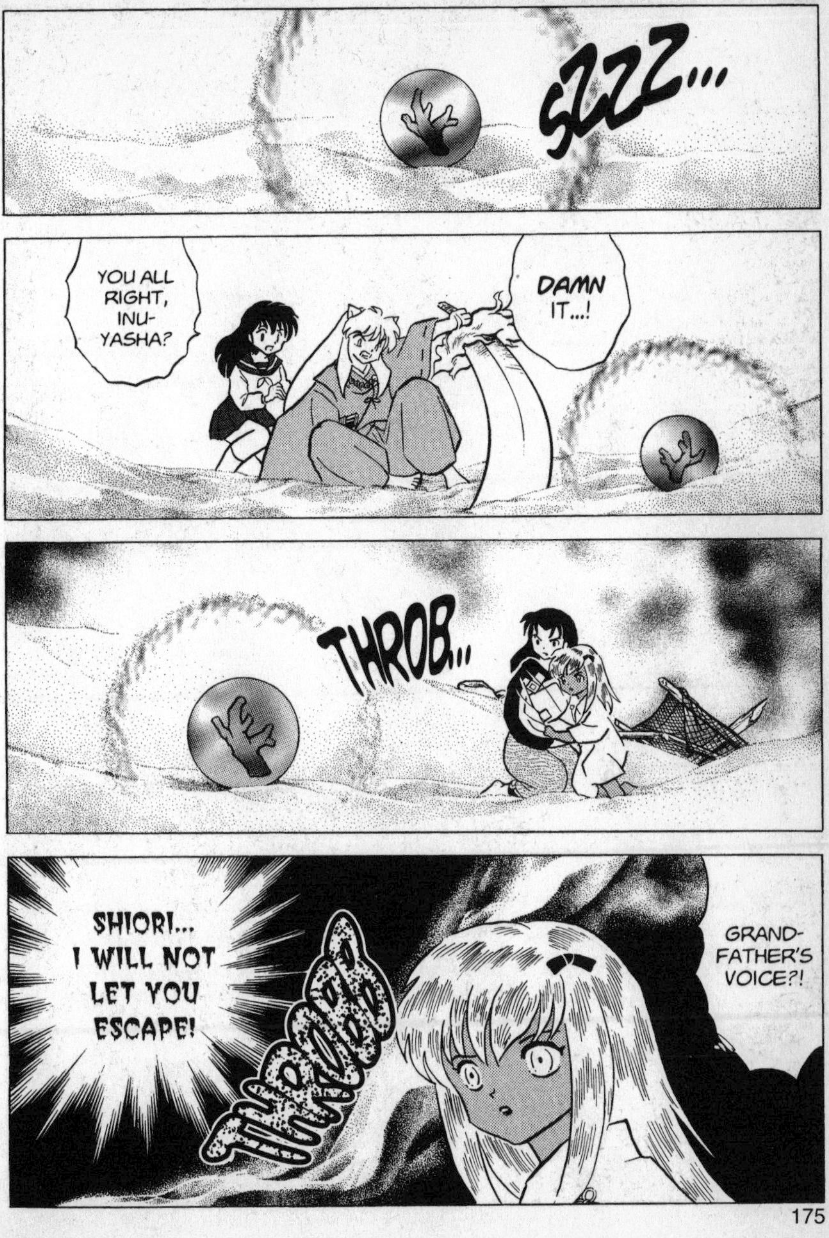
SZZZ...
YOU ALL RIGHT, INU-YASHA?
DAMN IT...!
THROB...
SHIORI... I WILL NOT LET YOU ESCAPE!
THROBBB
GRAND-FATHER'S VOICE?!

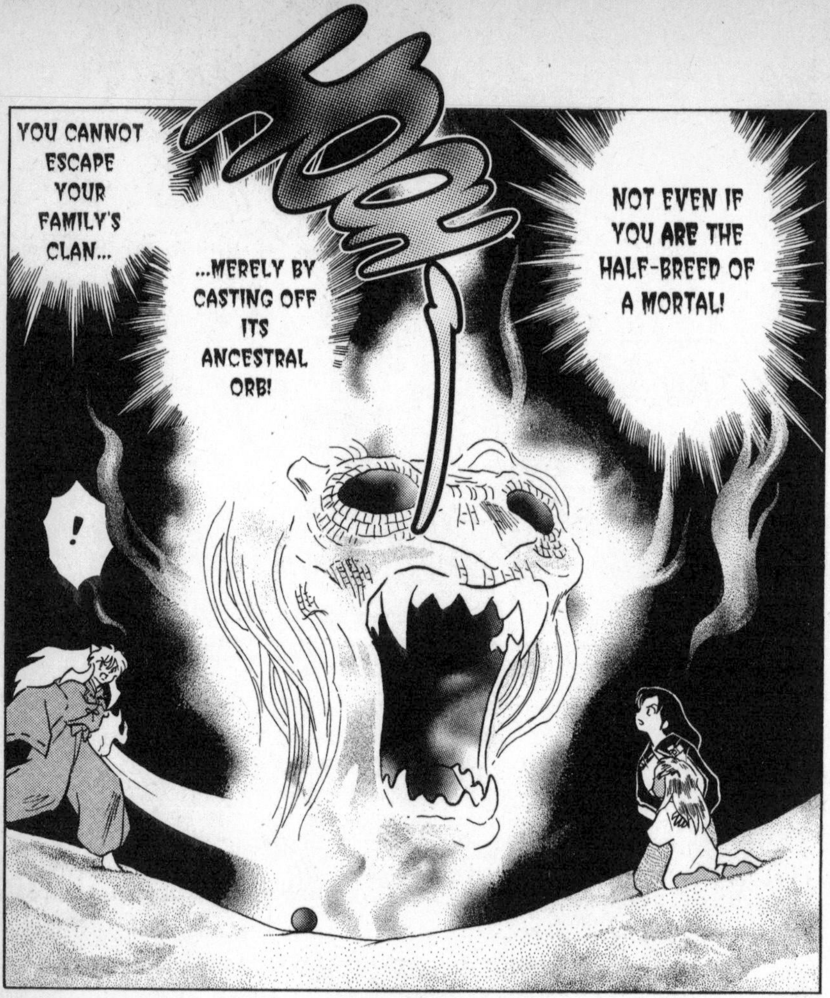
YOU CANNOT ESCAPE YOUR FAMILY'S CLAN...
...MERELY BY CASTING OFF ITS ANCESTRAL ORB!
NOT EVEN IF YOU ARE THE HALF-BREED OF A MORTAL!
!

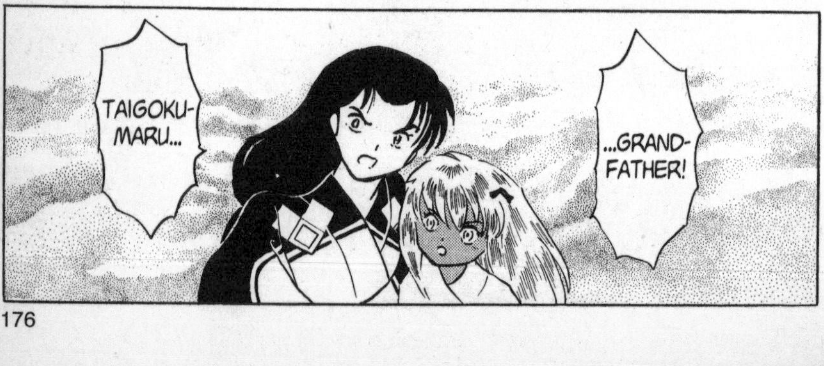
TAIGOKU-MARU...
...GRAND-FATHER!

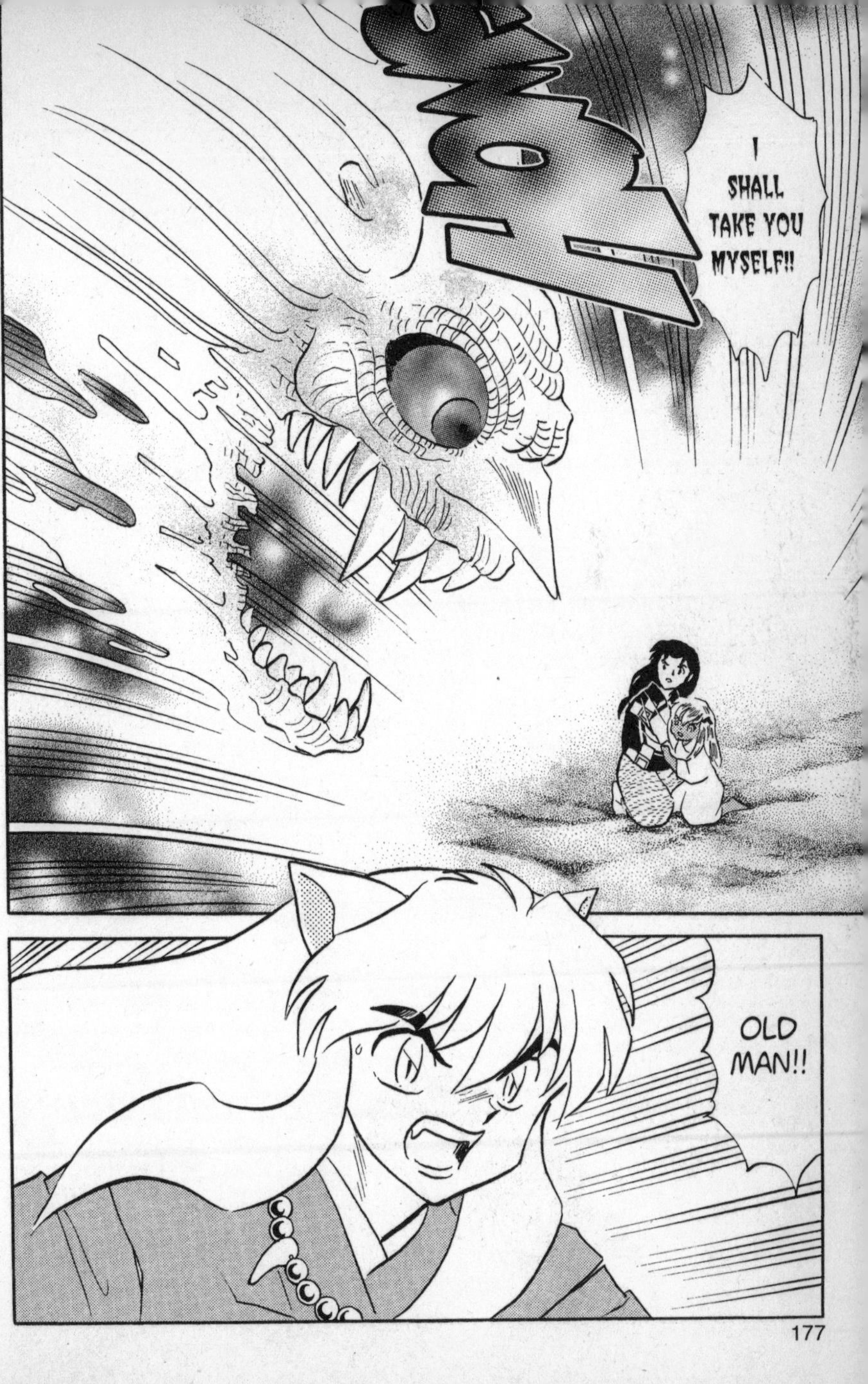
I SHALL TAKE YOU MYSELF!!
OLD MAN!!

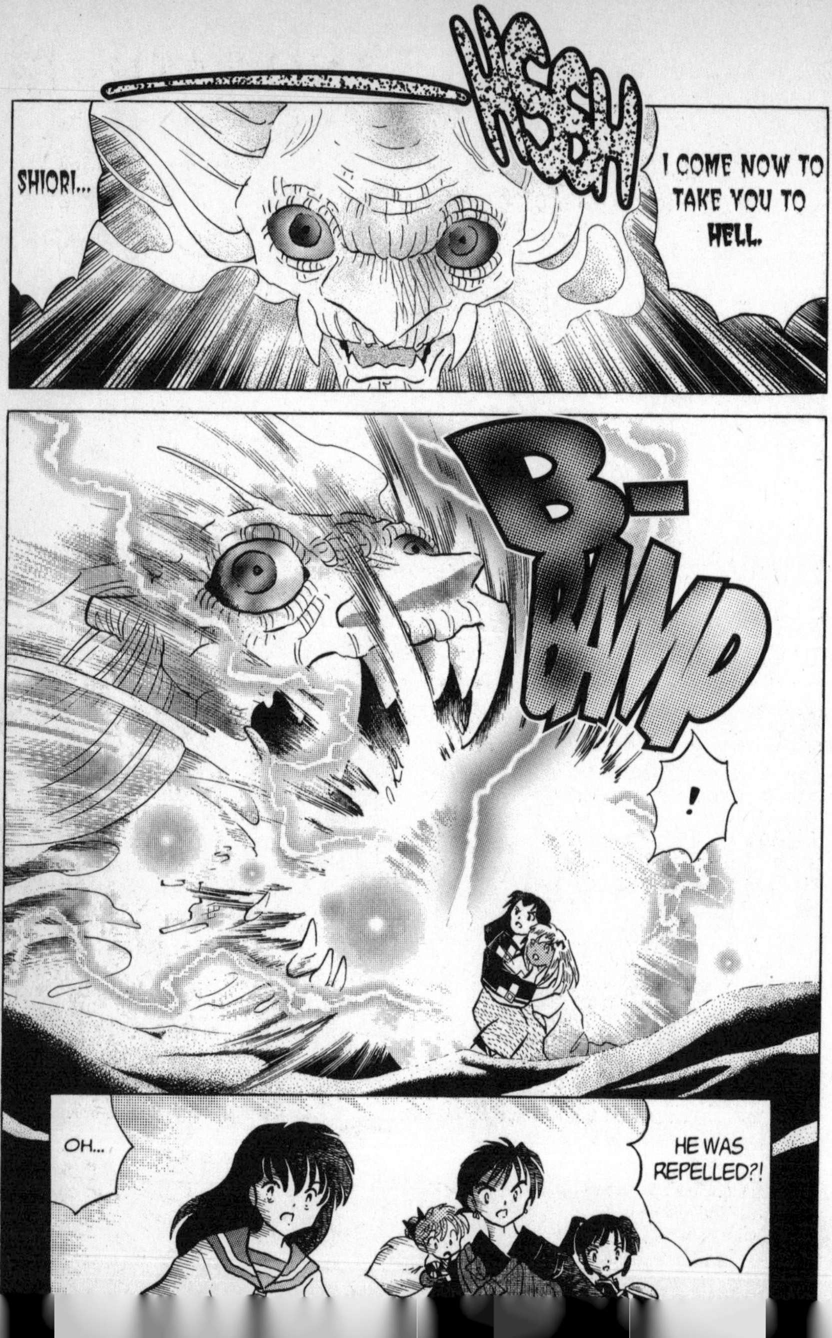
HSSH
SHIORI...
I COME NOW TO TAKE YOU TO HELL.
B-BAMP
!
OH...
HE WAS REPELLED?!

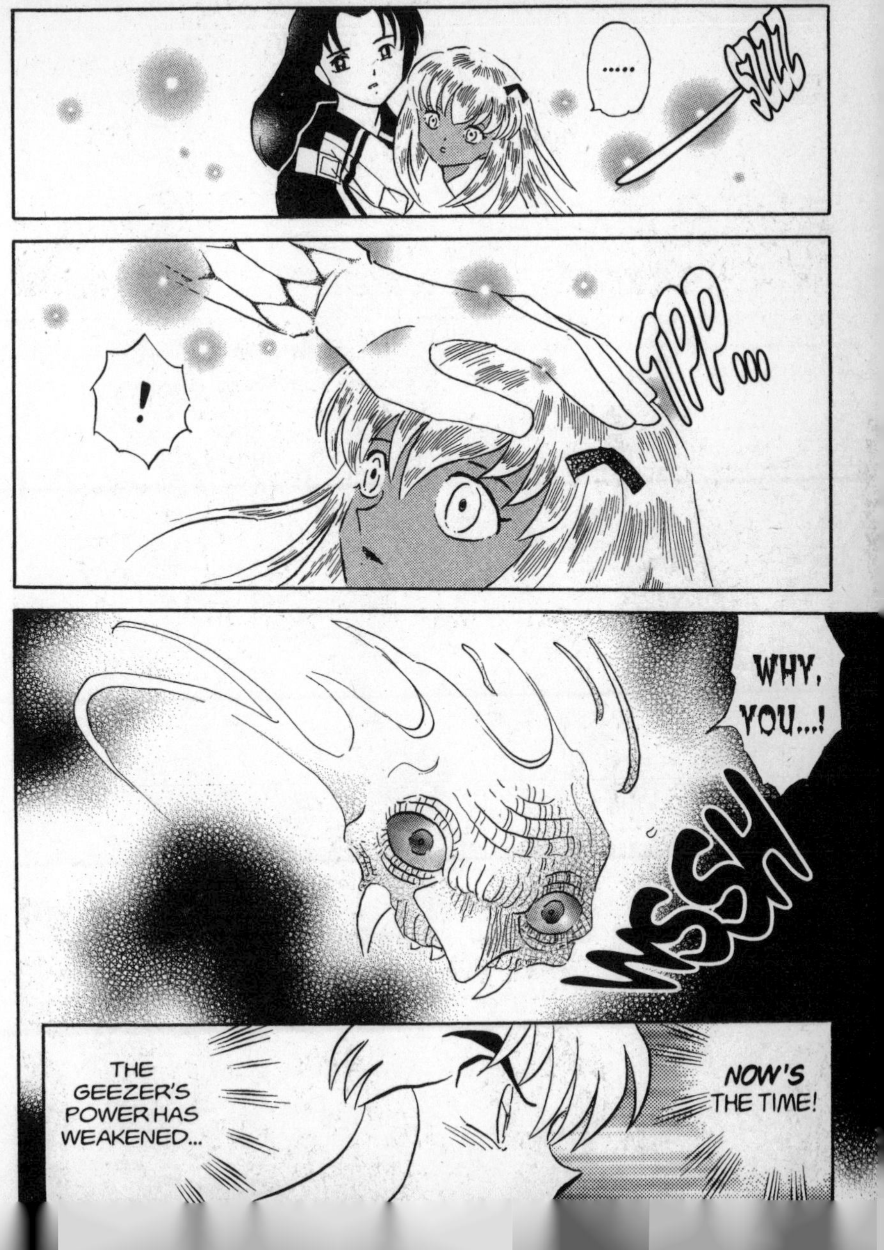
......
TPP...
!
WHY, YOU...!
WSSH
THE GEEZER'S POWER HAS WEAKENED...
NOW'S THE TIME!

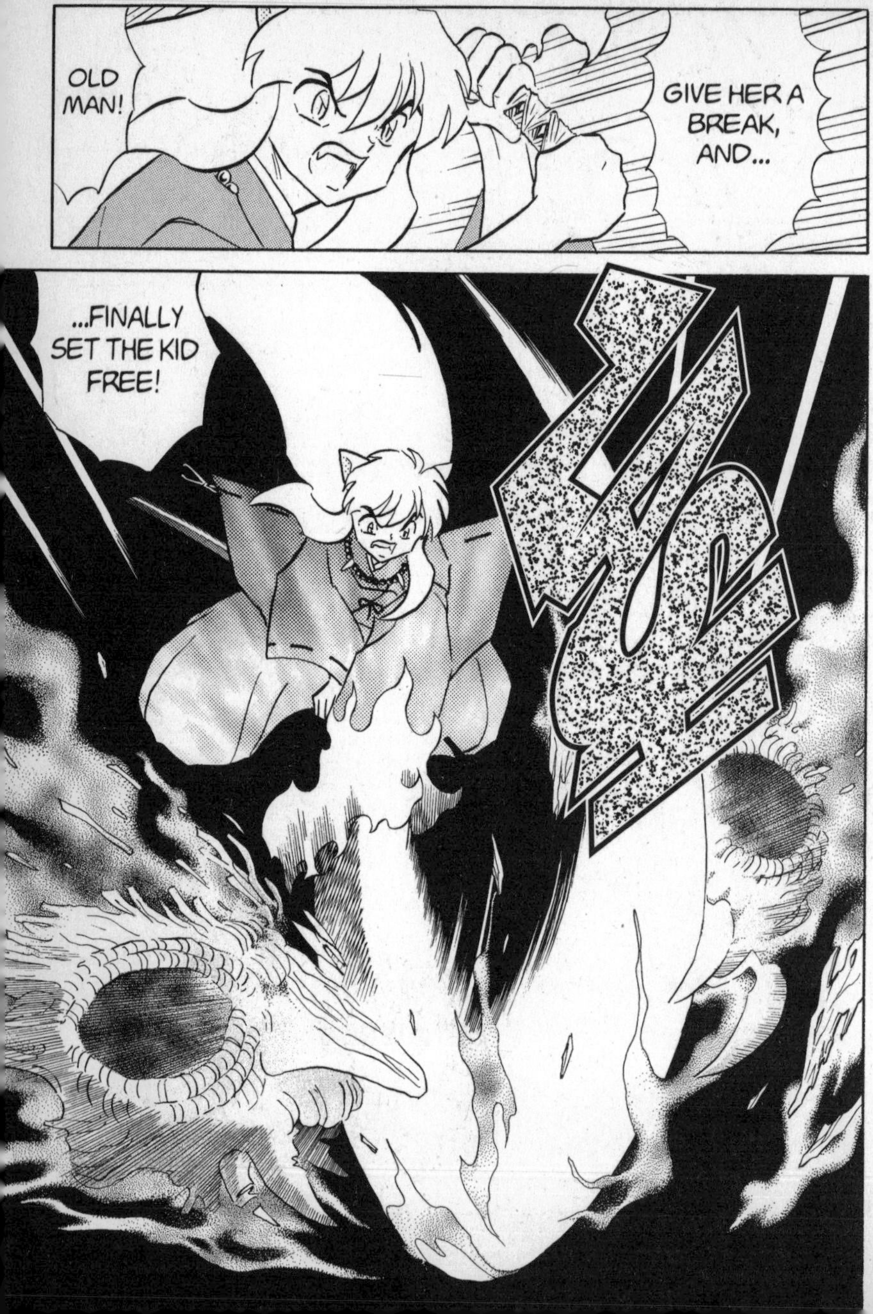
OLD MAN!
GIVE HER A BREAK, AND...
...FINALLY SET THE KID FREE!

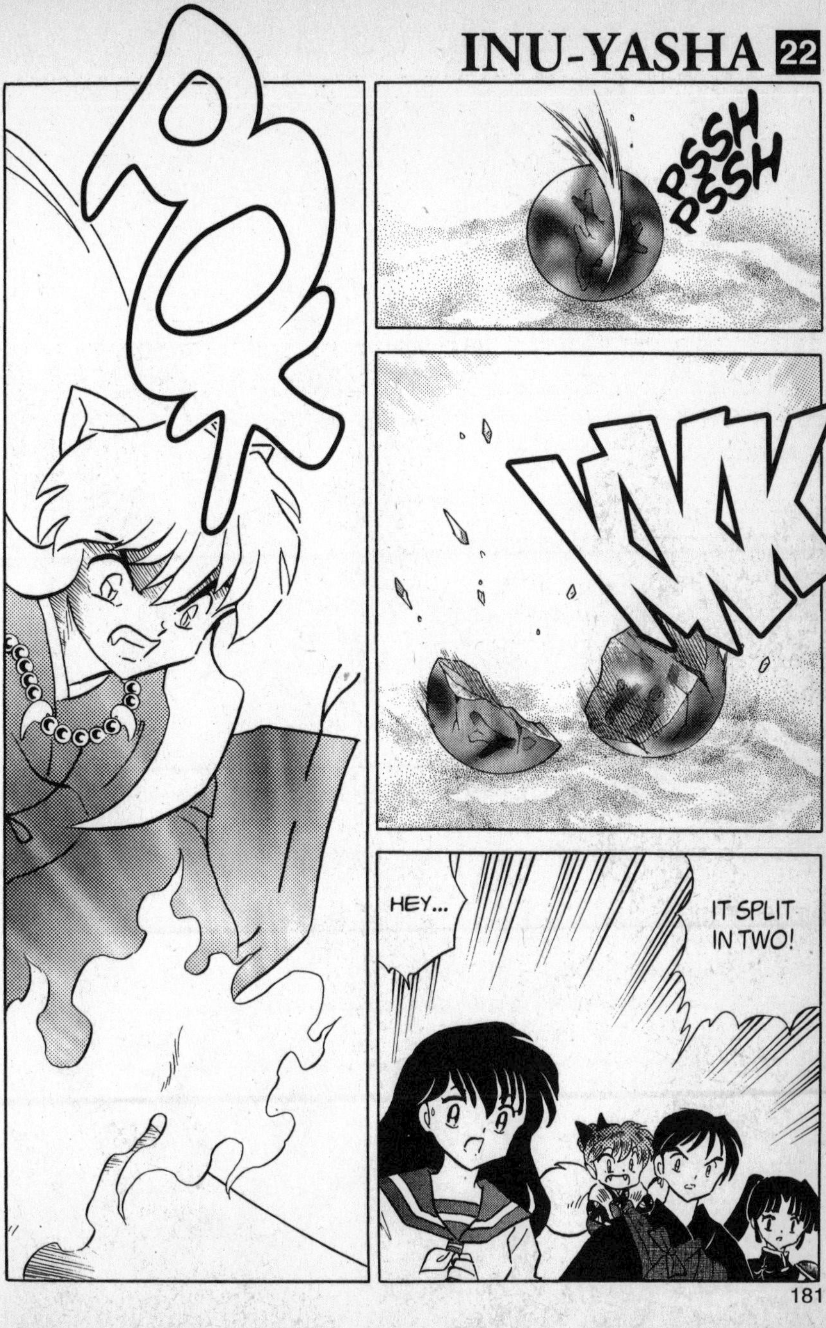
POK
PSSH
PSSH
HEY...
IT SPLIT
IN TWO!

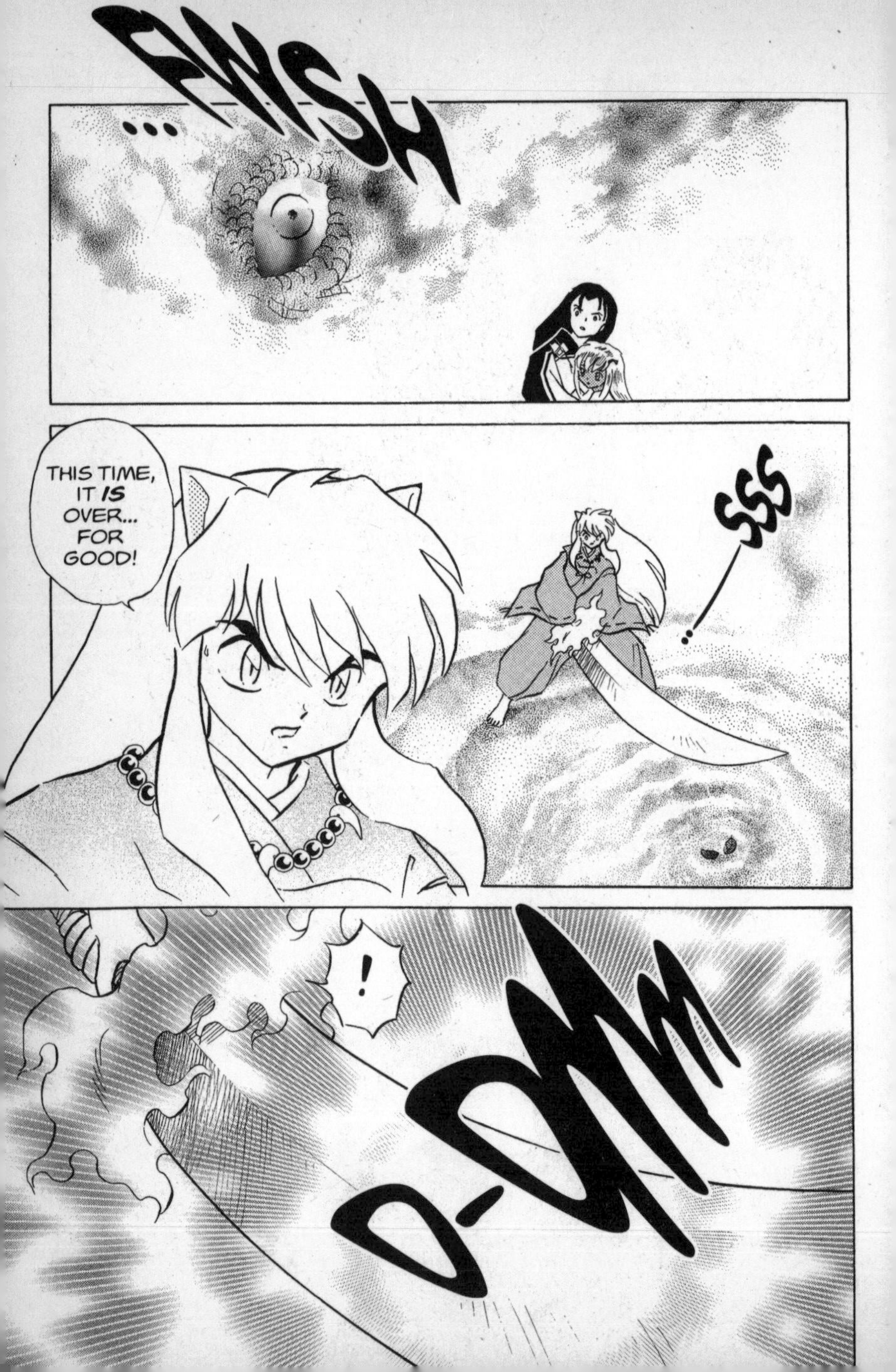
FWSH
...
THIS TIME, IT IS OVER... FOR GOOD!
SSS
!!
!
D-DMM

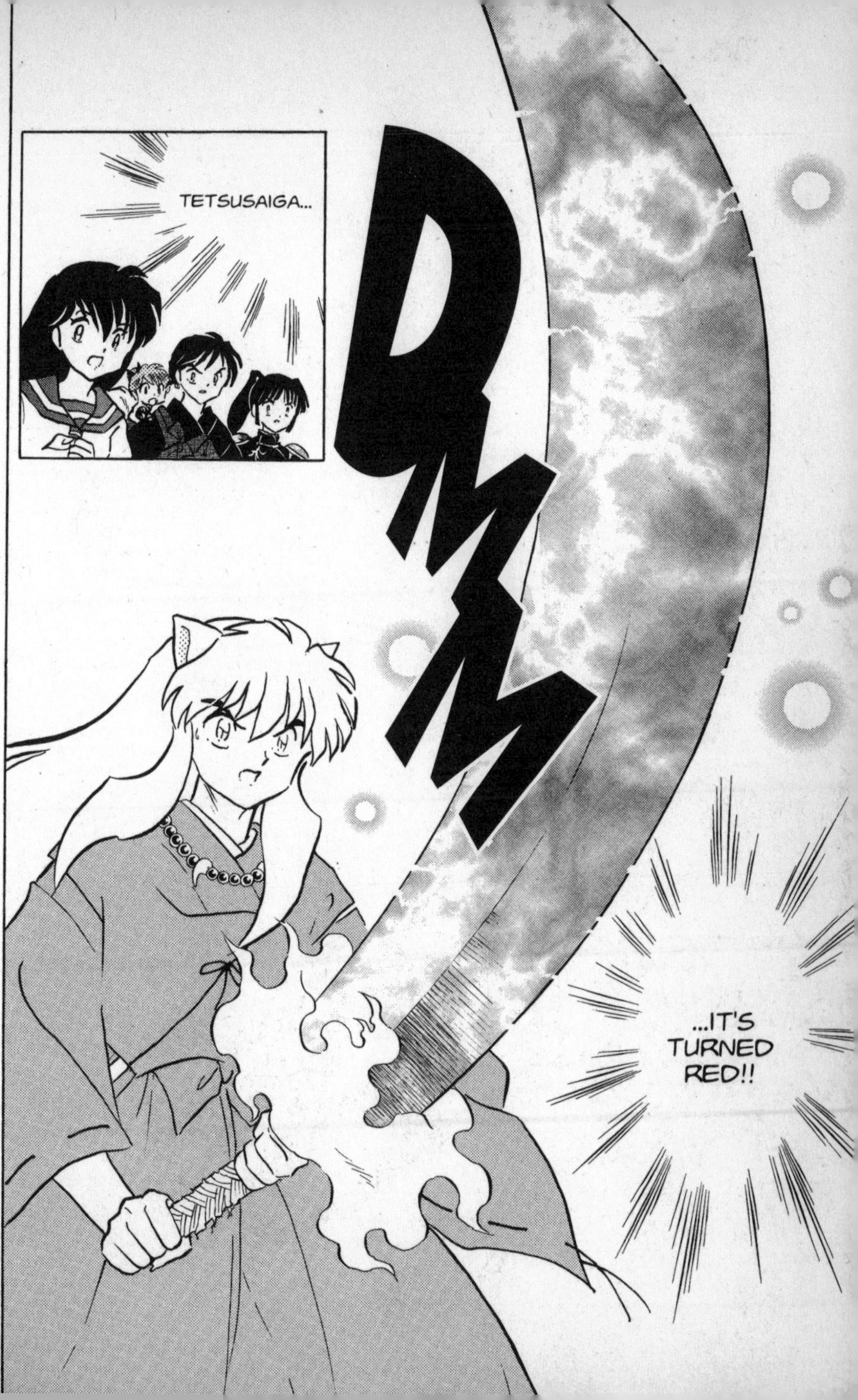
TETSUSAIGA...
DMMM
...IT'S TURNED RED!!

TETSUSAIGA ABSORBED THE SPHERE'S POWER...

WHICH MEANS THE BLADE...HAS BECOME *STRONGER!*

SHIORI...

.....

THANK YOU.

BUT...*YOU'RE* THE ONE WHO HELPED *ME.*

WEAKENING THE OLD GEEZER'S POWER...

THAT WASN'T SOMETHING I DID.

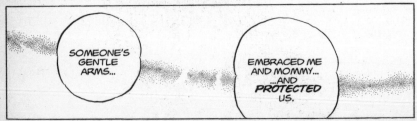

SOMEONE'S GENTLE ARMS...

EMBRACED ME AND MOMMY... ...AND *PROTECTED* US.

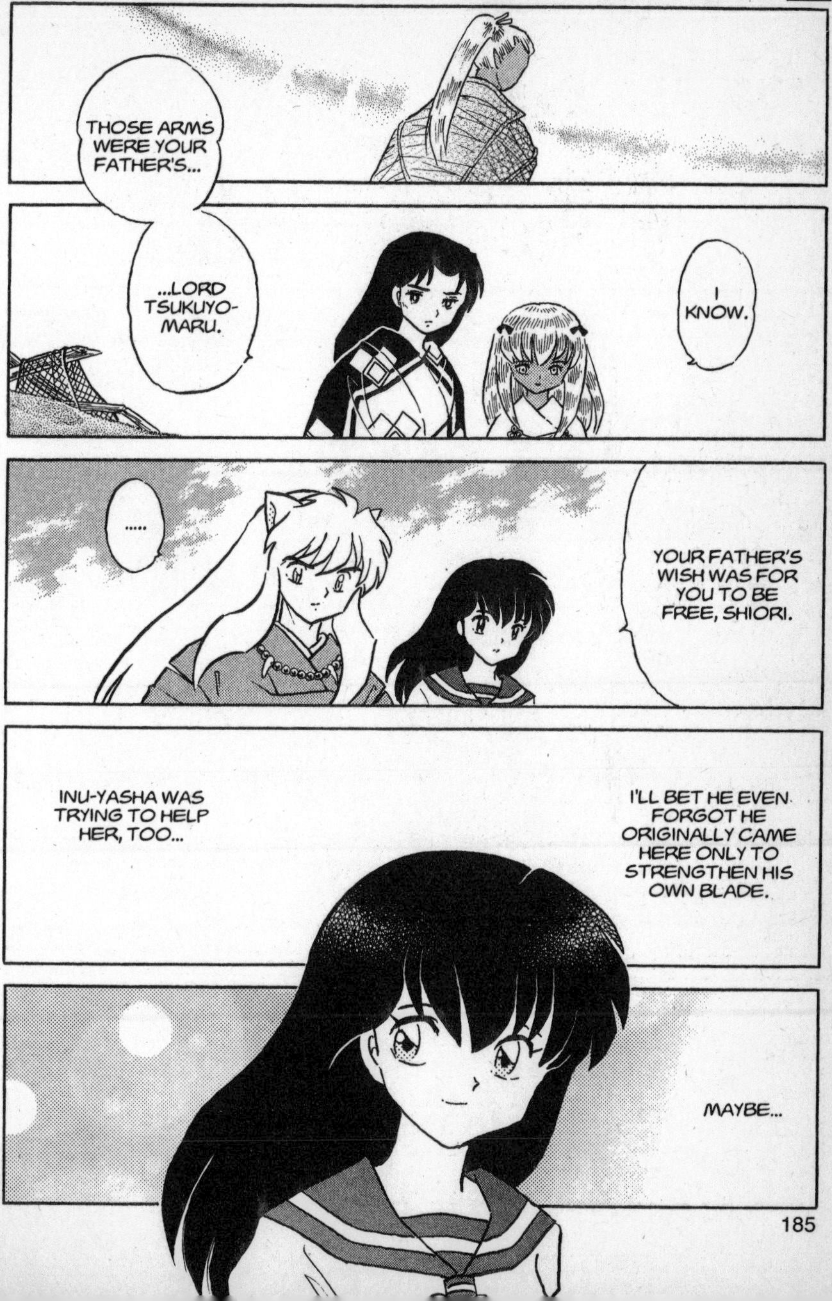
THOSE ARMS WERE YOUR FATHER'S...
...LORD TSUKUYO-MARU.
I KNOW.
.....
YOUR FATHER'S WISH WAS FOR YOU TO BE FREE, SHIORI.
INU-YASHA WAS TRYING TO HELP HER, TOO...
I'LL BET HE EVEN FORGOT HE ORIGINALLY CAME HERE ONLY TO STRENGTHEN HIS OWN BLADE.
MAYBE...

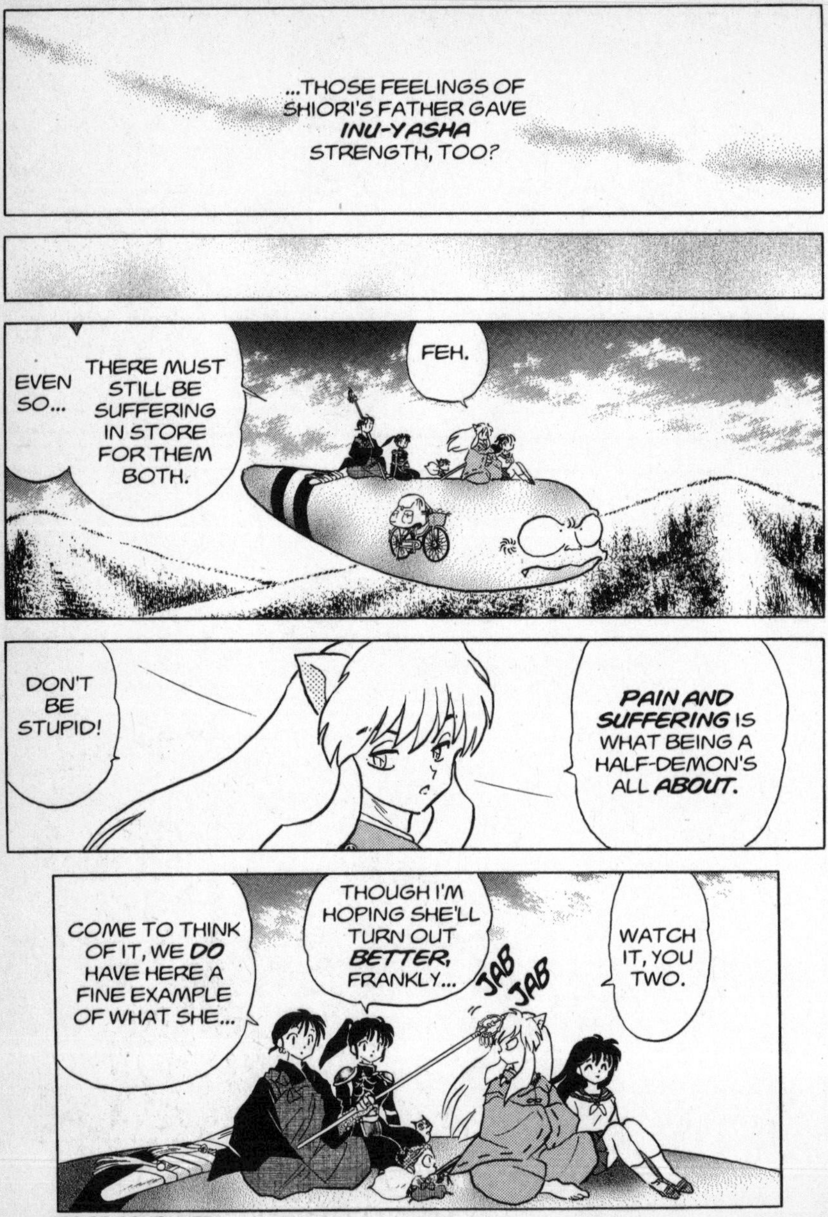
...THOSE FEELINGS OF SHIORI'S FATHER GAVE ***INU-YASHA*** STRENGTH, TOO?
EVEN SO...
THERE MUST STILL BE SUFFERING IN STORE FOR THEM BOTH.
FEH.
DON'T BE STUPID!
PAIN AND SUFFERING IS WHAT BEING A HALF-DEMON'S ALL ***ABOUT***.
COME TO THINK OF IT, WE ***DO*** HAVE HERE A FINE EXAMPLE OF WHAT SHE...
THOUGH I'M HOPING SHE'LL TURN OUT ***BETTER,*** FRANKLY...
JAB JAB
WATCH IT, YOU TWO.

TO BE CONTINUED...

About Rumiko Takahashi

Born in 1957 in Niigata, Japan, Rumiko Takahashi attended women's college in Tokyo, where she began studying comics with Kazuo Koike, author of CRYING FREEMAN. She later became an assistant to horror-manga artist Kazuo Umezu (OROCHI). In 1978, she won a prize in Shogakukan's annual "New Comic Artist Contest," and in that same year her boy-meets-alien comedy series URUSEI YATSURA began appearing in the weekly manga magazine SHŌNEN SUNDAY. This phenomenally successful series ran for nine years and sold over 22 million copies. Takahashi's later RANMA 1/2 series enjoyed even greater popularity.

Takahashi is considered by many to be one of the world's most popular manga artists. With the publication of Volume 34 of her RANMA 1/2 series in Japan, Takahashi's total sales passed *one hundred million* copies of her compiled works.

Takahashi's serial titles include URUSEI YATSURA, RANMA 1/2, ONE-POUND GOSPEL, MAISON IKKOKU and INUYASHA. Additionally, Takahashi has drawn many short stories which have been published in America under the title "Rumic Theater," and several installments of a saga known as her "Mermaid" series. Most of Takahashi's major stories have also been animated and are widely available in translation worldwide. INUYASHA is her most recent serial story, first published in SHŌNEN SUNDAY in 1996.

DITOR'S RECOMMENDATIONS

If you enjoyed this volume of InuYasha, then here's some more manga in which you may be interested.

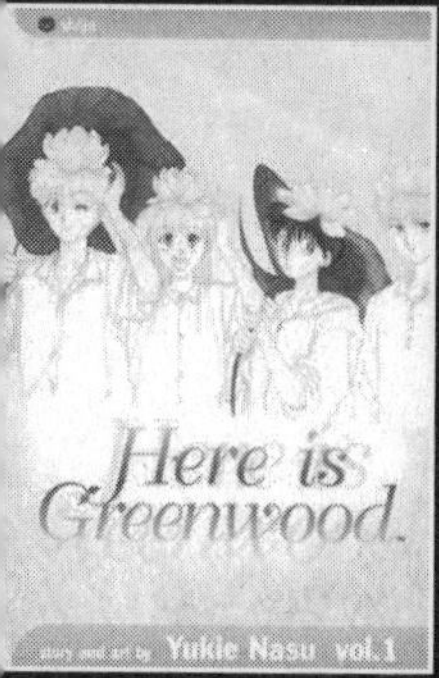
Here is Greenwood
story and art by Yukie Nasu vol. 1

HERE IS GREENWOOD

Aimed at a slightly older audience, perhaps, than most of Rumiko Takahashi's work, *HERE IS GREENWOOD* is exactly like Takahashi's *RANMA 1/2*, aside from the martial arts (none), the wacky hijinks (almost none), and the occasional depiction of the adult relationships among its students. Okay, aside from the fact that they both deal with high school boys, it's nothing like *RANMA 1/2*. But it's still cool!

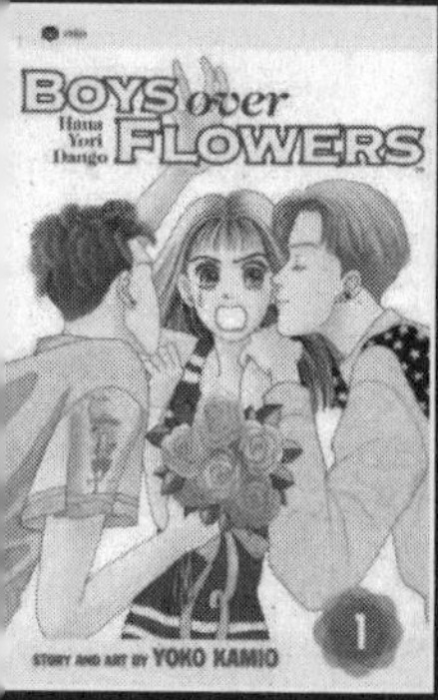
BOYS over FLOWERS
Hana Yori Dango
1
STORY AND ART BY YOKO KAMIO

BOYS OVER FLOWERS

Another tale of high school life in Japan, *BOYS OVER FLOWERS* (or "HanaDan," to fans) is not without its serious side, but overall tends to fall more in the "rabu-kome" or "love-comedy" genre.

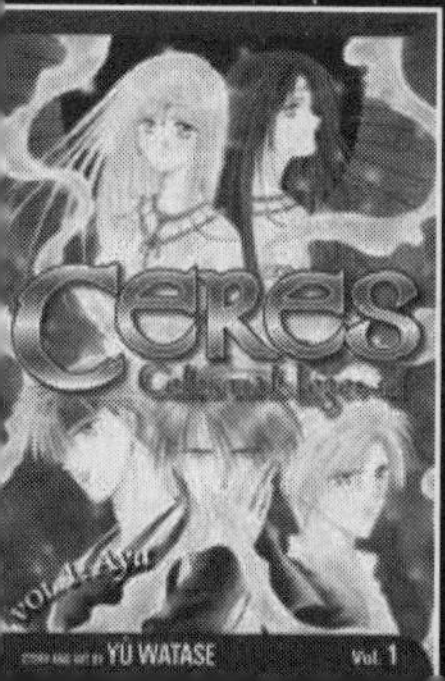
Ceres
STORY AND ART BY YU WATASE
vol. 1

CERES: Celestial Legend

Aya Mikage is a trendy Tokyo teen with not much else on her mind except fashion, karaoke, and boys. But a terrible family secret involving an ancient family "curse" is about to make things a lot more difficult.

COMPLETE OUR SURVEY AND LET US KNOW WHAT YOU THINK!

☐ Please do NOT send me information about VIZ products, news and events, special offers, or other information.

☐ Please do NOT send me information from VIZ's trusted business partners.

Name: _____

Address: _____

City: _____ **State:** _____ **Zip:** _____

E-mail: _____

☐ **Male** ☐ **Female** **Date of Birth** (mm/dd/yyyy): ___/___/_____ (Under 13? Parental consent required)

What race/ethnicity do you consider yourself? (please check one)

☐ Asian/Pacific Islander ☐ Black/African American ☐ Hispanic/Latino

☐ Native American/Alaskan Native ☐ White/Caucasian ☐ Other: _____

What VIZ product did you purchase? (check all that apply and indicate title purchased)

☐ DVD/VHS _____

☐ Graphic Novel _____

☐ Magazines _____

☐ Merchandise _____

Reason for purchase: (check all that apply)

☐ Special offer ☐ Favorite title ☐ Gift

☐ Recommendation ☐ Other _____

Where did you make your purchase? (please check one)

☐ Comic store ☐ Bookstore ☐ Mass/Grocery Store

☐ Newsstand ☐ Video/Video Game Store ☐ Other: _____

☐ Online (site: _____)

What other VIZ properties have you purchased/own? _____

_____

How many anime and/or manga titles have you purchased in the last year? How many were VIZ titles? (please check one from each column)

ANIME	MANGA	VIZ
☐ None	☐ None	☐ None
☐ 1-4	☐ 1-4	☐ 1-4
☐ 5-10	☐ 5-10	☐ 5-10
☐ 11+	☐ 11+	☐ 11+

I find the pricing of VIZ products to be: (please check one)

☐ Cheap ☐ Reasonable ☐ Expensive

What genre of manga and anime would you like to see from VIZ? (please check two)

☐ Adventure ☐ Comic Strip ☐ Science Fiction ☐ Fighting

☐ Horror ☐ Romance ☐ Fantasy ☐ Sports

What do you think of VIZ's new look?

☐ Love It ☐ It's OK ☐ Hate It ☐ Didn't Notice ☐ No Opinion

Which do you prefer? (please check one)

☐ Reading right-to-left

☐ Reading left-to-right

Which do you prefer? (please check one)

☐ Sound effects in English

☐ Sound effects in Japanese with English captions

☐ Sound effects in Japanese only with a glossary at the back

THANK YOU! Please send the completed form to:

NJW Research
42 Catharine St.
Poughkeepsie, NY 12601

All information provided will be used for internal purposes only. We promise not to sell or otherwise divulge your information.